WORDS
AND
WORLDS

WORDS AND WORLDS
A LEXICON FOR DARK TIMES

EDITED BY VEENA DAS AND DIDIER FASSIN

DUKE UNIVERSITY PRESS · *Durham and London* · 2021

© 2021 Duke University Press
All rights reserved
Cover designed by Aimee C. Harrison
Text designed by Matthew Tauch
Typeset in Whitman by Westchester Publishing Services

Library of Congress Cataloging-in-Publication Data
Names: Das, Veena, editor. | Fassin, Didier, editor.
Title: Words and worlds : a lexicon for dark times / edited by Veena
Das and Didier Fassin.
Description: Durham : Duke University Press, 2021. | Includes
bibliographical references and index.
Identifiers: LCCN 2020041472 (print)
LCCN 2020041473 (ebook)
ISBN 9781478013259 (hardcover)
ISBN 9781478014164 (paperback)
ISBN 9781478021476 (ebook)
Subjects: LCSH: Language and languages—Political aspects. |
Words, New—Political aspects. | Sociolinguistics. | Language and
culture.
Classification: LCC P119.3.W57 2021 (print) | LCC P119.3 (ebook) |
DDC 306.44—dc23
LC record available at https://lccn.loc.gov/2020041472
LC ebook record available at https://lccn.loc.gov/2020041473

CONTENTS

ACKNOWLEDGMENTS

The essays that compose the present volume were prepared for and discussed at a workshop held with the contribution of the Nomis Foundation at the Institute for Advanced Study in Princeton. We are thankful to its School of Social Science as well as to the Anthropology Department at Johns Hopkins University for their administrative support. We especially express our gratitude to Donne Petito for her efficacious assistance, to Laura McCune for her gracious organization of the event, and to Munirah Bishop for her scrupulous copyediting of the manuscript. We are grateful to the two anonymous reviewers solicited by Duke University Press for their astute comments and to Ken Wissoker for his critical support.

INTRODUCTION
FROM WORDS TO WORLDS

DIDIER FASSIN AND VEENA DAS

The idea of this intellectual enterprise came out of a conversation in the gloomy context of the spring of 2017. As we were evoking our perplexity and dismay with respect to the ongoing political crisis in the United States, we realized that we had both commented on it in earlier public interventions using the figure of the return of the "grotesque" in politics (Das 2017; Fassin 2017). Like many others, we had been deeply troubled by the election of the new president, against the background of the rise of populist, nationalist, and xenophobic parties in Europe and beyond, but we were in addition disappointed with most of the hastily elaborated and often contradictory analyses made of it, whether in terms of discontent with globalization, racist backlash, cultural war, identity politics, economic protectionism, nationalism, or fascism. Our parallel discussions of the grotesque, based on both Michel Foucault's ([1999] 2003: 11) reading of it as "the fact that, by virtue of their status, a discourse or an individual can have effects of power that their intrinsic qualities should disqualify them from having," and on Alfred Jarry's ([1894] 2003) disruptive character Ubu, tried to unsettle our habitual understanding of politics in a time when the ridiculous and the odious were simultaneously legitimized as forms of governing through the person of the sovereign, to whom they paradoxically gave more power. But rather than formulating a definitive interpretation, which we did not have anyway, we used this troubling figure as a pretext to question the contemporary moment in a different way and destabilize the categories that we use to contemplate the world. As our conversation went on over several weeks, we thought that there might be some merit in extending and deepening our reflection so as to avoid the dual problem of Eurocentrism, since the debate tended to be exclusively focused on the West, and presentism, since it seemed frozen by the fascination of current events. There was certainly something unique about what was happening here and now, and it was essential to recognize it as such. But this uniqueness, full of sound and fury, could also serve as a spark to initiate a broader undertaking, imagine other geographies, and provide alternative genealogies. This is how the project of *Words and Worlds* came into being.

The dystopian transformation of contemporary societies, of which we had caught a glimpse, has now expanded to various parts of the planet and to diverse domains of human activities. What seemed to be an aberration has become a new norm. The delusional politics of a Trump is echoed by the delirious spectacle of a Bolsonaro and a Duterte. Nationalism becomes exacerbated as the former's "America First," Modi's chants, and Orbán's slogans aggressively resound. Religious discrimination serves as a trivialized mode of governing, from the Muslim ban in the United States to the persecutions against the Rohingya in Myanmar, the oppression of the Uighurs in China, and the wily judicial tactics of amendments to the Citizenship Act in India that would disqualify Muslims from taking their rights as citizens for granted. White supremacy finds increasingly overt expressions in Charlottesville, Virginia, as well as in Christchurch, New Zealand, and Halle, Germany. The lives of migrants and refugees do not seem to have more worth at the border with Mexico than they have in the Mediterranean Sea and on Nauru Island. Neoliberal polities abandon political liberalism to privilege authoritarian policing and repress opposition. With capitalism unleashed, inequalities reach new heights and climate change threatens the future of the planet. On a daily basis, forged news and alternative facts promoted by state leaders and disseminated via social media supplant the traditional relation to authenticity and actuality. We acknowledge that not all these transformations appeared all at once, but they became increasingly visible and unrestrained: the ordinary spectacle of politics across the globe. To apprehend this dystopia, we do not need to invent neologisms but simply to vet our old vocabulary. This is what *Words and Worlds* is about.

Each chapter of the book is organized around a term that we take as part of a political lexicon. Since the idea of a lexicon is sometimes collapsed with that of a keyword format, it might be helpful to spell out the differences in the ways these ideas have come to be used in recent years to delineate different features of social life and its representation. Although there were classic precedents of using words strategically to specify a domain of life for analysis, especially in Germany with the Schlagwortforschung, research on buzzwords, initiated by Richard Meyer, and the Begriffsgeschichte, history of concepts, developed by Reinhart Koselleck (Bondi and Scott 2010), the keyword approach is most closely associated with the work of Raymond Williams. His enterprise had started with a list of sixty words that was to be an index to his book *Culture and Society*, but the proposal had to be dropped for reasons of space. As he recalls in the preface to his later book on keywords, he expanded the list over the next twenty years and wrote short entries against each word so that the 60 words grew to 127 and included both words in common use, such as *family* and *culture*, and words more specialized, such as *hegemony* and *dialectics* (Williams [1976] 2014). In a fascinating discussion about what he means by a vocabulary, he recalls that on his return to Cambridge after the war, he had the uncanny feeling, shared by many others, that something in the use of language had shifted: "We just don't speak the same language" (11). It was not simply that some new words had entered people's vocabularies but that the weight of different words had shifted. For instance, he evokes how earlier the word *culture* was not used very often in Britain and was reserved for discussing questions of aesthetic taste and judgment. After the war, perhaps due to the exposure to North American ways of talking, people in England had begun to refer to culture as a quotidian term; today it is not uncommon to hear such expressions as *the culture of parking* or *the culture of corruption*.

Do these words then circulate in different discourse communities? Is the increasing resort to such platforms as Twitter or Facebook by authors to promote their own work an indication of the democratization of knowledge, or is this an indication of the grotesque—the Ubu-esque as it seeps into disciplinary discourses similar to the processes described by Foucault ([2003] 2006) for nineteenth-century psychiatry in France, when tokens of power came to stand for disciplinary authority? These are vexing questions, and we argue that one of the ways to address them is through careful attention to the formation of concepts and their political plenitude. We use the notion of a lexicon to indicate that words are not sovereigns to parse out separate regions of the real as much as they are nodes crisscrossing each other through which flux and movements in highly volatile milieus such as that of our contemporary world might be given expression.

To return to the keyword approach, it is clear from Williams's writing that he was himself uncertain as to whether the keywords he identified were separable semantic units—pivotal words, which had distinct boundaries though they might spill over different domains of social life—or whether it would be more useful to construe larger units such as catchphrases or whole sentences. For instance, one could think of the way J. L. Austin

([1962] 1975) uses phrases such as "I pronounce thee" or "Enough is enough" to argue that words have force, wield effects, and are thus forms of action. The growth of web semantics as a field in its own right has brought forward new questions in the way words come to be treated as keys to unraveling important social processes. Here, too, it is not easy to decipher whether the appropriate units of analysis should be keywords identified as those which are statistically determined to be frequently used and whose rise or decline would indicate changes in social domains, or should one look at longer recurrent expressions or lexical grammatical patterns, since meanings of words could vary depending on the pattern identified? For instance, the term *democracy* might appear within different clusters across regions or in different periods of time. When paired with rights, consent, voting, minorities, it points to possibly, albeit not inevitably, an aspirational politics, but when occurring within darker constellations such as those of corruption, deals, torture, and populism, it might point to a different set of anxieties. It would be the work of social analysis to lay bare the processes through which words and worlds come to be articulated by filling up the picture through a robust attention to context, so as to avoid sheer nominalism.

Although computational methods have opened up some interesting ways to decipher certain aspects of political ideology from text data using keywords, the impulse to take these findings as more objective or more scientific needs to be treated with caution. As Hao Yan, Allen Lavoie, and Sanmay Das (2017: 1) point out, even when algorithms perform well in data set cross-validation tests, generalizing from different data sets, such as congressional records and conservative or liberal media sites and wikis, is "surprisingly negative" for North American politics. This does not mean that such methods do not have potential to develop but that a robust cross-disciplinary conversation and critique is essential to think of the very meaning of political speech and its relation to both concealing and revealing regions of political life. The history of political talk in North America and elsewhere is not necessarily that of slowly unfolding tradition but of confrontation, argument, and exercise of power. As Daniel Rodgers (1987) observes, political commentators were acutely aware of the function of political rhetoric to cover up the hidden agendas, the secret deals, the hand in the till. The normativity in the usage of words, the use and abuse of language cannot be surmised from statistical frequencies alone until the context in which data are generated in the first place receives close scrutiny. Thus data generated in, say, congressional records that pertain to strategic use of language might belong to one kind of language game, while the conservative or liberal media websites might be oriented to different modalities of communication and expression.

In a very different but crucial direction, one can explore keywords not within a language but across various languages through the delicate problem of translatability. Such endeavor leads to being attentive to divisions, differences, and transports among same or similar words in related languages, which have a history of overlapping preoccupations and mutual influence. Interestingly this approach often provides a new intelligibility of these words within one's own language. An exemplary text for considering such tensions is the *Dictionary of Untranslatables: A Philosophical Lexicon* (Cassin et al. 2014), which takes words and concepts to be part of a network within which dislocations, projections, and distortions are the normal fate of words and concepts as they move from one field to another. Such awareness leads to being mindful of the kernel of untranslatability, namely, the fact that our concepts might embody not only what is in circulation but also processes of doubling and mirroring, inflections that have been forgotten, intruders that have generated new connotations, terms that do not have their fields of application anymore—in other words, the whole hurly-burly of what Wittgenstein ([1953] 2009) called forms of life.

So, although we asked each contributor to write on one specific topic, all of them were invited to consider how different topics were interconnected, what kind of life these words acquired as they burrowed their way deep into the fabric of contemporary politics, economics, culture, and more broadly society. Far from seeking a reduction of reality to concepts from which experience has been expunged, we hope that their contributions cut into the many conversations on neoliberalism, authoritarianism, surveillance, disorders of democracy, risks of planetary extinction, and the crisis of trust in the presentation of facts differently than the overdetermined frameworks assuming that some single overarching concept can provide a key to characterize the widespread sense of disquietude or the feeling of business as usual.

Whereas we were propelled into this project by the pressure of the events of 2017, we were acutely aware, having worked in very different regions of the world, of the ludicrous claims that somehow the world had changed now that the United States or Europe felt threatened by unrests, protests, and movements of different kinds within or at their borders. If the timing we chose for this project was driven by the shock expressed all around us, our lexicon did not assume that the contemporary was best sensed in events occurring in these regions of the world. We understand the emergent character of the contemporary (as distinct from the actual) but do not go along with the conceit that all innovation (for good or bad) would happen in the West while the rest would merely be producing replications of so-called Western innovation.

Our project in this sense was also oriented in a distinct direction, since it did not consist in establishing a dictionary of concepts understood as neutral intellectual tools. Rather, we understood such an approach to be reductionist and potentially dangerous; conversely, we had to start with commonsense terms so as to challenge some of our usual prejudgments. Our sentiment was, indeed, that some of these concepts were perhaps exhausted for having been overused and needed a burst of fresh air in which to flourish again. They had been circulating for a while without being called into question, and the current events suddenly made many of them appear as what they were: obsolete or, at any rate, frozen. If something positive could therefore come out of the present crisis, it might be the endeavor to query what we take for granted. The revisiting of the words that we use to better inhabit our worlds participated in such an endeavor. Scrutinizing the terms that serve to talk about what is going on without our even realizing that they may not express what we try to think and exploring their meanings and histories in various traditions and diverse contexts could give us a chance to refresh our perspective on the most serious issues of our time. If, as W. H. Auden ([1947] 2011: 15–16) writes in *The Age of Anxiety*, "the world needs a good wash and a week's rest," so do perhaps our ways of representing it, and we should not be, in his words, these "near-sighted scholars" who have uncritically "defined their terms." The task is undoubtedly immense, and our modest attempt can be only part of a larger collective effort. Moreover, while it is timely and imperative, it should be conceived of in the *longue durée*. Thus the sense of urgency that was ours when we started this project was converted into what we hope will be a long-lasting and open enterprise.

This proposal is all the more necessary since the often-praised instruments supposed to apprehend the present and forecast the future, from big data analysis to algorithm-based predictions, have spectacularly shown their limits. Moreover, they are as subject to ideological manipulations and rhetorical trickeries as old-fashioned rumors were. While recognizing the new avenues that such approaches open up, we are cautious of the over-reliance on the assumption that there is one magical key that will open all doors to reality. Critical approaches to the contemporary world and its problems such as those suggested here have been increasingly under attack or simply deemed passé, but we contend that they are not sedimented ruins of earlier times or simply subjective expressions of longings for days gone by. They are powerful repositories of modes of thinking that are being continuously sharpened by the call to respond to critical developments in the world. In these disquieting circumstances, we considered important that various disciplines engage in a dialogue beyond their epistemological differences so as to enrich our comprehension of the present moment as well as its ramifications in the past.

Thus the contributions to this volume come from anthropology, history, geography, economics, philosophy, political science, legal studies, and public health. Various methods are used, from philology to genealogy, from ethnography to historiography, from statistics to hermeneutics. The spatial decentering involves countries on five continents, from Sudan to Russia, from Colombia to India, from Cameroon to the Netherlands, from Saint Lucia to the United States, several chapters moving beyond national borders across the planet and others being in some way deterritorialized. Each author was instructed to discuss the self-evidence of the term in question and to propose an alternative reading of it—or better said, to put it to work within specific contexts in which it would uncover distinct realities. Rather than rushing in to offer readymade interpretations of contemporary predicaments, our idea was to arrive at different formulations of the issues at stake. Instead of right answers to provide, we looked for better questions to ask. This implied the recognition of points of ignorance, blind spots, and false certainties ensuing from the way we select problems, devise standards of substantiation, or adopt particular styles of reasoning. Ours was definitely not a claim that we would be able to understand the world but that we would be able to approach it otherwise.

....

In the opening chapter, Veena Das unexpectedly questions knowledge. More precisely, she is interested in its dark side as it is revealed in catastrophic moments of mass violence. But rather than separating, as is often done, the inordinate knowledge about the traumatic loss and the everyday knowledge related to smaller crises, she affirms the importance of apprehending both as intimately linked. To illustrate her claim, she analyzes two cases in depth. The first one, known as the Jeju incident, concerns massacres perpetrated in 1948 by the military government of South Korea with the support of the military administration of the United States against the residents of Jeju Island who were protesting the splitting of the country. The second one, during the Partition of India, regards the large-scale brutalization of both Hindu and Muslim women, comprising abductions, conversions, rapes, and murders that took place from 1947 on. In both cases there has been a long period of silence and secrecy with a late official recognition of the facts that had occurred in the form of discourses attempting to legitimize authorized versions, divide victims and traitors, and celebrate heroes and heroines. Contrary to this reification of knowledge through oppositions between truth and falsity and affirmations of certainty and positiveness by the authorities, ethnography uncovers the hesitations and indeterminacies in the production of knowledge within society, especially among those who have suffered from these extreme forms of violence. Investigations into the available archives as well as rituals honoring the dead offer more complex, more sensitive, and more appeasing access to unstable, contested, and often intolerable knowledge.

Discussing in a less tragic context the present fate of *democracy*, Jan-Werner Müller starts with a paradox since democracy seems to be almost universally claimed and at the same time increasingly deemed threatened. According to him, explanations of this paradox generally oscillate between a return of the past and the emergence of novel radicalities, with some searching for historical analogies and others tracking down new political theories. But the anxiety generated by this tension has also called into question the foundations of democracy inasmuch as it empowers the people through the right to vote yet rejects outcomes that might be seen as deleterious to the democratic project itself, such as electing leaders who institute authoritarian measures. Interestingly, such criticism is symmetrical to that of the populists who believe the people are deprived of their power by the elites. Both interpretations therefore give rise to a further interrogation: Who counts for the people? Whereas, from a liberal perspective, democracy formally engulfs the population in its entirety, populism distinguishes the so-called real people from the rest, on the basis of racial, ethnic, religious, or even political criteria. The populist position is contradictory not only with regard to the liberal one but with the very principle of democracy. However, its force, especially when it is in government, is to respect the letter of the democratic law while violating its spirit, thus embarrassing its critics. Many authoritarian and nationalist regimes across the planet can indeed present themselves as democratic, but just as easily, genuine democratic experiments in places outside the West can be excluded from theories of democracy on the grounds that these do not correspond to the hegemonic paradigm—not only from these theories but also from what counts as facts pertaining to these theories. Consider US projects of destabilizing democratic regimes in order to place authoritarian leaders more open to colonial projects of extraction in new guises, and then ask why these practices, authorized by democratic governments in North America or Europe, are not part of the facts that theories of democracy must account for. More generally, as Müller argues, since liberal democracies are not implementing the values they claim, beginning with the triptych *liberty, equality, and fraternity*, which has been receding in recent decades, it becomes all the more convenient for nondemocratic forms of polities to wear the mantle of democratic honorability. Thus democracy is surely endangered now not only by its populist challengers, as is often thought, but also, and perhaps even more, by its liberal champions.

The present flourishing of authoritarianism calls for an examination of *authority*, which Banu Bargu commences with a strong claim. For her, the multiplication of forms of authoritarianism in a time when its traditional forms, that of the father and the priest as well as that of elders and corporations, have declined should be regarded neither as a mere excess of authority nor as a nostalgia for past authority but as a consequence of a void of authority. Indeed, for Bargu, modern democracies are characterized by a structural deficit of the authority of the people, which is the corollary of the conflation of authority and power on the side of the state. This argument was already formulated by Hannah Arendt, for whom the erosion of authority, understood as what produces obedience without the exercise of coercion, paves the way to authoritarian regimes. It is also developed in a genealogical perspective by Giorgio Agamben, who affirms that, whereas in ancient Rome the authority of the Senate and the power of the people were distinct, authority and power have converged in modern societies. Such evolution, theorized and defended by Thomas Hobbes, was contested by Jean-Jacques Rousseau and Karl Marx, who viewed it as the usurpation of power by those who govern to the detriment of the people. As Bargu shows, the contemporary appeal of populism relies precisely on its denunciation of this deprivation of the people's power. In its right-wing manifestation, the leader occupies the empty space of lacking authority in the name of the people. In its left-wing expression, political participation is demanded by the people, but the leader often takes over.

The populist call to the people obviously poses the question of *belonging*. The definition or the delimitation of who counts as people is crucial in nation-states, as argued by Peter Geschiere. Remarkably, for him, the language of autochthony, which presumes that some have a precedence over others, are entitled to special rights, and can exclude those deemed allochthones, is commonly in use in the Netherlands as well as in Cameroon, and we could add in France, Germany, and the United States as well as in India, China, Australia, and South Africa, to name a few countries. This distinction between those who belong and those who do not has its roots, he reminds us, in Greek antiquity. But it also has a more recent history. In the colonial world, in particular in the French colonies, the differentiation between natives and nonnatives became part of the form of government, whether power was preferably delegated to the indigenes or to the immigrants. In Dutch society, it is when the guest workers became unwelcome that the new terminology appeared, being supposedly neutral but actually racialized as it applied essentially to non-Western populations. However, Geschiere affirms, it is at the end of the twentieth century, after the fall of the communist regimes, that the language of autochthony and allochthony decisively prevailed. In Africa it became a way of building constituencies and led to dramatic ethnic conflicts, with a linguistic twist opposing Francophones and Anglophones in Cameroon. In Europe it fueled xenophobic policies and divided the political landscape, with a religious twist as Muslims became the principal object of suspicion. However, this distinction between those who belong and those who do not relies on the construction of imaginary communities that invent false genealogies and build true enmities.

In contrast with such potentially or effectively bellicose attitudes, *toleration* offers a powerful response to the coexistence of differences, be they ethnic or religious. This is Uday Mehta's argument based on his reading of the writings of Gandhi, whose ideas about how to live with differences are nevertheless better thought of as "forbearance." As Mehta notes, following the constitutional settlement in 1950 in India and over the past seventy years, the constitutional norm of secularism, with its own, somewhat idiosyncratic model of religious pluralism, resulted in the relatively stable coexistence of democracy and nationalism, because both were seen as accepting and vouching for the country's prolific religious and cultural diversity. Yet he also alerts us to the disquiet often expressed in India with this model as a "haunting"—the sense that India's secularism and nationalism were not as "pure" as the nationalism based on the ideal of a single language, single religion, or cultural homogeneity seen to be typical of European nationalism. Recently the belligerent claims of a strong Hindu nationalism have weakened the constitutional principles of a democracy and a secularism that were welcoming of cultural and religious diversity. Violence against Muslim minorities, such as in the growing numbers of crowds lynching Muslims or use of political thugs to silence protests of such violations, has become blatant and open, while the passing of the notorious Citizenship Amendment Act in 2019 has put in jeopardy the very idea of India as a constitutional democracy. In this context, Mehta's revisiting of the philosophy of Gandhi, one of the world's major thinkers, is important. To do so, he juxtaposes Gandhi and two European modern philosophers on the question of how to manage religious difference and delineates the profound differences in perspective. In the wake of bloody civil wars based on sectarian distinctions within Christianity, Hobbes considered that only the state could ensure the settlement of such conflicts, while Locke trusted individual respect for such private matters but relied on political mediation in case of tensions. Both therefore connected religion and security, arguing for an external interference when security was threatened by dissensions in the name of religion. Conversely, for Gandhi the coexistence of various religions was a fact that society had to deal with independently of considerations of security, accepting the possibility of conflicts and trying to minimize them without the intervention of a third party, not only because the third party was the British colonizer but also because of his distrust of the state form itself as a guarantor of peace. In his view, toleration was not a value but merely reflected the evidence of the coexistence of religions, and secularism was not inscribed in a teleological narrative but simply manifested through actual facts. Such a radically different view might seem like a form of modest pragmatism. Yet it involves a deeper philosophy that puts its trust on the pull of a spirituality-based forbearance—after all, Gandhi's notions of satyagraha, or insistence on truth, had fortified the most ordinary of people to stand up to British power with no other weapon than a body ready to receive violence. Yet today Gandhi's ideas appear archaic, and an important question is how to understand the difficulties of sustaining such notions of frugality, forbearance, and nonviolence in a context in which the state might perform its secular mandate in the letter of the law, while it is common knowledge that such claims are just smoke and mirrors.

But is the analysis of the state the best way to think about *power*? It is this question that Alex de Waal addresses. Being interested in the various centers of gravity both at a global scale and within national borders, he takes Sudan as an important case study for his analysis. In this country the state is viewed as weak and contested but also as a source of rent and an object of robbery. Civil war has been raging for most of the sixty years since independence, with the humanitarian crisis in Darfur as the climax, ending with a peace agreement. This, too, though, eventually appeared to be a fool's game and soon broke down. Through a quasi-ethnography of the power relations at play during the negotiations between actors of the conflict, including international ones, de Waal shows how, in such contexts, politics literally becomes a marketplace in which power is a mere commodity. But this marketplace is dark and disorderly, thus generating brokerage, intimidation, and opacity of information. In short, it is a deal-making place—as some leaders elsewhere also define politics—in which transactions over private enrichment can be made to appear like pursuit of public goods. Far from the Weberian interpretation of the state as having the monopoly on the legitimate use of physical force, so-called fragile states such as Sudan should be regarded as oligopolistic, with a multiplicity of rivals involved in the exertion of violence and the pillage of public goods. But, according to de Waal, beyond these local games that have ravaged parts of the African continent, such heterodox analysis calls for a revision of most contemporary theories of the state in the so-called Global South. One could, however, wonder whether these neglected dimensions of political theory, such as disorder, lawlessness, or illegibility, should not be extended to Western states, not only for the disruption and chaos that these states create in other parts of the world—think of Iraq or Libya—but also for the various forms of predatory governance encountered in the very metropolitan world.

It is an extreme form of disorder that Julieta Lemaitre explores: *war*. Indeed, the war in Colombia, considered the longest civil conflict of the twentieth century, opposing the government and the paramilitaries to the guerrillas, has devastated the country for more than half a century. However, being described as low intensity, it has not received the international attention that the more than 200,000 casualties and five million internally displaced persons would have deserved. Writing in the aftermath of the conflict that long peace talks finally ended, Lemaitre contrasts the legal discourse of human rights and humanitarianism and the public narrative of suffering and victimhood with the ordinary experience of women who fled their homes and found refuge in the city. Their experience is one of fear of suspicious neighbors and threatening youths as well as of difficult attempts to recover minimal forms of agency, one of previous collaboration with various groups engaged in the civil war as well as of awareness of the persisting role of mafias benefiting from the support of allegedly disarmed actors of the conflict. Neither international organizations nor national institutions take this into account, as they assume a definite separation between war and peace and a clear distinction between accountable soldiers and innocent civilians, and as they emphasize the return of the rule of law and the need for reconstruction. Such analysis goes beyond the specific case of Colombia and calls for a critical take on the political and moral simplifications at work in processes of postconflict settlements, in which the actors are all too eager to find arrangements at the cost of the complex and disturbing truths they prefer to ignore.

No less complex and disturbing truths may arise from the interpretation of *revolution*, as Behrooz Ghamari-Tabrizi shows. Establishing a parallel between two almost concomitant facts, namely, the onset of the Iranian Revolution against the shah and his Western supporters and the debate around the French Revolution in Parisian intellectual circles in the background of the discredited communist regimes, he suggests that ironically the real event occurred at the very moment when the historical concept was waning. As the specter of an apparently irremediable ending in terror or totalitarianism loomed, the imaginary of a possibly different world carried by the revolutionary project seemed to dissolve with the discovery of the atrocities perpetrated in its name and the dictatorial regimes to which it led. But this dissolution appeared not to be ineluctable, and the Arab uprisings awakened anew the utopian hope of radical change, soon contradicted by the unfolding of the events, however, at least in Syria and Egypt. Returning to the Iranian Revolution, its ideological project was primarily a religious one, which Foucault describes in terms of political spirituality. The objective of the revolutionaries was not only to transform society, its inequality and its injustices, but also to transform themselves. Yet, Ghamari-Tabrizi argues, their political theology was difficult to apprehend from a Western perspective, as the creative and inspired dimension of the revolt was buried under representations of dogmatic backwardness and refusal of progress. In contrast, the Arab uprisings were almost immediately read on both ends of the global political spectrum in terms of rejection of authoritarianism and a democratic turn toward the liberal values of the West. Hence, the Arab Spring was designated in reference to the 1848 Spring of Nations and the 1968 Prague Spring celebrated by pundits and politicians in Europe and North America, at least until the election of Mohamed Morsi. More generally, the question posed is that of the frequent incapacity of observers to read such events in their own historical context, which leads to the betrayal of their meaning, as the actors' intentions are lost in translation. Here, too, the question of what constitutes success and what constitutes failure is important to consider, for, if history does not belong to the victors, we might ask what residues these political aspirations leave by way of political sensibilities that might become dormant, waiting for some other occasion or form to be reignited. In other words, we could argue that there is no such thing as dead experience.

The problem of intelligibility is also at stake in the approach to *corruption*, a morally loaded word omnipresent in the contemporary world. In her study of the practices that are designated as such in Russia, Caroline Humphrey emphasizes that *corruption* refers to both the description of an act and a judgment about it but also that the act itself can receive very different interpretations depending on the perspective adopted. Thus, at a global level, international organizations produce statistics and establish rankings among countries; at a national level, each state develops its specific criteria and prescriptive discourses; and at an intimate level, individuals make evaluations regarding what they deem wrong. These perspectives can radically differ. For instance, as Humphrey explains, civil servants consider that they are entitled to obtain the best possible share of the state's resources in return for their services, and they do so according to their position in the bureaucratic hierarchy. Beyond their salary and their housing, they benefit from various forms of privilege granted by the state and of rent extorted from people situated in a lower estate. From a global perspective, these practices are generally understood as corruption. From the national perspective, they are codified, considered legal while other practices such as bribes or kickbacks are illegal. From an intimate perspective, people produce their own assessment, blaming these acts only when they are not executed according to one's rank or when they are in excess of what is expected. But on the whole, rather than being individually determined, the privileges and rents are part of a system. For example, the sum required to get a job is distributed along the hierarchical chain but also entails the necessity of illicit incomes for the new employee. Such practices reveal an economic system in which values and affects are sufficiently shared within society to allow the reproduction of these practices.

At first sight, one could think of *openness* as inscribed in a symmetrical moral economy that rejects opacity and calls for transparency. It is this widely proclaimed ideal that Todd Sanders and Elizabeth Sanders challenge. While openness seems to work hand in hand with democracy, as whistleblowers lay bare the dangers threatening citizens and journalists correct fake news through their fact-checking, a closer examination of the implementation of this ideal shows that it has more complicated and more ambiguous implications than one often imagines. The controversies around Wikileaks leave no doubt about the potential political stakes, but it is the domain of science that Sanders and Sanders choose to explore with two interesting case studies. The first one concerns the 2009 Climategate in Britain. This scandal followed the release of thousands of private electronic documents of environment experts discussing their results; used by climate skeptics, the leak became a major contribution to the denial of global warming, but it also served to challenge the traditional scientific norms of confidentiality and secrecy. The second case study pertains to the 2017 HONEST Act, passed by the US Congress, which requires that the Environmental Protection Agency renders all the scientific data and studies on which it makes its decisions publicly available. Deemed dishonest by numerous scientific institutions, the act was regarded as one more example of the war on science, since the legislation implied the release of sensitive information and opened the way to corporate interventions, as had previously been the case for the tobacco industry. In a time when openness is consensually presented as a public good and a democratic practice, these two examples demonstrate its downside and, in the end, the manipulation to which any such supposed ideal can be submitted.

Another success story in the global parlance is *resilience*. Noting the rapid dissemination of the word in environmental debates, Jonathan Pugh inscribes it in a broader evolution of world development policies. After a long period of intervention at the governmental level through structural adjustment and state-building programs, international agencies, notably those of the United Nations, turned to what they referred to as civil society, supporting nongovernmental organizations and developing microfinance projects. The most recent addition of this turn was resilience, defined as the capacity of a community or a society to transform itself to better adapt to new challenges. The term stemmed from physics, later flourished in psychology, and was eventually adopted in policies, in particular around environmental issues. In this last context, small islands and their inhabitants appeared to epitomize the necessity and urgency of contemporary resilience as global warming menaces their very existence, with sea level rising and powerful hurricanes multiplying. But as Pugh shows, the conceptualization of the problem in terms of resilience has come down to transferring the responsibility of the management of these threats from those who produce environmental changes to those who endure them. In the wake of the reception of the so-called ontological turn, it has resonated with a romanticized version of the noble savage, whose resilient mode of living is presented as an alternative to Western lifestyles and a response to the dangers related to the Anthropocene. Simultaneously every scene of destruction becomes also a scene of possibility within a form of capitalism in which such terms as disruptive technologies are seen as major sources of innovation. In contrast with a real estate market that does not expect to build for the long term in this context but sees natural destruction as an opportunity for short-term gains, we have to rethink the Anthropocene as a context for new forms of production that create value, not destructive consumption.

In most of these discussions, one tends to lose sight of a crucial element: *inequality*. Considering it at a global level, Ravi Kanbur analyzes its evolution from a dual perspective, which, interestingly, provides two sets of symmetrical results. On the one hand, inequality between nations, measured in terms of per capita national income, has declined in the past quarter-century, largely due to spectacular growth rates in countries such as China and India, although even Africa has benefited to a certain degree from the economic boom. On the other hand, inequality within nations, estimated via decile segmentation or Gini index, has increased in many countries, including the United States and most of Europe as well as China and India. But while, on the whole, the diminishing inequality between nations represents three-fourths of the global inequality among human beings, the income gap between rich and poor countries remains formidable. The unequal fortune depending on where one was born, which is called *citizenship rent* on the lucky side and *citizenship penalty* on the unlucky, appears to be a logical incentive for international migration, Kanbur explains. However, migrants making up only 3 percent of the world population implies, first, that the immense majority of people in the world live in the country where they were born and, second, that anti-immigrant angst is partly the result of manipulations of public opinion. Indeed, while economists, using both historical and present data, discuss the consequences of migration for the host country in terms of national income and natives' wages, it is clear that the debates about the opening of borders and the emotions mobilized around immigration have more than economic grounds. The backlash against cross-border migration, particularly in Europe and the United States, is a question of values and affects, of moral sentiments and political imaginaries. Thus the link between inequality and migration concerns not only those who leave their country in search of a better life but also those in the host country who observe with apprehension the growing disparities that impact their lives as a result of the national policies conducted by their government.

In the end, if one word dominates the vocabulary of current concerns, it is *crisis*. As it serves to name a multiplicity of issues, its ubiquity and polysemy are both striking and problematic, Didier Fassin argues. The term itself originates in ancient Greek, with the dual meaning of a pivotal moment in the evolution of an event and of the evaluation of this event in order to adjudicate it. In other words, it associates an objective and a subjective dimension; a problem can actually exist, but it becomes a crisis only when it is problematized as such. But what happens when the two aspects are disconnected, when a serious issue remains ignored or, on the contrary, when an issue is fabricated or amplified? Such discrepancies call for an analysis in terms of authorship, Fassin argues. In the first case, the question is who has the authority to declare a crisis; the problem of police violence in the United States existed and was recognized as such by the African American populations who were victims of it long before it became a crisis when acknowledged by society at large. In the second case, the question is what the declaration of a crisis authorizes; the problem of the rise in crime was artificially created by conservative politicians in France to generate reactions of fear, justify law-and-order policies, and ultimately obtain electoral gains. A critical approach to crises therefore does not take them for granted but addresses the relations of power as well as the logics of interest at work. But the inflation in the use of the term to describe multiple states of affairs suggests a more general interrogation. Does it signal a mere trivialization of the idea of crisis or, on the contrary, suggest the existence of a world in crisis? These two interpretations are not exclusive. The banality of the term does not preclude deeper anxiety. Whereas it certainly has different meanings in various geographical and social contexts, today's prevalence of the language of crisis should not be overlooked. It certainly characterizes a form of life that involves a particular relation to time and action, a sense of urgency and disempowerment, a perplexity about the present and alienation from the future.

By a remarkable coincidence, as we were making our final revisions to this volume, the world entered an unprecedented moment as the coronavirus pandemic brought most countries on the planet to an almost complete halt. Much to our dismay, many of the disorders of democracy and governance that are discussed in the chapters that follow, including questions of scientific uncertainty and secrecy, the spread of false information, challenges to democracy, calls for resilience, and the unveiling of disparities, presented themselves now in a vocabulary of unprecedented crises. Ironically, in many places of the world the pandemic came on the heels of other crises and became an opportunity for many governments either to use obsolete legal mechanisms to expand their powers or to create new forms of surveillance, many of which (but not all) received either open or tacit popular support. This is hardly the place to offer a detailed analysis of the global dimensions of the coronavirus pandemic or the very different ways in which measures to deal with it have impacted different kinds of populations. However, the difficult relation between science and politics that it has revealed must surely elicit serious responses from social scientists. First, the dominance of epidemiological models might have hidden from view the fact that these models explicitly excluded any consideration of ethical or economic consequences of policy choices (Das 2020a; Manski 2020). Second, given the disproportionate adverse impact on vulnerable populations such as the poor and migrant communities, one would have expected that discussion of social and economic inequality would move to center stage in public policy, yet there are few signs that such shifts will happen (Fassin 2020; Dorn, Cooney, and Sabin 2020). Finally, one must realize that many uncertainties with regard to the numbers of people infected or infection fatality ratios of COVID-19 are a result of the lack of sufficient testing in nonsymptomatic populations. Thus this uncertainty is itself produced by the shortages of testing kits, of protective equipment for frontline health workers, and failure to plan for keeping supply lines open. Said succinctly, the natural and the social cannot be parsed apart, nor can the devastation of this pandemic be understood without understanding the slow erosion of health infrastructures and the decline of safety networks that had made everyday life itself perilous for the vulnerable groups most affected by the pandemic and the modes of its management. This is the sober note on which the last chapter of this book concludes, as we are thrown into yet more dangers to the social fabric of many societies.

KNOWLEDGE   1

VEENA DAS

At first sight it might seem puzzling to place the word *knowledge* within a lexicon for a dark time since the concept of knowledge is linked in the popular imagination with such noble pursuits as the search for truth. After all, the current disquiet around the ubiquity of prevailing falsehoods that pass for the truth relates not only to possibilities opened up in the era of big data but also to the fact that even heads of state can no longer be held responsible for spreading falsehoods. Thus the "Fact Checker" feature at the *Washington Post* reported that as of October 30, 2018, President Trump had made 6,420 false or misleading claims over 649 days of his presidency (Kessler, Rio, and Kelly 2018).[1] These blatant, in-your-face falsehoods by the president and the enthusiasm of his supporters for his "ability to tell it as it is" are attributed to a decline in the nature of democratic politics and in the moral ethos of our times. Yet it is important to remember that Michel Foucault's ([1999] 2003) concept of the grotesque (to which we alluded in the introduction) alerted us to the fact that the grotesque refers not only to degraded sovereign power but also to the way expert knowledges establish their authority, not on the strength of reason but through tokens of power. Foucault famously showed that truth is not simply there waiting to be discovered but rather makes its appearance on a scene under very specific circumstances that can give it very different meanings and significance. In religious and theological imagination, this pursuit of knowledge is not a simple, innocent affair but has a dark side. My efforts in this chapter are to track the dark side of knowledge by an attentiveness to the way knowledge is secreted in everyday life, especially in relation to catastrophic events. I explore only one aspect of this dark side of knowledge, what I call inordinate knowledge, that subjects have to bear and that has consequences far beyond the act of merely knowing the attributes of an object such as knowing that Everest is the highest mountain.[2]

In his characterization of inordinate knowledge, Stanley Cavell (2010: 84) describes it as "excessive in its expression" and contrasts it with knowledge that is "mere or bare or pale or intellectualized or uninsistent or inattentive or distracted or filed, archived knowledge." As I understand it, each and every adjective here points to a region of knowledge within which the subject has yet to discover which aspects of knowledge matter to her and where her attachments lie. I hope to show in the rest of this chapter that the boundaries between what knowledge is pale or bare and what it is that comes to carry the possibilities of excessive expression do not lie in any absolute characteristic of forms of knowledge. Rather, it is the way in which knowledge enters the realms of the social, becomes weighty with consequences for those who are in possession of knowledge or those who have to endure what they cannot ignore, that it moves from being pale and bare to dark and filled with plenitude. I present two case studies of catastrophic events and their folding into everyday life with a view to showing how the different modes of knowing as means of navigating the catastrophic and the everyday lead us to see that inordinate knowledge is not simply knowledge *about* an object in some neutral kind of way within a reality that can be held to be stable. Reality does not have that frontal character; it is not something we might watch before us or something that intrudes from the outside, but it exists around us like the atmosphere. Reality is deeply embedded within context, if we understand context not simply as an external frame secured through an indexical relation to time and space markers, but rather like the weaver's loom that is discerned within the cloth it weaves. Thus modes of knowing do not simply represent objects; they also constitute the objects of knowing, or efface them, in a manner that profoundly affects how one comes to inhabit a new reality.[3]

The Catastrophic and the Everyday: Modalities of Knowing

In his discussion of the fragility of the everyday and the possibilities of destruction and possible recovery the philosopher Piergiorgio Donatelli (2015) thinks of two different routes. The first route is that on which an extraordinary event of traumatic loss functions as both an event and a figure of thought. In contrast with (or parallel to) this view of life as vulnerable to catastrophic events, Donatelli draws attention to the kind of destruction that consists of small, recurring, repetitive crises that define everyday life itself or are grown within the everyday. Rather than taking these two routes as different ways of arriving at the everyday, I propose to look at the everyday and the catastrophic as mutually braided.

The twentieth century has been often characterized as a century of genocides. The imperative to contest the story of collective violence from the point of view of victims and survivors has been an important part of this story. Yet there is also the worry that victim stories lead to a kind of voyeurism (Kleinman and Kleinman 1996; Mookherjee 2015) or that the ubiquity of a trauma narrative substitutes critical engagement with the structural forces of inequality or discrimination by a psychologizing of experience and of subjectivity (Fassin and Rechtman 2009). But the neat divisions between knowledge that claims its authority on the basis of subjective experience and that which relies on objective criteria and evaluation through distancing procedures (Minow 1992, 1998) give way to entanglement of the subjective and the objective if we pay attention to the manner in which subjectivity itself gets suffused with technical bureaucratic languages.

An impressive literature has emerged on mass violence, genocide, and acts of violence committed in the shadow of war. I offer a discussion of two different contexts in which the issues of law, bureaucratic procedures, and violence are posed. The first is the context of organized massacres in Jeju Island in South Korea from 1947 to 1954, which brings into focus the question of officially imposed silence about state executed violence (Park 2010). It also shows the work that the legal recognition given to the term *victim* came to perform in the lives of the kin and community of the dead, but this category (of the victim) is not transparent. Rather, the bureaucratic legal forms through which the victim status is produced align with very different kinds of knowledge—shamanic, ritual, genealogical—to generate different kinds of affects. In this case, the survivors absorb all kinds of socially concealed knowledge that might remain hidden, through which social life is sought to be repaired. State recognition of the brutal violence done to a population seen as marginal does not take the form of victim testimonies as in truth and reconciliation commissions—yet the pressure on families to press for state recognition of the harms done to them was crucial in the context in which the stigma of being traitors to the national cause continued to suffuse social life with bitter divisions, imposed silences, and incredible obstacles for survivors to mend the ruptures in generational connections.

The second case study I offer is that of the massive sexual violence committed in communal riots in the context of the Partition of India in 1947. The division of India into two independent and composite nations, India and Pakistan, was a formative event for both nations,[4] but it was also one of the most violent events in history, marked by massive intercommunal killing, rape, and abduction of women. However, what these events produced then was not the category of "victim"; the legal categories that came into operation were "refugees," "evacuee property," and "abducted persons." The Constituent Assembly, an elected body that met right after independence to write the Constitution of India, which enacted new laws and ratified the colonial laws that would continue to be operative in independent India, debated the legal mechanisms for the recovery and rehabilitation of abducted women and children. Later I track how the state's intervention in this recovery and rehabilitation process constituted a masculine imaginary of the nation and how the category of the abducted woman seeped into the everyday life of families and communities. (For a detailed discussion, see Das 2007.)[5]

I must confess that there is an asymmetry in the manner in which I came to choose these two cases for discussion. In the case of the Jeju massacres, about which I had known very little, it was reading Han Kang's (2016) novels, especially *Human Acts: A Novel*—a haunting and even terrifying novel based on the uprisings and massacres in the southern city of Gwangju—that led me to a visit to Jeju Island and Gwangju to meet with different scholars and theater activists to understand something of these events. If I write about these events now, it is as an act of tribute to the Korean scholars and activists who have struggled with these issues for many years.

In contrast, the case of the abducted women is a topic I had worked on for many years; these events were also tied to my personal history. But however many years I spend on these themes, there is a lot I don't know and perhaps cannot know. Recently my eldest grandson, Nayan, asked me if I could tell him about a historical event that had changed the course of our family life. His fictionalized account of my responses to his questions inspired me to think more about how a woman (me) now in her seventies would rake the fallen leaves of language and literature to re-create experiences she had as a baby—experiences of loss that she could not have comprehended then. I hope this asymmetry is not simply an irritant but yields interesting insights. For instance, how does my own understanding of violence and the overwhelming and intimate knowledge I gathered about the way violence done to women seeps into the most intimate aspects of relations make me a different kind of reader of Kang's almost unbearable rendering of loss, narrated not only through the living or through ghostly apparitions of the dead but also in the voice of dead bodies dissolving into stinking masses? I do not have answers to such questions, but I hope the juxtaposition of these cases might be seen not simply as a means for making heuristic comparisons between two external situations that are both similar and different but also as a way that the anthropologist absorbs such overwhelming knowledge and the experiences that haunt her outside the disciplinary frames.

Were the Jeju Massacres an "Incident"?

What is known in official parlance as the Jeju 4.3 incident is actually much more ambiguous in terms of its antecedents and the continuing violence it unleashed in subsequent years that went unacknowledged until 2000. That is the year when the National Committee for Investigation of the Truth about the Jeju 4.3 Events was finally established, followed by public apologies for the brutalities committed against the inhabitants of Jeju between 1947 and 1954 and the imposition of complete censorship on the survivors and witnesses of the brutal massacres. Announcing 14,028 victims, the first report of the commission was published in 2003, following an official apology by President Roh Moo-hyun. His subsequent participation in a service in 2006 in commemoration of the events paved the way for public discussion. Jeju residents vigorously contest the idea that the brutalities and subsequent imposition of taboos on the discussion of Jeju violence can be simply treated as an "incident" with a defined beginning and an end.[6]

Although an agreed narrative of the details of the events that transpired under the general heading of the "Jeju uprising" as well as the heterogeneity of the experiences of residents living in different parts of Jeju is only now beginning to emerge, I give a very broad description based on, among others, Merrill (1980) and Park (2010). Park divides the insurgency into six phases. He identifies the period of Jeju uprisings as occurring between 1947 and 1953, first under the administration of the US Army Military Government and later under President Syngman Rhee's leadership. Started as part of the independence movement against Japanese colonial rule, the movement escalated into a full-scale insurgency or uprising in the course of a single year. Park attributes the radical escalation to rivalry between mainland police forces and the local constabulary, along with a complete misreading of events taking place in Jeju by the officers of the military occupation and later by the leadership on the mainland. A major obstacle in rendering a fuller picture of these events has been the paucity of publicly available documents and sometimes the exclusive reliance of scholars on English-language documents produced by the military occupation.

Residents of Jeju had been among the most active protestors in Korea against Japanese colonial occupation that had lasted thirty-five years. Following the Japanese surrender to Allied Forces on August 15, 1945, there was a period some consider a time of relative peace, while others describe continuing violence and confusion. In any case, arbitrary arrests and police action against Jeju Islanders followed when plans for the unification of the two divisions in Korea under American and Soviet trustee status failed. Islanders began to organize protests against the proposed elections in South Korea, suspecting that these separate elections would lead to a permanent division of the country (see, for instance, Cumings 2016; Shin, Park, and Yang 2007; Kim 2014). While there were several incidents of police firing indiscriminately on protestors and arbitrary arrests in the preceding months, April 3, 1948, is considered the official start of what came to be characterized as an armed uprising. There is no agreed narrative about the character of this uprising: Was it a *struggle* led by the Jeju division of the South Korean Labor Party (SKLP) against the US Army Military Government's involvement in plans to divide Korea permanently? Were these protestors unruly rioters? Or had the Jeju division of the SKLP been infiltrated and was acting as the fifth column on behalf of a communist insurgency? Or were they, or many of them, just children with rusty weapons playing war? What is clear is that the military government in conjunction with the US military administration responded with ruthless and disproportionate force to suppress the uprising by unleashing a large police force flown in from the mainland. Extreme right-wing paramilitary groups joined in. Mass slaughter of villagers, especially of men, took place, and whole villages were erased as punishment for participation in the uprising. The Korean sociologist Sungman Koh (2018) notes that labeling the protests "treason" enabled massacres and violation of human rights by governmental forces to continue, and even to escalate in 1954–57. Estimates of the number of people who were killed vary, but about 10 percent of the population of Jeju Island was killed—the absolute number estimated at thirty thousand.[7] After South Korea's April Revolution of 1960, which overthrew the Rhee government, there was a brief period when the terms for the dead shifted from *red guerrillas* and *rioters* to *guiltless survivors* and *innocent victims*. However, the military coup of 1961 that installed the Park Chung-hee government again led to the extreme stigmatization of the dead; even the expression "innocent deaths" was banned from use in public (Koh 2018; Park 2011, as cited in Koh 2018).

It is only relatively recently (January 2000), after the shift to a democratic government in the 1980s, that the Jeju 4.3 incident received official recognition in South Korea with the Establishment of the Special Act of Investigation of the Jeju 4.3 Incident and Recovering the Honor of Victims (the Special Act), charged with uncovering the truth of the Jeju incident. Finally, two separate official apologies to the bereaved families and survivors offered by President Roh Moo-hyun, in 2003 and 2006, signaled that the period of treating the Jeju incident as a taboo subject was over.[8] The government also installed the Public Peace Park, allowing (as Koh [2018] says) what was a secret history to pass into the public discourse and public history of South Korea. Within the larger complex of issues, such as those pertaining to transitional justice, the Special Act also introduced a new mechanism for determining and separating the recognized victims from those who could not be incorporated as victims into official history. What impact did this provision of the act have on the processes of ritual commemoration and of familial memory, which seemed to take the official categories to be salient for repairing genealogical ruptures? Was the bureaucratic mechanism successful in imposing its own reality on the reality of survivors, especially in relation to their obligations as kin and as descendants? What different forms of knowledge were marshaled to overcome this division between officially recognized victims and traitors, solidified by the certifying process of a government anxious to undo past wrongs?[9]

Ritual Knowledge and Its Adjacent Realities

When thousands of people are massacred and buried in mass graves, how do families grapple with this brutal severing of the knowledge that connects one generation to another (Kim 2019)?

One powerful model of how rituals respond to the presence of unknown dead—physically proximate though not socially known—is offered by Heonik Kwon (2006, 2008), who shows how the holes created in the connectivity of the social tissue, as in the indeterminacy introduced into genealogical knowledge, are sought to be repaired by improvisations introduced in rituals by stretching them in new directions. Kwon shows how the unknown dead (usually pictured as the unknown fallen soldier) are imagined as hungry and thirsty ghosts whose anguish is the cause of innumerable dangers and misfortunes to the living. The living cannot offer the dead solace because the unknown dead cannot be placed within the grid of genealogical knowledge necessary to make them benign ancestors. In the case of villages in Vietnam (notwithstanding important regional variations), one ritual technique was to make ancestral shrines under shamanic instruction for these unnamed soldiers who have been forced into an existence as ghosts. Families were instructed that such shrines were to be placed outside the domestic space in order to distinguish between known ancestors and the strangers who died in these foreign lands but who still needed rituals to placate their conditions as ghosts. Yet the difference between kin and strangers, ancestors and ghosts, turns out not to be absolute, since the war also created estrangement between kin who might have fought on opposite sides, sometimes unknown to each other. The hospitality offered to the stranger could also become a way of reincorporating the estranged kin. Kwon's consoling story of hospitality is a wonderful example of what I have called "ordinary ethics" (see Das 2012; Lambek 2010), but in treating the ritual and shamanic knowledge as completely independent of the distortions by secular power, the argument elides one important aspect: the intertwined nature of bureaucratic power and ritual action. Does this elision have consequences for understanding the administrative grotesque—the various mechanisms instituted and carried out by pen-pushing bureaucrats of issuing or denying certificates, acknowledging or disavowing any knowledge of the whereabouts of the disappeared, or of places where the dead are haphazardly buried that have to be contained or transformed through shamanic knowledge and ritual manipulations?

A powerful essay by Koh (2018) shows how modern bureaucratic procedures, even in their benign incarnations, sometimes tear apart the continuity of generational connections and how the work of ritual to restore connections is engaged. It is interesting that the interplay between the designation of a dead ancestor as "victim" or as "traitor" through procedures authorized by the state meets the visceral knowledge that descendants bring to bear on the experience of their kin such that ritual creates an alternate form of knowing that does not directly contest the state's production of public knowledge of events but still creates a story diagonal to it.

Koh describes the motivation for his essay as providing a description of how bereaved families scattered throughout Jeju and in Osaka, whose relatives were massacred in the police and military operations, engaged the state through the Special Act to obtain documentation with regard to their status as victims, and how they pacified the dead through ritual commemoration. He characterizes the knowledge that the descendants had of their deceased relatives as "experiential knowledge" and contrasts it with the impersonal knowledge of the "April 3 Incident" as it is embodied in national narratives. An example of these national narratives is found in the names of victims inscribed in the Peace Park in Jeju to commemorate the event and to acknowledge wrongful killing. But what does the public proclamation of some who died as victims, even as it excludes others who are characterized as traitors, do to the experiential knowledge that Koh is talking about? Clearly the term *experiential* as an adjective does not take us to the realm of experience; it refers more to the different ways we come to know something rather than to the experience of *carrying* that knowledge. Yet it is not as if the anthropological discussions on experience, which rely on a rather simplistic notion of the inner or on contrasts between sensory impressions and cognitive models of realty, will solve the complex issues (see Das 2007, 2020b). For now, I suggest that it would be helpful to see what kinds of issues came up for the survivors in this particular milieu. After all, talk about the unknown dead in a milieu in which ancestors and ghosts are not simply distant and abstract concepts but are felt with every sinew of the body, who come to haunt the descendants through dreams and apparitions, is not the same as the talk of ancestors in contexts in which the relation to the unknown dead (e.g., the fallen soldier) is commemorated primarily through national rituals.[10] Even though one might regard the rituals as "performances" in both cases, the swirling affects in each case might be very different.[11]

The case study I present from Koh's work involves members of a family he calls D, identifying different members with a combination of the letter *D* and a number, ranging from D-1 to D-10, spanning three generations. The events center around D-4, who was a primary school teacher and a member of the local branch of the SKLP who had participated in several protests over arbitrary police and military actions in 1948. He was targeted for surveillance and was repeatedly imprisoned and released. In order to save himself from police intimidation, he had tried to escape to Osaka following the lead of his two brothers, who had already managed to migrate as stowaways, but D-4's plans failed and he escaped to the mountains to evade the police. As exemplary punishment and a warning to the community, his parents, his wife, and later he himself were shot dead, as witnessed by the community and his young children.

The surviving members of the family were now split: the two brothers in Osaka were adopted by Japanese childless couples and in time became naturalized Japanese citizens; the surviving children of D-4 were brought up by their grandparents but with the stigma of guilt by association of being antinational. After years of silence around the massacre of their family members, the story of reclaiming their dead relatives as ancestors began with the passing of the Special Act in 2003 and the public apologies issued by the president of the republic in 2005.

The Special Act included provisions by which families could register their dead kin in the Family Register maintained by the state and apply for victim status to be accorded to these dead relatives.[12] Article 2 of the Special Act, according to Koh, defined eligibility as "civilians rendered deceased, missing, or with a post-event disorder by the Jeju 4.3 incident or imprisoned," provided that the deaths had occurred in the legally approved period of March 1, 1947, to September 21, 1954. However, the question of who was to be considered a genuine victim was resolved only in 2002, when the Constitutional Court ruled on a clause that created exceptions to the effect that key executive members of the Jeju branch of the SKLP, as well as ringleaders of the armed guerrillas, would be excluded from victim status as they did not deserve the protection of the republic. However, clear evidence was to be provided of these antinational activities for the clause to apply.

A large number of people in Jeju made petitions on the basis of this provision. Koh reports that after reviewing the petitions the committee found that 84.4 percent of those massacred were killed in punitive operations by the army or police (see also Kim 2014). In the case of the D family, after years of silence and secrecy during which ancestral rites were conducted in the most clandestine manner by the survivors, D-7, a surviving daughter, and her brother, who had escaped to Osaka, tried to formally register the deaths of her grandparents and her parents in the family register.

As discussed, one of the provisions of the Special Act was geared toward allowing bereaved families to apply for victim status for their dead relatives. Accordingly, D-7 and her brother submitted documents detailing the deaths of their grandparents and parents and asking for victim status to be accorded to them. After a lapse of four years, the investigating committee did certify the two grandparents and the mother as victims, thus exonerating them from charges of being part of the communist insurgency. But D-7 and her brother failed to get victim status for their father, who fell under an exceptional clause applying to those who were members of the Jeju branch of the SKLP. D-7 recalled that when she visited the Peace Park where names of victims are publicly displayed and realized that the tablet that had her father's name had been replaced by an empty tablet, she was devastated that her father would not have a place among the tablets for his parents and his wife.

After consultations with a shaman the D family decided to build a semipublic family mausoleum where the graves of all their dead would be placed together so that D-7's father would be united in memory with his parents and his wife. Although for purposes of official records the brother and uncles who had migrated to Osaka and had become Japanese citizens would not have counted as descendants in the Family Register, by using documents from the time when they were in Jeju, they avoided being struck from the register. D-7 and her brother were thus able to bring home the dead who would otherwise have become, in time, like the ghosts described by Kwon, who roamed the streets because there were no identifiable descendants to take them home.

I have described this case from Koh's essay in detail because it provides an important illustration of the entanglement of state-produced knowledge and ritual knowledge. Here the term *victim* does not appear as an appeal to the authority of subjective experience or in the context of providing testimony to a truth and reconciliation commission, or even as part of the victim statement during the sentencing phase of a trial, as in US courts (Minow 1992). Instead it becomes the qualifying condition for genealogical connections to be maintained in imagining kinship as constitutive of the relations between the living and the dead. What I find most compelling in Koh's analysis is the way ritual requirements for specific identities to be accorded to the dead (victim or traitor?) become a means of authorizing the knowledge produced by the state.

The entanglement of different ways of knowing and classifying—that of the bureaucrats (victim or traitor?) and that of the shaman (ancestor or ghost?)—makes *victim* not only a legal category but also one that becomes a defining condition for the efficacy of rituals for ancestors and for shamanic knowledge to function. The inordinate character of knowledge appears in this world as the unbearable burden of not being able to convert your dead kin into ancestors, consigning them to a ghostly existence. In the case of the D family, there were clearly the affects generated through the children's knowledge of how exactly their parents had died (shot before their eyes), as well as having to carry with them the stigma of being children of traitors. The recognition they sought from the state in terms of acknowledgment of the harms done to them is more toward the restitution of the good name of their ancestors, so that the ancestors can rest peacefully in death, and less in terms of the discourse of transnational justice or human rights—although as Don Selby's (2018) work on human rights in Thailand shows, the latter discourses can find their footing in religious discourses. In the end, the state failed D-7 and her brothers, but the construction of a family mausoleum with the help of shamanic knowledge made the cruelty of the state's form of knowledge more bearable to the descendants.

In contrast, the Partition of India did not produce the legal category of victim but that of the abducted woman, which has a long history in the political imaginary as well as in the mythological imagination in India.

The Abducted Woman, Dark Knowledge, and the Occult

As mentioned earlier, the Partition of India in 1947 was a founding event in the history of the subcontinent. Independence for India and Pakistan and freedom from the bondage of colonial rule came along with massive displacement of populations on both sides of the newly drawn border. The nationalist movement had generated demands from the Muslim League for a separate homeland for Muslims, who feared that despite the promises made by the Indian National Congress, that as a secular republic India would honor the rights of all religious minorities, including the Muslims reduced to a minority in the new country. While precise figures on population loss in the Punjab are a matter of some debate, recent estimates calculated on the basis of the census reports of 1931, 1941, and 1951 of India and 1951 of Pakistan put Partition-related population loss either through direct death or forced migration in the range of 2.3 million to 3.9 million.[13] A complete religious homogenization took place at the district level of the affected states (see Hill et al. 2008), although nationally India has the third largest population of Muslims in the world, which shows that migration of Muslims was limited to certain areas in the north.

In addition to widespread murder and looting, one aspect of the communal riots during Partition was the large-scale violence against women. According to the fact-finding report by the government of India (Khosla 1989), the number of women abducted was 100,000. The Constituent Assembly of India that met in the transition period to ratify older legislation and enact new laws paid special attention to the task of recovery and rehabilitation of abducted women. The major legal instrument enacted was the

Abducted Persons (Recovery and Restoration) Act of 1949. Several administrative mechanisms were put in place for implementing the provisions of these agreements. Social workers and other officials were trained to conduct search operations, and anecdotal evidence and some accounts available in the archive suggest that some families did report missing women. In general, however, the searches were conducted rather like spy operations: officials in disguise collected nuggets of information from villages and from women who were either forcibly kept by or were hiding with their abductor's family (see, for instance, Patel 2006). There is not much evidence available on what happened to the abducted women who were restored to their original families. Yet the secrecy with which the events of abduction and restoration were treated lent an uncanny quality to the everyday as it became a public secret that a family might well have a woman who was abducted and forcibly converted at that time.

I offer some instances of how this uncanniness of the ordinary sometimes broke into public knowledge, leading to improvisations through which such breaches of the "normal" were navigated and contained within kinship relations. The "publics" the families had to negotiate in terms of knowledge of a woman's abduction and possible rape were not anonymous publics but those made up of extended families and kin groups where the woman's reputation mattered for such things as marriage prospects (Das 1976). Ideas of purity and honor were crucial for containing what I call "poisonous knowledge" (Das 2007) secreted by such collective events as the large-scale abduction of women. In her work on the national discourse on rape in Bangladesh after the war of independence in that country, Nayanika Mookherjee (2015) draws a compelling picture of the way publicity generated by nationalist projects that recognized the raped women as *biranganas* (war heroines) and honored them in national media hid other kinds of knowledge that had to be carefully navigated at the level of local norms pertaining to the family and the village community.

Among the network of Punjabi families that I studied, no one explicitly acknowledged a family member's abduction and possible rape. This was not so much a question of repression and taboo as one of determining what kind of protection could be offered by silence about the past. Yet the distinction between silence and speech was not absolute. I have described elsewhere (Das 2007) how subtle insults could be folded into fraught kinship relations such as those between a woman and her husband's mother. Thus Manjit, one of my respondents who was very close to me, described how her husband's mother might allude to an aphorism—for example, "There is

nothing to be proud of a woman's body; a woman eats the dung of men"—
referring to a cultural understanding of sex as especially polluting for a
woman. However, Manjit also knew that her mother-in-law was making
a subtle reference to Manjit's history of having been rescued by the army.
By avoiding any reference to what had happened to her in that period, her
mother-in-law avoided a direct insult and its consequences. But this did not
take away the sting of the indirect insult. Yet the knowledge that there were
women who had been rescued and hence had a tainted history provided a
force field within which suspicion about the purity or respectability of a
family would find expression in all kinds of indirect ways. Such knowledge
also challenged what it was to genuinely care for a wife or a daughter-in-law
whose Muslim origins might have been papered over but could erupt into
consciousness, announcing an "otherness" to a close relative with whom one
had inhabited a life.

Mohammad Sayeed (2017) describes a case in which the caretaker of a
Muslim graveyard was approached by a Hindu family who wanted their
mother who had just died to receive a burial instead of the ritual cremation
that is traditional for Hindus.[14] The woman's daughter, the main person
negotiating this delicate situation, told the caretaker that their mother had
been extremely frightened of fire and hence did not want to burn after she
died. Although the imam of the mosque adjoining the graveyard refused
to allow the burial because of the communal tensions it could create, the
caretaker contacted the gravedigger, who agreed to arrange for the burial
provided the family agreed that it would be accompanied by the performance of Islamic rituals and prayer. The woman was buried after the caretaker found some pious Muslim women in the neighborhood who would
give the body its last bath and an imam who would conduct the funeral
prayer, *salat-al-janazah*, which seeks pardon from God for the dead person
and for all Muslims. The Hindu family participated, standing a little apart
at first but then invited to join the small congregation of Muslims. What
made this ritual somehow appropriate for the dead woman was the implicit understanding that there is always a possibility that hiding within
the folds of a Hindu family is a Muslim woman who has never been able to
shed her attachment to Islam.[15] Sayeed attended the funeral but was not
able to converse on this topic with the family, so we cannot know how the
family navigated this clandestine knowledge with other kin or neighbors.
However, this compelling case gestures toward a register of rituals in
which the other might well turn out to be the self in a manner analogous
to the way in which a shrine for the unknown dead, in the cases Kwon

describes for Vietnamese villages, may turn out to offer refuge to an unknown ancestor.

The acceptance of a certain degree of ignorance as essential for life also means that the state-mandated appellations, such as that of the "abducted person," simply do not carry the same weight as the appellation of "victim" did in the context of Jeju. Perhaps the absence of commemoration sites or public memorials for victims of the Partition is related to an implicit acknowledgment that a sharp opposition between victim and perpetrator was simply not possible. However, there are other registers on which the memory of abduction of women leaves its traces—for example, in Urdu and Punjabi literature. As in ordinary life among Punjabis, here too there is no direct narration of the stories of abduction—only hints and omens in which one can find oneself addressed by a literary voice that has absorbed these events.

One of the giants of contemporary Urdu fiction, Saadat Hasan Manto, left an indelible mark on the literature of the Partition. One of my early reflections on the violence of the Partition brought in Manto's short stories—especially "Khol Do" (Open It) and "Fundanen" (Tassles)—as testifying to the distortion of everyday language and its bodying forth, departing from the usual analysis of literary texts in terms of the contents of representation (Das and Nandy 1985; Das 2007). Since then, Manto has become a central figure not only in the understanding of the experience of Partition but also for insights on the bodily nature of language itself (Lemons 2019). Here I evoke another author, a poet far less well-known in the English-speaking world but a much beloved poet on both sides of the border in Punjab. Shiv Kumar Batalvi does not address the travails of the Partition directly, but his poetry is suffused with exquisite portraits of grief and the sense that kinship relations themselves have become lethal—even the most loving ones. Sometimes when Batalvi takes the female voice or speaks from the female region of the self, his poetry becomes a searing testimony to the sense of villainy that taints masculinity, a heritage I cannot help but think traces the Partition violence left in the social body.

Here is a couplet from one of his poems, "Ki puchde o haal fakiran da," freely translated:

Kabran udikdiyan mainu
Jyon putran nu mavan

Graves lie in wait for me
as mothers await the return of sons. (Batalvi 2009)

The love of a mother for her son is considered in Punjabi life to be the purest expression of love, yet here kinship relations migrate into poetry to suggest that even the purest love is contaminated by exhaustion with life. The other couplet I offer is in the female voice addressing the mother:

Mayen ne mayen
Main ik shikra yaar banaya

Mother oh mother,
I made a hawk into my lover. (Batalvi 2009)

The multivalence of the term *yaar* would have allowed the line to be translated as "I befriended a hawk," except for the erotic imagery and sensuous words. The following lines come after a description of her laying out a bed for love in the moonlit night:

Tann di chadar maili ho gayi
O palangi pair jo paaya

The (unstained) sheet of my body became tainted
when he stepped on this bed of love. (Batalvi 2009)

The poem is incredibly sad for Punjabi ears not only because it ends with the hawk lover taking flight, never to return to the *vatani* (the home, the nation), but also because a sense of the taint of male villainy is suffused in the poem—as if that feeling is never going to be erased from Punjabi life. In addition to hearing snippets of these poems during my fieldwork, I was also privy to many other stories in which figures of the occult appeared, such as the ghosts of women who committed mass suicide to protect the honor of their families. An example was that of the seductive female ghostly spirit Padmini (a Hindu name, also the protagonist of the Sufi romance *Padmavat*), who attached herself to an *amil* (Islamic healer), which I describe elsewhere (Das 2015a). In the story of the restless spirit of Padmini, I was told, a famous guru offered to conduct her cremation so that she could find peace, but she contemptuously dismissed him, saying that even he, with all his powers, did not possess the ability to assuage the grief of the brutally violated women. These are forms of knowing in which reality is not directly confronted either by legal or ritual mechanisms but seeps into the interstices of ordinary life, both present in and absent from explicit discourse of any kind.

Conclusion

In choosing to think of the dark side of knowledge through the notion of inordinate knowledge, I have tried to bring into focus the ways in which we might avoid the trap of binaries such as knowledge and ignorance, truth and falsity, certainty and indeterminacy. The challenge I face is not to carve out a global path from uncertainty to certainty, as if the battle against skepticism could be won once and for all. Instead I have tried to attend to regions of knowledge that can cause us to change the questions we ask, not asking for formal solutions to problems of indeterminacy because of the finitude of knowing subjects or veiling of objects, but seeing how inordinate knowledge is contended with—locally, diurnally, and repeatedly. Relying on two case studies to ask how catastrophic events secrete knowledge in the everyday, I have asked how this knowledge is endured or contested, concealed or revealed, and what are the rhythms of these movements.

I contend that some of the most difficult issues we face today as citizens or as relational beings concern this dark side of knowledge. As citizens, how do we deal with the knowledge that torture is regularly practiced as part of the security apparatus of many democracies, if not within the country for reasons of legality than by outsourcing it to autocratic governments where it might be legal or, in any case, easier to execute? What responsibility do we bear for these practices that are before our eyes—that we cannot help but know about? Other forms of inordinate knowledge secreted in the everyday relate to our personal lives. As relational beings, how do we reveal the extent of sexual violence or violent histories of our families to our children and our grandchildren? The women on Jeju Island made their responses in terms of the cultural repertoire of their own societies relating to the care of the dead. Women in Punjabi families offered small acts of care as their response to unspeakable horror, almost waiting for life to knit itself back slowly, pair by pair. This is not to belittle the state rituals of commemoration or witnessing or offering public apologies—these are very important, as we saw in the Jeju case and as we have seen in cases of genocide, apartheid, and several other atrocities that human beings seem able to perpetrate. However, there are many different routes to the difficult tasks of repairing life, and it is important to document and acknowledge these different modes of engaging with inordinate knowledge.

One of the most intriguing remarks in Wittgenstein's (1980: 46e, emphasis in the original) *Journals* is the following: "The whole planet can suffer no greater torment than a *single* soul." I do not pretend to understand this remark in its fullness, but it evokes for me the necessity of embracing a mismatch between harm and healing, between not knowing and shading your eyes from what you cannot help but know. Instead of a rush to judgment, the pressure on anthropological knowledge is to place oneself within the realities of catastrophic and quotidian knowledge rather than confronting it as if from the outside.

Notes

I am very grateful to my coeditor, Didier Fassin, and to the participants in the workshop on "Words and Worlds," held at the Institute for Advanced Study, Princeton, in September 2017, for their astute comments and support for this project. I want to thank the Academy of Korean Studies, Seoul, for their kind invitation to participate in the conference "Envisioning Humanities in the Era of Great Transformation of Civilization" in celebration of their fortieth anniversary at Seoul. To all the scholars and performance artists at Jeju and Gwaingju (especially Kyung-man Cho, Kang-eui Park, Eun-sook Kim, and Sungman Kho) who graciously gave me the opportunity to discuss their work, I am more grateful than I can say. Dr. Young-Gyung Paik showed true friendship in the way she opened paths for me to participate in the intellectual milieu of South Korea and shared many important insights; I cannot thank her enough for her generosity. To my colleague and friend Clara Han, with whom I have shared many discussions on Korea, *dhanyavad*—thanks. And finally, to Youjoung Kim and Sojung Kim, my grateful thanks for their comments and ongoing discussions of the vibrant intellectual life in South Korea.

1. The "Fact Checker" feature of the *Washington Post* reported that as of July 9, 2020, the number of false or misleading claims made by President Trump had gone up to 20,055 in a period of 1,267 days.

2. Even such a simple statement might be complicated if we think of how the height of the mountain matters differently for a student answering a geography question and for a climber planning an expedition (see Benoist 2010).

3. I am not taking any position here on realism or on the autonomy of objects. The issues I examine relate to how inordinate knowledge finds expression in the social milieu, something we are likely to miss if we confine our definition of knowledge exclusively to what is produced or communicated only within officially recognized institutions charged with producing and communicating knowledge, such as laboratories and classrooms.

4. While it is often recognized that Pakistan emerged as a new independent nation as a result of the Partition of India, many scholars fail to register that India too emerged as a single nation whereas earlier it was a patchwork of princely

states with varying degrees of sovereignty that existed along with the territories under the British Empire.

5. One could think of the parallel in the Korean case of the massive sexual violence done to "comfort women" by the occupying Japanese forces, but the Korean government did not allow this issue to come up in the public domain. Only since 1990 have women come forward with their experiences, and despite an official apology from Japan, the issue continues to be the subject of considerable debate between Korea and Japan. The contrast in the attention paid to women as subjects of the state points to different ways the nation constructs itself as a masculine entity.

6. I am very grateful to Youjoung Kim, who wrote an excellent term paper on this theme for my 2019 class Anthropological Tone in Philosophy.

7. My point about the catastrophic nature of this violence is not about numbers alone. Obviously the scale of murders or of mass deaths matters, but reducing everything to scale might fail to capture the specific nature of the terror experienced. For instance, in this case, taboos on any reference to the dead created an aura of fear and suspicion and an inability to mourn that extended more than five decades.

8. The taboo on talk of deaths or disappearances of relatives was experienced in the mainland in different ways. Nan Kim (2016) notes that the anticommunist sentiment was so strong in South Korea that relatives feared making inquiries about untraceable kin would turn up the scandalous knowledge that some lost kin had migrated or chosen to stay in North Korea. Kim writes that even at officially staged events of "reconciliation" between divided families, initially each side felt compelled to perform the politically correct discourse—communist or anticommunist.

9. There is an impressive body of literature on the Jeju 4.3 incident, but unfortunately I do not read Korean and hence have been dependent on the English-language literature that sees these events in the light of issues pertaining to transitional justice and the global form of the truth and reconciliation commission (see, for instance, Shin, Park, and Yang 2007). Heonik Kwon and Seong Nae Kim (2018) make a compelling case for understanding popular religious sentiments and the importance of what they call a "religious-public sphere" in understanding the specificity of Korea and the legacies of the Cold War. There is little doubt that much social action and knowledge are generated outside the state apparatus—yet, as I hope to show, the bureaucratic logic of the state does not remain a separate sphere but becomes enfolded within the commemorative practices.

10. I do not mean to suggest that rituals for ancestors are the only context in which the unknown dead present dilemmas to descendants. Feelings of grief and sorrows that float around without a definite plot have also been noted in

the context of family lore in which parents hide the deaths that disappear from official remembrance.

11. For an elaboration of this point, see Das 2014.

12. Family registers were maintained by the state and local government and were initially organized around the head of the household and his descendants. Women shifted after marriage from the father's family register to that of the husband. The Civil Code of 1958 led to changes in that after the death of the head of the household, names of the eldest son and his descendants stayed in the original register, and new registers were started for younger sons, who could now become heads of household. A new family law in 2005 abolished the family-based register so that each individual now registers with the state as an individual (see Shin 2006). This shift is seen as a victory for feminist groups, but I have not found any work that discusses its implications for ancestor worship or for shamanic knowledge.

13. Initial calculations contained, for instance, in the fact-finding report headed by Justice Khosla had put the numbers of people killed at 200,000 to 250,000.

14. It is only the bodies of saints and of infants that are given a burial in accordance with Hindu funerary rituals. Cremation is conceived as the final fire sacrifice that completes the cycle of sacrificial rituals initiated by the householder in fulfillment of his obligation to maintain the cosmic order of the world.

15. Learning that a close relative had a hidden history tied to large historical events can come as a shock, creating ripples in what looked like the smooth waters of everyday life. The Turkish human rights lawyer Fethiye Çetin (2012) describes how she learned on her grandmother's deathbed that though her grandmother had always performed the role of a pious Muslim woman, she was, in fact, an Armenian girl abducted by a Turkish Muslim military officer and now desired a Christian burial—something her granddaughter was not able to accommodate at that time. However, Çetin bravely went on to discover her Armenian relatives and to create an Armenian Turkish extended family.

DEMOCRACY

JAN-WERNER MÜLLER

We live in paradoxical times. *Democracy*—the word, at least—commands almost universal assent; virtually no leader on the global stage fundamentally disavows the notion. Even the Chinese leadership occasionally claims that they are realizing a more perfect form of democracy (in contrast with, for instance, the United States).[1] What Perry Anderson (2000) wrote at the dawn of the new millennium still seems plausible today: "For the first time since the Reformation there are no longer any significant oppositions—that is, systematic rival outlooks—within the thought-world of the West; and scarcely any on a world scale."[2]

Yet, at the same time, there is tremendous anxiety about the fate of democracy, to an extent we have not experienced for perhaps half a century.[3] That anxiety can be backed up with data: political scientists have diagnosed a global "democratic recession," which is to say, the overall number of democracies around the world has been declining steadily. According to some observers, surveys reveal an increasing disaffection with democracy among citizens, or at least growing indifference (a finding that is said to apply especially to millennials in the West; Diamond 2015; Foa and Mounk 2016).[4] But it's not just numbers: there is a kind of speechlessness, or at least confusion, vis-à-vis politicians who claim to be democrats but do not seem quite to live up to that claim. Should figures like Hungary's Viktor Orbán or Turkey's Recep Tayyip Erdoğan be called "illiberal democrats"? After all, they themselves officially profess allegiance to democracy. Or are they better understood as "populist authoritarians"? Is a twentieth-century vocabulary of dictatorship, or even fascism and totalitarianism, still helpful in making sense of the present?

Long-established democracies are certainly not exempt from the uncertainty about what to call and how to classify threats to their political systems. Here various issues, particularly rising inequality and anxieties about increasing immigration, are often cited as causes—even if the answer to the question "Causes of what, exactly?" has remained rather unclear. There has been talk of "erosion," "sliding," and, in the words of the Canadian philosopher Charles Taylor (2017), a process of "slipping away" of democracy.

It is a striking peculiarity of the way we talk about democracy today that, on the one hand, threats can be personalized very easily: it's the strongmen, from Trump to Putin. On the other hand, what supposedly explains the rise of the strongmen appears rather amorphous, drawn-out "developments." To be sure, these can be pinned on particular people—usually "liberal elites." But this framing of "crisis" also means that there is not one dramatic moment of democracy's quasi-official end, as would be the case with a military coup, for instance.[5] In any case, it is not so obvious that any particular policy challenge can really be said to have "caused" the supposed "erosion" of democracy—especially because these challenges are ubiquitous and yet have not produced the same outcomes everywhere. In many ways, today's pervasive talk of a "crisis of democracy" hides more than it reveals.

The situation really is paradoxical, then: officially, democracy seems still the only game in town; the word keeps being claimed and affirmed almost universally. But it seems less and less clear what the rules, let alone the intended results, of the game are supposed to be. The worry is that de facto we live in a de-democratizing world and that somehow we lack the words—or rather, concepts—to grasp what is happening.

What the Hell Is Going On? Three Implausible Answers

Our current state of uncertainty has elicited three prominent responses: first, an almost desperate search for historical analogies; second, an attempt to show that there actually are new antidemocratic political philosophies (and that they can be defeated intellectually and ultimately also politically); and, third, a more or less openly voiced set of views by liberals (in the widest sense; I do not mean the partisan American understanding here) that contemporary problems with democracy are, in the end, the voters' own fault—with the more or less openly voiced conclusion that democratic decision-making should be restricted, since democracy is just too precious to trust the people with it.

One obvious way to find one's bearings in the present is to say, "This reminds me of something we know." Once we have our historical analogies in place, we can comfortably use our position of knowing the outcomes of certain historical episodes to distill and distribute the supposed "lessons of history." There are numerous problems with this search for analogies and the resulting manuals of how to act politically in the present. One is not specific to our age: as James Bryce famously observed, the chief practical use of history is to liberate us from plausible historical analogies. For the most part, analogical reasoning is likely to mislead us. What might be special about our age, however, as Tony Judt once observed, is that we have become extremely skillful at teaching the *lessons of history* but very bad at actually teaching *history*. Most high school pupils might come up with three bullet points encapsulating the takeaways of twentieth-century history; very few would be able to articulate a halfway plausible argument about what motivated people to act in different ways in, let's say, 1932 or 1933.

In any case, there is no reason to think that today's threats to democracy resemble attacks on democracy that we know from the past. It's a fair guess that all those citizens who—with good intentions, no doubt—rushed out after November 8, 2016, to purchase *1984*, *Animal Farm*, or *The Origins of Totalitarianism* stopped reading after a few dozen pages (if they had expected some readily applicable message). Fascism and Bolshevism are not being revived in our era; less obviously, one of the reasons we are not witnessing a second coming of the antidemocratic past is that today's actors bent on undermining democracy are also trying very hard to learn from history. And that means that they know full well that massive human rights violations, which are bound to remind international audiences of twentieth-century dictatorships, should ideally not be part of a repertoire of techniques to establish and maintain nondemocratic rule. (In that sense, the recent open brutalities of Erdoğan are a sign of weakness, not of strength.) Precisely because we would recognize certain patterns from history, these patterns aren't there. But that doesn't mean that nothing is happening.

It is also a specific legacy of the twentieth century—especially the Cold War—that we assume political argument to be structured around the ideas of prominent thinkers of some sort. The first imperative for many observers today appears to be *Cherchez le maître-penseur!* Hence what one might call "instant intellectual history" is prominent in our day. The best way to make sense of Trumpism? Even now, the man to watch and listen to is Steve

Bannon (and his more or less secret reading list, which includes figures like the Italian traditionalist Julius Evola, a major inspiration for the European New Right). Bannon drops the name Evola once and, instantly, a learned article by one of our many excellent intellectual historians has given the key to our age. Want to understand Putin? Look for the philosophical power behind the throne of today's quasi-czar and you find Alexander Dugin (or, even less plausibly, Ivan Ilyin, recently identified by the historian Timothy Snyder [2018] as the fascist homunculus inside the Russian president). Need to understand today's self-declared antiliberals in eastern Europe? Must get a summary of the books by Polish Platonist Ryszard Legutko!

Such instant intellectual history takes it for granted that we are dealing with political actors inspired by comprehensive worldviews; it also often assumes implicitly that citizens are eager for such worldviews and elect leaders because they espouse them. These assumptions simply aren't warranted. To be sure, more or less prestigious names are being dropped here or there and can serve as signals about political orientations; in that sense, the name-dropping is important, even if the point is not the imminent translation of some comprehensive worldview into practice. But then the crucial question is, A signal directed at which audiences? And why do these audiences matter? Especially in Russia—a prime contender today for a great power with philosophical pretensions—the name-dropping appears more about satisfying committed nationalists (and, to some extent, *siloviki*, the representatives of the national security state) than an indication of the actual sources of policy.[6]

It is not hard to see why liberal political theorists in particular have inadvertently been building up what they take to be their opponents into the kind of serious thinkers that in fact they're not; after all, it gives them something to work with. It is also easy to see why liberals have sometimes almost casually adopted the view that ordinary men and women are ready to be seduced by illiberal ideologies. After all, since the early nineteenth century suspecting the masses of being up to no good has been the default position of liberalism. The rather clichéd invocation of the supposedly *democratic* double disaster of "Brexit and Trump" gives liberals license not to hold back when it comes to reviving the prejudices of nineteenth-century mass psychology: people are just irrational, or at least horrendously ill-informed. What has in effect become a kind of intellectual "democracy defense industry" has a range of recommendations—but the truly effective weapon against the nondemocrats, or so it seems, is to restrict democracy (or at least the number of elections where something is actually decided):

in the United States various gatekeepers should be re-empowered so that the Trumps of this world can be kept out of the primaries (see, for instance, Rauch and Wittes 2017).

Populism against Democracy?

The only likely response liberals crying "It's the people's fault" will ever get is populists' "It's the elites' fault." Let me offer a different account of today's endangerment of democracy by populism—one that is not focused on individual people and political mentalities and that resists an inflationary use of the term *populism*. Contrary to what is often said and written today, not everyone who criticizes elites, not everyone who can count as a political "insurgent," is automatically a dangerous populist. After all, any civics textbook would instruct us to be vigilant with the powerful; keeping a close eye on elites can in fact plausibly be seen as a sign of authentically democratic engagement by citizens. Of course, when in opposition, populists criticize governments. But, crucially, they also claim that *they and they alone* represent what populists often call "the real people" or "the silent majority." As a consequence, they denounce all other contenders for power as fundamentally illegitimate. At stake is never just a disagreement about policy or even values, for that matter—which is of course completely normal (and, ideally, productive) in a democracy. Rather, populists immediately personalize and moralize every conflict: the others, they insist, are simply "corrupt" and "crooked." They allegedly do not work for "the people" but only for themselves (i.e., the establishment) or multinational corporations or the EU or what have you. In this respect, Trump's rhetoric during the 2015–16 presidential campaign was an extreme case—but Trump was not really an exception. All populists in one way or another engage in the kind of talk we heard from Trump about Hillary Clinton (and which we still heard when he called opposition members who do not applaud him "un-American").

Less obvious is that populists insinuate that all citizens who do not share their conception of "the people" and hence, logically, do not support the populists should have their status as belonging to the proper people put into doubt. Think of Nigel Farage, leader of the UK Independence Party, claiming, during the night of the fateful referendum, that Brexit had been a "victory for real people" (CNN 2016); he implied that the 48 percent who voted to stay in the EU might not be quite real—which is to say: not part of the real British people at all. Or think of Trump announcing at a campaign rally in May 2016, "The most important thing is the unification of the people—because the other people don't mean anything" (Flores 2016). So the populist decides who the real people are, and whoever does not want to be unified on the populist's terms is completely and utterly excluded—even if they happen to have a British or a US passport.

So the crucial indicator, if that's the right word, of populism is not some kind of antiestablishment sentiment; criticisms of elites may or may not be justified, but they are not automatically something problematic for democracy. Rather, what matters is populists' antipluralism, their claim to the absolute moral monopoly of representing the people. They always exclude at two levels: at the level of party politics they present themselves as the only legitimate representatives of the people, and hence all others are at least morally excluded; less obviously, at the level of, if you like, the people themselves, those who do not share the populists' symbolic construction of the "real people" (and, as a consequence, do not support the populists politically) are also shut out. Put differently: populism inevitably involves a claim to a moral monopoly of representing the supposedly real people—and also inevitably results in exclusionary identity politics. This is not to say that all politics appealing to or, for that matter, constructing identities (and most forms of politics do, of course) are therefore populist. But the populist strategy is to—sooner or later—reduce all political questions to the one question, Who truly belongs? Who is a part of that homogeneous authentic collective that populists always imagine?

There is an obvious link with nationalism here, particularly ethnic nationalism. But nationalism and populism are not the same thing (and neither are nativism and protectionism). Populists need some kind of "content" to explain who the real people really are—and ethnos is an attractive contender. But the content can be different, as long as it allows populists to make a claim to exclusive representation of the authentic people (let's say, the authentic Bolivarian people, in the case of Hugo Chávez) and to completely delegitimate all other contenders for power. Arguably one of the most ingenious (and despicable) strategies has been Trump's: as Thomas Meaney (2018) has argued, he complemented the construction of the Muslim-as-enemy that preceded his rise in 2015–16 with a suspicion of "fake Americans," wannabe Americans—primarily Hispanics—who seek to pass but actually pose a threat from within to the real American.

Note that populists can do significant damage to a democratic political culture even if they are never in government. After all, populist parties that do not do so well at the polls have to face an obvious contradiction:

How can it be that the populists are the people's only morally legitimate representatives and yet fail to gain overwhelming majorities at the ballot box? Not all populists do opt for what might seem the easiest way out of this contradiction—but plenty do, when they in effect suggest that one should think less of a *silent* majority and more of a *silenced* majority. By definition, if the majority could express itself, the populists would always already be in power—but someone or something prevented the majority from making its voice heard. Put differently: populists more or less subtly suggest that they did not really lose an election at all, but that corrupt elites were manipulating the process behind the scenes. Now, of course, anyone can criticize the US election system; in fact, there's clearly plenty to criticize. And, once again, such criticisms can be a sign of good democratic engagement. What is not compatible with democracy is the populists' claim that comes down to saying, "Because we did not win, our system must be bad and corrupted." In this way populists systematically undermine the trust of citizens in their institutions—and thereby damage a given political culture, even if they never get anywhere close to the actual levers of power.

Not all populists will necessarily resort to something like conspiracy theories to explain away their failures. At the very least, though, they will be tempted to make a distinction between the *morally* and the *empirically* correct outcome of an election. (Think of Orbán after losing the 2002 parliamentary elections claiming that "the nation cannot be in opposition," or consider Andrés Manuel López Obrador, after his failed bid for the Mexican presidency in 2006, arguing that "the victory of the right is morally impossible"—and declaring himself the only "legitimate president of Mexico" [Bruhn 2012].) Populists will keep invoking an amorphous "real people" who would have made a different political choice. For instance, the losing candidate in the 2016 presidential elections in Austria, the far-right populist Norbert Hofer, claimed about the winner, the Green politician Alexander Van der Bellen, that he had been "counted correctly, but not elected" (*gezählt, aber nicht gewählt*) (*Die Presse* 2016); in other words, Hofer insinuated that his opponent had indeed received more votes, but that nevertheless he had not really been chosen (as if a real choice could somehow happen by acclamation or some other process not involving the secret ballot). As the German constitutional lawyer Christoph Möllers has put it, there is a difference between *counting* majorities and *feeling* majorities.[7] Populists will tend to play off sentiments against numbers, not recognizing that, in the end, numbers, and the process of correctly counting, are all we have in a democracy.

It might seem from what has been said so far that all populists live in a kind of political fantasy world and hence are bound to fail in practice. Many liberal observers think that populists offer only very simplistic policy prescriptions that will quickly be exposed as unworkable, or even that populists, deep down, are afraid of actually winning because they are clueless about what to do next. Conventional wisdom has it that populist parties are primarily protest parties and that protest cannot govern, since, logically, one cannot protest against oneself: antipolitics cannot generate real policies. More specifically still, if populists are all about anti-elite rhetoric, they will by definition have to cease being populists once they have acquired power and themselves become the political elite.

The notion that populists in power are bound to fail one way or another—or that they will necessarily moderate—is comforting. It is also an illusion. In fact, what we have seen emerge in recent years might well be called a "populist art of governance." Not uniform, to be sure, but sharing enough clearly recognizable elements. For one thing, while populist parties necessarily protest against elites, this does not mean that populism in government will become self-contradictory. All failures of populists in government can still be blamed on elites acting behind the scenes, whether at home or abroad. (Here again we find the not so accidental connection between populism and conspiracy theories.) Many populist victors continue to behave like victims; majorities act like mistreated minorities. Erdoğan would present himself as a plucky underdog; he'd forever be the street fighter from Istanbul's tough neighborhood Kasımpaşa, bravely confronting the old, Kemalist establishment of the Turkish Republic, long after he had begun to concentrate all political, economic, and, not least, cultural power in his own hands. One side effect of the summer 2016 military putsch has been to reinforce this self-presentation as struggling with the people against the visible and invisible forces of evil—the military and the "Gülen network"—as opposed to the face of a sultan-in-the-making, holed up in his pretentious presidential palace.

When populists have sufficiently large majorities in parliament and when countervailing forces (be they institutions or mobilized civil society) prove too weak, they try to build regimes that might still look like democracies but are actually designed to perpetuate the power of the populists as supposedly the only authentic representatives of the people. To start with, populists colonize the state itself. Think again of Hungary and Poland. One of the first changes Orbán and his party, Fidesz, sought after coming to power in 2010 was a transformation of the civil service law so as to enable them to place loyalists in what should have been nonpartisan bureaucratic positions. Both Fidesz and Jarosław Kaczyński's Law and Justice party (PiS) also immediately moved to diminish the independence of courts (and, arguably, managed to abolish it completely). Media authorities were captured; the signal went out that journalists should not report in ways that violate the interests of the nation (which were equated with the interests of the governing party). Whoever criticized any of these measures was vilified as doing the bidding of the old elites or as being outright traitors. (Kaczyński spoke of "Poles of the worst sort" who supposedly have "treason in their genes" [Lyman and Berendt 2015]). Moreover, like Napoleon III, populist leaders would typically counter any criticism by jurists or journalists with the question "Who elected you?" and describe the press as an "illegitimate rival of the public authorities" (Napoleon III) or as "the enemy of the American people" (Trump) (Rosanvallon 2018: 112).[8]

Such a strategy to consolidate power is not exclusive to populists, of course. What is special about populists is that they can undertake such state colonization openly: Why, populists can ask indignantly, should the people not take possession of their state through their only rightful representatives? Why should those who obstruct the genuine popular will in the name of civil service neutrality not be purged?

Populists also engage in the exchange of material and immaterial favors for mass support, what political scientists often call "mass clientelism." Again, such conduct is not exclusive to populists: many parties reward their clientele for turning up at the voting booths. What—once more—makes populists distinctive is that they can engage in such practices openly and with what appear to them to be authentic moral justifications: after all, for them, only some people are really *the* people and hence deserving of the support by what is rightfully their state. Without this thought it's hard to understand how Erdoğan could have politically survived all the revelations about his regime's corruption, which had started to come out in 2013.

Some populists have been lucky to have the resources to build up entire classes to support their regimes. Chávez benefited crucially from the oil boom. For regimes in central and eastern Europe, funds from the European Union have been equivalent to oil for some Arab authoritarian states: governments can strategically employ the subsidies to buy support or at least keep citizens quiet. What's more, they can form social strata that conform to their image of the "real people"—and that are deeply loyal to the regime. Erdoğan enjoys the seemingly unshakable support of an Anatolian middle class that emerged with the boom under his AK Party (and that also embodies the image of the ideal, devout Turk, as opposed to Westernized, secular elites, and as opposed to minorities such as the Kurds). Hungary's Fidesz has built up a new group that combines economic success, family values (having children brings many benefits), and religious devotion into a whole that aligns with Orbán's vision of a "Christian-national" culture.

There is one further element of the populist art of governance that is important to understand. Populists in power tend to try to discredit protests by civil society as comprehensively as possible. For them such opposition is a particular symbolic challenge: it potentially undermines their claim to exclusive moral representation. Hence it becomes crucial to argue (and supposedly "prove") that what looks like civil society is not civil society at all, and that what can seem like popular opposition on the streets has nothing to do with the real people. This gives a clue as to why Putin, Orbán, and PiS in Poland have gone out of their way to try to discredit NGOs as being controlled by outside powers (and also legally declare them to be "foreign agents"). Trump, for his part, tweeted about "paid-up activists" when citizens came out against his proposed "Muslim travel ban."

Populists have also used protest to prolong and deepen the culture wars on which all populists thrive: they point to a minority that is allegedly not part of "the real people"—in fact, the protestors are actively betraying the homeland, according to the populists—and reassure their own supporters that they are the real, righteous people (which is why Bannon did not say something absurd when he claimed that "the resistance" was "our friend" [Sherman 2017]). The lesson here is of course not that citizens should refrain from protest; it is only that one has to be aware of how swift and sophisticated populists are when it comes to incorporating protest into their own narratives to justify their exclusionary identity politics.

In a sense, populists try to make the unified people in whose name they had been speaking all along a reality on the ground, by silencing or discrediting those who refuse Putin's and Orbán's representative claim (and, sometimes, by giving them every incentive to exit the country and thereby to separate themselves from the pure people: 500,000 Hungarians have left in recent years). Thus a PiS government or a Fidesz government will not only create a PiS state or a Fidesz state; it will also seek to bring into existence a PiS people and a Fidesz people. In other words, populists create the homogeneous people in whose name they had been speaking all along: populism becomes something like a self-fulfilling prophecy.

Populists' Worlds—and How the Words We Use to Describe Them Fail Us

There is a distinct danger here of homogenizing very different phenomena, when in fact the political worlds created by populist leaders display significant differences: Orbán is not Narendra Modi, who is not Erdoğan, who is not Trump. Still, the family resemblances are discernible enough, and, ultimately, we find ourselves, I would argue, in front of *one* populist family.

The words used to describe that family picture matter. First, the ubiquitous language of *retrogression* and *backsliding* is at least somewhat misleading. It suggests that we are going back to something we already know (Huq and Ginsburg 2018). To be sure, it is important to capture a development over time, which is implied by *retrogression* and *sliding*. Also, the comparison between point A and point B in time on the basis of measurements and checklists is meaningful (even if there is much to be criticized when it comes to a mechanical application of checklists; Scheppele 2013)—so if countries drop down on various rankings and indices, that can be an important finding. But usually the master metaphor is not just "sliding down" but indeed "sliding backward"—when there are in fact no clear precedents for what we are living through. The point bears repeating: one of the reasons there are no obvious precedents is that populist-authoritarian leaders also have the benefit of hindsight; they know that nothing they do should too obviously remind global audiences of mass human rights violations as witnessed in the twentieth century.

Second, for many observers a default concept used to grasp various forms of regime change in the present has been *illiberal democracy*. Such a designation is highly problematic both on a normative-theoretical and a strategic level. It is questionable on a normative level because it assumes that holding elections is a sufficient threshold to have democracy (and, by implication, only the rule of law, civil rights, and the protection of minorities are under threat or already damaged in an illiberal democracy). Such a framing overlooks that in populist-authoritarian regimes rights that are constitutive for democracy as such—most obviously free speech and free assembly, but also media pluralism—are effectively curtailed.[9] Put differently, it is not just liberalism that suffers here; it is democracy itself that is purposefully damaged. *Illiberal democracy* suggests—falsely—that democracy is really left intact.

Orbán and other supposed "illiberal democrats" have often managed to reframe criticisms of their attacks on democracy and the rule of law as mere subjective value choices. Liberals, Orbán in his defense of an "illiberal state" (or what in 2018 he declared to be the project of a "twenty-first-century Christian Democracy" [DW.com 2018]) will charge, simply do not like the Hungarian government's conservative family policies, the assertion of strong nation-states inside the European Union, and, most of all, the rejection of immigration and the settlement of refugees (see, for instance, Furedi 2018). Now one can legitimately disagree about these issues in a democracy. But by focusing all attention on them, Orbán has remade what should be a debate about basic democratic institutions into yet another culture war (with an appeal to conservatives everywhere in Europe to join his side, since, in the eyes of one of his intellectual supporters, his concept of illiberal democracy "is most congruent with the Burkean version of conservative thought"; Furedi 2018: 117).

Once the conflict has been declared a matter of seemingly subjective value commitments, the tables can be turned. It becomes easy to accuse the liberals of being the real illiberals: even though they are supposed to be the defenders of diversity, they cannot tolerate an ethnic nationalist like Orbán who seeks to deviate from a supposed Western mainstream of multiculturalism and "the anti-nationalist political culture of the EU" (Furedi 2018: 117). Hungary is even said to have "become the object of cosmopolitan resentment" (74).

Put simply: one can have many legitimate *policy* disagreements in a democracy. But policy is different from polity: with the latter, basic democratic rights either are respected, or they are being purposefully undermined, as in Hungary, Poland, Turkey, and elsewhere. By accepting the terms suggested by actors hostile to democracy and by focusing on ideological-cultural conflict, liberal democrats have failed to capture this difference.

On a strategic level, liberals then needlessly concede the "d-word" to authoritarians—which, for the most part, is the word, the political prize, they really want. (Leaders in Kazakhstan, Azerbaijan, and so on do not care very much whether or not Western observers find them liberal.) Moreover, in the case of a figure like Orbán, *illiberal democrat* is reason to rejoice for the Hungarian leader—after all, that is his proud designation for himself. What gets lost in this culture war about "liberal globalism" is the fact that democracy itself has been purposefully damaged.

It is also worth remarking that, specifically in the European context, "illiberal democracy" results in a kind of division of legal-political labor in which the nation-state is by default left with "democracy," whereas, when absolutely necessary, the liberal repair crew from Brussels, that is, EU bureaucrats, will fly out to fix the rule of law. Obviously, we should not fashion our theoretical concepts to fit political PR purposes—but there is every (including normative) reason for the European Commission, as the official "guardian of the treaties," to claim the mantle of democracy-defense for itself, as opposed to just being a kind of supranational—and, for many people, by implication, paternalistic—watchman for liberalism.

Third, populist-authoritarian regimes have generally opted for a strategy of *rule by law* (or, as some observers have put it, "autocratic legalism").[10] They have been painstakingly legalistic in pursuing what I called the populist art of governance. To be sure, much of what they have done violates the spirit of the law—but not the letter.[11] Here it is insufficient to claim that just some informal norms are being violated. The norms in question are not just ones of civility or a default preference for constitutional softball (cf. Levitsky and Ziblatt 2018). They are ultimately based on the imperative to preserve pluralism and the possibility of a polity to change course on second thought. (I am echoing here the political theorist Nadia Urbinati's understanding of democracy as the "politics of second thoughts" [Runciman 2015].) Norms allow political actors to gain distance to themselves and are based on a rational form of reciprocity (rational, that is, as long as one can expect to rule and be ruled in turn and accepts regular turnovers in power as legitimate); this is one function that the new authoritarians most clearly seek to disable.

In response to criticisms, many of these new authoritarians have also sought to weaponize comparative constitutional law: through decontextualized, ahistorical comparisons, they have sought to demonstrate that critics, such as the EU Commission or the Venice Commission, are insufficiently attentive to the sheer variety of models for constitutional democracy—or just plain hypocrites. Such a strategy has often been complemented with use of "constitutional identity" as an additional weapon or, more precisely, a shield to deflect criticism from the outside (see, for instance, Uitz 2015, 2016).

Fourth, and to coin a phrase, it's also the economy, stupid. Populist-authoritarian regimes today do not comprehensively mobilize societies in the name of grand ideological projects; that is one of the obvious differences with fascism. True, they hold up ideals of the "real Turk," the "real Hungarian," and even, to some degree, the "real American"; in that sense, they do involve larger cultural projects. (The education systems and culture industries in Turkey and Hungary, for instance, have been profoundly re-shaped in accordance with such collective self-representations.) But these more or less coercive attempts at permanently establishing a particular form of cultural hegemony have gone hand in hand with much more mundane practices of self-enrichment. These are at least partly explained by the fact that the absence of any countervailing powers makes capturing state institutions for economic gain an irresistible proposition.[12]

Lack of constraints makes self-dealing with a veneer of legality possi-ble—and then in turn reinforces the need to capture the legal apparatus so as to avoid punishment in the future. If everything came down to ideol-ogy, populists would not have to fear losing power so much; after all, they nominally subscribe to democratic values. Crucial is the fact that populist leaders at least in some cases have created extended "political families" that, in authentic mafia style, pledge absolute loyalty in exchange for ample material reward and, crucially, protection into the indefinite future.[13] As a Hungarian observer points out, "The main benefit of controlling a mod-ern bureaucratic state is not the power to prosecute the innocent, it is the power to protect the guilty" (quoted in Frum 2018: 53).

Ideology can function here partly as a reliable indicator of political-familial submission; less obviously, going along with provocations and outrageous norm breaking by the leader becomes a litmus test for those whom one reasonably suspects of actually still believing in proper demo-cratic standards. Norm breaking can thus also become a way to compro-mise members of the political family—and their conformity in turn estab-lishes reliability and trust (a perennial problem for the original form of the mafia).[14]

Another, less obvious aspect of such new "mafia states" appears to be the following (I say "appears" because what I present here is what I take to be a plausible hypothesis, not a claim with a firm empirical basis at this point): as Ernst Fraenkel (2017) famously demonstrated, the Nazi state was not characterized by complete chaos and lawlessness; there were plenty of areas of life where "arbitrary domination" would have seemed an absurd description, given that so much proceeded in "normal," predictable ways: marriages were concluded and annulled, business contracts were writ-ten and enforced, and so on. Alongside these large areas of legal normal-ity, however, there was always the threat of the "prerogative state," which could act in completely unpredictable and of course unaccountable ways. Fraenkel coined the term *dual state* to capture this particular configuration of legal normality alongside naked exercises of power.

What if today we are again faced with "double states," except that the realm of politics, broadly speaking, in many respects remains one of normality (plus some legal-looking manipulations), whereas one's fate in the economy is subject to arbitrary decisions? Or perhaps not so arbitrary—for if it is indeed the case that loyalty to the extended political family becomes crucial for any kind of economic success, then punishments are foreseeable. At the same time, these practices are not so easily detectable by outside critics, for they can always be disguised as having been dictated by economic or financial necessity. It will be hard to prove that such mechanisms of ensuring compliance with a populist-authoritarian regime are really at work—but it seems a reasonable hypothesis to explain how such regimes remain quite stable in the absence of direct political repression.[15]

Weaponizing the economy is only one part of an explanation of the persistence of populist-authoritarian regimes. Another part—in fact, an absolutely crucial one—is the capture of the media by such regimes. That capture does not have to be complete; on the contrary, an obvious total Gleichschaltung would too easily remind both citizens and outside observers of paradigmatic twentieth-century dictatorships. It is enough that major TV channels and local papers communicate the right messages; discontents remain free to blog on obscure websites and organize the occasional demonstration. Also, "the right message" does not have to mean propaganda; often enough, the right message is factually correct and, crucially, it mainly serves to displace the news that could be embarrassing for the regime.[16] In this regard, the United States is certainly already closer to such regimes than many European democracies. The fragmentation into different public spheres with sometimes completely different forms of "news coverage" encourages the ongoing culture wars that populists positively require.

What's to Be Done in Dark Times for Democracy? Some Tentative Thoughts

It is often rather too casually asserted that "the rise of populism" must be a symptom of deeper, underlying problems with democracy. On a very abstract level, this is obviously true: what has happened over the past decade or so is not random. But things also cannot be quite so simple that whatever one can plausibly find on a laundry list of pernicious developments, from rising inequality to capture of the political process by powerful economic interests, automatically explains everything about populism. Some more effort in understanding is required.

No populist agenda can advance without making it plausible that the polity is split into corrupt elites on the one hand and, on the other, virtuous, homogeneous people—and, crucially, that some people simply do not belong in the polity at all. Where this kind of dualist image is not present, we might be dealing with real political pathologies, but one should refrain from using the designation *populism*. Even where it is present but political actors do not present themselves as the only representatives of the people, and hence deny the legitimacy of all other contenders for power, we should also not employ *populism*: Jeremy Corbyn and Bernie Sanders may speak of the many and the few, but criticizing an establishment or even an oligarchy is not the same as the moralized antipluralism that I have identified as a crucial characteristic of populism. Where such a moralized antipluralism exists, we should not just look for indications of "economic anxiety" or cultural rifts, or irresponsible entertainers masquerading as news anchors,[17] but ask how exclusions, as presented by populists, can become plausible at all.

We need to distinguish two challenges. One is a strain on—or sometimes de facto breakdown of—the social contracts underlying democracies, with the likely result of both political freedom and political equality diminishing (Giebler and Merkel 2016). The second can be summed up as a *crisis of mediation*. This notion partly refers to profound changes in the media environment, which has always been a crucial part of the institutional infrastructure of democracy, but it also concerns the apparent problems of the institution that used most successfully to mediate between citizens and the political system: political parties.[18]

The particular challenge is that these two fateful developments reinforce each other, and, arguably, it is only by going back to the basic structures of democracy—and refashioning them in an appropriate manner—that we can meet the challenge. *Refashioning* is not to suggest that all was well beforehand. Part of the problem with public discourse today is that what one might crudely call a liberal mainstream warns that democracies are dying—and then leftists answer that democracy had never really been born. Liberals implore us to defend the institutions we have, and the radical left reminds us that these institutions bear deep imprints of racism and sexism—not to speak of the evils of capitalism. Both sides have a point, and doing justice to both simultaneously is precisely the challenge.

Democracies involve a delicate mixture of conflict and cooperation. They make room for conflict in such a way that disagreement is not seen as complete delegitimation of the other side or an indication that one side aims at the total political (or even physical) destruction of the other side. They also promise a sense of collective mastery for a people as a whole. Moreover, they are a form of institutionalized uncertainty: no one can say conclusively that only they represent the people; no political or policy outcome can be predicted with certainty, since democracy is always a dynamic process; and the terms of democracy themselves can be renegotiated democratically (which means there is also no final certainty about the form of our democracy) (see Lefort 1998; Przeworski 1991). A social contract involves a commitment to particular forms of these very general principles; on a practical level, this means, above all, self-restraint when it comes to occasions when the winner might take all.

It is clear that in a number of countries that delicate balance between conflict and cooperation has been disturbed (what in the United States is sometimes rather misleadingly referred to as *polarization*). The notion of a loyal (and legitimate) opposition is no longer accepted. Sometimes it is the powerful who deny the legitimacy of their opponents or blatantly violate democratic norms because they fear their power is slipping away (for instance, in the face of demographic change, as in the United States); sometimes it is groups that have steadily been losing influence and for whom such denial is more a sign of desperation. New movements and parties might help to restore the legitimacy of a system, even when they are officially committed to overcoming that system (think of Podemos in Spain, for instance); after all, it might become possible to have an existing system reflect underlying conflicts in a society, so that even the losers can live with the outcome. (Democracy is not about everyone getting what they want; it's about everyone having a chance to make their case.) But such de facto reform might be the exception; more common is the experience that substantive inequality leads to highly unequal participation, which in turn reinforces inequality and hence less and less commitment by a whole range of citizens to anything like a sense of an actual social contract.

Put more bluntly: the truth in today's populist rhetoric is that some of the rich and the powerful really are seceding from the rest of society—for it is unclear why they need most other citizens at all.[19] They don't need them as soldiers (as was still the case during the Cold War); they don't need them as consumers (for consumers can also be elsewhere around the globe); and, with automation, they need them less and less for providing basic services.[20] Ancient Greek democracy became a reality when Athens needed the hoplites to fight wars; it was clear to everyone why they had to be in it together. But today this is far from obvious. Nor is the answer to a less idealistic question: Why is this form of political pluralism, where everyone has a chance of ruling or being properly represented, advantageous and hence acceptable for all?

"Social contract" does not equal social harmony. Democracy needs conflicts, but the conflicts need to be represented in such a way that "partners to the conflict" do not end up excluding each other from the polity. "People versus elite" is by no means the only or even just obvious way to organize conflicts; the fact that we now seem stuck with this dualism is a sign of the failure of parties and party systems, which in turn points to deeper structural problems with the social contract.

The other fateful development concerns the institutional infrastructure of democracy. Let me focus here on the media for a moment and leave aside parties. It has been tempting to redescribe the latest structural transformation of the public sphere in terms of individual dispositions or conduct: the notion of "post-truth" in particular has de facto allowed the unrestrained rearticulation of prejudices about the "irrational masses." Alternatively, the supposed emergence of a "postfactual age" has been explained with a kind of technological determinism, as if the business models of Facebook, Google, and others were simply given by "technology" as such, when in fact polarization and ignorance have turned out to be big business; of course, this new pessimism about technology is only the flip side of the enthusiasm about the inevitably democratizing effects of the internet, which was based on the same deterministic assumptions.[21]

There was no golden age of purely fact-based political debate. Still, for all the lamentations in an earlier age of mass democracy (just think of Walter Lippmann), there was arguably more of something identifiable as a common public.[22] In our time, it has become much easier to drop out of the public altogether or to live in separate, highly partisan public spheres. (Add to that the fact that the number of professional journalists is declining dramatically in many countries, so that the actual quality of *any* of the fragmented public spheres is likely to be lower; meanwhile, the number of people working in PR is steadily increasing.)

Notice how the fragmentation of the public sphere also helps those engaged in the art of populist governance. If plenty of citizens never hear about particular scandals produced by the political family, dissatisfaction, let alone protest, is rather unlikely. For instance, when former US attorney general Eric Holder tweets that, in the case of Robert Mueller being fired, "the American people must be seen and heard—they will ultimately be determinative" (@EricHolder, December 17, 2017), the tacit assumption is that we can all hear and see each other. Everyone loves a Danish fairy tale where it takes just one child to say that the emperor is naked—but the premise of Andersen's story is that everyone can hear the child.[23] All models of protest and, more specifically, civil disobedience rely on the notion that protestors and disobedients can appeal to a larger public in the face of serious injustices (see Rawls 1973; and Habermas 1985; see also Smith 2011).[24] That notion cannot be taken for granted anymore.

Democracy as ideal and as practice is not done yet. But it suffers from a number of serious structural challenges. A threat in the face of which we all realize again that "we are in this together" is imaginable but is not something for which one wishes. Broad-based political mobilization remains the best second-best option, though how entrenched interests will react in an age when "nation-state containers" do not so obviously contain them has yet to be tested seriously.[25]

The crisis of the mediating institutions that have made representative democracy work since the nineteenth century—political parties and professional media—can logically result in radical experimentation, which shows that these institutions really can be replaced. An experiment of this sort has been undertaken by the Five Star movement in Italy: this self-declared "antiparty" seeks not only to create an online direct democracy but also to do away with journalists (whom the movement's founder Beppe Grillo has always accused of being as corrupt as *la casta* of politicians). There are reasons to think that this attempt at achieving what Urbinati (2015) has termed "direct representation"—based on the abolition of all intermediary powers but not of the principle of representation as such—is de facto only producing mass plebiscites on the internet. But democracy, as John Dewey held, is about "experimentalism"—hence, prima facie, experiments ought to be given a chance.

A more conventional way forward is obviously just the replacement of establishment parties with new or at least renewed parties. One might criticize much in Corbyn's Labour and in Podemos, but in some ways these more limited experiments (in programmatic innovation or, for that matter, renewal) show that there might yet be life in the party as a political form. Here too, though, it is hard to see real transformation without massive popular—not populist—involvement.

Notes

I am grateful to the participants in the "Words and Worlds" gathering in September 2017, Veena Das and Didier Fassin in particular, and also to an audience at Yale Law School in February 2018. Parts of this chapter draw on my books *What Is Populism?* (London: Penguin, 2017) and *Democracy Rules* (New York: Farrar, Straus and Giroux, 2021).

1. The contrast with the twentieth century is less dramatic than often assumed today: at least since the First World War, most major powers claimed to realize a form of democracy. (Even the Nazis sometimes advanced peculiar notions of "Germanic democracy" as opposed to what they portrayed as Western plutocracy.) See my *Contesting Democracy* (2011).

2. This is not to deny that de facto (and, often enough, in explicit statements behind closed doors) business elites are more than happy with today's authoritarian alternatives to democracy.

3. Think back to the Trilateral Commission's report on the crisis of democracy in the mid-1970s or Jean-François Revel's long-forgotten *Comment les démocraties finissent* (1983).

4. As Adam Przeworski (2018: 131) observes drily, "Inferring the stability of democracy from responses to survey questions is a publicity stunt, not a valid scientific procedure."

5. That perception is not as new as it's sometimes made out to be. Samuel Huntington (1996: 8) already argued in 1996 that "erosion" and not "overthrow" was the real danger. Never mind that *crisis* in the original Greek sense actually does signify a life-or-death moment; there cannot really be such a thing as a "drawn-out crisis."

6. I am indebted to Guillaume Sauvé and Ivan Krastev for discussions on this point.

7. Personal communication with the author.

8. Some further language by relevant actors: János Lázár, one of Orbán's right-hand men, speaks of a "majoritarian democracy . . . where there is no need for democratic brakes and counterweights"; Polish justice minister Zbigniew Ziobro justified his decapitation of the courts by saying that Poland is "a democracy . . . not a court-ocracy." See Will Freeman, "Colonization, Duplication, Evasion: The Institutional Strategies of Autocratic Legalism" (on file with author); and BBC *News* 2017.

9. The point here is not to subsume liberalism under democracy—there are plenty of tensions, as many theorists, sometimes, but not necessarily, inspired by Carl Schmitt, have insisted. But any serious attempt to separate them has to end up with a conceptual division along the lines I am suggesting here (which

is also why notions such as "democracy without rights"—in contrast to a liberal "rights without democracy"—do not really make sense). See also Ober 2017, which offers a similar conceptual separation.

10. On this point I am indebted to my colleague Kim Lane Scheppele (paper on autocratic legalism on file with author). See also Ginsburg and Simpser 2014; Landau 2012; and *Verfassungsblog* 2017.

11. To be sure, that point can be overstated. Hungary, where the governing party held a supermajority large enough to change the Constitution at will, is probably the best example for autocratic legalism; in the case of Poland, there has been plenty of blatant illegality (just think of the government's outright refusal to publish certain decisions by the Constitutional Tribunal). The best analysis of the Polish situation is now Sadurski 2018.

12. Theoretically this development is well illuminated by Max Horkheimer's notion of a "racket society." See, for instance, Horkheimer 1985 and 1947.

13. By far the best analysis is provided in Magyar (2016). A consequence of this mafia approach is that all political conflicts ultimately become *personal* conflicts—a dynamic clearly visible with figures like Trump and Orbán.

14. See in particular the work of Diego Gambetta.

15. I am indebted to my colleague Kim Lane Scheppele for discussions on this point.

16. Margaret Roberts (2018) has emphasized that fear—the targeting of specific journalists and dissidents—plays an important role, but so does the generation of friction and flooding, which disorients audiences or just buries the wrong news or messages.

17. Sean Hannity describes himself as an "opinion journalist" and an "advocacy journalist" (Shear 2017).

18. Still the best account: Mair 2013.

19. This analysis is compatible with Polanyi's, which has justly seen a renaissance in recent years.

20. I am indebted to Ivan Krastev for discussions on this point.

21. Empirically the problem is severe segmentation, not credulity vis-à-vis "fake news" or "junk news" across the spectrum. See, for instance, the report on polarization and "junk news" by Oxford's Computational Propaganda Project (Narayan et al. 2018).

22. On fragmentation of news coverage in the 2016 presidential election, see Faris et al. 2017.

23. Perhaps this rendering isn't entirely faithful to the original tale. There, after all, not everyone can hear the child, but everyone can hear someone else (whom

they trust) repeat the truth the child has uttered; the crowd is not segmented along any kind of epistemic or moral lines.

24. A creative attempt to rethink civil disobedience under present conditions is de Lagasnerie 2015.

25. Tooze 2018 highlights the possible change of the very foundations of politics, from a system of nation-states to an "interlocking matrix" that, as of now, privileges a corporate oligarchy.

AUTHORITY 3
BANU BARGU

Today we are witnessing a flourishing of authoritarian leaders, often situated at the helm of populist movements that threaten existing democracies. From Turkey's Recep Tayyip Erdoğan to Nicolás Maduro in Venezuela, from Hungary's Viktor Orbán to Evo Morales in Bolivia, charismatic leaders challenge the ruling elites and existing mechanisms of representation, mobilize the masses, and manage to conquer power. Even though they come to power by challenging the political establishment, on grounds of its corrupt ways, elitism, and overly bureaucratic, procedural, and even oppressive modes of governance, once in power they often skillfully consolidate their position by monopolizing the political sphere at the expense of their opponents and erode institutional checks and balances, which they view as constraints on the popular will that they claim to embody.

If the authoritarianism of such leaders appears on the extreme end of the spectrum of populism, having successfully taken and monopolized power, there is a host of other figures who have enjoyed significant electoral victories and multiplied their popular appeal in the past decade without, however, being able to consolidate power. From Marine Le Pen's failed but alarming bid for the French presidency to the increasing votes for Geert Wilders's Freedom Party and Matteo Salvini's Northern League often stealing the spotlight from its erstwhile coalition partner, the Five Star movement, it appears that most democracies are facing a problem of rising authoritarianism, as the growing antagonism against existing political elites is combined with support for exclusionary ideologies such as racism and xenophobia. The result is a call for greater protectionism, both economic and political, and a growing impatience with legality and proceduralism.

As trust in existing democratic institutions declines, they are also eroded by the very people whom they are supposed to serve.

However, what complicates these instances of authoritarian resurgence around the world, often in remarkably different contexts, is that, paradoxically, authoritarianism seems to be the result of democracy and enjoys strong popular support, with leaders of these movements or parties commanding a wide, and widening, appeal. In fact, as Ernesto Laclau's (1977: 106–7) prescient theorization of populism teaches us, populist movements build on the main antagonism between the "power bloc" and "the people" as a collective subject conceptualized as the "underdog" (166). For Laclau, the appeal to "the people" can come from both the right and the left; that is, there can be "a populism of the dominant classes and a populism of the dominated classes" (167, 173). Whereas left-wing populist movements effectively combine the popular contradiction with the discourse of class struggle, right-wing populist movements deny the class component and work to neutralize class conflict (Laclau 1977: 195–96; Hall 1988: 49).

More recent scholarship on authoritarian populist movements and leaders (Panizza 2005; Mudde and Kaltwasser 2013; de la Torre 2014; Moffitt 2016; Müller 2016) underscores the appeal to "the people," evoking the spirit of democratic participation and popular sovereignty, often against their usurpation or torpidity in increasingly stale and corrupt democratic systems. Even if they offer different explanations for these movements, these studies converge in drawing attention to a very prominent, if also contradictory, feature in their discourses and practices, namely, that this appeal to "the people" goes hand in hand with attempts to hierarchize, repress, and exclude segments of the population. Further, these movements offer a challenging combination of what is often viewed as a perversion or excess of "authority," followed by the masses' unquestioning obedience and, simultaneously, if also contradictorily, a strong desire by the same masses to have a real say in politics, one they increasingly feel is denied them by way of traditional mechanisms of political representation and participation. As such, authoritarian populism presents a curious phenomenon that cannot easily be situated as Left or Right, democratic or undemocratic. As Jan-Werner Müller (2016: 11) has put it, "Populism is something like a permanent shadow of modern representative democracy." For most observers, populism is a danger, or in Nadia Urbinati's (2014) phrase, a "disfiguration of democracy." For others, it can be a way of achieving political hegemony (Laclau 1977: 108), a response to the crisis of neoliberalism and an attempt to "recover and deepen democracy," especially if it is claimed by the left

(Mouffe 2018: 5). For still others, even the most progressive forms of populism are not immune to the dangers of authoritarianism, making it impossible to write authoritarianism off as merely a right-wing phenomenon.

The dual and ambivalent character of populism, especially authoritarian populism, presents an interesting *political* problem because it emerges at a time when the advent, dissemination, and internalization of modern conceptions of equality have led to the dissolution of traditional forms of authority on a wide scale. The personal authority of figures such as the father, the priest, and the teacher, as well as the communal authority of family elders, religious institutions, and occupational corporations, have waned in many parts of the world, though in uneven ways. This general leveling has opened up greater possibilities of political participation for ordinary people. However, even though people might historically be at their most powerful in terms of rights and liberties, greater access to power, and more accountability from their representatives, authoritarian populism indexes a general feeling of loss—of voicelessness, victimization, and inequity. Neoliberal reason exacerbates atomization and encourages the reintroduction of personal and familial values to the public sphere in the name of freedom (Brown 2018: 18–23). Neoconservative politics advocates traditional forms of authority, especially by way of the radicalization of religious identities, the return to family values, and the embrace of cultural and economic nationalisms along with anti-immigrant and racist discourses.

At the same time, the ambivalent relationship between authoritarian populism and democratic politics presents an intriguing *theoretical* problem concerning the role of authority. While the meaning of authoritarianism appears obvious as the opposite of democracy, a closer investigation of its link to the concept of authority reveals a more complex picture. Authoritarianism is often viewed as the aberrant usurpation and abuse of political authority. Sometimes it is explained as a function of the popular desire for an effective leader whose authority can be trusted before the unknown in times of change and widespread insecurity. Alternatively, it is seen as a popular expression of dissatisfaction with modernity, resurging as a stubborn remnant of a bygone era that refuses to disappear despite the egalitarian turn in politics. In my opinion, we should interpret authoritarianism neither as the reflection of mass psychology in search of a leader nor as the remainder from the past. Instead of an excess of authority to which such causes may lead, I submit, contemporary authoritarianism should be understood as the consequence of a lack, a void of authority—at least, of a certain kind of authority—in contemporary politics: *the authority of the people*. Such a recasting renders the seemingly obvious opposition between authoritarianism and democracy more ambiguous.

This chapter takes the rise of authoritarian populism in the current political conjuncture as its *worldly* point of departure and approaches its ambiguous nature vis-à-vis democracy by way of a *wordly* inquiry that zeroes in on the concept of authority. Focusing on authority as one of the central concepts of our contemporary lexicon, I aim to make the case that the very dualism that characterizes authoritarian populism is, in fact, closely related to the problems that surround the concept of authority, particularly in its relationship to power and the popular will, and its role in our political landscape. In order to problematize authority on its own terms and defamiliarize the link between authority and authoritarianism, I begin with the different definitions of authority prominent twentieth-century thinkers have offered, noting their consistent attempts to differentiate authority from power. I then give a brief account of the trajectory of the concept of authority in modernity, sampling the discursive sources of its conflation with power and the resultant problems. Finally, I examine the ways in which two prominent thinkers of politics—Jean-Jacques Rousseau and Karl Marx—have reckoned with these problems by proposing alternative paths to think about politics.

My analysis of authority leads me to the observation that populisms today cannot be understood without reference to a *structural deficit* at the heart of modern democracies based on political representation. In a nutshell, this structural deficit is not about the *power* of the people; rather, it is about the *authority* of the people. It designates a constitutive problem: even though the authority of the people is continuously invoked as democracy's primary source of legitimation through appeals to the authorship of "the people," their authority is subject to practical and institutional erosion and erasure by the functioning of the same regime. At the root of this structural deficit is, I argue, the conflation of authority with power in the context of modern sovereignty, which takes its inspiration from a dominant tradition of state theory inspired by Thomas Hobbes. Discontent with the structural deficit of *popular authority* in contemporary democratic regimes creates fertile ground for populist movements, especially those in which charismatic leaders effectively usurp the democratic desires of the masses to fill the void of popular authority.

....

There is a striking commonality among the prominent thinkers of politics who have pondered the meaning of authority. Each has insisted on the importance of distinguishing authority from power and violence, on the one hand, and urged to complicate the simplistic binary of authority versus freedom, on the other. Accordingly, the distinguishing feature of authority as a form of domination is that it involves *voluntary* submission by the dominated. Hence any attempt to understand authority as unfreedom is inadequate at best. Similarly, while the relationship of authority involves a clear hierarchy and thus a differential of power, the fact that authority is not based on coercion or the threat of violence changes the meaning of that power differential, imparting to it a certain *legitimacy*. In this light it is not possible to think about authority without reference to a constellation of other concepts, such as power, volition, coercion, hierarchy, and legitimacy, which are necessary to map its coordinates in the modern lexicon.

Hannah Arendt, for example, offers one of the most intuitive, albeit negative, definitions of what authority is: neither force, nor persuasion. Arendt (1961: 92–93) remarks: "Since authority always demands obedience, it is commonly mistaken for some form of power or violence. Yet authority precludes the use of external means of coercion; where force is used, authority itself has failed." Emphasizing the perceived legitimacy of authority, Arendt problematizes the alleged incompatibility between authority and freedom.[1] She contends that because both liberals and conservatives construe freedom and authority in opposing terms such that when one advances, the other recedes, they fail to identify the political problem of the twentieth century in which *both* freedom and authority have receded with the rise of mass politics—whether in the form of revolutionary dictatorships or fascist governments (100).

For Arendt (1961), the rise of totalitarianism and the erosion of established systems of political representation have to be read against the background of the dissolution of relations of authority. "Authority has vanished from the modern world," she acutely announces (91). The crisis of authority, encompassing particularly "prepolitical" and traditional forms of authority, such as those located in the family and at school, has important effects on democratic politics, insofar as it is these forms, according to Arendt, that undergird and make possible a public sphere that is based on agonistic equality and that enables the experience of freedom. The crisis of authority, albeit indirectly, also leads to the conflation of authoritarianism with totalitarianism. Arendt insists on the distinction between these terms, arguing that "even the most draconian authoritarian government is bound by laws" (97). Unlike totalitarianism, where violence is substituted in place of authority, she argues that the power of authoritarian governments is nonetheless bound by a transcendent source of authority (such as religion or tradition) that not only imparts to them their legitimacy but also acts as a check on them. Thus, for Arendt, while totalitarianism is the result of the crisis of authority, authoritarianism is mainly the replacement of democratic legitimacy with another source of legitimacy. As a counterpoint to the crisis of authority, Arendt attempts to salvage a political conception of authority, which she deems necessary for democratic politics. She does this by unearthing the Roman roots of authority, understanding it as a relation to foundations that offers a necessary permanence against the transience of human affairs (95).[2]

Arendt's reflections on authority constitute a good starting point because they trouble any linear connection between authority and authoritarianism, just as they deny the wholesale condemnation of authority as such. In her worry about the erosion of authority paving the way to totalitarianism and quest for an alternative political authority qua durable foundations to counteract it, Arendt perhaps overestimates the distinction between totalitarian and authoritarian regimes, missing the continued role played by legal authority in both. More importantly, she does not consider the ways in which authoritarianism can be legitimated democratically, as well as on other grounds, which is the main paradox that authoritarian populist movements present to us today. Nonetheless, Arendt's conceptual work is important because it invites us to hold authority apart from power, while attending to different sources of authority and their implications for democratic politics.

Deeply informing Arendt's account is Max Weber (1978), who notes the multiple modalities of authority and systematizes them by offering his seminal threefold classification: legal, traditional, and charismatic authority as ideal-types. Legal authority is the most rational, founded as it is on rules and the commands of those who hold office according to those rules. Traditional authority is founded on the legitimacy of established traditions and those issuing commands according to those traditions. Finally, charismatic authority depends on the "exceptional sanctity, heroism or exemplary character of an individual person, and of the normative patterns or order revealed or ordained by him" (215).

Weber's typology (1978: 212) rests on his demarcation of authority as a distinct "mode of exercising 'power' or 'influence'"—one that is not reducible to power. Also translated into English as "domination" or, more precisely, "legitimate domination," *authority* (Herrschaft) is defined by Weber as "the probability that certain specific commands (or all commands) will be obeyed by a given group of persons" (212). Weber posits that domination is a concept "more precise" than power (Macht), which is "the probability that one actor within a social relationship will be in a position to carry out his own will despite resistance, regardless of the basis on which this probability rests" (53). Whereas power qua the imposition of one's will can proceed by *any* means, including violence, authority understood as securing obedience to one's commands requires an essential component: *voluntary* participation on the part of those who obey. Hence, for Weber, the distinguishing quality of authority is that obedience entails "a minimum of voluntary compliance" (212). While this volition could arise from a multitude of different motives—out of habit or custom, affective ties, material interests, or ideological reasons—the presence of willing compliance, regardless of the reasons for it, suggests that those who comply recognize the authority as *legitimate*. It is this belief in the legitimacy of rule, more than any particular motive, that lies at the source of voluntary compliance and provides the guarantee for the preservation of authority.

Both Arendt and Weber are keen to demarcate authority from other forms of power. In a similar way, Alexandre Kojève's (2014: 27) posthumously published reflections on authority put the contrast in the starkest terms: "Exercising an Authority is not only something different from using force (violence), but the two phenomena are mutually *exclusive*. Generally speaking, one needs to *do nothing* in order to exert Authority. The mere fact of being compelled to call on the intervention of force (violence) proves that no Authority is involved here." These interventions hammer in the distinction between power and authority and cast doubt on the facile claim that authoritarianism is simply an excess or surplus of authority. Instead they point us toward another possibility, namely, that the power of the people, organized in the state form, requires the voluntary supplement of obedience to imbue that power with legitimacy. Whether generated by a legal order, tradition, or popular participation, such authority is crucial for the power embodied in the state not to be reduced to force, embodied in a repressive apparatus composed of the ensemble of institutions of violence—the police, the army, prisons, and borders.

....

For many thinkers, the crucial distinction between authority and power draws inspiration from history, in particular from the Roman republic, where the Senate was the bearer of authority versus the people as the source of power. This form of government, which, according to Giorgio

Agamben (2003: 78), presents a model in which "*auctoritas* and *potestas* are clearly distinct, and yet together they form a binary system," has largely been supplanted with a modern model in which power and authority converge (Fueyo 1968: 213; Agamben 2003: 75).[3] The conceptual distinction between authority and power has lasted long after the Roman Republic and was still a large determinant of medieval politics. In this dense, multilayered, and complex political and social landscape, the plurality of powers, with their different sources of authority—religious, familial, local, communal, traditional—remained dispersed and often at odds, even if power and authority were not always mutually exclusive (Brunner 1992).

The historical turning point is the emergence of the modern state as the centripetal, monopolizing apparatus not only of political power but also of multiple sources of authority. Authority depends on continuity with the past and permanence of social relations, but modernity is characterized by the idea of self-founding and the constitution of the political anew (d'Allonnes 2006: 78–79). Accordingly, in order to justify its demand for obedience at the expense of other sources, the modern state had to generate its own—singular—source of authority. In the history of Western political thought, this decisive historic break finds its most potent expression in Hobbes's work. In an effort to argue against the multiple sources of authority, Hobbes advances a theory that begins in the void, a "state of nature," from which he can stipulate the self-institution of the state, one that derives its authority only from the individuals who collectively constitute it. He thus revolutionizes the theory of the state by proposing *popular authority* as its foundation, but he does so by conjoining the idea of popular authority with the collective power of individuals. This move is accompanied by the shift in the location of sovereignty away from personal qualities of any particular ruler to the "seat of power," thereby also depersonalizing the source individuals must obey as the expression of their own power. As a result, sovereignty becomes the general name of a relationship of command and obedience, whose basis resides in the right of life and death, or what Hobbes sometimes refers to as the power of the "sword." Despite what the sword would tend to imply, sovereignty is not purely coercive but also has legitimacy because it is "authorized" by individuals and follows, at least logically, from their consent. For Hobbes (1996: 114), sovereignty is a "common power, to keep them in awe, and to direct their actions to the common benefit," but it is not reducible to coercion precisely because it is produced by the *voluntary* agreement of individuals who want to escape the war of each against all.

Even though Hobbes is at pains to emphasize the voluntary basis of this founding agreement, he is under no illusions that obedience should necessarily arise out of anything other than fear, whether this is the mutual fear of individuals in the counterfactual state of nature or their fear of the sovereign, whose office, once constituted, can channel the wrath of the commonwealth upon those who disobey its rules from within the commonwealth as much as upon those who threaten the commonwealth from without. Fear, of course, is only the negative expression of self-interest, which, in the last instance, is self-preservation—though even Hobbes (1996: 86, 111, 114) at times seems to suggest that, in addition to the basic desire of self-preservation, the "desire of such things as are necessary to commodious living; and a hope by their industry to obtain them," that is, the prospect of a "more contented life," are also among the incentives for obedience. The Hobbesian model of state does not discriminate between fear or love, interest or ideology, in determining the legitimacy of rule; these widely different reasons for obedience do not impact its voluntary character.

Thus, in proposing popular authority as the source of voluntary obedience and the legitimating force of the new state, Hobbes expands its affective foundations to ensure its generation as part of the production of sovereignty. Furthermore, he amalgamates popular power and authority, inscribing this amalgamation as a constitutive feature of the process of the production of sovereignty. Thus, in his theoretical formulation of the social contract, Hobbes combines two moments into one: (1) the constitution of a collective entity that can compel obedience with the threat of violence with (2) the simultaneous production of the legitimacy of that entity, which justifies why obedience should be readily given to it once constituted. The amassing of the power of a multitude of individuals into a "unity" that is "the people" and the conferral of this power to the sovereign proceed hand in hand with the production of popular authority and its transfer to the sovereign. *Authorship* is the mechanism that enables the collapse of these two moments.

For Hobbes, the act of authorship is inscribed within a relationship of representation (Pitkin 1964). The sovereign, as an "artificial person," represents the words and actions of those individuals who author the sovereign into being. Thus, when the sovereign acts, his acts are binding upon the author because "the actor acteth by authority" (Hobbes 1996: 107). Ultimately this mechanism of representation is an ingenious device that captures the willful agency of the masses without, however, necessitating their collective action, except in the founding moment of the commonwealth. As the masses author themselves into "the people," their constitutive multiplicity and disunity is counteracted by the unity of the "actor" they authorize to act on their behalf. If they come into being by their own act, they exist only through the actions of the sovereign.

Hobbes thus inscribes in the polity what I call a *structural deficit* at the very moment of its institution, when "the people" as a collective agent disappears in the product of its own construction—sovereignty. Because the collective subject's existence is absolutely dependent on its representation by the sovereign, the initial "authorization" that imbues this immense power with legitimacy remains in effect as long as sovereignty endures. This originary consent cannot be retracted except by way of rebellion and then only at the cost of drawing upon those who rebel against the rightful wrath of the sovereign. Even then the legitimacy of rule remains intact because the use of violence against insurgents is simply the means of exercising already legitimate power, means whose legitimacy is also authorized by the ends to which they are directed. Hence Hobbes's (1996: 117–18) way of resolving the democratic paradox—in which the sovereign may well have to defend the commonwealth against the masses that constitute it and turn the collective might of those masses against themselves—is to assert, simultaneously, the logical necessity of the unilateral and irreversible act of authorization, on the one hand, and the logical impossibility of the sovereign to act against the interests of those who authored him into being, which would amount to individuals violating their own preservation, on the other.

If Hobbes's Leviathan appears as an authoritarian commonwealth in which subjection to the sovereign's commands does not permit any dissidence, the reason should be sought less in the *excess* of authority usurped by the office of the sovereign than in the *erosion* of the founding authority of the people, which supplies legitimacy to the office of the sovereign in the first place. This structural feature is not unique to Hobbes but practically animates, to different degrees, contemporary polities organized on the basis of state sovereignty. Hobbes's argument merely lends state sovereignty a sophisticated and modern justification. This justification is to attach, irrevocably, the founding authority of the people to the existence of the sovereign as their representative. Logically, then, while Hobbes can and did grant that a sovereign might not be "equitable" in his decisions and may sometimes err, he can never grant a right to contest such decisions on the grounds that such a right would amount to retracting popular authority from the seat of the sovereign, thereby undermining the constitutive mechanism that generates the legitimacy of the commonwealth.

To this claim the objection that the contract is a mythical construct is not as damaging as it is thought to be, precisely because Hobbes (1996: 132–36) admits that defeat in war or conquest can similarly fulfill the same function as that of a consensual founding. Hobbes's discussion of "commonwealth by acquisition" shows that legitimacy, which is crucial for the likelihood that the sovereign's commands will be obeyed, can just as well be produced ex post facto by the constitution of a rule-bound order. In the absence of a consensual founding, legitimacy can have a source other than the constituent power of the people that is implied in their authorship role. Hence Hobbes has no problem justifying different forms of sovereignty (democratic as well as autocratic) as long as each maintains the ability to provide security through a rule-bound order. This is because, for Hobbes, the presence of *any* rule-bound order is better than none. As a result, even though Hobbes suggests consent as the new source of legitimacy for the modern state and thus bestows us with the concept of popular authority, he quickly resituates authority away from "the people" and in the unitary and centralizing apparatus of the modern state that acts as the guarantor of a rule-bound order. Sovereignty thus becomes the violent supplement of authority, one that subsumes popular authority and takes precedence over it, even though it is a product of it.

Even if the ontological dualism of anarchy versus sovereignty in Hobbes's theory were to be rejected, the specter of authoritarianism that arises from the erasure of popular authority cannot completely be expunged. The critical amendments to Hobbes's theory of sovereignty proposed by John Locke, for example, are a case in point. Locke (1988) liberally imagines a sovereign who is subject to their own laws; he affirms and even absolutizes individual rights; and he stipulates the possibility of revolutionary contestation and thereby the reassertion of popular authority (at least in extreme conditions) precisely because he rejects anarchy as the automatic alternative of a commonwealth and embraces the existence of a community both prior to the foundation of the commonwealth and potentially subsequent to its dissolution. This community can pass judgment on the sovereign's actions as well as on the normative content of the rule-bound order; it can even remake the order when the order is no longer tolerable. However, until the moment the reassertion of popular authority arrives, albeit only after "a long train of Abuses, Prevarications, and Artifices, all tending the same way, make the design visible to the People" (415), the possibility of authoritarian rule remains largely intact through the mechanism of the prerogative (375–77), which functions in a way that erodes popular authority, by allowing discretionary acts by executive power, acts that are outside and sometimes against the laws made and legitimated on the basis of popular authority. Hence despite the increasing liberality of theories of sovereignty, the structural deficit of popular authority continues to imprint them insofar as the conflation of power and authority remains a dominant feature of their modern articulation.

In spite of his attempt to demarcate authority from power, at least analytically, Weber (1978: 54) inserts himself in this dominant tradition when he puts forth his famous definition of the state as the "compulsory political organization with continuous operations [*politischer Anstaltsbetrieb*]" whose "administrative staff successfully upholds the claim to the monopoly of the legitimate use of physical force in the enforcement of its order." This famous definition affirms the conjunction between authority and force within modern state sovereignty. Weber is, of course, fully aware that the authority of the state can have different sources (and, conversely, that not every authority is necessarily exhausted in the state, despite the Hobbesian fantasy). However, for Weber, most befitting of the modern state is, undoubtedly, the legal source. Legal authority derives its legitimacy from the fact that it transposes authority to an impersonal order in which the persons exercising power are themselves also subject to rules of the same order.[4] With its administrative staff, whose members are hierarchically organized according to clearly defined competencies and technical specializations, who are completely separated from ownership of the means of administration, and who work by a distinctive formalism bound by rules, legal authority is the most rational, predictable, and efficient form of domination (223). By emphasizing the rationality of submitting to the impersonality of a rule-bound order and administrative machinery, Weber takes the core insight of what Hobbes had provided in a particularly authoritarian inflection to its logical conclusions.

Two critiques are most relevant to the problem of collapsing authority and power in the modern state, a problem Weber inherits from the Hobbesian formulation of sovereignty. First is Weber's tendency to attribute legitimacy to domination in a legal order purely on the basis of its rule-bound nature as a rational form of political organization. The problem here is Weber's silence on the normative content of those rules that regulate conduct—indeed, many legal orders can have a deficit of legitimacy if their laws are considered unjust (Habermas 1975). Such rule-bound orders are all the more vulnerable to alternative claims of authority. The second critique is that Weber's tripartite typology of legitimate domination fails to include a very important fourth type: democratic legitimacy (Arato 2017: 16–18). To correct this deficit and address the conflation of power and authority in the theory of the modern state following the Hobbesian tradition, it is crucial to turn to an alternative tradition, constituted by thinkers of democracy and radical politics who have creatively addressed both the question of the normative content of the legal order and the problem of democratic legitimacy. Here, I turn to the political thought of Jean-Jacques Rousseau and Karl Marx as two important representatives of this alternative tradition. Looking closely at Rousseau's critical intervention, by way of his keen recognition of the problem of legitimacy, and Marx's critique of modern sovereignty, I would like to highlight how these two thinkers have not only grappled with the problem of authority but also pointed us toward different pathways to think about politics. These pathways also constitute new venues to think through the relationship of authority and authoritarianism in the modern state.

....

Rousseau's work insightfully articulates the first critique advanced against the Hobbesian tradition, already questioning a mere equivalence between legality and legitimacy in his forceful exposure of the originary social contract as illegitimate. This is because, as Rousseau (1993: 97–99) argues in the *Discourse on the Origin of Inequality*, even though the Hobbesian-Lockean contract establishes a legal order, it institutionalizes class-based inequalities and cannot offer "civil liberty" in place of the natural liberty it destroys. Rousseau's normative indictment of such an order cannot be clearer: "Such was, or may well have been, the origin of society and law, which bound new fetters on the poor, and gave new powers to the rich; which irretrievably destroyed natural liberty, eternally fixed the law of property and inequality, converted clever usurpation into unalterable right, and, for the advantage of a few ambitious individuals, subjected all mankind to perpetual labour, slavery, and wretchedness" (99).

It is true that Rousseau (1993) inherits many of the formulations advanced by Hobbes regarding the nature of sovereign power, such as its indivisible, absolute, inalienable, unlimited, sacred, and inviolable nature. However, his conception of sovereignty nonetheless diverges from the Hobbesian version (and its more liberal iterations) for two reasons. First, no source of sovereignty is acceptable other than that which follows from the constituent power of the people. "Sovereign authority" (193) always refers to the authority of the people. Legitimate rule cannot grow from conquest, enslavement, or usurpation, as would be permissible in Hobbes, simply because it manages to institute a legal order. Against the assumption that legality automatically generates legitimacy, Rousseau's principal intervention is to appeal to a different source: the principle of *democratic legitimacy*. It is only by direct popular participation in the making of the rule-bound order that the laws gain their legitimacy. Since obedience is given not to an arbitrary power that imposes rules but to one that is authored by the collective of which every individual is part, Rousseau reasons, the conflict between liberty and obedience is eliminated in favor of a higher form of liberty in the polity (196). Rousseau thereby suggests one way of addressing the structural deficit of popular authority found in its dominant Hobbesian counterpart.

Second, the role of the people is not confined to the moment of founding (as in Hobbes), nor limited to moments of crisis, dissolution, and decline (as in Locke), but made permanent as the source of sovereignty through the general will. Authorship, once again, is the favored metaphor to indicate the agency that flows from "the people." Rousseau (1993: 212) argues, "The people, being subject to the laws, ought to be their author: the conditions of the society ought to be regulated solely by those who come together to form it." The authorship of the people, however, is not conceived as a one-time "authorization" in the founding moment, relegating "action" to the political representative, as in Hobbes, but a recurrent one, unrestricted even by any laws the people may have already chosen to give themselves.

However, Rousseau's principle of democratic legitimacy cannot eschew the conflation of power and authority, this time of "the people." Having insisted on the difference between force and authority—might makes no right—how can Rousseau ensure that the unbounded will of "the people" does not lead to illegitimate laws, abuses, or eventual withering away by the intervention of partial interests, representatives, and other forces?

Three mechanisms aimed at addressing the problem of conjoining power and authority emerge from Rousseau's (1993) democratic theory. First, he insists on the separation of powers, especially that between the legislative and the executive, in order to ensure that the potentially boundless combination of power and authority that inheres in "the people" is functionally limited solely to the making of the laws. The enforcement of those laws, which inevitably requires judgment on particular matters as well as the use of force, is assigned to the government (229–30, 261, 264). Rousseau thus reinstitutionalizes the separation between authority and power he collapsed in theorizing popular sovereignty. Despotism, then, akin to contemporary forms of authoritarianism, is when the government acts on its own authority instead of that of "the people" (233). Crucial to note is that the government arrogates sovereignty not by the usurpation of *power*, which it already has in its hands by the people's entrustment, but by abrading and usurping *popular authority* (259–60).

The second mechanism that Rousseau (1993) introduces is the enigmatic figure of the legislator as the structural inverse of "the people." The legislator is attributed superhuman qualities, such as superior intelligence, wisdom, lack of worldly ambition, and dedication to distant glory. If this otherworldly wisdom affirms the legislator's legitimacy of standing to propose a constitution, his worldly acumen, which can adapt the laws to the character of the people for whom they are crafted, assures the constitution's longevity. This combination of qualities endows the legislator with utmost authority, even though the legislator is absolutely not to have any power, "for if he who holds command over men ought not to have command over the laws, he who has command over the laws ought not any more to have it over men" (214). Just as "the people" have authority to make laws but not the power to enforce them, the legislator has authority to suggest the laws but not the power to legislate them. As with the first mechanism, Rousseau attempts to isolate institutionally an authority that is pure—not contaminated with power and not open to abuse.[5] Hence the paradoxical formulation: "In the task of legislation we find together two things which appear to be incompatible: an enterprise too difficult for human powers, and for its execution, *an authority that is no authority*" (215, my emphasis).

The third mechanism that Rousseau proposes to counteract the conflation of power and authority in democratic sovereignty is through the inculcation of a republican morality. Rousseau believes that with appropriate customs, mores, and values, with the pervasive force of public opinion, citizens can acquire habits that guide their decisions in ways that will ensure the justness of the laws. Aware that the initial authority of the legislator drafting the laws can wane over time or require updating according to changing circumstances, that the authority of the legal order can dwindle with injustices and problems in execution, and, finally, that the authority of "the people" can erode by the influence of particular wills over the general will, Rousseau (1993: 228) appeals to the force of habit (let us say, the authority of tradition) to complement democratic legitimacy. With properly republican mores, "the people" can act as a self-correcting, even self-bettering, agent and keep public power in its rightful path.

Rousseau's proposals constitute an important attempt within a radical democratic imaginary to grapple with the consequences of the Hobbesian conflation of authority and power in modern state sovereignty. Rousseau's deeply democratic commitments steer him away from the path of political representation in order to preserve the authorship function of "the people." His analysis suggests that authoritarianism is about the usurpation of popular authority. The mechanisms he proposes to prevent the erosion of popular authority rework different kinds of authority into the picture: the charismatic authority of a legislator and the traditional authority of mores. Even if these solutions might not be fully satisfactory, Rousseau nevertheless reminds us that authority and freedom can go together and that the success of a democracy hinges on making sure that the authority of "the people" is not simply a principle to appeal to but one to keep intact and to protect against its potential erosion and usurpation.

....

Another response to the Hobbesian conflation of power and authority is offered by Marx's critique of modern state sovereignty. In the young Marx, one finds a ready acceptance of popular sovereignty, which derives its legitimacy from the authorship of "the people" as the first condition of modern democracy. Inspired by Rousseau, Marx (1978: 20) exalts democracy as the "essence of all state constitutions" and argues that in all other constitutions, the state continues to be an alienated entity, an abstraction that does not coincide with its material referent in the actual life of the people but that dominates and confronts the people as if it were not their product. Democracy reflects the self-determination of the people in their actuality.

However, Marx soon moves from this underdetermined embrace of democracy to expose problems with formally democratic constitutions in light of their class character. Most significantly, political representation is considered to facilitate a process by which the interests of the dominant class have come to stand in for common interest (the Rousseauian "general will"). Thus Marx reconceptualizes political representation as the mechanism by which the authorship of "the people" is diluted and popular authority as the legitimating source of the legal order is diminished to the point of simple lip service. In Marx's hands, political representation becomes the means by which popular power is usurped and exercised as *class* power.

In *The Class Struggles in France*, Marx (1978) welcomes the proclamation of the republic in place of constitutional monarchy as signifying the dissipation of the independence of the state from society but registers its class character in the brutal suppression of the workers in the June insurrection. Once the "veil" of neutrality of the constitutional monarchy is gone, the dominant class in civil society becomes the politically ruling class. Designated with such terms as the "bourgeois republic" and the "republic of the rich," the French state is characterized as aiming "to perpetuate the rule of capital, the slavery of labour" (590), thus as an instrument of class rule. In *The Eighteenth Brumaire*, Marx becomes even more explicit: "The bourgeois republic signifies the unlimited despotism of one class over other classes" (602). Instead of the bourgeois republic, Marx argues for a "social republic" that allows for an opening of the political form and the possibility of reclaiming "the people."

The struggle for the "social republic," though brutally repressed by the state, reappears on the stage of politics with the Paris Commune: Marx (1978: 631) calls it the "direct antithesis to the empire." He depicts the commune as the dialectical consummation of the relationship between the republic and democracy: all governmental functions are elective; members are chosen by universal suffrage and for short terms, and they are revocable at any time; they are mostly workers and receive only workmen's wages as compensation for public service; education is free and public; and in place of a standing army, a popular militia is substituted. The commune, in Marx's interpretation, is the political form that best expresses its social content, that is, its foundation in "the people," understood, however, not as an undifferentiated mass but in class terms, where the working poor constitute the social makeup. Marx thus exalts the commune as the *republic of labor*, the "self-government of the producers," "the political form at last discovered under which to work out the economic emancipation of labor" (635).

It is possible to isolate three mechanisms in Marx's analysis of the commune that respond to the problems brought forth by the problematic of modern state sovereignty. First is the advocacy of a plenitude of powers that eliminates the distinction between the legislative and executive functions of government. For Marx, the commune is the new political form in which state power, corrupted in its republican form into the class power of the bourgeoisie, can be appropriated back to the hands of "the people." The commune restores popular power, while changing its class character to reflect the composition of the social body whose majority is the working class, and enables the unfettered use of this power. In this proposal, we see Marx moving in exactly the opposite direction from Rousseau, who tried to relocalize authority and power in distinct apparatuses of the legislative and the executive. With Marx, the problem of the conflation of authority and power is addressed by intensifying and infusing this combination with the political will and unity of the working class, the very people that have hitherto been denied both.

A second mechanism is to predicate the legitimacy of the commune not only on its class content but also on its explicit goal of eliminating the gap, the standing distance, that forms between the constituent power of "the people" and the congealed form of this power in the hands of government. As part of this aim, the role of political representation is highly restricted and tied to the imperative mandate rather than the free mandate for each elected representative. The imperative mandate is buttressed by techniques such as immediate recall, short terms of service, and compensation for service at working wages as mechanisms to ameliorate, if not to eliminate, political representation tout court. As a result, it is thought that popular power will not be subsumed in its own creation and that the dilution of popular authority through representation can be reined in.

Finally, the most important mechanism that Marx proposes against the political oppression arising from the usurpation of the people's power and authority by the state is to imagine sovereignty beyond the horizon of the modern state. Reconceptualized as self-determination, the sovereignty of the commune is exercised by the social body. In order to prevent the formation of a new Leviathan, especially given the plenitude of powers, not only is representation tied to strict limitations but the standing apparatuses of the state, such as the army, are also either eliminated or severely circumscribed. Marx (1978: 633, my emphasis) argues, "While the merely repressive organs of the old governmental power were to be amputated, *its legitimate functions were to be wrested from an authority usurping pre-eminence over society itself,* and restored to the responsible agents of society." The commune is considered "expansive" as opposed to repressive; it permeates the social body instead of standing above and against it as a constraining, "parasitic," and violent force; and it aims at expressing the masses' creative and limitless desires instead of suppressing them. Marx celebrates this novel constitutional form as a curiously self-negating format that both affirms the authority of "the people" and remains most conducive to their freedom (633). According to Marx and in the subsequent radical political imaginary, it is thus the dismantling and eventual disappearance of the state-form that constitutes the ultimate solution envisioned to counteract the structural deficit of modern democracies that arises from the erosion of popular authority.

....

For Rousseauian and Marxian critiques of the dominant state tradition, the missing link between authority and authoritarianism is the *authority of "the people"*—the principle that both thinkers acknowledge as the legitimating force of government. Popular authority is, as they sharply disclose, usurped by those claiming to act in the name of "the people" and exercise its collective power, often against the people itself. If such usurpation is enabled by the conflation of power and authority in the contractual origin-myths of sovereignty, it congeals in the apparatuses of the modern state. Within the problematic of modern state sovereignty, democracy, especially through its proceduralist development, bureaucratic management, and dependency on dominant mechanisms of political representation, is hollowed from within. This generates and increasingly exacerbates what I have called the *structural deficit* in the polity, the discrepancy between the appeal to "the people" and the actual erasure of popular authority. Whether this deficit is expressed by the disappearance of "the people" as a collective political actor at the very moment of its institution in the product of its own activity or by the gradual attenuation of the influence of "the people" through the establishment of a standing distance between government and the authorship of "the people" is relatively unimportant. The general tendency points us toward a widespread contradiction between the centrality and simultaneous precarity of popular authority in modern states, both theoretically and practically. The critiques advanced by Rousseau and Marx highlight this structural deficit in the dominant tradition in stark terms. They also offer us alternative political imaginaries that challenge the given configuration of existing democracies, advancing proposals that recognize and attempt to address the problem of authority. If their proposals, quite different as they are from one another, such as institutionally separating authority and power, on the one hand, and merging them beyond the state-form, on the other, seem remote from a satisfactory answer, they nonetheless remind us that authoritarian populism need not be the only response to the crisis of democracy.

How, then, might the contradictory role of authority in the mythologems and theories of modern sovereignty analyzed here along with their democratic and radical critiques help us account for and possibly think beyond authoritarian populist movements today? How do Erdoğan, Orbán, and Trump fit into a similar narrative about the crisis of democracy? How should we interpret their *electoral* successes in democracies that they submit to the harshest criticisms and understand why, despite their exclusionary, repressive, and hierarchical political discourses and practices, they also continuously appeal to "the people"?

Obviously, Weber's category of charismatic authority goes a long way in explaining how populist leaders are able to generate loyal and ardent followers. However, even if the argument for the mass appeal of charismatic leadership has a certain allure, especially to problematize a popular need to identify with authority, it does not always compellingly address the social dynamics and contradictions that create such a need or exacerbate it in the first place. In other words, the theory of charismatic authority is by itself insufficient to account for the emergence of populist movements, focused as it is on the authoritarian leader and the leader's relation to the obedient masses. This approach also tends to ignore the Janus-faced feature of populist movements, especially their claims to democratic legitimacy, often against established democratic regimes that should ostensibly derive their legitimacy from the same popular source. When Trump rallies the crowds, for example, or when the masses pour into the streets in an effort to resist the attempted coup d'état against Erdoğan, popular support for these leaders cannot simply be explained away by the masses' captivation with charisma or readiness to identify with the leader, even if these dynamics should be taken into account.

To interpret the rise in neoconservative politics embodied by charismatic leaders at the helm of populist movements as a cultural and political backlash to the earlier waves of egalitarianism is another plausible explanation. It turns our focus to the social context of modern democracies in which the advent, dissemination, and internalization of modern conceptions of equality, especially with the impact of anti-authoritarian movements since the late 1960s, have led to the dissolution of traditional forms of authority on a wide scale. In response, for all those who are disaffected by the loss of status, privilege, and prestige, it is not difficult to pinpoint the allure of the slogan "Make America Great Again," for example, or the ambitious invigoration of neo-Ottomanism under Erdoğan's rule. These appeals have an unmistakably backward-looking, nostalgic quality to them as an embrace of the past, however invented, and its relatively stable social roles and accepted hierarchies, predictability, and glory, in order to problematize the issues, weaknesses, and insufficiencies of the present. However, while the search for tradition, community, and hierarchy identifiable in the resurgence of religious identities, family values, and nativist discourses sheds light on the strivings of populist movements to restore a status quo ante, this interpretation too is insufficient insofar as it fails to explain why they are nonetheless based on a strong desire by the masses to act in a political capacity, a desire that takes for granted the achievements of egalitarianism and modernity on a large scale. Even if this desire is expressed in the form of an appeal to the past, it is undergirded by the present difficulties of imagining and enacting a different future.

These interpretations do not exhaust all those available to us, thanks to a growing and vibrant body of scholarship. However, my analysis points us to a different, and neglected, dimension, one that emphasizes the role of popular authority. The desire of the masses to take the center stage in politics and assert their authority appears increasingly unrealizable through existing mechanisms of political representation that are ostensibly in place to guarantee popular participation. What authority's role in the political lexicon animated by the dominant state tradition teaches us is that the conflation of power and authority in the institutionalization of modern sovereignty installs a growing gap between popular authority and power. The intensity of this gap differs according to context, of course, but its presence is constitutive of the hegemonic form of representative democracy upheld by sovereign power. Contemporary populism thrives in that very gap.

Populist appeals to "the people" as a collective subject share an implicit understanding of the erosion of popular authority in established democratic systems where the dominant measures to address the legitimacy problem, such as routinized channels of political representation, established bureaucracies, and checks and balances, have effectively diminished and diluted the originary role of the *authorship* of the people that animates the sovereignty of these systems and guarantees the normative content of the rule-bound orders they hold up. They build on the experience of loss when "the people" whose authority and collective power are the fountain of legitimacy for modern sovereignty finds itself reduced to irrelevance, having increasingly become an empty signifier that is constantly appealed to but without any real voice. The originary authority of "the people" has been appropriated and turned against the masses, with the whole might of their collective power.

While the opposition between "the people" and the "power bloc," which appears alien, indifferent, and even hostile to popular demands, dominates the self-representation of populist movements, this representation often reframes the problem as one of *power*. However, as I have argued, what is very much at stake is the *authority* of "the people." The appeal of populism becomes all the stronger because people want to reclaim their authority precisely at the moment of its decline. In right-wing variants, the leader steps into the void of popular authority on behalf of the masses and usurps their representation in the name of giving voice to them. In more egalitarian versions, the masses attempt to reassert their authorship without mediation, thereby demanding to rethink political representation and the state-form. Either way, through appeals to "the people," the populist narrative mobilizes the masses to occupy the stage of politics once again, a stage held up by their power but over which they have lost authorship. At stake in these appeals is not only the kind of legal order that "the people" will author but, more crucially, authoring "the people" itself. Who will claim this authorship? This question is the terrain of the political battle today. And it is only through the practical, insistent, and collective exercise of this authorial function that democracy might break its current mold.

Notes

1. For an in-depth analysis of authority in modern political theory within the problematic of freedom, see Marcuse 1972.

2. Arendt (1961: 127–28) considers authority as strongly tied to the Roman origins of the concept, which denotes the experience of foundation and its sacredness. However, the specific form of authority that she considers to have been lost with modernity is not simply the Roman form but the reworking of this form with Greek philosophy by the Catholic Church so that it comes to denote not only the idea of the beginning but also transcendent standards.

3. Here Agamben (2003) follows Jesús Fueyo (1968), for whom the convergence of authority and power in the modern concept of sovereignty is a constitutive source of confusion and inconsistency in the modern theory of the state.

4. Weber departs from Hobbes, for whom it would have been a logical contradiction to have the sovereign obey its own commands, and steers closer to Locke in this amendment.

5. This is because the people "is often deceived" (Rousseau 1993: 203) or does not always see what the common good is: "The general will is always upright, but the judgment which guides it is not always enlightened" (212).

BELONGING

PETER GESCHIERE

4

In 1990 George H. W. Bush triumphantly announced a "new world order," a slogan that seemed to fit those years. Others—Gorbachev, Rajiv Gandhi—had preceded him. In 1992 Francis Fukuyama even announced "the end of history" because of the definitive victory of capitalism. These visions of what the new world order would be about certainly differed, but they had in common that they conjured a future of increasing global flows and cosmopolitanism. Instead, the post–Cold War world turned out to be haunted by communal conflicts and a return of values earlier considered to be parochial in which belonging—with exclusion as its fixed complement—and issues of cultural difference were to become matters of life and death. The global dimensions of this shift were brought home to me when in the early 1990s in my own country the Dutch quite abruptly began to define themselves as *autochtonen* at the very moment when this term wreaked havoc in many parts of West Africa—the part of the world where I work as an anthropologist. In several countries—Ivory Coast, Cameroon, East Zaire/Congo—the language of *autochtonie* with its inevitable implication of the need to exclude the "other," the *allogène*, the *allochtoon*, triggered bloody confrontations or even drawn-out civil wars.

A spectacular example is still the plan for an "opération d'identification et de recensement électoral" in Ivory Coast announced in 2002 by President Laurent Gbagbo, just after his rise to power on an autochthony ticket. The plan—launched in a context of a bloody civil war between the North and the South about who "really" belonged to the Ivorian nation—was to oblige all persons in the country to return to their "village of origin" in order to prove their citizenship. As a certain Seri Wayoro, "director of identification" for this operation, explained its aim: "Whoever claims to be Ivorian must have a village. Someone who has done everything to forget the name of his village or who is incapable of showing he belongs to a village is a person without bearings and is so dangerous that we must ask him where he comes from" (Marshall-Fratani 2006: 28).

The use of such notions in the Netherlands and elsewhere in Europe has had, until now, less bloody effects. Still, it is striking how the same concepts have great mobilizing power—one could speak of a *visceral* appeal—in completely different situations. Autochthony seems to express a kind of arch-belonging: how can one belong more than by claiming to be "né de la terre" (born from the soil) (Loraux 1996)? Following this notion in its quite different trajectories in the present world can therefore help to gain deeper insights into what in comparative perspective can be termed a "global conjuncture of belonging" marking the "post–Cold War moment": variable issues and tendencies in different parts of the world converging in making belonging a crucial issue (Geschiere 2009; Piot 2010).

Indeed, it was not only in francophone Africa or the Netherlands that the language of autochthony came to play such a prominent role. Striking is, for instance, the increasing currency of the term in English. When, just after 2000, I started to present papers on the issue for anglophone audiences I was invariably told that this is a foreign term, hardly used in English. But more recently the notion seems to have acquired the status of a buzzword in English as well. It is increasingly current not only in academic publications but also in the everyday language of journalists, politicians, and people in general. It is all the more important to emphasize that the omnipresence of the term and of similar notions of belonging in the present-day world glosses over conflicting scenarios and different trajectories. For instance, in the two countries on which I focused in my book, Cameroon and the Netherlands, the term not only has a different history, but also the grievances involved in making it a hot-button issue are very different. Yet, as said, the same language (one's own people first; immigrants are "liars" who are soiling the purity of the ancestral lands, etc.) is capable of stirring up deep emotions. It is their apparent self-evidence—their natural truth—that gives these notions a visceral force. Returning them to history and its contingencies might help to highlight ambiguities in what seems to be crystal clear.

After a brief historical sketch, focusing on a few key moments in the long history of these notions, I propose to explore why they acquired new vigor in recent contexts ("the post–Cold War moment"). Next I will address a paradox that recurs in all contexts, despite much variation, between a promise of total certainty and a practice of deep insecurity.

Behind this paradox might be the close association of autochthony, and belonging in general, with both entitlement and resentment. A claim to be autochthonous—or more generally to belong somewhere—implies that one is entitled to certain advantages. And it is this implication that makes the language of belonging so often a language of resentment. Even in situations where autochthonous groups are clearly in the majority and/or in power, it is a language of nostalgia and loss (McGovern 2011).

Genesis: Classical Athens

Indeed, while working on my book, the complex historical vicissitudes of the notion became ever more intriguing to me. As said, I started to work on autochthony because I was struck by the coincidence that the same jargon quite abruptly became so politically charged in such different contexts as Cameroon and the Netherlands. However, following the central notion of autochthony turned out to be quite an adventurous journey. I had certainly not expected that it would take me to such widely different spots in the world and in history—like some sort of magical bird, turning up in unexpected places. But its starting point is clear: classical Athens of the fifth century BC.

Athenian citizens of the fifth century BC—the city's golden age, the time of Pericles, Euripides, and Plato—were prone to boast of their *autochthonia* as proof that their city was exceptional among all the Greek *poleis*. All other cities had histories of having been founded by immigrants. Only the Athenians were truly *autochthonos*—that is, born from the land where they lived. This was also the reason Athenians would have a special propensity for *demokratia*. The classical texts—Euripides, Plato, Demosthenes—are surprisingly vivid on this aspect. To the present-day reader, it might come as a surprise to read in the text of these venerated classics the same language of autochthony that is now so brutally propagated by Europe's prophets of the New Right (and others). An unexpected performance in the French Assemblée Nationale in 1990—just after Bush Sr. celebrated his new world order—shows how relevant these old ideas are for present-day issues.

In that year Madame Marie-France Stirbois, member of Parliament for Jean-Marie Le Pen's Front National—France's party for the extreme right that was to become so successful two decades later under Le Pen's daughter Marine—surprised her colleagues by delivering a passionate speech about classical Athens and the way in which Euripides, Plato, and even Socrates defended the case of autochthony (Loraux 1996: 204). Apparently her fellow representatives were somewhat surprised as, until then, Stirbois's interventions had not portrayed such an in-depth interest in the classics (or any academic subject, for that matter). Clearly another sympathizer of Le Front National, probably a professor at the Sorbonne, had written the speech for her. The incident inspired Nicole Loraux, a leading classicist, to look into the history of Athenian autochthony.

At first sight, the Athenian claim to autochthony seems to be as natural and as unequivocal as, for instance, the claims of the former president of the Ivory Coast, Laurent Gbagbo, that one needs to distinguish *Ivoiriens de souche* (literally, "Ivorians from the trunk") from later immigrants (Jean-Marie Le Pen used the same term for the French). However, Loraux (1996) shows that a return to the classical locus of autochthony is rewarding since it highlights the tensions and inconsistencies of this apparently unequivocal notion in particularly striking ways. The following examples testify to both the vigor and the complexities of autochthony in Athenian thinking.

In *Erechtheus*, one of Euripides's most popular tragedies, the playwright has Praxithea, King Erechteus's wife, offer her own daughter for sacrifice in order to save the city: "I, then, shall give my daughter to be killed. I take many things into account, and first of all, that I could not find any city better than this. To begin with, we are an autochthonous people, not introduced from elsewhere; other communities, founded as it were through board-game moves, are imported, different ones from different places. Now someone who settles in one city from another is like a peg ill-fitted in a piece of wood—a citizen in name, but not in his actions" (Euripides 1995: 159–60).

Heavy language under heavy circumstances. The play's story is that Athens is threatened with destruction by a Thracian army invading Attica. The Delphi oracle has prophesized that King Erechtheus can save the city only by sacrificing one of his own offspring. The king seems to hesitate, but his wife shows him what autochthony means in practice: "This girl, not mine in fact except through birth, I shall give to be sacrificed in defense of our land. If the city is captured, what share in my children have I then? Shall not the whole then be saved, so far as is in my power?" (160).

Euripides's tragedy was based on a myth, placed in a mythical time, but it was clearly topical to Athens's situation in 422 BC, when the play was first performed. At that time, the city was at the height of its naval power, but it was already locked in mortal combat with its archrival, Sparta. Indeed there was good reason for celebrating Athenian uniqueness at the time. In other respects, Praxithea's words must have seemed straight to the point for the audience. Her scorn of a person "who settles in one city from another" being like "a peg ill-fitted in a piece of wood" no doubt had special meaning in fifth century Athens, where the majority of the population were seen as foreign immigrants (*metoikoi*). Adding to the scorn, quite a few immigrants were wealthier than the true Athenian citizens.

With Plato, Athenian autochthonia seems equally self-evident. He lets Socrates improvise a funeral oration celebrating Athenian uniqueness in no uncertain terms: "The forefathers of these men were not of immigrant stock, nor were these their sons declared by their origin to be strangers in the land sprung from immigrants, but natives sprung from the soil living and dwelling in their own true fatherland."[1] As in Africa, funerals, and more notably funeral orations, were a high point in the expression of Athenian autochthony. In general, autochthony in Greece, as elsewhere, was linked to heavy ritual in which the earth plays a key role. Such rituals seem to confirm the idea that autochthony was a long-standing trait of Athens. Yet Loraux warns that in the Athenian case—as elsewhere—the claim "to be born from the soil" amounts to a denial of history, which is always about movement, as is true also in Athens.

For Loraux, the classical texts thus highlight the basic impossibility of autochthony implying a constant struggle with a history that undermines the apparent self-evidence of chthonic belonging. Hence, in Athens as elsewhere, there was great uncertainty about "authentic" and "fake" autochthony: an obsession with purification and the unmasking of traitors hiding inside. Such uncertainties make the notion, despite its apparent self-evidence, a fickle basis for the definition of citizenship—a problem all too relevant for autochthony's present-day trajectories. If in classical Athens a fellow citizen would publicly put in doubt your *autochthonia* and therefore your citizenship, you could challenge him in the council. If he was put in the wrong, he would lose his citizenship and risked being sold as a slave. Yet taking the matter to the council was risky: if *you* were found to be in the wrong, *you* would lose your citizenship and *you* could be sold as a slave. *Autochthonia* could always be contested—a warning for our times as well.

History (1): A Colonial Version of Autochthony

Autochthony's tortuous trajectories on the African continent were directly shaped by the colonial intermezzo. The term was abruptly introduced on the continent by French colonials around 1900, when they were struggling with the question of how to administer the vast territories they had conquered in a few decades in West Africa. Indeed, in the French colonial conception, developed during the penetration into the West African Sudan in the 1880s and 1890s, *autochtonie* was to become the very first criterion for bringing some order into the confusing proliferation of all sorts of diffuse groupings—some more or less integrated in larger state-formations, others constantly splitting up in segments—that confronted the new conquerors. Autochtonie was to become the basic principle for the French alternative to British indirect rule. While to the British it seemed increasingly vital to discover the "real" chiefs in order to base the native administration on them, the French were initially rather bent on circumventing at least the higher chiefs, who in some parts of the Sudan had offered determined resistance. Instead, homogeneous *cantons* had to be formed, populated by the same *race* (here used in the sense of what today is called an ethnic group) and administered by local power-holders who would constitute the building blocks for *le commandement indigène*. Therefore it was urgent to discover— within the confusing medley of groups and subgroups—the real *autochtones*.

A typical example is provided by the huge, three-volume book *Haut-Sénégal-Niger* by the French ethnographer-administrator Maurice Delafosse ([1912] 1972), who was to become very influential in the building of the French colonial empire. A recurrent principle in the book is that "some *indigènes* are autochthons, whereas others are definitely not" (280). And thus a vital question in his encyclopedic description of the various groupings in this area is whether a certain group is or is not autochthonous. Striking in this context is that, despite his determined search for autochthony, Delafosse is clearly much more interested in migrating groups. Invariably, once he has finally found an autochthonous group, it gets only a short description in a somewhat condescending language. They are qualified as *malheureux*, poor and backward (238). In contrast, Delafosse devotes more than forty pages to, for instance, the Peul/Dyula ethnic conglomerate, clearly fascinated by their peregrinations throughout West Africa and their reputation as empire builders.

This makes his book a striking example of a widespread colonial paradox, of crucial importance to the vagaries of autochthony and belonging in postcolonial Africa. On the one hand, colonial authorities emphasized the urgent need to "fix" the local populations: only thus would it be possible to administer them—and more specifically levy taxes and labor. The principle that the new administration should be built upon autochthon groups, the true locals, fits this localizing accent. Yet, on the other hand, most colonial governments showed in practice a clear preference for migrants, qualified as more energetic and entrepreneurial—and therefore much more interesting for launching projects. In practice, their formal preference for truly local groups foundered rapidly on this penchant for migrants among the new colonial authorities who tended—just like Delafosse—to oppose the latter's dynamics to the locals' indolence and resistance to change. In many areas the French soon became inclined to appoint chiefs from these more "enterprising" groupings over "backward" locals. Yet the initial preference for autochthonous groups did introduce the term and its counterpoint, *allogènes*, as some sort of primal criterion in the French colonial context.

One of the reasons the term flourished in the new setting is that it easily articulated with distinctions already existing locally, though these had often a quite different tenor. Indeed the varying trajectories of the autochthony notion, also inside Africa, offer another example of the ways in which colonial terms were appropriated locally, acquiring a dynamic of their own. Especially in the interior of the West African Sudan local patterns of organization turned around a complementary opposition between "people of the land" and "rulers"; the latter were (and are) often proud to have come in from elsewhere and refer to their external origin as their justification to rule. Yet the "priest of the land" still forms a ritual counterpoint to the chief of the ruling dynasty. To the French ethnologists, *autochthony* was an obvious term to describe this counterpoint position.

A good example is the vast literature on the Mossi (the largest group in present-day Burkina Faso). For generations of researchers, this opposition in Mossi society between what they termed *autochtones* and "rulers" became a central issue inspiring highly sophisticated, structuralist studies. But this was not the meaning that came to the fore with so much force in the 1990s with democratization in this part of Africa. One of the main targets of the upsurge of autochthony in neighboring Ivory Coast was precisely these Mossi immigrants who were supposed to have taken the land of the "autochthons" of the rich cocoa belt in southern Ivory Coast. In this version of the term—as in the version propagated by Delafosse—an autochthon is certainly not a subordinate; on the contrary the reference to the soil expresses a claim to priority, to possession of the land and thus the right to exclude strangers. Clearly, despite its self-evident or even "natural" appearance, a term like *autochthony* can take on very different meanings in different contexts and times.

For the African continent the colonial background provided a common framework. All the African situations that are nowadays the scene of particularly fierce confrontations around autochthony, belonging, and the exclusion of "strangers" are deeply marked by the paradox of most colonial regimes that, on the one hand, insisted on fixing and territorializing people—which implied a determined search for autochthons who "really" belonged—and, on the other, demonstrated a constant favoring of migrants.

History (2): Autochtonie, the Dutch Version

In the Dutch case, autochthony's history as a political term is much shorter. It was abruptly introduced in 1971 in the context of growing worries about labor immigrants (at the time commonly called *gastarbeiders*, literally "guest laborers"), when the Dutch began to realize that many of these "guests" did not intend at all to return to their land of origin. Typical was that the counterterm, *allochtonen*, was first introduced in the debate. The label of *autochthonen* emerged as a reactive self-identification.

The Dutch trajectory was not that different from that in other European countries. As elsewhere, the urgent demand for labor for a new spurt of industrialization had led already in the 1950s to recruitment of labor, first from the northern side of the Mediterranean and later also from the southern side. But special was the tenacious denial that the Netherlands had become an *im*-migration country. The destructions of the grim occupation by the Germans (1940–45), the vivid memory of mass unemployment in the 1930s (which lasted relatively long due to the peculiarities of Dutch financial policy), and the general conviction that the Netherlands was overpopulated (in the 1950s I was still taught in school that we were the most densely populated country in the world) made the government insist that we were an *e*-migration country. The consequence was a terminological void. Incoming groups could not be called (im)migrants in formal documents. The tenacity with which civil servants erased such terms from all documents led to an uncertain search for alternatives. As such, *gastarbeiders* (guest laborers) became an oxymoron in the 1970s, when it became clear that people, especially those from the southern side of the Mediterranean, had come to stay. For some time (ethnic) minorities became the official label, but this was soon criticized as condescending. In 1971 the term *allochtonen* emerged for the first time. But it was only after 1990 when the Centraal Bureau voor de Statistiek (CBS; Central Bureau for Statistics) adopted this notion that the term became current. From then on official demographic statistics were published in terms of *allochtonen* versus *autochtonen*.

The adoption of this term was defended as choosing a neutral, scientific term (indeed it was current only in geography, where it had natural connotations: allochthonous stones, etc.), so that it could help cool down discussions that became ever more heated. It is striking, however, how quickly this supposedly neutral term—like its counterpart, *autochtoon*—acquired a deep emotional connotation. Ever since its formal acceptance—and, as elsewhere, the fact that it was taken over in official statistics was the crucial turning point—any proposal to abandon it met with almost hysterical reactions. It became nonetheless clear that there were many problems with it: the haphazard way in which Western and non-Western *allochtonen* were distinguished; the criterion that one counted as *allochtoon* if one of the four grandparents was not born in the Netherlands (which meant in practice that mixed marriages multiplied the number of *allochtonen*); and especially the biological fixity of the term, which made integration basically impossible. (Can an *allochtoon* ever become an *autochtoon*?) It was only in 2017 that the CBS finally dropped the terminology from its official statistics. But the language is still very much around despite its divisive implications (Geschiere 2009: ch. 5).

The Post–Cold War Moment as a Turning Point

The discussion so far may give an idea of the kaleidoscopic riches of the history of notions like autochthony. The language can break through at highly different moments in time and in space, being used as a gloss of very different oppositions. In Europe it came to be about race and religion; in Africa it expresses, now especially, a struggle over the control of the state and (urban) land. Yet the language imposes implications and tensions of its own. It is striking, for instance, that in both contexts I have sketched, the 1990s were a turning point: they brought a return-with-a-vengeance of angry languages that were supposed to belong to the past. In both contexts Piot's emphasis on the post–Cold War moment as a watershed that might be as significant as the decolonization transition after the Second World War is highly relevant. And so is his warning that these more recent changes pose as much of a theoretical challenge precisely because their implications—new, rhizomatic forms of state formation, new religious ferment, economic dynamism escaping formal controls—remain so utterly confusing.

It may be important to highlight how surprising in retrospect the comeback of languages of soil, rootedness, and exclusion was. In Africa the first decades after independence (for most countries around 1960) were deeply marked by the ideal of nation-building and a concomitant defense of the unity of national citizenship. In Cameroon, for instance, under the first president, Ahmadou Ahidjo, who ruled until 1982, *autochtone* became an increasingly dangerous notion. Several politicians who continued to use it were accused of *subversion*—undermining the unity of the nation—and sent to Tcholliré, the horrible concentration camp, far up north, where Ahidjo neutralized his opponents. Similarly, if people in the Dutch context had predicted in the 1970s that only two decades later Dutch *autochtoon* culture would become a hot issue, they might easily have become an object of ridicule. In the 1970s we knew that the future would be about class conflict and exploitation; we believed that nationalism had had its day. Clearly it is important to take into account the temporality of these ideas, all the more since they often present themselves as timeless givens. Why, then, did notions of belonging and identity take on so easily powerful exclusionary implications in different parts of the globe over the past two decades?

Africa: Land Scarcity, Democratization, Decentralization

Several factors can explain the quite sudden return (with a vengeance) in many parts of Africa of the colonial distinction of groups as autochthonous and of others as "strangers." A long-term problem is of course the growing land scarcity in many parts of the continent. Anthropologists often emphasize the inclusive tendencies of African social formations and the emphasis on "wealth-in-people" in a context where land is an open resource so that it is rather the ability to attract people that makes leaders real "big men" (Guyer 1993). But access to land has become increasingly limited, especially in the more populated parts of the continent, where the spread of cash crops (notably cacao and coffee) made for a more permanent use of the soil.

The Ivorian example has to be understood against the background of a constantly expanding "cacao belt" in the forest in the south of the country running up against the limits of available land. The bitter civil war that rocked this country around 2000 was about excluding migrants from the north as "strangers," while only one or two generations earlier they had been welcomed as clients to reinforce the labor force under "traditional" arrangements of "tutelage"—an incisive turn, with clear parallels in neighboring Ghana and Nigeria. The Ivorian example highlights also the tragic confusions triggered by such a reversal. Instead of a unilineal change from a "traditional" closed system to a more open "modern" configuration, there appeared to emerge a return to "tradition." However, some used this seemingly traditional turn to realize new forms of mobility. In Ivory Coast young "autochthons" who claimed to restore their "traditional rights," which had been squandered by their elders, created roadblocks where they extorted fines from "strangers," but often they used this money to buy a plane ticket to France (Chauveau and Bobo 2003).

However, the abruptness of the turn in the early 1990s has to be seen also in the rapidly changing global context. For Africa, it was especially democratization and decentralization as some sort of neoliberal twin that had profound implications for everyday life. Both had the quite unexpected effect of making the village—one's rural belonging—again of vital importance for urbanites, some of whom had lived for generations in the city. Democratization—in most countries abruptly realized by a combination of internal and outside pressures—meant a sudden return of the power of the popular vote. The impact of the end of the Cold War was particularly direct here. Unable to continue playing off the West against the East (or vice versa), one-party dictators could no longer profit from the almost unconditional support of their external allies and had to concede to internal pressures. The one-party model, excluding opponents by various forms of direct and/or organizational coercion, was no longer viable. Regimes had to look for new ways of marshaling the popular vote. Appealing to apparently deep-seated feelings of local belonging became a tempting strategy in this respect.

The Cameroonian example is particularly telling here. Within a few years the former one-party regime made a complete switch, from a determined celebration of national unity to the promotion of local autochthony—which until then had been severely reprimanded as sowing division and discord. Even more surprising was that, against all odds, this regime thus succeeded in staying in the saddle. Cameroon's Paul Biya is now one of the longest in power—thirty-eight years as of 2020—among African presidents. Clearly the radical switch in the early 1990s did pay off.

While under one-party rule politicians had been strongly advised not to try to build up their own local support—they had to realize that they depended only on the favors of the top party people—the regime now ordered its civil servants to do exactly what had been anathema before: campaign in their regions of origin and thus make their own people vote for the president and his party. At the crucial presidential elections of 1992 this tactic was not very successful. Only after strenuous rigging—reason enough for most EU countries to withdraw their support, except of course France (there were close personal links between Biya and François Mitterrand)—could Biya declare himself to be the winner. From then on, the regime used its control over the state machinery to stir up "autochthonous" protests in the various regions, thus prying apart the opposition and coming out of all subsequent elections as the victor with ever larger margins. The new constitution of 1996 included in its preamble a plea for the recognition of local forms of belonging—a notion that would have been considered "subversion" and an attack on the unity of the nation only ten years earlier.

Clearly the particular articulations of democratization and notions of autochthony can vary. As shown, it inspired President Gbagbo in Ivory Coast to launch the idea of a "national operation of identification" in a desperate effort to purify the nation of any foreign element. In Zambia political rivals succeeded in excluding former president Kenneth Kaunda from running again with the simple claim that he "really" descended from strangers.[2] But everywhere the return of democracy made the village of origin and affirmation of one's local belonging again of crucial importance.

As important as democratization was the drastic shift in the policies of global development agencies like the World Bank, the IMF, and other major donors: from an explicitly statist approach to an equally blunt distrust of the state. While up to the early 1980s it seemed self-evident that development had to be realized through the state, and that therefore strengthening the state and nation-building by the new state elites were the first priorities, the state was subsequently seen no longer as a pillar but rather as a major barrier to development. Especially after the World Bank's 1989 report on Africa—again, not by coincidence at the very moment that the Cold War was ending—*bypassing the state*, strengthening *civil society* and NGOs, and notably *decentralization* became the buzzwords. But just as democratization turned out to create unexpected scope for autochthony movements, the new decentralization policy and the support of NGOs made the affirmation of one's local belonging crucial. Simplistic applications of the idea of decentralization automatically raised questions of who belonged or did not belong in a given area: people identifying as autochthonous to the region tended to exclude others who had come later from the new-style development projects. The funding available for NGOs led to a bewildering proliferation of organizations, often with a retired civil servant as the initiator and strongly locally based—thus again raising the question of who was in and who was out.

Important in all this is that such developments cannot be dismissed as merely political games, maneuvers imposed from above by shrewd politicians or well-meaning "developers." Political manipulations and external interventions by politicians and development agencies certainly play a role, but they work only because the very idea of local belonging strikes such a deep emotional chord with the population. Indeed, the force of the emotions unleashed by a political appeal to autochthony is often such that it threatens to sweep the very politicians who launched it right off their feet. This is, for instance, vividly illustrated by the increasing importance, throughout the continent, of the funeral "at home" (that is, in the village of origin). In 1995 a Cameroonian politician, Samuel Eboua, then the country's éminence grise, put it very succinctly: "Every Cameroonian is an *allogène* anywhere else in the country . . . than where his ancestors lived and . . . where his mortal remains will be buried. Everybody knows that only under exceptional circumstances will a Cameroonian be buried elsewhere."[3] In many African societies the funeral has become a key moment in a precarious balancing of mobility and belonging. A striking aspect of urbanization in many parts of Africa is that, at least for quite some time, it did not lead to a definitive choice between city and countryside, but rather created what anthropologists have called "a rural-urban continuum" (Geschiere and Gugler 1998). Urbanites, even those who are born in the city, are keen to maintain a base in the village, building a house and planning to retire there. Their insistence that they ultimately belong to the village has ideological overtones and is balanced by a certain reluctance toward village life in practice. But the need to be buried there is at the very core of such ongoing involvement.

This is the background to the spectacular forms funerals are taking in many parts of Africa. They are increasingly turned into a true festival of belonging—often to the clear discomfort of urban elites who dread such occasions when the villagers can get even with "their brothers" from the city. Marked by a proliferation of all sorts of "neotraditional" rites that often involve great expenditure, these occasions show how deeply rooted this obsession with belonging is in society, but also what a complex balancing act between returning and maintaining distance it requires from urban elites. For many regions, there is a direct link between, on the one hand, the growing preoccupation with local belonging in a context of democratization and decentralization and, on the other, the increasing exuberance of the funeral "at home" (Monga 1995).

It may be important to emphasize the *neo*traditionality of such customs. The well-known case of *Burying SM* in Kenya (see Cohen and Atieno Odhiambo 1992) offers a striking example of this. The funeral of S. M., a famous lawyer in Nairobi, led to a fierce fight—finally decided in the national Court of Appeal—between his Luo clan and his Kikuyu widow over where the corpse should be buried. The widow wanted to bury S. M. at their sumptuous farm in Nairobi and emphasized his identity as a modern Kenyan citizen. But the representatives of his clan insisted that modern or not, S. M. was a Luo and that a Luo should be buried "at home." Yet, surprisingly enough in view of all this emphasis on "custom," Jaramogi Oginga Odinga, the grand old man of Luo politics, sided with the widow and declared that this stress on burying at home was new to him. According to him, the Luo, as an expansionist group, used to bury their dead in the areas where they migrated to in order to confirm new claims.

In other respects as well, the custom of burying at home shows an impressive capacity for innovation. It is striking, for instance, how easily this obligation spans the new distances created by the increasing frequency of transcontinental migration, thus producing new efforts in balancing mobility and belonging. In anglophone Cameroon people now celebrate what they call *bush-fallers*, adventurers who try to cross the Sahara just hoping to be lucky. There is a word play here: *bush* stands for Europe or any other rich part of the world; *falling* evokes the image of the hunter, who leaves on an adventure and returns with big prey. However, this metaphor also has a flip side: there are many mythical stories about hunters who found a fertile spot in the bush and stayed there. So the relatives who stay behind double their efforts to make sure the *bush-faller* will not forget where he really belongs. New forms of mobility seem to engender new strategies of belonging (Alpes 2017).

The ease with which the family networks of belonging, with the funeral as a central moment, now bridge distances on a new, global scale highlights the emotional depth to which slogans about autochthony, belonging to the soil, and the need to defend the ancestors' fief appeal. A major challenge in studying autochthony and the politics of belonging is therefore how to relate political manipulation by elites and deep emotional involvement among the people, since the combination of both seems to be at the heart of the conundrum of belonging and exclusion that is becoming so central in our supposedly globalizing world.

Europe: Belonging and the Culturalization of Citizenship

In Europe similar pleas for protection of the autochthons against immigrants had different effects. In almost all countries it led to a rapid unfolding during the 1990s of parties that are grouped under the label of the

New Right: Le Pen's Front National in France, Filip Dewinter's Vlaams Blok/ Belang in Flanders, Lega Norte in Italy, and more recently Alternative für Deutschland. In the Netherlands it was individual politicians, first Pim Fortuyn and subsequently Geert Wilders—whose party has the quite original form of a party with only one member, Wilders himself—who mobilized enduring support after 2000. But in all these countries it was clear—from the electoral successes but also from new turns in the public debate—that this populist discourse, employed with great rhetorical skill by the politicians, touched a deep chord among a considerable part of the population. One consequence was a determined move to the right by middle-of-the-road parties. Viewpoints that were considered to be extremist only fifteen years ago are now quite common in public presentations of the leaders of the more established parties, clearly with the aim of restricting electoral losses to the New Right.

A special effect of these developments was a "culturalization of citizenship": an increasing emphasis on issues of belonging that seemed to make socioeconomic aspects of immigration fade into the background (Duyvendak, Geschiere, and Tonkens 2016). Paul Scheffer's influential 2000 article, "The Multicultural Drama," in the NRC (supposedly the most intellectual among the Dutch newspapers) pleaded for the necessity of an "enforced cultural integration" of allochtonen: the cause of all the problems was less their disadvantaged economic position than their refusal to adapt to Dutch culture. The challenge became therefore to clearly define this Dutch culture to which immigrants had to adapt. This turned out to be less easy than expected because of the receding tenor of autochthony discourse—a general characteristic: what seems to be evident recedes as soon as one tries to fix it.

Ever since 2000 Dutch policies on integration have produced a whole instrumentation in order to test immigrants' belonging: *inburgeringscursssen* (literally, courses to "encitizenize"), *burgerschapsexamens* (citizenship exams), a "canon" of Dutch history, and so on. Especially the struggle to formulate such a canon highlights how difficult it is to give substance to what should be a firm pillar of belonging. In her mission statement the Dutch minister of culture clearly defined the aim for such a canon: it should promote integration and citizenship education among the younger generations. However, she installed a committee of mainly historians, and they turned out to be quite cautious in this respect. Their report warned against exaggerated expectations: a canon could certainly not be imposed; if coupled with national pride it could easily constrain people's view; therefore it should not be equated with a Dutch identity. The committee even expressed doubt concerning the notion of a "national identity" as such. A canon might be associated with *inburgering* (learning to be a citizen), but even here the committee was prudent: this should not be seen as the main motive behind its canon. Its main aim had rather been to formulate a canon "of the country in which we live together . . . offering society a common framework of reference for mutual communication and for operating as a Dutch person in the world . . . a canon for Boulahrouz and Beatrix . . . (respectively a then famous football player of Moroccan descent and the former Queen of the Netherlands)" (Geschiere 2009: 160).

Clearly the committee was very conscious of the risk that a canon might imply a fixing of something (culture?) that is always in flux. It proposed a quite original solution for this by constructing its canon from a series of "windows" rather than from specific events or facts. Each of its fifty windows opens up to a ramification of stories and links with related topics and aspects. Thus the committee hoped to have provided a common but open framework for the teaching of history, which could constantly be adapted to changing circumstances.

The reactions were, of course, highly diverse. Spokesmen who had already defended the idea of such a canon were especially disappointed. No wonder. To put it simply, they had asked for "memory"—the minister's assignment to the committee to produce a canon that would "promote integration and citizenship education" clearly suggested this. But she left this task to professional historians. Thus the result was "history"—pluralistic and with due attention to ambiguities. A standard reaction in the press was that the committee had missed its chance for not daring to couple history to national identity in a time when there was a deep need for this.

Similar defusing effects marked the other mainstay of the new policy for forceful cultural integration of immigrants. Minister Rita Verdonk promised to further impose *inburgeringscursussen* (courses for citizenship) and a citizenship exam. Here again the main issue became how to define the culture that immigrants had to be integrated into. Typical were the confrontations around a film, *Naar Nederland* (To the Netherlands), that was to play a central role in information for potential migrants. Officially the film was to provide a realistic idea of what to expect in their chosen country; however, critical voices soon commented that the aim seemed to be deterrence rather than information.

Early in 2005 the ministry launched the first version of the film, shown only behind closed doors. Soon rumors circulated about two moments in the film: a shot of two men passionately kissing each other after they had been officially married by the mayor of their municipality and a longer shot of girls sunbathing topless on the beach. This led to fierce protests. Some people commented that the aim of the film was clearly to deter Muslim immigrants, to whom such scenes were supposed to be particularly shocking. However, there were also loud protestations from autochtonen who thought it was a shame to characterize Dutch society with such scenes. And for a considerable part of the Dutch population topless sunbathing and same-sex marriage, especially if this leads to two males kissing each other in public, are almost as shocking as they are for many Muslims. The minister reacted by ordering these scenes taken out of the film. But this led to more loud protests, now particularly from gay action groups: same-sex marriage had been officially recognized in the Netherlands, the first country in the world to do so; deleting this scene from the film would mean that the minister was hiding Dutch reality and giving in to Muslim prejudices.

In the end, the film became part of the package immigrants have to study for their *burgerschapsexamen*. However, Dutch embassies in several countries warned that they would have difficulty if they circulated what locally was seen as pornography. So now two versions of the film are offered: one that includes the scenes and another one without them. The vicissitudes of the whole project show again the evanescent quality of Dutch culture. Like autochthony, it seems to be so clear at first glance, yet the harder one tries to formalize it, the more elusive it becomes.

The tug-of-war over the film also may indicate why some even speak of a "sexualization of citizenship." Especially in Western European countries debates about belonging are increasingly focusing on the role of women and the refusal of homophobic attitudes. During a presentation at Groningen University (in the north of the Netherlands) in 2008 Judith Butler even referred, with clear irony, to the special position of "the promiscuous male gay as the pinnacle of modernity" (compare Butler 2008). The scene of the two men kissing each other on the mouth to seal their marriage suggests that any homophobic utterance will disqualify an immigrant for Dutch citizenship.

Autochthony may seem self-evident to its protagonists, but its self-evidence dissolves as soon as it has to be captured. Still, the idea itself remains powerful enough to impose clear shifts among established political parties. In a lecture in 2017 that attracted considerable publicity the Christian Democrat leader Sybrand Buma—one of the main pillars of the present government—stated categorically, "It is not us who have to change, but the newcomers. . . . Our tradition, our culture and our values are so beautiful . . . we cannot allow that they will be watered down. . . . Respect for diversity has never been an aim in itself." Fifteen years ago this would have been the language one expected from a New Right leader. Now it comes from the leader of a centrist party. We are very far from one of the wisest voices in the debate over integration: Kwame Anthony Appiah's plea (2005, 2006) that we need "common stories" in order to live together, but that these stories must address diversity and allow for conversation across differences.

Autochthony as a Denial of Mobility: Searching for an Impossible Purity

I have highlighted the ambiguities surrounding discourses of autochthony and localist belonging. Often presented as self-evident or even natural— which is crucial to their capacity to convince—such ambiguities are highly historically circumscribed, subject to constant shifts, and allowing for highly variable articulations with other discourses on nation, race, ethnicity, indigeneity, or religion. Yet, as I said, the discourse has implications of its own that create unexpected *rapprochements*, despite all differences. A common trait of special importance might be this receding quality since it triggers a paradoxical combination of a promise of basic security—how can one belong more than if one is born from the soil?—and a practice of visceral insecurity. After all, this belonging can always be contested and outdone by someone who claims to belong more. It is this worrying combination that gives autochthony discourse a nervousness that emerges everywhere, despite kaleidoscopic differences, and gives it a violent potential.

Claims to be autochthonous are haunted by memories of earlier movement that become guilty secrets. In his seminal analysis of polemics about who is autochthonous and who is not in present-day Goma, on the border between Rwanda and eastern Zaire, Stephen Jackson (2006) speaks of "nervous languages." Such nervousness marks all the examples quoted earlier. The apparent self-evidence of chthonic belonging is always balanced by a strenuous concern to unmask "fake" autochthons hiding within the community—leading all the more easily to violence since the traitors are inside. As Radio Mille Collines kept repeating prior to the genocide in Rwanda of 1994, "The cockroaches are amongst us." A Cameroonian friend, normally a staunch defender of autochthony, summed up such uncertainty in a more everyday way, after he was suddenly outdone by a rival for a political function when the rival was seen as more autochthonous: "This autochthony thing is terrible: you can go to bed as an autochthon and wake up to find you have become an *allogène*."

However, precisely because of its fuzziness other readings of notions like autochthony and their effects on everyday life are possible as well. In an article based on his research in a secondary city in Burkina Faso, Mathieu Hilgers (2011) contests my characterization of autochthony as a more empty notion (in comparison, for instance, with ethnicity). In his research area, as in other parts of the West African Sahel, autochthony classifications have acquired a substance of their own. It is very possible that there are variations in this respect. In Cameroon, for instance, *autochthony* remains very much a colonial term (hence its suspect aura during the decades of nation-building). In many parts of the Sahel it was grafted upon older notions with a longer history—such as more or less clearly institutionalized forms of tutelage or land shrines respected for their sacredness (see also Lentz 2013). Such older notions can serve as pegs that make for a less fuzzy delimitation of notions of autochthony and more substantial institutionalization.

In a similar vein Jean-Pierre Chauveau (2003), a leading scholar on recent autochthony struggles in Ivory Coast, protests against a tendency in the literature to reduce the notion of autochthony to its rhetorical and ideological instrumentalization, leading to a pejorative view and neglecting its realities in everyday life. He is certainly right that debunking autochthony or other discourses of belonging as false history is of limited use. The question is rather why the term has such mobilizing power in very different circumstances and what realities it constructs on the ground (Geschiere 2009: ch. 6). Chauveau masterfully analyzes how autochthony has become a reality in Ivorian politics; the same applies to Cameroon. However, the question remains how far such constructs can escape the receding tendency, highlighted earlier, which seems to be given with the very notion of autochthony as a denial of history. The classical Athenian example, of how easily a man could lose his citizenship if rumors started to circulate that his autochthony was fake, is telling (Loraux 1996: 195).

Autochthony seems to imply a denial of migration as an omnipresent reality. This makes it basically a search for the impossible purity of an "Otherless universe" (Mbembe 2000: 25). Hence the basic insecurity that seems to mark so many discourses on belonging. It can always be contested. Is this the secret of why even in situations where self-identified autochthons are clearly in a dominant position the discourse bears a heavy mark of resentment and loss (McGovern 2011)? It is these two aspects—their historical contingency hidden under apparent self-evidence, and the link with an entitlement under threat—that give discourses of belonging a strong potential for violence in the present-day world.

Notes

1. See Loraux (1996: 39) and Détienne (2003: 21) on Plato's *Menexenus*.

2. Donald Trump, US birther-in-chief, could learn a lesson from these Zambian manipulations.

3. Interview with *Impact Trbu Une* 5 (1995): 14.

TOLERATION 5

UDAY S. MEHTA

This essay explores the connections among religious toleration, secularism, and security. The main questions are of a theoretical nature, relating to different understandings of religion, their relationship to security, the logic of religious conflict, and the role of political and social arrangements in mediating such conflicts. But it is also motivated in part by the unmistakable ascendency of tensions and conflict in religiously plural societies, where majoritarian assertiveness threatens norms of toleration and secularism—typically by invoking a concern with national identity and considerations of security. This is conspicuously the case in the recent developments in India.

From the early expressions of the anticolonial struggle and the articulation of nationalism in the late nineteenth and twentieth centuries, religious majoritarianism in India was an argument that was kept in reserve—never entirely absent as a potentiality, and yet never fully asserted as a political and cultural actuality. Following the constitutional settlement in 1950 and over the past seventy years the constitutional norm of secularism resulted in the relatively stable coexistence of democracy and nationalism because both were seen as accepting and vouching for the country's prolific religious and cultural diversity. Unlike many other "purer" expressions of nationalism in Europe and elsewhere, where the nation was presumed to be anchored in some shared unitary attribute such as religion, language, or ethnicity, in India democracy and diversity were the main constituents of a mutually supporting alloy of both the nation and the republic. But this constitutional alloy, a kind of forbearance, was always haunted by the proximity of the "purer" and more typical form of nationalist assertion in which the nation and the constitutional regime had independent sources of legitimacy. This was the specter in response to which secularism as a political norm was articulated. The fact that secularism has been such a contested aspect of Indian politics is at least partially explained by the dual burden it has always borne of being a buttress for the very existence of the nation, while also being a conspicuous part of its political idealism.

The election of Narendra Modi as prime minister in 2014, and again more emphatically this year, with a huge parliamentary majority, and as the leader of a party (Bharatiya Janata Party; BJP) that has historically favored a Hindu and religiously majoritarian conception of the nation, challenges the stability of this original and established constitutional norm. During his term, with what appears to be predictable regularity, there have been various dramatic incidences of rape, lynching, and other less spectacular forms of aggression, the revoking of the special status of Jammu and Kashmir (article 370 of the Indian Constitution) typically directed at Muslims though also at other minority groups. These incidences, along with explicit and veiled expressions of Hindu nationalism by the prime minster and other high officials, have highlighted the need to reconsider the question of religious toleration and secularism. The stakes are considerable, precisely because religious and majoritarian claims have always had a reserve potential to lay claims on a national narrative and thus put into question its pluralist and secular orientation.

....

In a broad sense, secularism refers to a set of political arrangements that profess to help secure the peaceful coexistence of diverse religious beliefs and practices. It has a special significance under conditions where various religious groups live together and where conflict is thought to be motivated to a significant degree by the beliefs and practices of such groups. In this rather direct sense secularism and religious pluralism are linked with security, understood as the absence of pervasive conflict, and hence they are also enmeshed with other ideals, such as justice, material well-being, and the pursuit of happiness, because these ideals are assumed to be reliant on the absence of widespread conflict.

This conceptual connection between secularism, religious pluralism, and security mirrors an intellectual history in which they assumed a theoretical and practical centrality, at roughly the same period in the seventeenth century. Among English political thinkers, such as Thomas Hobbes and John Locke, there was a firm consonance of opinion that religious pluralism and security were closely connected, despite the two philosophers' differing assessments of the effects of religious beliefs in motivating conflict, and despite their differing views on how to manage such potential conflict. Both Hobbes and Locke and, more broadly, the main strand of modern political thinking place a very high value on security and hence on anything that potentially motivates conflict.

There are plainly various ways of conceiving of religious diversity and the conflict associated with it, along with the familiar mandate of toleration and secularism. These various conceptions stem from different normative positions, histories, and experiences and vouch for different modes of existence. This point has been richly elaborated in recent writings, which point to the ways toleration and secularism are historically conditioned, and which further suggest that claims to their presumed universality are too easily overdrawn and perhaps limited by their own provincialism.[1]

I share and endorse this broad historicist claim, but the main purpose of this chapter is different, even though it follows from this historicist orientation. My focus is on certain ideas and experiences that acknowledged the fact of religious and cultural diversity but did not conceive of that fact, and the challenge it posed, as requiring a commitment to the abstract value of toleration and the political response associated with the term *secularism*. As I argue, the main reason for this stemmed from a different assessment of the consequences of religious conflict and a different valuation of security.

In the Indian context of the twentieth century these ideas were most forcefully elaborated by M. K. Gandhi. Gandhi took religious diversity to be an established and long-standing feature of the civilizational experience of India. But the implications which he believed to be implicit in this were very different from those in the predominant tradition of modern European and nationalist thinking. His objections to secularism and to the abstract idea of religious toleration were integral to his alternative understanding of religion, religious conflict, and an altogether different valuation of security and the role of social constraints in mitigating conflict. Gandhi's demurral in giving priority to political forms of redress was part of this broader alternative understanding.

....

The commitment to toleration and secularism is in many ways an anticipatory response to what are taken to be the implications of religious diversity and the conflict associated with it. Such an understanding of conflict underlies the modern response to the fact of religious diversity. But such responses are conditional on a particular grammar of thinking about religious diversity, the importance of security, and the role and the rationality of the state.

The English Civil War in the seventeenth century, in which religious conflict among sectarian Christian groups was a central feature, is the decisive experience in conceptualizing the rationality of the state and the logic of conflict.[2] Hobbes articulated the importance of this experience with a clarity that explains its enormous influence, even in traditions that modify his preferred absolutist conclusions. For Hobbes, there were four crucial features relating to religious diversity and the conflict associated with it. First, because religion involved matters of individual faith and salvific concerns—the "inner realm"—it sanctioned private judgments, which included judgments about ways of living one's life and valuations regarding what made it meaningful. This implicated religions with the troubling potential of encouraging radical forms of individuality and alternative conceptions of social and political order, even when they professed to be doing the opposite. Second, in the context of the sixteenth and seventeenth centuries, sectarian distinctions within Christianity had become the basis of hardened group identities. Third, these various sectarian groupings, by professing a claim to religiously and historically sanctioned authority, vitiated the possibility of establishing what for Hobbes was the only credible form of political authority, which had to be unified, singular, and, in the main, secular. Finally, and this is what was most crucial, the combined effect of the previous points made compromise or a modus vivendi impossible among diverse religions or sects, and hence produced, and had the permanent potential to produce, a form of conflict and insecurity that was devastating to all forms of social order, and at the limit, to life itself. It was this predicament that led Hobbes to conclude that neither individual volition nor the traditional authority of religious groups could produce the order requisite for any form of social enterprise. What was therefore essential was the displacement of religious authority as the grounds for public obedience. What mattered in terms of the structure of the state was the status of being a citizen, and one could be a citizen only by being the subject of a sovereign.

For Hobbes, the lesson of the Civil War was that it shattered the illusion that society through its various regulatory authorities could be self-regulating and that it could produce a stable form of order that could thwart the pulsating effects of human nature and the passions to which human beings were prone. Instead only a political dispensation in which the state had the power to be the authoritative mediator of conflict could produce order, peace, and security. Another way to put this is that the problem of authority had to be wholly subsumed under the category of political sovereignty. Locke had a different view of religion in which it was a private matter relating to the individual's salvific beliefs, and for that reason it did not, as Hobbes assumed, necessarily produce mayhem and widespread conflict. Given this in many forms of religious belief and practice were beyond the magistrate's authority and merited toleration. But even with Locke's more circumspect view of religious conflict, the limit to toleration was set by considerations of "the safety and security of the commonwealth" (Locke 1950: 45).[3] Hence, as with Hobbes, the matter of religion required the mediation of political arrangements, which alone could secure the requisite kind of public security. A version of this Hobbesian and Lockean narrative, I argue, becomes central to the constitutional founding of the modern Indian state, which lays out the broad mandate of secularism in India.

My purpose in recalling Hobbes and Locke and their view of religious conflict, the role of the state, and the importance of security is to set up a contrast with Gandhi. The contrast operates on many registers. At the broadest level, nothing like the historical experience or an imagined version of the English Civil War informs Gandhi's thinking. Instead the experience through which Gandhi thinks of the past and the present is the effects of modern civilization, which have to do mainly with the revaluation of technology, security, self-understanding, patience, and courage. Perhaps surprisingly, given Gandhi's views on nonviolence, he does not, at least not as a primary consideration, associate the deleterious and deforming effects of modern civilization with war, massive devastation, or anarchy. Gandhi does not think of security and the preservation of life as foundational ideals, either for individuals or for communities, and hence he does not give them the primacy that characterizes much of modern political thinking. He thinks of order not in terms of something that requires a single agent, like the state, that can secure it by having the power to intervene in every eruption of conflict and disorder. The sort of order that matters to him is written into the weave of society and extant social norms, at least before they had been ravaged by the effects of modern civilization. He thinks of conflict, including religious conflict, as amenable to persuasion and compromise, in the way that interests are thought to be, and when such persuasion and compromise fail, he imagines the ensuing conflict as something that tends in any case to limit itself. It is not of necessity escalatory, because it is not spurred by passions that are beyond individual volition or social constraints. For Gandhi, religious diversity is simply a fact, in the Indian case a long-standing and largely unexceptional fact. It is a fact about the distinct religious languages and visions through which people imagine their life and what makes it meaningful. It is not, in the main, a fact about the contesting claims regarding authority and power of different religious groups. The threat that the diversity of religions poses—and he does not think of it as a permanent or underlying threat, is of occasional disorder, but never of social devastation. Unlike the tradition of thinking from Hobbes to Weber and on to contemporary realist thinkers, that has taken anarchy to be the necessary and immediate counterpoint to the absence of political order, Gandhi does not think in terms of such Manichaean contrasts because, as I have said, he finds the extant basis of order in the diffused patterns and minutiae of social practices. Late in his life Gandhi was even prepared explicitly to countenance the possibility of anarchy in India, which, despite that prospect, did not warrant imperial intervention (Devji 2012: chap. 6). And finally, for Gandhi religion simply is the language through which individual self-understanding and self-transformation is made possible. It represents those deep inner convictions and that faith through which individuals explore their own selfhood. And crucially it is this feature that gives to religion the potential to facilitate mutual understanding among different groups, without requiring a commitment to the abstract value of toleration or the backstop of a unified and powerful state.

To get a fuller sense of Gandhi's views on religious plurality and conflict one needs to consider passages in *Hind Swaraj* where the issue is explicitly considered. Gandhi's interlocutor (in *Hind Swaraj*) raises the matter of the deep enmity between Muslims and Hindus, and how this commonly accepted claim undermined the potential unity of the nation and threatened its aspirations to independence from imperial rule. Gandhi disputes both the alleged nature and depth of the enmity and the specific sort of unity that self-rule required. India, for Gandhi, had a unity that predates the arrival of the British. It was a unity that included the coexistence of various religions and a long history of assimilation: "If the Hindus believe that India should be peopled only by Hindus, they are living in a dreamland. The Hindus, the Mahomedans, the Parsees and the Christians who have made India their country are fellow countrymen, and they will have to live in unity if only for their own interest. In no part of the world are one nationality and one religion synonymous terms: nor has it ever been so in India" (Gandhi 1909: 52–53). For Gandhi religious diversity and a basic unity of coexistence, underwritten by civilization's rhythms and not unitary power, are simply facts. They are part of the warp and weft of an ancient land, and for him they provoke none of the anxiety that they do in his nationalist interlocutor. Neither religious diversity nor the sort of unity Gandhi has in mind is freighted by any necessarily troubling implications; nor for that matter is he buoyed by a high idealism that the presence of religious diversity may point to. Again, they are merely facts, banal and scattered in their obvious familiarity. Hindus and Muslims, Gandhi points out, have survived and prospered under rulers of each faith. They are part of a syncretic way of life that has points of mutual contact and divergence. What matters is simply that "those who are conscious of the spirit of nationality do not interfere with one another's religion" (52). The unity Gandhi vouches for is a shared "mode of life" and not a shared national form to facilitate a superintending form of political governance (48). It is a unity tethered to civilizational routines of common and conflicting interests and social norms. It does not have, and does not need, in the manner of the typical nationalist and imperialist, clearly defined political boundaries or a clear font of power and obligation.

On the matter of the alleged deep enmity between Hindus and Muslims Gandhi (1909) is again almost cavalier in his denial of such an enmity. Instead he thinks of the enmity (and conviviality) as occasioned by contingent circumstances that almost always admit of indifference, negotiation, and persuasion. Even on the freighted matter of the killing of cows by Muslims he says he would "only plead" with Muslims; that is, it is not for him a political matter to require the blunt power of the state, to refrain from such acts, notwithstanding the reverence that he, as a Hindu, felt toward cows. "[But] if he [the Muslim] would not listen to me, I should let the cow go for the simple reason that the matter is beyond my ability" (54). Gandhi's apparent pragmatism in this sentence does not call into question his own religious convictions. In some other context one can well imagine him being willing to die for those convictions. But his point here is that he does not take the difference between the Muslim attitude toward the cow from his own Hindu reverence for it as sanctioning an escalation of that difference. Gandhi knows and accepts the fact of the occasional conflict between Hindus and Muslims. But what is striking is the degree to which he views such conflict as having no necessary or deep escalatory potential:

> I do not suggest that the Hindu and the Mahomedans will never fight. Two brothers living together often do so. We shall sometimes have our heads broken. Such things ought not to be necessary, but all men are not equi-minded.

When people are in a rage, they do many foolish things. These we have to put up with. But, when we do quarrel, we certainly do not want to engage counsel and to resort to English or any law courts. *Two men fight; both have their heads broken, or one only. How shall a third party distribute justice amongst them? Those who fight may expect to be injured.* (57, emphasis added)

What is most striking in this and many similar passages is Gandhi's casual equanimity about the conflict between Hindus and Muslims. There is no suggestion that the conflict stems from a deep friend-enemy animus in which the depth of the antagonism can be, or should be, the foundational ground of a political construct that makes possible a unity forged around that construct. Gandhi never gives an account of such conflict in which it arises from the essential nature of the two religions, or indeed from anything that has a deeper motivational basis. His thought is strikingly free of such underlying mandates, just as it is free of the mandates of political economy or those of class conflict. Instead, in the examples he gives, the conflict is almost always occasioned by, and limited by, a narrow set of contextual considerations. In Gandhi's rendering the conflict is merely a foolish act motivated by prosaic anger, a kind of schoolyard brawl that will run its course, without any implied or necessary escalation, and following which, one assumes, the patterns of social conviviality and distinction will reassert themselves. Even the possibility of heads being broken, and hence of violence, does not occasion any special concern. Neither does the possibility that perhaps only one party's head gets broken, and hence that the initial conflict may have been between unequally matched opponents. In Gandhi's view such things, sometimes, just happen. They are acts of almost childlike folly with no grave religious or historical logic underlying them. They are not part of a cascading momentum that embodies as its immanent consequences dire implications about the war of all against all or social devastation. Gandhi never imagines such a pandemic eventuality in the Indian context.

But what did deeply trouble Gandhi, and what at numerous times in *Hind Swaraj* and elsewhere he returns to, is the idea that such conflict required the mediation of "a third party." Gandhi is insistent in his refusal to countenance such mediation, be it the law with its warrant of justice, or the imperial state as the guarantor of peace, order, and a progressive historical alignment, or the national state as it vouches for equality and a representational sanctioned form of acting on behalf of the public interest. Elsewhere in the same chapter of *Hind Swaraj* Gandhi (1909: 57) writes, "We

[Hindus and Muslims] should be ashamed to take our quarrels to the English," making it clear that for him the issue of seeking mediation, where the warrant for the mediator lay in its superior power, was fraught with both psychological and ethical considerations. At its root, for Gandhi, all such forms of mediation eviscerate the natural and potential integrity of the self by holding out the lure of abstracted forms of substitution, which only third parties can supply and which make their mediation essential. Even Gandhi's extended diatribes in *Hind Swaraj* against lawyers, doctors, and modern forms of travel are part of the same worry regarding mediation and the effects it has on the self. They interject a dependence, which Gandhi thinks is the hidden essence of modern civilization, in which the security and deepest values of the self become reliant on abstracted projections of power.

Secularism for Gandhi was at root a form of mediation, which required conceiving of toleration as an abstract value alongside other similarly conceived values. Its mandate was the rationality of the state and the presumption that religious conflict was escalatory and that it could be thwarted only by a superior power. Toleration conceived as an idea or a value was essentially linked to this mandate. But for Gandhi toleration in many ways was not a normative value, at least not in the sense that it becomes a standard by which the state mediates between it and other values or deploys it to mediate between the practices and beliefs of various religions. Instead it is simply a description of the fact of religious diversity as Gandhi saw it exemplified in the course of Indian civilization. It did not require conceptualizing toleration as a value, understood as a normative ideal that had to be supported by the state (the third party), because the fact that it referred to was itself not burdened by the harrowing implications, which secularism as an instrument of the state and toleration as a value were meant to manage.

Gandhi not only disagrees with his interlocutor, but the root of that disagreement is that he does not share the specific anxieties as they relate to religious diversity, its expected effect on conflict, and the need for a nationalist political unity. Gandhi is indifferent to these anxieties, even though he has other deep worries relating to effects of modern civilization. To put the matter in a broader context, Gandhi is indifferent to precisely the sort of worries that motivated Hobbes in the context of the English Civil War and that underlie the grammar of political thinking in the post-Westphalian context and that would go on to obsess nationalists like Vinayak Savarkar as they pondered the effects on nationalist aspirations of minorities in general, and religious minorities in particular. Gandhi believed that it was precisely these sorts of anxieties that were borrowed from another way of thinking and another context—a context that did not capture the reality of India, where, moreover, the borrowing itself was an adventitious anticipatory response, which would put into motion an undesirable set of consequences.

....

The main point that I have been urging can be summarized as follows. Secularism and the linked idea of religious toleration rely on a conception of conflict, which as a matter of historical fact drew on the crisis of the English Civil War and which in its underlying logic, at least implicitly, is deemed to be a universal fact, thus becoming part of the essential grammar of the state. In this understanding, religious conflict is necessarily escalatory and devastating of social order and security. For that reason, its effects can be moderated or managed only through the mediation of the state and the power at its disposal. One characteristic feature of such management is the state's commitment to religious toleration, which of course can take many institutional forms. Toleration refers to permissive attitudes toward religion, but in the specific sense that it receives its warrant from the state. Given this widely held view of religious conflict, secularism becomes all but mandatory, as does the need for a unified state. The rationality of the state, or what amount to the same thing, the presumed conditions on the basis of which the state is deemed to be rational, is reliant on a particular conception of religious conflict and a linked conception of the special priority of security as an individual and collective value.

But if, in the manner of Gandhi, one does not subscribe to this understanding of conflict and to the special priority of security, a range of options open up that do not turn on a political settlement or on the power and unity of the state. On this view, religious toleration, understood as a value, and secularism as an orientation of the state cease to be mandatory because they refer to a different history with different implicit potentialities and a different grammar of thinking (Bilgrami 2014: 3–57). For Gandhi these options included forms of social organization that were scattered and decentralized; where conflict was quotidian (and not motivated by something essential) and persuasion common; where security of individuals and the collectivity were valued but did not have a trumping primacy because they were not associated with the devastation of all forms of sociability; and where toleration was not an abstract value but referred simply to the long-standing experience of living with religious diversity, and where what was normatively crucial was the preservation of such forms of living together.

Gandhi vouched for these alternatives even after it was clear that the end of imperial rule in India would culminate in the birth of two nations whose mode of managing religious diversity was going to be starkly at odds with his own understanding. Indeed for Gandhi it was precisely the resort to the idea of civil war, the deep and unending basis of the conflict between Hindus and Muslims, and more broadly, the constant resort to the proximity of crisis, and hence the imperative need for a unified state that narrowed the options to the point that only partition could be thought of as creating the conditions in which the state, or rather two states, could perform the appropriate form of mediation.

In the context of the late 1940s in India, when independence was acknowledged to be fated and when the constitutional form of the future state was being considered by the Constituent Assembly, it was precisely the language of crisis, disunity, and religious strife that came to haunt public deliberations. It was from these deliberations that the idea of religious toleration and secularism came to be taken as mandatory. The invocation of crisis, strife, impending disunity, sectarian divisions, and the prospect of mayhem are ubiquitous in the reflections of Indian Constituent Assembly debates. The British imperial authorities had themselves grounded the legitimacy of their rule as the sole basis for avoiding chaos and mitigating the sectarian crisis that would result from their departure. Especially in the early speeches of the assembly, when a broader context was being imagined, the invocation of crisis constituted a haunting background to the deliberations.

From a political and constitutional perspective nations have to articulate themselves as singular entities. It points to the crucial significance of the singular collective pronoun "We, the people," as authorizing the constitutional project. In terms of constitutional salience, unity is understood not as a social or civilizational category, the way Gandhi thought of it, but rather as something that refers to a political form. Unity, as Carl Schmitt pointed out, was the essential and permanent precondition and aspiration of the modern form of the state. In many ways, the generative crucible of modern constitutions and modern politics turns on the metaphor and the idea of destruction and creation. As a coupling, it is the font of that particular disposition by political power and becomes, or at least projects itself as, the singular and redemptive energy of a society.

The idea that political power emerges from the site of destruction or that it should need such an image for its self-generation is revealing of the nature of political power itself. At a broad level, it points to the fact that power has a strained if not antithetical relationship to the past. In constituting itself through an act of clearing it is markedly different from social authority, which, as Weber emphasized, typically relies on continuity as its mode of self-authorization and legitimacy. This is a theme that informs the Indian Constituent Assembly, though often with ironic touches. The assembly, as is well known, was full of speeches and references to India's glorious and multifarious pasts. One can recall Nehru's many invocations of India's five thousand years of history and traditions (which he often characterized through the metaphor of weight, thereby also suggesting burden), or Dr. Radhakrishnan's frequent references to India's ancient republican traditions, or the countless other occasions in the assembly when the civilizational luster of India was mentioned usually with triumphal pride. And yet, and this is the irony, the dominant temper of mind in the assembly was revolutionary, for which the challenge was to build a new society on the ruins of the old. It was that thought that guided the assembly from its start to its conclusion and for which the state and political power was deemed to be the necessary instrument. The metaphor of building, of creating something new, runs through the assembly's deliberations. When, for example, Nehru in the resolution regarding "aims and objects" invokes, with commendation, the American, French, and Russian Revolutions it is because, as he says, they "gave rise to a new type of State." For that new state to have the stature and power requisite for the crafting of a new society, the past had to, quite literally, be past. It could survive only as something on which the state could do its work, as though it were an inherited one-dimensional coda, but not as a living force that infused the present.

······················

Gandhi, as I have indicated, expressed a dissenting view to this entire form of thinking, which was of a piece with his reluctant support of constitutionalism and the need for unity expressed around the mediating power of the state and the narratives of crisis that underwrote it. But there was also another aspect of these narratives whose focus was the social. There is a family of familiar accounts, often linked with the magisterial work of Norbert Elias on the civilizing process, in which civility referred to the slow accretion of new domestic and public practices, which produced what came to be known as a civilized society. The broad impetus for this was the intermingling of new groups of peoples who had to accommodate each other's differences. Over time this produced a society that displaced the older language of etiquette and manners along with feudal and aristocratic norms, and thus paved the way for an ascending liberal and commercial world.

Gandhi abstained from these broad narratives of society and social development. He was indifferent to the historicism that is essential to these narratives, because nothing of any importance in Gandhi turns on the logic of historical development. This did not mean that he thought of human beings as living in some timeless zone of immobility—only that he did not accept the typical social and political narratives that history offered up as the bases of individual and collective self-fashioning. He did not, for example, think that Indian civilization had to, or should, conceive of itself as bound to a teleology whose inevitable outcome was the nation-state or a condition of economic modernity. Correspondingly he abstained from endorsing the driving frictions that are internal to these historical narratives, accounts such as class struggle, the increase of the productive forces, the logic of capitalist development or imperialist expansion, or the impulse to enlarge the domains of social and political freedom through constitutional commitments. Such abstention did not make him indifferent to social and economic woes such as deprivation, gross inequality, exploitation, or the abuse and abridgment of rights. It was just that his views on these matters did not share the causal logic that typically organizes such narratives.

Gandhi abstains from these accounts for a very simple reason. He was never drawn to the idea of society as a project in need of wholesale refashioning. His thought is not spurred by the Manichaean contrast that underlies and guides the vision of so much of modern political and social thought, whereby the only alternative to political order is the asocial and diabolical ravages of anarchy. It is not that Gandhi accepted or commended every extant aspect of society. He clearly did not, as is obvious from his work on the problem of untouchability in the Hindu caste framework and many other social woes. But even on these matters his emphasis is not on producing "a wholly" new kind of society marked by a radical rearrangement of social relations or ruptures in the existing patterns of life. He took society, like religion, to be a given, a fact, which despite its vexations and tribulations had the tensile capacity to produce an order from within and which had the resources for managing conflict among groups and for engendering mutual understanding and self-transformation. Gandhi was never taken with the dream of a new kind of society or of a new kind of man. His vision comes from a palette that draws from the materials of ordinary life. He could and did imagine a society with different hues and shapes, without, nevertheless, replacing the palette itself. It was from this broad philosophical orientation that he challenged the idea of secularism and conceived of religion as having a different potential for individuals and for the diverse groups that made up society.

....

I want to return to how Gandhi understands the role of religion, its link to toleration, and what he deems necessary to its flourishing. In the final chapter of *Hind Swaraj* Gandhi makes the following observations and claims:

> You English who have come to India are not a good specimen of the English nation, nor can we, almost half-Anglicized Indians, be considered a good specimen of the real Indian nation. If the English nation were to know all you have done, it would oppose many of your actions. The mass of the Indians have had few dealings with you. If you will abandon your so-called civilization, and search into your own scriptures, you will find that our demands are just. Only on condition of our demands being fully satisfied may you remain in India, and if you remain under those conditions, we shall learn several things from you, and you will learn many things from us. So doing, we shall benefit from each other and the world. But that will happen only when the root of our relationship is sunk in a religious soil. (Gandhi 1909: 115)

Gandhi was concerned with three issues in this passage. The first is the fact that the English in India and the half-Anglicized Indians betray their real and best national traditions and inheritances. They are quite literally poor moral specimens of the genus of which, in the present, they are taken to be representatives. Regarding the former group Gandhi believes that their actions would be disapproved of by the English nation were it to become fully aware of them. The English in India operate in a moral penumbra and perpetrate a kind of moral subterfuge against the English people. It is a subterfuge that is not fully evident to Indians because few of them have any dealings with the English. The theme is one of self-betrayal and moral occlusion, by both the English and the Indians.

The second issue relates to the conditions that distort the mutual understanding between the two groups. The reason for this distortion is the extant context of their interaction, the imperial context, but Gandhi does not name it as such, with its conspicuous association with a regime of unequal power and racialized differentiation. As a general matter, in his more reflective writings Gandhi avoids the term *imperialism*. It is too narrow for his purposes and places the accent in the wrong place, by pointing primarily to a political turpitude. Gandhi's purposes exceed the political relationship by pointing to something deeper that underlies and disfigures it. Instead he identifies the context through a broader reference, to "your so-called civilization." It is modern civilization that confines the relations between the English and the Indians on a plane that vitiates their ability to learn from each other. The reference to mutual learning or understanding, almost by its banality, is telling because it suggests that something as elemental as mutual and genuine learning among different groups is made impossible by the mediation of modern civilization. Here in a sense it is modern civilization that is the "third party." What Gandhi has in mind are the grand historical narratives that are wedded to a conception of progress and a corresponding belief in differential civilizational elevations. He is contending that such narratives make mutual learning impossible because they are premised on the immaturity of one group and the temporal assurance of a particular outcome, that is, even if a conversation between the English and the Indians were to occur. It is also what makes it difficult for the English to appreciate the justice of the demands being made by the Indians, because a particular conception of justice has already been written into those historical narratives. Instead Gandhi suggests that mutual learning and the claims of justice would become clear only if the English sought guidance in their "own scriptures" rather than in the warrant of history.

And third, in a more prescriptive voice, Gandhi writes of the conditions that could rectify both the hindrances in the way of mutual understanding and the self-betrayal within each group. Regarding these conditions he speaks of the essential need to return to scriptures and of rooting the relationship between the English and the Indians "in a religious soil." Again the reference is quite general. Gandhi does not invoke specific religious doctrines that might be common to Christianity and the Indic religions and that might serve as the basis of an interfaith framework of understanding. The idea is not of an overlapping consensus that grounds mutuality. Gandhi's primary concern is with the need for a self-searching that is internal to each group. On his view a return to scripture is essential to this self-searching. But he is insistent that only a relationship anchored in a religious seedbed holds the potential of both groups overcoming their respective self-betrayal and of learning from each other. Moreover, in this repositioned relationship between the English and the Indians, he says, the broader world would learn from their interaction, and suggestively, there would also be the possibility, to which in this passage, as elsewhere, Gandhi makes explicit reference, that there might be no reason for the English to decamp from India.

The themes of self-betrayal, the distortion brought about by modern civilization, and the need to anchor mutual relations in the language of scripture and religiosity are a digest of the broader issues that matter deeply to Gandhi. Their substance is obviously intertwined. They suggest both a positive purpose and a refusal to think in familiar terms. Gandhi is refusing the categories that by the early twentieth century and with re-doubled zeal in the decades that followed had come to suffuse the discourse of imperial relations from both sides. He does not, for example, speak of exploitation, inequality, racism, differentials of power, absence of political representation, economic immiseration, quotidian forms of violence, or the warrant and urgency of national independence—even though, in dif-ferent degrees, all these mattered to him. Similarly, from a positive per-spective, he does not engage with the idea of progress, the integration of India and the world, of a modernity that moved India away from feudal and obscurantist norms and which carried the imprimatur of science, the pros-pect of democratic self-governance, and other mandates of a progressive future. As he comes to conclude his discourse on home and self-rule, all these categories seem at best secondary to his ultimate purposes. Instead his summation, both critically and positively, points to the importance of scriptures and the language of religion. It is the muffling and displacement of this language that obscures what for Gandhi is the most basic and essen-tial fact of the empire and of modern civilization—namely, that it imperils the moral hygiene of both the English and the Indians.

There is something puzzling about this invocation of religion and the thought that it alone could redeem the appropriate link between the En-glish and the Indians. Why is Gandhi so insistent that a relationship fraught with so many obvious political, economic, moral, and cultural vexations should not, as the typical nationalists insisted, be conceptualized in those familiar terms but instead through the language of scripture and religion?

Gandhi's views on religion and his own religiosity are highly complex. This is not the context to propose even a cursory summary of their com-plexity. What is relevant is that he associates religion in its diverse forms as something given, into which one is, as it were, arbitrarily cast. Gandhi's main preoccupation is with infusing the mundane aspects of life with meaning and moral depth, which for him turns ultimately on religious considerations that have to do with submission, where submission itself is not understood in terms of a willed act or a choice but rather as something that "seizes" the person, and that therefore suggests a form of surrender. This is a thought familiar to many religious traditions regarding how faith is understood. Faith is not chosen but is constitutive of believers. They give themselves up to it. To paraphrase Wittgenstein, we take hold of a picture (or a narrative) of which faith is a part and hence we become believers. Faith does not frame the picture or hold the narrative together as something prevenient to it. It is simply one part of it. I think this view broadly captures Gandhi's own understanding of religion and faith in which the sovereignty of the individual as an agent (chooser) is, if not wholly denied, never crucial to having faith or being religious. In this sense, it is linked with Gandhi's understanding of the social as a prevenient mesh of interconnections. This is what allows Gandhi to affirm different religions as being of equal sanctity, while always claiming to be a devout Hindu himself, and it also explains his opposition to missionary attempts to change people's religion.

For Gandhi religion is similar to one's family, one's social location, and even one's caste. They make up the habitus that marks out the patterns of individual and social embodiment. Religion, with a special poignancy, constitutes the language through which a bounded horizon is navigated and made meaningful to individuals and communities. It limits choice but also deepens its potential application. Gandhi never identifies religion as the basis for forging a homogeneous unity that could serve as a buttress to the nation or to any broad collective identity. He thinks of religion in terms of faith, which makes possible coexistence, without having to lean on shared identities that must almost of necessity be secured and invigilated by a third party. It is instead a diverse inheritance, the grammar and the minutiae through which the pursuit of self-knowledge is carried out in the practice of everyday life. That practice, because it involves a deep and constant attunement to the question of who I am, places a high premium on patience. Its sternest vigilance is directed at those everyday activities such as diet, sexual desires, material strivings, and abstracted forms of political expedience, where the underlying passions are likely to distract attention from the self, and where, moreover, there is a heightened possibility of a vicarious lure.

Patience is the idea that backs Gandhi's refusal to assent to the urgencies that mark what I have called the grammar of modern forms of political thinking. It denies the abstraction and the resort to the future that is a necessary feature of all forms of instrumental reasoning. It does not sanction the logic of history or of politics because they are typically inattentive to a deep and unhurried moral and psychological vigilance. The patience Gandhi urges insists on that vigilance even in the face of manifest moral violations and injustices that were common in the empire, but equally conspicuous to institutions such as the Hindu caste system. It constrains the avarice for power. It moderates the Hobbesian hubris that the world is an artifice wholly of our creation. It mitigates the potential feelings of resentment, anger, humiliation—in a word, of alienation—that stem from having our hopes thwarted in the present. It restrains the urgency that underlies most forms of violence. It renders fluid the categorical nature and the structures that rely on distinctions such as friend and enemy, insider and outsider, and other compacted identities such as class, caste, race, or ethnicity, all of which ultimately require the mediating intervention of the state. The concentration it does demand is always on the present and on the self, both of individuals and of collectivities. It operates in a register that is not drawn to the grandiosity of changing the world, or rather, it imagines such change as occurring from actions that are attuned to the question "What am I doing to myself?"

....

On this view, the problems that arise from the fact of religious diversity can be resolved within the extant social framework because it is deemed to have the flexibility to admit of conflict and conviviality, and because it is not confronted with, nor does it promote, compacted religious identities, and finally because it is not fastened to the form of security that, to the extent that it can be realized, requires the constant presence of a superintending power. It relies instead on the extant social and religious grammar for exploring the here and the hereafter. Gandhi saw in that grammar the resources to contend with the challenge of religious diversity. In contrast, the view in which toleration and secularism are thought to be essential relates to the political imperatives under which the fact of religious diversity has to be "managed" by a state, which of political necessity is concerned with issues of national unity, norms of fairness, the advancement of the public interest, and the logic of accountability and representation. Under these imperatives, religious diversity must be rendered in a form amenable to the mediation of the state—with its own distinctive urgencies. Among the ways in which the Indian state and judiciary have refashioned religions is by giving them a defined shape and associating them with "essential doctrines" and practices, all of which assume their specific form through the contestations of representation, conflicts over resources—in brief, the mediation of politics.

For the most part, religious identity in India (and elsewhere) is now thoroughly constituted through the functioning of the state. Perhaps this mutual embrace of politics and religion makes some form of secularism all but mandatory. Gandhi's reflections on religious coexistence refer to an era when religions had not ceded authority to the state and when the state itself had not penetrated all domains of social life. They also belong to an era when religions, perhaps more than any other social identifier, could articulate a self-confidence that was not reliant on narratives of victimhood, the logic of history, or the calculus of representative power—narratives that comport with the rationality of the state, especially those that profess to be representative. These narratives of fragile identities now saturate religious discourse, even when they proclaim them with feigned confidence and stridency. Perhaps all this renders mute the terms in which Gandhi conceived of the challenge of religious diversity and coexistence. There is no denying that he thought in terms of categories that now have an archaic quality to them. But they merit reconsideration at a time when the familiar terms in which the challenge of religious diversity and abstract invocations of toleration feel fatigued and the promise of secularism seems constantly to be entangled within a web of political and juridical hubris, and which in any case tilts in favor of religious majoritarianism. Perhaps what makes Gandhi relevant today is that he thought religiously, and that he could imagine a world in which such thought did not produce religious identities or religious states. There is a conception of toleration in this vision, which thwarts the worst impulses of religious majoritarianism along with its reliance on a narrow and pure form of nationalism and its hyperbolic conception of security.

Notes

1. Much of the recent writing on secularism and toleration is anchored in an appreciation and critique of Charles Taylor's (2007) magisterial work *A Secular Age*, which details the path of Latin Christianity. See Warner, VanAntwerpen, and Calhoun 2010; Bilgrami 2016; Bilgrami 2014: chaps. 1 and 2; and VanAntwerpen 2007. There is of course an older literature on secularism that is also attentive to its historical particularity. Talal Asad (2003) in his classic book, *Formations of the*

Secular: Christianity, Islam, Modernity, articulates an important position that questions the presumed universality of secularism. Michael Walzer's (1997) book *On Toleration* is also deeply attentive to the different regimes and norms of toleration. Also see Rajeev Bhargava's (1998) edited volume *Secularism and Its Critics*.

2. Hence the story is quite different in the French or German intellectual traditions. In France, the king and the royal court in Paris acted to evacuate the mediating social and untidy institutions on what was a preemptory basis. I am grateful to Didier Fassin for pointing this out to me in an e-mail.

3. Locke (1950), of course, limits toleration on other grounds that relate to atheists and Catholics and Muslims.

POWER 6

ALEX DE WAAL

There is no current theory of political power that is not also a theory of the state. With a few notable exceptions, such theories presuppose a singular locus of gravity and source of illumination, around which the various subjects of our study rotate. That theoretical and empirical center of gravity is the state, whether conceptualized as Leviathan, sovereign, the dominant institution for governing public affairs, legitimate public authority, political settlement, rules of the political game, or the central source for generating fields of power (Schmitt [1922] 2005; Khan 2018; North 1991; Leftwich 2015; Lukes 2005; Foucault 1978; Bourdieu 1994). Whether hegemonic or contested, and regardless of the contingencies of the historic processes whereby it was produced, the state as singular phenomenon dominates our imagination, our vocabulary, and how we perceive other social phenomena.

Maintaining a singular center for our theoretical field is, I suggest, insufficient for our current predicament. We need to conceive a plurality of forms and sources of power, including "wild" power that is outside the state, perhaps opposed to it, perhaps illegible and unpredictable. Notably, power is becoming a tradable commodity: we need a theory and an imaginary of the political market and what it may entail.

Our current state-centrality is firmly drilled into our perceptual apparatus. Socialized and schooled in the public order of late modernity, we not only "see like a state" but also *feel like a state* (Scott 1998; Fassin 2015): in the same way that our brain has a sense of the position of our limbs, so too we have an intuitive sense of how the parts of the body politic should be connected to each other. We *feel* that political power is properly the orderly governance of a society's affairs. Those schooled in modern societies feel that the rules, mechanisms, and institutions—especially the uniformed services—that administer an orderly public life *are* the state.

Pierre Bourdieu (1994: 4, emphasis in original), who took a lead in articulating a challenge to the inevitability of the singular conceptualization of the state, nonetheless conceded that it served as *"the culmination of a process of concentration of different species of capital*: capital of physical force or instruments of coercion (army, police), economic capital, cultural or (better) informational capital, and symbolic capital. It is this concentration as such which constitutes the state as the holder of a sort of meta-capital granting power over other species of capital and over their holders."

Ernest Gellner, who more than any other Anglo-Saxon political scientist brought the sensibilities of the ethnographer of the postcolony to the analysis of the dominant sociopolitical forms of our time, circled around the challenge of whether and how we might think differently about nations and states—but could not escape the gravitational pull of Weberian stateness. Having critiqued the Weberian definition of the state, he wrote, "The idea enshrined in this definition corresponds fairly well with the moral intuitions of many, probably most, members of modern societies." He continued, "Weber's underlying principle does, however, seem valid *now*, however strangely ethnocentric it may be as a general definition" (Gellner 2006: 3–4, emphasis in original). Gellner's italicized *now* hints at the fact that for the historical ethnographer, the chronocentrism of late modernity is no less "strange" than a Euro-American ethnocentrism. The state, and its sibling concepts of "sovereignty" and "legitimacy," have an enduring mystique—they are, qua Carl Schmitt, hand-me-down theological concepts.

In this essay I suggest that contemporary history has other ideas. There are *several* centers of gravity in our political-scientific solar system, and we should adjust our eyes to the wavelengths of the light they emit.

Four historic trends make it urgent to retheorize and reimagine. The first is the much-heralded decline of the West, especially the United States, vis-à-vis China and its rival model of the state. The East Asian state is identifiably a rule-bound sovereign order, differing from its Western counterparts in that it is politically illiberal. Though the rise of China may be a threat to a liberal world order led by Western states, it poses less of a threat to theories of statehood, other than denting the self-assurance of the Anglo-Saxon political science academy (and demanding that it become less monolingual). The second trend is the failure of Western military and aid interventions in the so-called fragile states on the peripheries of Europe and America, and the associated intellectual retreat of state-building theories to "good enough" stabilization (Mac Ginty 2012). The third is the normative shift in US politics, in which "disruption" has been transformed from the conservatives' deepest fear to the overt and aggressive agenda of those in power. The last is the set of risks associated with the reckless pursuit of domination over the planetary ecology, namely, the Anthropocene (Beck 2016; Orr 2016). This includes the closing of the environmental frontier and the escalating dangers of new pathogens becoming pandemic (Ewald 2011). There are limits to the exploitation of the global commons.

My empirical starting point is an ethnography of subaltern elites at the interstices of the current global (dis)order. Building on Lila Abu-Lughod's (1990) use of resistance as a diagnostic of power, I study the contours of power through the actions of subaltern brokers who possess it in small amounts. Adapting Bourdieu's "central bank" metaphor, my protagonists are retail currency dealers who trade in small quanta of power, from which they nonetheless extract sufficient marginal returns to be able to gain a profitable political livelihood. To adapt the "rules of the game" metaphor beloved of many political scientists to the real and metaphorical multilingualism of the world outside the metropole, these brokers are playing different language games at the same time, earning translation rents by leveraging the subtly different meanings that adhere to close homonyms in different languages.

Thus in Sudan—the case I explore here—the rules of the political game are peculiar and diverse. There are different imaginaries of stateness: the state in Sudan sees, hears, and feels differently from that in France or Britain. It is a state contested in many different ways. Sudanese do not agree on their history, their boundaries, their laws, the relationship between religion and politics, or of course their future. It is a state felt and lived through the practices of its agents—civil servants and soldiers, diplomats, administrative chiefs, financiers, journalists, jailors and prisoners (Fassin 2015)—each of whom is politically multilingual. From the indeterminacies of translation arise innovations in the political craft: the most skilled traders are not only transactional rentiers but also artisans who can create new objects, sometimes even works of art. Thus a political entrepreneur can create a political fact out of the contours of a norm.

But from these interstices another distinct feature of power is clear. This is power at or beyond the frontier: *commandement* (Mbembe 2017), rule-breaking arbitrary power (Schmitt [1922] 2005), or the "deals space" in which an individual transaction has neither value as precedent nor meaning within a set of rules (Pritchett, Sen, and Werker 2018). This is power at the front line of conquest, robbery, or trickery, where quanta of power are transformed from one condition (typically a set of local rules) into another (a commodity to be traded, an instrument in a hierarchy). Our broker may reckon that local power is underpriced and can be bought up cheaply, or underdefended and can be coerced, or both. Such power may come to constitute a state, but that is not the face that it shows to those it subjugates, defrauds, enslaves, or kills, and any such state that emerges cannot properly be imagined without also imagining what it has destroyed. It is also *wild* power: the barbarian power exercised by those beyond the boundaries of the state, but also the savagery of those whose possession of sovereign privilege places them above law and beyond order.

No people subjected to colonialism can possess a singular or unironic imaginary of stateness: as Walter Benjamin (1968: 257) observed, "The tradition of the oppressed teaches us that the 'state of emergency' in which we live is not the exception but the rule." Alongside the state imposed by the colonizer, shaped of course by the colonial encounter and the locals who served and subverted it, there is the imaginary of alternative stateness. This is the starting point of W. E. B. Du Bois's (1903) Pan-African critique of modernity as "double consciousness" and James Scott's (2017) attempt to write the "barbarians" back into the history of states. To modify Benjamin's (1968: 255) enjoinder to the historian to empathize with the defeated, the colony will contain voices that possess "the gift of fanning the spark of hope in the past . . . convinced that *even the dead* will not be safe from the enemy if [the enemy] wins." It follows that any political broker in the postcolony should be literate in at least two political languages, and—to draw on Achille Mbembe (2017: 130–31)—a master of spectacle, dramaturgy, and polymorphism.

But let us simultaneously focus more tightly and also step back to see this system in its totality. At the granular level, indeterminacies of translation, incommensurability of games, arbitrariness of transactions are the stuff of "real politics" everywhere, though seen most clearly at those friction-laden boundaries where different models of stateness scrape alongside one another. From a great distance, what we see is an array of differently constituted polities, including those that contrive to be illegible to colonizing states or that escape any classification of "stateness" at all, which wander wildly in different elliptical orbits around a star system that is itself in disorder. In short, alongside a (revised, nonsingular) imaginary of statenesses we also need a theory of its opposite, which we can gloss as "disorder."

Theory from the Interstices: Darfur, Sudan

Sudan achieved an ambiguous independence in 1956: nationhood meant different things to different members of the political elite. For Prime Minister Ismail al-Azhari, who engineered the parliamentary vote to bring forward independence from Britain, the creation of the republic was a modernizing project. For many in his Unionist Party, it was a stepping-stone to the unity of the Nile Valley, that is, political union with Egypt. For his parliamentary rivals, the Umma Party, it was the country's second independence: they dreamed of reviving the indigenous millenarian Mahdist state that had driven out the British and Egyptians in 1885 and established an independent Islamic state for thirteen years. The southern Sudanese members of Parliament supported the independence vote because they had been promised that there would be a federal system in which the southern region, severely underdeveloped and culturally distinct, would be able to run its own affairs. The failure to deliver on that promise led to civil war, which lasted until 1972. The de facto constitution during this time was the state of emergency. A second civil war broke out in 1983 and lasted twenty-two years. Peace talks between the Sudanese government's ruling National Congress Party (NCP) and the largest and most prestigious rebel group, the Sudan People's Liberation Movement (SPLM), based in southern Sudan, ended with the signing of the Comprehensive Peace Agreement in 2005.

An indeterminacy of translation was the original sin of the CPA. The title Comprehensive Peace Agreement means different things in the two languages, English and Arabic, which, according to the decision of the parties and the mediators, are equally definitive for interpreting the text. The 260 pages of the agreement include six protocols and two implementation matrices signed from 2002 on. Putting them under a single cover made the text "comprehensive." The CPA was also intended as the template for second-ranking agreements to resolve the wars in Darfur and eastern Sudan, and for recommencing the stalled "south-south dialogue" of internal reconciliation among southern armed groups and political parties. The text also contained provisions for national elections that were expected to bring into government all the civilian opposition parties that had constituencies underrepresented in the CPA's power-sharing formula.

The Arabic translation of "comprehensive peace agreement" is *al itifag al salam al shamil*. The first two words (meaning "peace agreement") are unproblematic. But the third—*al shamil*—implies a sealed completeness. It shares a root with *shumuliya*, "totalitarianism," and *al da'awa al shamla*, "the all-encompassing religious call to God," an Islamist project of societal transformation pursued a few years earlier. Unsurprisingly and perceptively, many Sudanese saw the CPA not as a charter for inclusiveness but, on the contrary, as an exclusive carve-up by the NCP and SPLM.

The ambiguity was well understood by the Sudanese leaders who signed the CPA. They asked their lawyers to pore over the text, but their intentions were not to follow the extraordinarily complex provisions according to the implementation matrices but to use the document for political change: it was a negotiated political *un*settlement (Bell and Pospisil 2017). President Omar al-Bashir repeated the mantra "The CPA is our Bible, our Koran" several times, and like a holy book, the document was seen as a charter for authority—and like such a scripture, its interpretation was contentious. Bashir and SPLM leader John Garang had several different possible ways of exercising their power and realizing their visions. Garang, for example, was simultaneously holding out the possibilities of national unity and the separation of the South—of imposing the SPLM's "New Sudan" vision on a weakened Khartoum by force of arms (partly through the war in Darfur) and launching a new party with the (Islamist) vice president Ali Osman Taha—and also hadn't ruled out making a coalition with other opposition parties. Throughout the long civil war, Garang had been betting on several horses at the same time, and peace was no different. The Islamists were similarly capable of developing parallel political initiatives at the same time; indeed their mentor and sheikh, Hassan al Turabi (out of power in 2005 but nonetheless influential), was famous as a political chameleon. For the Sudanese political elite, "feeling like a state" was not a commitment to a singular, well-ordered circuitry of power but rather a range of possibilities for becoming a state—a kind of political synesthesia.

The Darfur war had begun as a sideshow to the long-standing north-south war; Darfur flared up just as the older war was approaching its negotiated conclusion. It was a product of the ambiguity of the political reshuffling and the half-promises made at the time, as well as a legacy of famine, war, and disruption in the 1980s (Flint and de Waal 2008). Secular Darfurians, inspired by Garang and receiving military support from the SPLM, escalated their insurgency because they saw it as the best means of obtaining leverage in the national political carve-up. Darfurian Islamists, who had joined the government in the 1990s in the hope that the Sudanese Islamic state would be color-blind and that their status as Muslims would outweigh their standing as non-Arabs, also rebelled. The two groups, the Sudan Liberation Movement and the Justice and Equality Movement, coordinated well while they were winning, but not when the government turned the tables.

Khalil Ibrahim, the leader of the Justice and Equality Movement, was a master of political multilingualism and keeping his options open. The Arabic and English versions of Khalil's manifesto, the *Black Book of Power and Wealth in Sudan*, are substantially different documents, speaking, respectively, to Islamist and secularist audiences. Khalil shifted his alliances and political programs several times; he played a game of strategic delay in the (reasonable) assumption that another roll of the dice would be possible in different circumstances. His troops had rear bases and political headquarters in (successively) Chad, Eritrea, and Libya, and he was on his way to relocate to South Sudan when he was killed in an airstrike in 2011.

The government counterinsurgency was ruthless, and during 2003–4 more than forty thousand Darfurian civilians were killed violently, a humanitarian crisis set in train that claimed the lives of several times that number, and over a million were forced from their homes. The scale and savagery of the slaughter rapidly generated international outrage, including the influential Save Darfur Coalition in America, which labeled the atrocities "genocide" and called for military intervention. The United States, the United Nations, and the African Union had no stomach for sending troops to occupy Darfur and implicitly remove President Bashir from power, especially as he had just signed a peace deal for South Sudan. The international power brokers compromised on peace talks, mediated by the African Union, and pressure for a UN peacekeeping force.

Intense negotiations to resolve the war were held from November 2005 to May 2006 in the Nigerian capital, Abuja, between the government of Sudan and the Darfur rebels. By this time the SPLM had joined the government as a junior but influential partner, and the core tenets of the CPA had been incorporated into the Interim National Constitution. The Darfur peace agreement that was being negotiated in Abuja would be a buttress to this central pillar. The mediation team began with the English-language (inclusive, democratic) reading of the CPA; the Darfurians began with the Arabic (exclusive, division-of-the-spoils) reading.

I was a member of the African Union mediation team that sought and failed to find agreement. In February 2006, on a flight to Abuja, I was reviewing the draft of a text for a power-sharing agreement for discussion by the delegates. The passenger in the next seat opened a ring-binder document that caught my eye: its title was "Power Distribution." He flipped to the next page and I saw a diagram with zigzag lines and icons of electricity pylons, at which point I lost interest in peeking over his shoulder. Nonetheless, it made me think of how the mediators were treating the allocation of political power among different parties in the same manner as an electrical engineer designing the infrastructure for delivering energy to different neighborhoods of a city. We used words such as *equity* and *capacity*. Our implicit model of power was the mechanics of a public utility, just as John Maynard Keynes had compared the economy to a plumbing system.

The mediators serving the African Union, along with the wider circle of UN staff, economists from the World Bank and development cooperation institutions, and scholars of political science and international development on consultancy contracts, were confident that the combination of diplomatic firepower, goodwill, and hard work drafting documents would yield an agreement. Collectively we had been sailing with the wind at our backs for a generation. The ordering of power of late modernity was, we assumed, the prevailing wind, which would get us to our destination without our having to relearn the half-forgotten seaman's skills of weathering squalls and tacking into the wind. We were wrong.

The negotiations for the power-sharing chapter of the agreement were conducted around a square table. The mediators sat at one end, and the parties on either side, with observers making up the fourth side. The preferred process would have been for the heads of the government and rebel delegations to produce their own shared proposals and then negotiate the points of disagreement. However, such was the distrust between the parties, and the fragmentation on the rebel side, that those kinds of discreet private negotiations were rare. What happened was that the text was drafted by members of the mediation team—mostly diplomats and lawyers—based on their best calculations of what would be workable for Darfur, and then presented to the parties for discussion. This was a frustrating exercise, as the negotiators seemed more interested in scoring political points than in finding areas of consensus. Finally, under a deadline imposed by the UN Security Council, the mediators simply put their text on the table, asked for proposed revisions, and then said, "Take it or leave it." The government delegation, headed by a veteran bruiser named Majzoub al Khalifa, took it. For him, the document itself was an emblem to be waved for the diplomats and the public, like the books ordered by the yard by a nouveau riche to furnish a library, their spines to be admired, their pages to remain unopened. For the rebel leader who did sign—a vagabond named Minni Minawi, elevated to undue prominence through American indulgence mixed with ruthlessness—it was the same. For the two rebel leaders who rejected the agreement, the document was the reverse: a symbol of travesty and betrayal. Abdel Wahid al Nur was vain and vacillating, convinced that the United States would impose a better deal if President George W. Bush were to hear the voices of the Save Darfur movement calling for military intervention. Khalil Ibrahim had already disengaged from the talks, having become entangled in an escalating civil war in Chad, which was about to become a disguised interstate war between Sudan and Chad; he thought that with Chadian backing he could impose regime change himself.

The 2006 Darfur peace talks failed. Two years later the Qatari government hosted new talks in Doha and openly adopted the formula according to which an expert document, written by UN consultants, was imposed on the parties. This time the proposals were backed by Qatari money, the extent of which was lavishly advertised during the peace talks themselves. The idea was that the Darfurians would be so incentivized by the funds on offer that they would write themselves into the blueprint.

Pushing this model harder didn't work either. There were many other things going on in the peace talks. The negotiations were multilingual, literally (Arabic and English were equally working languages) and also philosophically: the different logics of power had different grammars and indeterminacies of translation. There were different assumptions about how the quanta of power functioned, and about order and disorder. Above all, the Sudanese had trimmed their sails to a new prevailing wind, which was the marketization of politics. Political power was being traded as a commodity, and the mediators and state-builders were like naive and wealthy tourists, thoroughly outwitted by street vendors in a bazaar.

The Political Marketplace

Lenin famously and concisely defined politics as "who, whom": its elemental transactional component. This is the politicking of networks and influence, of deal-making, of ambition and betrayal. Raymond Geuss (2008) lamented that this kind of "real politics" has been too long neglected by political philosophers. Even in the most formal, rule-bound system of governance, politicking is a craft, and power not only grows out of the barrel of a gun and the vault of a bank but also flows from intangibles such as personal charisma and the skill of making deals.

The practical "real politics" of the Darfur negotiations were the bargaining in the hotel rooms, which involved dividing power into small enough parcels that could be bought and sold as in a bazaar (de Waal 2015). Khartoum's chief negotiator at the peace talks in Abuja was Majzoub al Khalifa, and he candidly explained to me his "real" task at those talks: to dispense his political budget in the political marketplace, to buy up sufficient loyalties to keep his president in power. He went through the motions of negotiating over the draft documents produced by the mediators, to keep the talks going and to keep the international community happy. But his political business was not transacted in the formalities of the conference room, but in his suite in the hotel, with his briefcase of cash.

Majzoub's particular skill was encyclopedic intelligence on every delegate and how to purchase allegiances at the cheapest prices. Some would settle for a straight monetary payment, especially if offered when that individual was strapped for cash to pay for something essential, such as a hospital bill. Some were embedded in local communities, for which a particular deal—maybe over a chieftaincy or an administrative boundary—would suffice. Those deals were typically less expensive, especially if he could recruit the rebel delegate as a broker who would be able to turn his gatekeeping role to personal profit. While the Sudanese general who headed up the cease-fire talks was preparing a detailed map of military positions and the physical terrain with its mountains and deserts, I imagined Majzoub with his own political market contour map that showed the localities where Darfur's rebel commanders could be bought up cheaply, and where they would have the leverage to extract more.

The political marketplace is more than a powerful metaphor; it is a description of actual power relations. In particular arenas, like peace negotiations between a well-endowed government and a fragmented and quarrelsome opposition, we see an auction of loyalties in which the chief buyer (e.g., Khartoum) is bidding for the loyalty of a number of subordinate players (the Darfur rebels), who can also turn to outside patrons to keep their asking prices high (in this case, Chad, Libya, and the United States). The negotiations are fast-paced, multisided, and transnational, and the deals are enumerated in hard currency—a bundle of characteristics that mark this bargaining as distinct from old-style patronage.

For a series of transactions to constitute a market, they must be sufficiently pervasive and systematic and exhibit price behavior that follows the laws of supply and demand. This is not just pervasive corruption or neopatrimonialism with dollars; it is a different kind of relationship between politics and governance. In the Darfur talks there was a marketplace, but at the time it wasn't clear to me whether this was created by the particular political ecosystem of the negotiations, in a claustrophobic jerry-built Abuja hotel, or whether it was part of a much bigger political market in which political services and allegiances are traded for material rewards. The answer, I concluded, was (mostly) the latter.

A political market can operate in a number of different ways, and this is where my anecdote about electricity comes back into play. Markets in fuel function in different ways, and so do markets in political power. We tend to see political power as a public utility (like electricity), something whose supply and price are set by a single provider, regulated in the public interest. In other words we think of political power as the exercise of governance through legitimate public authority. In some countries (paradigmatic Weberian states) this is the case. These are the limiting cases in which we cannot talk about markets at all, although there may be political transactions and corruption that both grease the institutional wheels and occasionally make the machine function improperly.

There are other forms of allocating power, following identifiably market logics, that are widespread and—I argue—increasingly dominant. In the years that followed the breakdown of the 2006 Darfur Peace Agreement, the Darfur political market operated as a field of free and open competition, with low barriers to entry and little regulation. In most places, the supply of firewood is organized in this manner: there are many small producers with small margins who compete, often on a part-time or seasonal basis. For about five years, the Darfurian political marketplace was open to any entrant possessing a few vehicles, some automatic weapons, and a satellite phone. He could set out his stall, advertise his wares, and become a political-military entrepreneur, renting his services, running freelance operations, building a reputation, and hoping for a generous buyout by one side or the other. We saw a version of what we might call a "conflict gig economy": several commanders, each of whom had twenty armed men and two or three vehicles, would coordinate a single operation, for example an attack on a market or a small garrison, overrun it and loot what could be taken, and then disperse. Those same commanders might find themselves in a different configuration, perhaps on different sides and shooting at one another, a few weeks later. There were enemies because there was fighting, not vice versa (Debos 2016). Reproduce these kinds of circumstantial bargaining at different, linked levels, and we have a political arena of extraordinary complexity. It would be impossible to map the bargains made, let alone predict them—but we could monitor price trends, such as the payout needed for a particular political service.

More often, the political marketplace should be seen as an arena of monopolistic competition, with high barriers to entry and the key actors able to manipulate supply, demand, and price—and influence the regulatory authorities as well. In his famous definition of the state, Weber used the word *monopoly* in the layperson's sense: meaning "sole provider." But for economists, monopoly refers to a situation in which providers are sufficiently powerful that they can influence the market, if not fixing prices then at least possessing considerable discretion over their level. This is how the price of gasoline is determined: the oil majors cannot set the price, but they can do a great deal to determine it over the short term and, with different strategies, over the longer term. ExxonMobil, Chevron, and others are rivals, colluding but also positioning themselves to outdo the other and sometimes take over their competitors. Economists call this "limited competition"; perhaps a more apt term would be *rivalrous oligopoly*.

It is notable that in many countries, the state's control of violence more closely resembles this oligopolistic, rivalrous model than it does the public utility model. This is a fusion of power as governance and power as "real" transactional politics, in which a dominant position is contingent on the skillful spending of a political budget, well-crafted use of force or threat of force, and ability to inspire confidence that political debts will be honored at a premium. This might also be called *functional kleptocracy*: a political order in which informal rules about who can take what are more important than law. In Sudan's capital and the relatively stable areas within a day's drive, this is how President Omar al-Bashir ran his political system. It was mostly rule-governed, but the rules could be difficult to discern from the outside—indeed they were deliberately opaque so as to raise the price of entry. There was an ever-present possibility of the most powerful actors, such as the president or the security chiefs, breaking any rules and simply stealing or killing with impunity.

The April 2019 popular uprising in Sudan began as a paradigmatic nonviolent civic protest in the tradition of the Arab Spring and Sudan's own prior Khartoum Springs, pitting a democracy movement against a military junta. Quickly, other logics of power surfaced. The man who seized real power was General Mohamed "Hemedti" Dagolo, an unlettered trader, commanding a nomadic militia bound together by lineage solidarity. Ibn Khaldun would have diagnosed the capture of civic authority by a nomadic horde. Hemedti's transnational business is based on gold trading (licit and illicit) and renting out forces to fight in Yemen and Libya, a model familiar from the nineteenth-century freebooting empires of central Africa. In twenty-first-century terms, he represents the capture of the state by a dynamic political-military-business enterprise, the occlusion of institutionalized authority by the political marketplace (de Waal 2019).

Is the political marketplace a phenomenon of the margins, confined to what are often called "failed" or "fragile" states such as Sudan? In these particular manifestations, that is certainly the case. But, I suggest, Sudan's wind chimes prefigure a change in the weather: political power is becoming a tradable commodity. The capitalist market economy has demonstrated enormous capacity for human advancement; no other mechanism of wealth creation has a comparable record. But the process, familiar to Marxist critique, whereby commoditization and marketization drive out other kinds of relations, has spread far beyond the material commodities of manufacture into the stuff of life, human attention, and the quanta of political power. In the formulation of Wolfgang Streeck (2014), the *marktvolk* have driven out the *staatsvolk*: civic governance and democracy are a matter of who controls the money.

The marketization of power is, I submit, the dominant political phenomenon of our time. It is transforming economies and ways of communicating and thinking on a scale and with an import comparable to the emergence of the modern state, with its hegemonic disciplinary capabilities, and in doing so is generating deep anxieties and pervasive disorder. The fusion of business and politics has reached an advanced stage in both the most marginal countries (such as Sudan) and the most powerful (such as the United States). This is "stateness" only at the furthest stretch of that term: it is better that we develop a different imaginary to understand this phenomenon. We can do so best by feeling our way into that dark twin of the state: disorder.

Imagining Disorder

Disorder has no place in the high scientism of the dominant epistemology of economics, sociology, and political science. Several concepts are fundamental to the social sciences: equilibrium, institutions, order, and development. In turn these are based on Pierre-Simon Laplace's "demon of mechanical omniscience." The implication is that any apparent disorder is either an unfortunate aberration and/or the manifestation of a deeper order. Thus the disordered society is one that is in a state of temporary aberration from the hegemonic order, its failures validating the legitimacy of the order from which it deviates. Theories of state failure and its euphemistic successor, state fragility, have neither explanatory nor predictive power in relation to the phenomena of armed conflict, social crisis, and institutional collapse. Rather, they are theories of state-building, drawn from an institutional-economics reading of metropolitan states and a handful of successful developmental latecomers, applied to postcolonies that have been destabilized in part through their position in the global order.

This, I suggest, is a vast gap. We need a theory of disorder. More than that, we need an imaginary of forms of disorder and a sense of what it means to see the world as a place defined by the lack of order. We need this especially because the commodification of political power breaks institutions and rule-governed systems, defies national and state boundaries, and elevates disruptive transactional politics.

There are many different kinds of disorder. Let me explore five generic forms (or formlessnesses): lawlessness, chaos, illegibility, designed instability, and disruption. This is not a typology, still less a theory, rather a set of devices for reimagining politics and power.

Lawlessness is the antithesis of the ordered state: it is wild power. It is a fearful, deeply normative construct. In Eurasia the historical referent is barbarians, especially nomadic pastoralists from the steppes and deserts and seafaring peoples from the north (Scott 2017). They are the definitive "other." Most societies have their Robin Hood myths, of the social bandit who robs from the rich to give to the poor, enacting vengeance on the greedy and callous. These figures exist in the geographical margins or distant in history; sometimes they were tamed in the end; despite being outlaws, their ethics are legible. Arab history is exceptional insofar as the synergistic enmity between the nomad and the settled lies at the heart of its political culture. In North America the primary historic referents for lawlessness are the Native Americans and the enslaved Africans; today they are immigrants and African Americans. But the American story is more complicated: central to the foundational American mythology is the settler-outlaw who tames the wilderness; he is both the personification of the new order and at the same time an outlaw. Many of the nineteenth-century hunters and rangers who "won the west," who extirpated the native tribes and defeated the Mexicans, were former Confederate guerrillas and members of the obligatory militia organized in the Southern states to repress slave insurrections. This is a frontier ethos, with roots in slavery, genocide, and private property in seized land. The narrative has since been nurtured by media and gun manufacturers, romanticized across the entire political spectrum, and has recently crystallized into the passion over the Second

Amendment to the US Constitution, which provides for the right to bear arms—bringing savage individual arbitrariness to the very center of the mythology of the founding of the republic (Dunbar-Ortiz 2018). For our purposes, the key point is that the political science fixation with institutions and laws overlooks its twin of an antistate ethos, deeply distrustful of the federal government and indeed of any institutions beyond the local.

Chaos has a particular meaning in the physical sciences that generates a metaphor that is helpful for our purposes. Chaos is not turmoil but refers to behavior that is fully determined and operates according to known principles but is nonetheless unpredictable and apparently random, owing to great sensitivity to small changes in initial conditions. A chaotic system can be understood but not predicted. Competitive markets are often chaotic in this sense. The chaotic movement of a liquid or gas can be turbulent, in that it retains a recognizable structure over time, while being unpredictable over short periods.

A rule-governed, institutionalized sociopolitical system may also become so complex that it is opaque to its creators. This is increasingly an issue with technical, economic, and governance systems that are administered through the algorithms of artificial intelligence systems. This level of complexity may be such that it is adjacent to chaos: an unexpected factor, internal or external, can generate a chaotic breakdown.

Illegibility is apparent disorder: it occurs when one is ignorant about the order that exists. The problems of political translation and multiple, rival rules of the game are cases of illegible orders rather than disorder as such. Some political orders are deliberately opaque to outsiders; a well-known case is the upland peasant societies of Southeast Asia, described by Scott as designed to resist state authority. "Barbarian" political authorities are typically illiterate, though rarely innumerate. The powerful can seek illegibility also, clouding arbitrariness in mystique. Insofar as an important element of power is setting the agenda, best done when discreet to the point of being indiscernible, so too the political leader who can select among the different possible political language games, which should be played at a particular moment, while recognizing that the others remain latent to be activated on other occasions, is master of the multilingual political domain.

Political science has played a role here in limiting our imagination of the possible. Let me give one example, which is a linguistic sleight of hand so routine and familiar that it is almost always overlooked. This occurs in the policy realm of postconflict state-building in countries such as Afghanistan, Iraq, and South Sudan. It is a switch from the Northian to the Weberian concept of a political institution; though close, they are analytically distinct. Douglass North's (1991: 97) definition of institutions is "the humanly devised constraints that structure political, economic, and social interaction. They consist of both informal constraints (sanctions, taboos, customs, traditions, and codes of conduct), and formal rules (constitutions, laws, property rights)." In subsequent writings, North himself assumes that the best institutions are Western Weberian ones, namely hierarchical rule-governed bureaucracies for the administration of public affairs, and almost all who follow in his footsteps, such as Acemoglu and Robinson (2012), make the same assumption. Yet it is a non sequitur. Anglo-Saxon political and economic institutions represent one particular form of institutionalized political life, which has been notably successful in the imperial metropole, but it is an elementary logical error to assume it is the only possible one.

As different "rules of the game" are tried out in different parts of the world, notably East Asia, and deliver the kinds of economic development and stability that economists like, at the same time as the shortcomings of Western-dictated formulae become more evident, economists and political scientists become more broad-minded in accepting what acceptable "institutions" might look like. This is less "disorder" than shifting toward another form of order. Other orderings may be less legible or involve stretching the metaphor of "rules of the game" beyond a place where it can reasonably reach. Subaltern and postcolonial studies are replete with examples. Scott (2009) writes of the peasantry's "art of not being governed." Africanist scholars describe how political orders have persisted in the face of destruction and turmoil so protracted and overwhelming that no overt societal coherence is possible and multiplicities of indeterminate orders are required for meaning to survive (Mbembe 2017; Guyer 2004). Jan Pospisil's (2019) study of the resolution of armed conflict, finely attuned to the real-world demands on mediators, brings into focus how the goal of a successful peace process is "formalised political *un*settlement"—ad hoc but well-crafted tools for avoiding an attempt at definitive resolution of the conflict and instead a incompletely-structured conversation that allows for the continued coexistence of those who have been at war.

Developing a metaphor from Scott (1998), sociopolitical order can be seen as an arrangement of political transactions that works, much like a forest is an ecological system that works. A Weberian state is one variant of that: a geometrically regular plantation of a limited number of species, which sacrifices sustainability and resilience for order and short-term productivity, regulated by impersonal "rules of the game." There are other variations of plantation, with different rules. There are also "wild" variants that have benefits that foresters are only belatedly coming to recognize, such as the transmission among the root systems of different trees of microbes that play a role in resistance to stress. In these variants the transactions that keep the collectivity functional depend on individual characteristics and positions rather than impersonal rules. (This is a rather fundamental challenge to definitions of politics that are premised on the "rules" metaphor.) It follows that some of these "orders," in their adaptable, overlapping, complex way, may be more resilient in the face of stress than their exactly ordered counterparts. They may not deliver the kinds of long-term economic growth so desired by Western policymakers, but they may turn out to be enduring.

The fourth cluster of forms of disorder we may call *designed instability*. This is the quasi-disorder of the functional kleptocracy, shifting corruption from the margins of political order to its center, the totem and taboo of the exercise of "real" power. It differs from the previous manifestation in that the architect of turmoil is a ruler or an elite in charge of a state. This has long been recognized as a ruling strategy in Africa (Chabal and Daloz 1999) and can be divided into distinct aspects: governing *through* disorder, governing *despite* an imposed disorder, and *managing* an elementary order in the midst of disorder. Within the (expanded) new institutional economics framework, this can be seen as a system that prioritizes the "deal space" as opposed to the "rule-governed space" (Pritchett, Sen, and Werker 2018), in which rules are enforced at the discretion of the ruler: "For my friends: anything. For my enemies: the law."

Last we have *(revolutionary) disruption*. On the political left, there is a long history of faith in the idea that a new order will arise from revolutionary chaos. One of the clearest exponents of such ideas was Jean-Jacques Rousseau, who proposed that virtue would prevail in a state of nature. Numerous leftists believed that it was necessary only to bring down the established order for a socialist Utopia to arise spontaneously; this was the motivation for the Russian anarchists in the late nineteenth century. Antonio Gramsci's much-quoted words from the 1920s reflect the leftist belief that a new order would certainly arise in due course, but perhaps not just yet: "The crisis consists precisely in the fact that the old is dying but the new cannot be born; in this interregnum a great variety of morbid symptoms appear."

A neoconservative version of the doctrine that disruption would usher in positive transformation informed the American administrators of Iraq in 2003: they fervently believed that if the institutions of dictatorship were dismantled, liberal democracy would automatically follow, as the end of history had been reached.

On the right, in fact, *disruption* has migrated from being a negatively marked word to a term of acclaim, a postdemocratic update on Joseph Schumpeter's "creative destruction" of the industrial capitalist era. In the writings of Ayn Rand and her followers, disruption and deinstitutionalization are ideologically constructed as liberty and renewal. Streeck (2016) dubs what will follow "the age of entropy." Borrowing from Gramsci's morbid "interregnum," he suggests that the current trajectory is toward "a prolonged period of social entropy, or disorder (and precisely for this reason a period of uncertainty and indeterminacy)" (13). Applying the categories of disorder I have developed, this is a combination of chaos, illegibility, and instrumentalized disorder, making a "postsocial society." Streeck continues: "A society in interregnum, in other words, would be a *de-institutionalized* or *under-institutionalized* society, one in which expectations can be stabilized only for a short time by local improvisation, and which for this very reason is essentially ungovernable" (13–14). Streeck's prognostication is for Europe, and he sees it as the product of the uncoordinated actions of political and commercial actors. In the United States a powerful coalition of libertarians, plutocrats, Silicon Valley billionaires, and would-be frontiersmen not only welcome but energetically promote such essential ungovernability.

Arguably, disruption is the fundamental character of democratic power, an anarchic subversion of any entitlement to rule on the basis of a social order. In the words of Jacques Rancière ([2005] 2014: 46–47), democratic power is "simply the power peculiar to those who have no more entitlements to govern than to submit." Democracy is therefore inherently disruptive and heterotopic, resistant to any institutional or juridico-political formulation, challenging oligarchic manifestations of power in whatever configuration they occur.

The Future of Power

The metropolitan academe has yet to grapple with the challenge of systemic disorders at the apex of power and the savagery of metropolitan rulemakers. Its own hierarchies, privileges, and paradigms would, of course, be threatened. The conceptual and perceptual apparatuses deployed by today's Western professoriate remain mostly faded relics from the era of state modernism. The imaginaries of stateness and sovereignty are hand-me-down prostheses, norms that became historical facts. The first rebuilding of the governing norms of the ship of state took place when imperial-industrial states secularized during the nineteenth century alongside the associated emergence of nationalism. Sovereignty and stateness shed most, but not all, of their theological DNA. With great effort, the most powerful European sovereign vessels were kept afloat during that reconstruction. The second rebuilding is happening now, as the commodification of power means that states are becoming political marketplaces, integrated across borders, dollarized, and disordered in many different ways.

Theory from the interstices is immediately relevant. Thus Mbembe (2017: 179) observes that the "Black" experience of the power of capitalism to dissolve social relations and subordinate humanity to a commodity is not confined to the racially and geographically defined margins, but is also occurring as capitalism colonizes its own centers. We can see this most clearly at the interstices of subaltern power. For the political trader operating at the interstices, understanding disorder is the secret to power, or to be specific, to brokering marginal gains in the quanta of power. Different logics of power have different grammars and indeterminacies of translation; those most skilled in the arbitrage will prosper. The commodification of power also has a disturbing implication that is already being realized on different continents. If power is indeed acquiring a price, then it follows that in some locations it will be underpriced relative to others, and those with sufficient political market intelligence will be able to map the contours of the global market and buy it up where the price is low. This can be done either literally, using cash to buy elections or offices, or metaphorically, by leveraging ideational and communications systems. The now-defunct social data company Cambridge Analytica and the mercenary political consultant Paul Manafort are among the most notorious of such transnational political service providers; those who follow their lead will surely be more discreet in their operations.

The commodification of power is not happening in isolation: the natural environment, the biological codes of life, human attention, communication, and learning are also being subjected to the same process. The market is hegemonic to a degree that no totalitarian state ever imagined; it represents disembodied power over social life and planetary existence more formidable than any institutions of government ever achieved. The capitalist imaginary is already dominant to such a degree that it is commonplace to observe that we can more readily imagine the end of the world than the end of capitalism (Fisher 2009).

The conceptual and perceptual apparatus for making sense of disorder in its variant forms is important for the academy and for any form of democratic politics, whether that is an exercise in salvage or transformation. Imagining a world of multilingual political orders is inherently emancipatory; understanding the dynamics of the political market is a necessity for rescuing power from the logic of commodification; and making sense of uncertainties and limits on understanding is vital if ours is to be an age that is not defined by all-pervasive anxiety. Building on Rancière ([2005] 2014: 97), democracy ultimately consists in the "singular and precarious acts" of contesting the entitlements to power by those with birth, money, force, or science.[1] To adapt Benjamin, our task is "fanning the spark of hope" *in the present*, which requires that we can seriously discuss and grasp alternative futures, turning aspirational norms into facts and making the political wilderness our home. Inspiring such democratic resistance and making possible such humane futures would be power indeed.

Note

1. Reference to "guns" added.

WAR 7

JULIETA LEMAITRE

Colombia is frequently portrayed as beset by decades of civil war. As Colombians begin to envision what the end of that war might entail, the country is producing a significant number of laws, policies, and programs focused on both peace and postconflict Colombia. The laws, enacting human rights protections, transitional justice, and reparations, define war as a conflict fought by armies, regular and irregular, that prey on innocent victims. These laws borrow heavily from international human rights and their merger with international humanitarian law, reflecting the point of view of a compassionate outsider intent on protecting victims of war crimes. They bring with them a rich vocabulary to describe war and its wages: extrajudicial executions, grave breaches of the laws of war, international war crimes, rights of victims, gender-based violence, crimes against humanity, transitional justice, restorative justice, and reparations, to name a few. Thus, in Colombia as perhaps in other places, in the aftermath of civil war it is legal regimes that are called on to provide a vocabulary and a narrative about war.

Faith in the laws' power to cement postconflict peace extends well beyond state capacity for implementation and enforcement through police forces, courts, and relief agencies. In places like Colombia, with an irregular presence of state institutions, and given their notable fragility in rural areas and shantytowns, the resource to legality is not based on faith in state power to enact democratic institutions. It is rather the resource to, or a desire for, legality as the language of reconstruction, mediating relations between civilians and institutions, providing rules for the emerging street-level bureaucracies, defining the aspirations of new social movements, clarifying and structuring what is normal and what is not in relationships between civilians (Lemaitre 2009).

Postconflict laws and institutions, widely covered by the media, provide a narrative in the sense of a definition of what is, quite literally, the norm: what the laws say is right and wrong. Human dignity is the premise of this norm, even if only in books, and as a result a rejection of the normality of violence and of the experience of war. It is faith in this claim, that violence and war are not normal, and faith in the alternative normality of human dignity, that fires the popularity of laws in Colombia, their recurrence in everyday conversations, their ubiquity in the media, and their power to define, in hindsight, the experience of war.

However compelling, the narrative that emerges from postconflict laws' depiction of normality remains in ambiguous tension not only with ordinary people's memories of war but also with ordinary language, cohabiting uncomfortably with submerged explanations of what happened during the war and on the importance (and hence the morality) of events during and after the war. It's not that the laws or the institutions created to implement them do not listen to ordinary people; quite the contrary, they insist on the importance of their participation, of their voices. But their voices are scripted to speak in a language that institutions emerging from the postconflict legal regime can comprehend; this includes civilians' self-identification as innocent, their rejection of all armed perpetrators, their rejection of war, and the careful legal measurement of the crimes defined as single events suspended in time. Human dignity, it seems, requires innocence, and suffering, defined in terms of the morality of peacetime in the liberal democracies of industrialized countries.

Postconflict laws and institutions that insist on civilian suffering and innocence during war, and on defining civil war as a time of great civilian suffering, do reflect reality. Civil war produces an enormous amount of civilian deaths and suffering; at times, it seems armies are spared the gunshots and the mortars and instead are aimed at those who bear no arms. Civilian moral agency, and probably that of many soldiers, is severely restricted if not suspended during war, limiting choices to the point that in many situations it seems irrational to demand responsibility for decisions taken during war.

Postconflict laws and institutions ignore the active role civilians play in war and the fluid boundaries between wartime violence and the violence that so often erodes peace in the years, sometimes decades, following a civil war. Civil wars, as scholars of this emerging field of studies have amply shown, are also wars among civilians. Not all unarmed victims of war are on the same side of history; some have also harbored deep hatred for each other. Some have, willingly or not, collaborated with the armies; some have benefited from their neighbors' losses, betrayed close friends and families, and enacted fantasies of revenge.

Postconflict laws and institutions ordering humanitarian relief also ignore civilian reconstruction after the war, the persistence and strength that allows survivors to rebuild their lives out of nothing. The ideal recipient of aid is destitute, and helplessness is rewarded with privileges by humanitarian legal regimes, while in practice it is only the most able who have access to perennially scarce resources and who redistribute them within the same networks of allegiance and partisanship that allowed for their survival during war. Admiration for strength and resourcefulness, for the virtues of gratitude and collaboration among survivors, is rejected by humanitarian legal regimes that take their values from the possibilities of peacetime in the liberal democracies of industrialized countries.

In the aftermath of civil war these facts—civilian collaboration with armies, the enmities among civilians, the hard work of reconstruction—have no legal meaning. Increasingly, as the legal discourse becomes more ubiquitous as the official language for war and its aftermath, these facts are on the way to losing their social meaning as well. This situation raises profound ethical dilemmas rooted in the tension between what is important for civilians fleeing the war and what is important for public officials whose worldview is embedded in human rights and humanitarian narratives. It also raises questions about the nature, and importance, of legal regimes after war, and whether or not we should respond differently.

This chapter provides an ethnographic approach to the way laws and humanitarian legal institutions attempt to provide social meaning in postconflict Colombia, written by a lawyer who has been both an observer and a participant in this process.[1] The chapter begins with a description of the wars that have ravaged rural areas, the settlements that have ended them, and the continuities between wars. This description also includes the postconflict legal regimes enacted to facilitate transitions to peace, their failure and successes. The chapter then focuses on a specific experience of war and its aftermath, that of internally displaced women. It examines women's stories about displacement, highlighting what these stories reveal about what matters to these women, and contrasting it to postconflict legal regimes' embrace of human rights narratives about the war. The conclusion claims there is a productive richness and subtlety in the experience, and it is lost in the legal account of war, and this loss can undermine the possibility of reconstruction.

Colombia's Twentieth-Century Wars: Breaks and Continuities

The civil war in Colombia has taken different shapes and intensities since the 1940s, exemplifying the porous boundaries between war and peace and the multiplicity of violence that undergirds a war. Notably, longtime tensions and episodes of political and community violence between liberals and conservatives exploded in the late 1940s in the midcentury civil war known as La Violencia—the Violence—as if there were only one. It ravaged the inter-Andean valleys with the ferocity of an ethnic conflict, with partisan identities replacing ethnicity, resulting in an estimated 200,000 civilian deaths. The conflict was successfully resolved by the 1959 power-sharing agreement known as Frente Nacional, with liberals and conservatives taking turns at the presidency and strictly sharing by half every post in the executive branch, from street sweepers and city councilmen to cabinet ministers and judges. Power sharing, enshrined in the constitution and a host of Frente Nacional laws, transformed the country by making partisan distinctions meaningless in a generation.

However, the Frente Nacional, while deeply transformative of old hatreds, excluded communists, a politically active minority with ties to the international movement. The exclusion of communists from the power-sharing agreement, and the global forces of the Cold War, led to the emergence of communist guerrillas in the 1960s and to a sixty-year war between the government—still controlled by the parties emerging from the old liberal-conservative divide—and various communist guerrillas. During the Cold War the communist guerrillas reflected their sponsors' allegiances, including the Sino-Soviet split, and the homegrown socialism inspired in the Cuban Revolution. International ties often meant also international support, and the United States too participated, training Colombian troops in global counterinsurgency tactics.[2] Anticommunist hatred and class warfare revived, at least in possibility, the desire to betray neighbors who were also enemies, and a quiet support for the covert antisubversive operations of successive authoritarian governments to the right, or for the spectacular use of violence by messianic revolutionaries to the left. Former conservatives found their place firmly at the right of the

Cold War, communists at the left, with the majority Liberal Party caught in an unstable center.

The end of the Cold War and the collapse of the Soviet Union in the late 1980s brought important transformations. Several guerrilla groups gave up their guns and joined an expanding democracy that eschewed the authoritarian rule of the Cold War period. Liberals led the adoption of a new constitution in 1991, embracing human rights protections as its beacon, creating a vigorous judicial protection for these rights, and creating new rules that allowed former communists access to power, effectively ending all vestiges of Frente Nacional and promoting human rights.[3] Overtly the rule of law appeared to be the way to end violence, not just political violence but other forms denounced by new social movements, including domestic violence, street and police violence against gays and lesbians, and the ubiquitous land theft of indigenous and ethnic Afro-Colombian lands.

In spite of the hope inspired by the adoption of the 1991 constitution, the war did not wane but instead intensified, morphing into a better-financed civil war fueled by a growing global economy. The legacy of the Cold War persisted in anticommunist operations, which included the emergence of counterguerrilla paramilitary armies. These armies were supported by a heterogeneous alliance of ranchers and large agribusinesses, cocaine traffickers, local politicians, and commercial interests, including transnational corporations. Brought together by guerrilla extortion and kidnapping, these allies also shared a vision of the economic possibilities of the rich inter-Andean valleys and a passionate greed for land and water. The triumph of "the free world" in the Cold War opened Colombia wide to the expansion of economic opportunities for those who could navigate global markets, both licit and illicit. Support for paramilitary armies financed mercenary training in counterguerrilla tactics, and soldiers learned to win hearts and minds through terror, severing heads and staging public torture, using local informants wearing masks to identify their left-leaning neighbors. It was an effective war, sometimes avidly fed by the same rural communities that suffered the most, by their greed and their betrayals.

Paradoxically the economic transformations supporting both the paramilitary expansion and the strengthening of the remaining guerrillas grew out of economic globalization and the market reforms also championed by the 1991 constitution. Oil, bananas, and palm-oil enterprises have all been linked to paramilitary armies, and the expanding cocaine and illegal mining markets supported both the paramilitary and the guerrillas. Guerrillas, especially the Revolutionary Armed Forces of Colombia (FARC), capitalized their growing share of the cocaine trade, an expansion that resulted in their control of large sectors of Colombia, especially the less populated rural areas. The war gained a clear economic dimension, and hundreds of thousands, soon millions of peasants fled, losing their land in the process. Armies forcibly displaced people both for territorial control and for land theft, concentrating rural property in a process so wide-ranging that today it accounts for over eight million acres of stolen land and over a million internally displaced families.[4] Displacement concentrated wealth, to be sure, but often, and this remains a silenced story, it funneled into the hands of neighbors and acquaintances of the same people who fled violence.

Congress passed new laws to respond to the changing situation. In 1997 the country adopted a groundbreaking piece of legislation, Law 397, which highlighted the humanitarian crisis created by forced internal displacement and responded to it by granting a generous list of rights to internally displaced people (IDP).[5] The law, however, had little implementation as the war raged with increasing intensity. In 2004 the Constitutional Court, following over five thousand demands for the protection of individual rights, known as *tutelas*, began an aggressive program of orders to the government to take action against the humanitarian crisis (Rodríguez and Rodríguez 2015). The court treated displacement as it would a natural disaster or an epidemic, ordering humanitarian aid as well as targeted poverty-alleviation programs, but never examining what it was people fled from, their relationship to each other or to the war they left behind. The approach was successful, and the government began to adopt more robust humanitarian policies and programs, making the Constitutional Court a hero among IDP for a few years.

By 2005 the dynamic of the war had shifted, with the balance favoring the state, supported by its paramilitary alliances. These alliances became a burden as human rights activists scrutinized them and as paramilitary use of terror was increasingly covered by the national press. The Colombian military, with US funds and training, slowly gained the upper hand, and the state pushed for the demobilization of an important section of the paramilitary. It did so, fittingly in the Colombian tradition, through legal reform: in 2005, under a law known as the Justice and Peace Law, paramilitary armies demobilized, receiving lenient sentences for detailed admissions of their crimes.[6] The Constitutional Court, and later Congress, modified the law into a regime that increasingly "placed victims at its center." Violence persisted, however, as former paramilitary armies turned to extortion and maintained territorial control, benefiting the economic interests that had financed them in the first place; at the same time, the remaining guerrillas fought both against the state and against criminal organizations attempting to gain control of cocaine trafficking. As former paramilitary commanders were tried by a fledgling transitional justice program, critics talked of a "transitional justice without transition" (Uprimny and Saffon 2006).

In spite of criticism, Colombians maintained their faith in legal reform to change the dynamic of violence. In 2011 Congress adopted a Victims' Law (Law 1448), which built on the rights already granted by Law 397 to create an ambitious reparations and restitution program for victims of civil war. The Victims' Law program includes humanitarian assistance, administrative reparations for victims, and land restitution for forcibly displaced people. The state used revenue from the spike in the prices of commodities to fund this ambitious reparations and pacification program, creating a complex bureaucracy that provided humanitarian assistance and individual reparations and also demanded victims be represented in municipal development plans and have preferential access to a wide variety of consistently underfunded poverty-alleviation programs and public services for the poor.

Finally, after four years of peace talks, the oldest and largest of the guerrillas, the FARC, entered legal politics after a complicated peace deal with the government, enshrined in a 2016 peace agreement. The peace agreement includes massive state investment in the peripheral areas formerly controlled by the FARC, as well as a specialized transitional justice system and focused interventions against coca cultivation and the persistent paramilitary armies. The legal regime necessary for the implementation of the peace agreement was still, in 2018, fragile, in spite of the recent creation of the transitional justice court; both hope and resistance revolve around legal reform.[7]

At the same time, a new war appears on the horizon, in a global context of prohibition: the war between the government and organized crime, a war that spans a variety of forms of territorial control by nonstate armed groups, as well as ideological tensions that remain in abeyance. The drug wars justify the maintenance of Latin America's largest and best prepared armed forces, and global rhetoric frames organized crime as the new insurgency, calling for increased militarization of police powers, the analogous use of counterguerrilla operations against drug cartels, and the "hearts and minds" approach to territorial control. Resisting global forces that push in this direction, however, Colombia has unofficially adopted a sui generis and generally successful state policy toward drug trafficking that has allowed democratic institutions to coexist with subnational shadow powers often financed by cocaine traffic and, at the same time, to slowly extend the reach of the Colombian state. Violence has decreased dramatically generally after the peace agreement but has increased in those areas of the country more strategic for the cocaine trade as well as on the border with Venezuela, where tensions with the Maduro regime, as well as mass immigration from impoverished Venezuela, continue to grow every day. In the next years, with the foreseeable end of communist guerrillas, both the persistent National Liberation Army (ELN) and the dissident FARC groups, and possibly with regime change in Venezuela, the situation might change this careful balancing act in ways that are difficult to predict today.

Faith in the ability of the legal system to address these changing conditions remains firmly rooted in recent history. Laws, including and perhaps especially the Constitution, are amended both to enact and to facilitate transitions: Colombians still remember the large-scale transformations enacted by the Frente Nacional, the 1991 constitution, and, on a lesser scale, by the Justice and Peace Law as well as by the Victims' Law. Throughout the decades postconflict laws and institutions have facilitated transformations, providing a narrative for a postconflict normality, but they have also coexisted with the persistence of the normality of violence. The archaeology of this dissonance sits, perhaps, uncomfortably on the tension between the words of the law and ordinary language.

War and the Words of the Law

As postconflict laws and institutions provide a narrative, they also create new social and institutional realities. The ambition of postconflict law reform is to name, and by naming create, a vocabulary and institutions to address the horror that seems to be outside its purview: genocide, perfidy, homicide against protected persons, to name but three names for the events of war. In this context, legal language engages in a careful negotiation with ordinary language: sometimes it remains sidelined by ordinary life, restricted to the realms of specialists; sometimes it is absorbed in it, providing words with which to speak about relationships and just deserts; sometimes both worlds and languages coexist uncomfortably.

This dissonance between the words of law and the language of ordinary life can represent an attempt to provide relief from the acute suffering caused by violence. For example, having a child that has been forcibly disappeared, with the legal framework both providing moral condemnation and assigning responsibilities within the political context of a dirty war, is a different experience from having a child that left one day for work or school and was never heard of again and to whom anything could have happened. The legal term *forcible disappearance*, the fact that it is a war crime, provides a partial relief from an experience that otherwise has no possible meaning in ordinary language. The legal regime is central to providing relief on many fronts: first, as material relief entitling families to reparations; second, as emotional relief in a community of survivors united by the legal description of the crime; and third, and perhaps more important, by providing meaning, naming events that otherwise have no name, and giving them moral and political significance.

An ethnographic approach to this operation, to the way the words of law provide social meaning, consistently reveals its limitations, both for the people whose experience is now named and for the state officials charged with the everyday responsibilities of making this language operational. Tensions consistently emerge between what the law considers important and what people consider important as they go about the ordinary business of surviving. The tension perhaps arises from what one of the Victims' Unit officials I interviewed described as "always arriving too late." The way she phrased it, the difficulty of her particular task of providing state-funded reparations was that "the state was always arriving too late"; that is, the state, at least in its incarnation as the state that speaks in the words of the law, is always arriving after-the-war, not only after the events themselves but also after people have survived on their own (Lemaitre 2019).

Between 2010 and 2016 I followed the lives of women who fled the war and the transitional justice and humanitarian relief bureaucracies that responded to them, "always arriving too late." An initial project, carried out with other people, interviewed, supported, and observed these women as they used legal words to engage government and NGO officials. Three other projects took me to the slums of Bogotá, where displaced people built neighborhoods out of nothing, to the Sierra Nevada, as both an indigenous community and a peasant community returned to their land after paramilitary demobilization, and to various NGO offices across the country, interviewing officers in charge of operating Colombia's response to the massive forced internal displacement.

The challenge that emerged from this process was how to unpack the misunderstandings that emerge from the limitations of law to name the experience of war and its aftermath. An important section of these disagreements, I have come to think, comes from the underlying definition of the experience of war as a sequence of violations, in legal terms, bracketing the experience of war as everyday life and the urgent questions about morality at the center of this experience. The imprint of human rights law on current laws regulating internal conflict means that war tends to be understood as a sequence of distinct events. After all, the thrust of human rights thinking, and lawyering, is to document fully at least one event of egregious human rights violations, generally more, but rarely much more. In order to identify these violations, single violations or their accumulation, legal reasoning requires events be taken out of context. The accumulation of violations attunes our moral compass to the identification of victims and perpetrators and to the actions that embody the violation and its patterns. The situations leading up to the events are left unspoken, as is the aftermath that cannot be framed as a human rights violation.

The difficulty for Western law in talking about civil war and its causes emerges from radical separation of war from everyday life, ignoring the chain of events that build into violence: a fight among neighbors, leading to malicious gossip linking a neighbor to the guerrillas, a lift one gives to tired soldiers at the side of a road, which is transformed into suspicion of collaboration with the government; young men who have nothing to do and dream of having a gun; envy of another's plot of land, or the ambition to rule, thwarted. These are the seeds of war, falling on fertile land. By the time the fact-finding missions ask questions, the forensic investigators excavate the mass graves, the state arrives and names what happened, it is always too late.

Civil War as Everyday Life

Civil war proper is defined as armed internal conflict, indicating the application of the laws of war (international humanitarian law; IHL) or, more specifically, of that small portion of the laws of war that regulate armies' behavior toward civilians. Whether or not human rights protections—more generous than IHL—are still applicable is a much-debated issue. In any case, for law, war is defined by the events that constitute a violation of the applicable legal regime, and extensive court cases and human rights reports describe in detail the horror-filled events that constitute specific violations of the legal regime.

The stories I heard from displaced women of their lives as they fled the war, stories told outside the need to establish their identity as victims before the law, presented a picture of the gradual erosion of the possibility of living a life one can recognize as one's own, of the possibility of raising children, of being a person one can live with, of losing one's *amor propio* (self-respect). This loss is endemic in the incapacity to protect and provide for loved ones, sometimes extended to a valued community of family and friends.

The decision to flee is frequently a decision that emerges not from the barrel of a soldier's gun, from ordinary life in war. The difficult decision to flee is a rebellion against the estrangement from one's life as one is unable to act in ways one can live with, rather than a response to direct threats from armed actors. One woman succinctly described it as "losing so much weight from nerves" when some of her neighbors were murdered and she had to flee, even though she herself was safe from retaliations. Former coca-growing peasants fled the army attacks preceding planes raining Roundup on their crops, promising famine, but declared instead they had fled from combat between feuding armies because the forms required to access subsidies did not include the possibility of fleeing from army actions to eradicate coca fields. Many flee when their children are on the verge of becoming attractive for insurgent armies, strong enough to carry guns, pretty enough to have sex with armed commanders.

Before deciding to flee many had already experienced the loss of self that comes from being unable to take care of oneself and others. Stories involve complicated forms of collaboration and resistance, leading to decisions to provide, or not, information, resources, enlisted children, to various armies in exchange for protection. Flight can come from failure. One rural teacher fled when, after years of talking her students into finishing middle school rather than joining the guerrillas, her rebellious eighteen-year-old son enlisted in the army. Her grief at a son who had "gifted himself to the army" was so great she could not get out of bed for weeks and had to be carried out in someone's arms like a baby. Another woman described giving her daughters to her brother to raise as his own, then fleeing to Ecuador. She had remained silent and watched while her husband was shot before her eyes, pleading for help. In other versions, she had fainted:

I lost my home, all of it. I lost my children, I lost my husband. My husband was killed. I lost my daughters, I gave them to my family to save their lives so I lost them too. Not literally, because they are alive, but they call my sister-in-law Mami. They are no longer mine. I could never bury my husband. I saw how they threw him to the river and I could never find him again. And that pain is perhaps the only thing in my life that never ends. Every time I remember, I remember how he asked for help, I felt so impotent. And I fainted. I was pregnant. I was young. I didn't have the courage to face those who were killing him.

For months this story, captured by a student on a recorder, haunted me. Why did she give away her daughters before she fled to Ecuador? Why did she never return and claim them? Why did it take her so long to finally reach out to them? The reasons are embedded in the long interview: she was not strong enough to mother them, so saving her daughters' lives required giving them away. This opens the door to many unanswered questions, including the reasons soldiers singled out her husband for murder; perhaps it was because she was a rural teacher, and it was not unusual in the war for paramilitary armies to single out teachers for punishment, especially rural teachers suspected of leftist sympathies. One can empathize with the guilt, the impotence, the deep erosion of the sense of oneself as a capable mother that comes with remaining silent and that might be rooted in other silenced circumstances preceding the event.

Another woman, a respected peasant leader in her region, told me in confidence that the paramilitary commander "me cogió en gracia," a phrase with an ambiguous meaning (loosely translated as "he found me entertaining"), denoting that he both liked her and liked to torment her. She feared the commander, despised the local boys who enlisted in the paramilitary army, and also described the commander as inordinately handsome and attractive. After accepting her standing in the community as a peasant leader and taking her at her word that she was not guerrilla, he asked her to identify whether a young man they had captured was local. She didn't know the boy, but clearly his life depended on her word. She says she lied and said she knew him, but the way she told the story ("on that occasion") entailed the possibility that at other times she hadn't lied. Once, the commander asked her to deliver the remains of a man they had tortured to death to his family, something she remembered with dread, without elaborating on what the family had said to her upon receiving the body. But when her teenage daughter had her *quinceañera*, this woman refused to invite the soldiers to the party, a decision that directly led to her being banished from town, leaving behind land and a life's worth of work, including the respect of the community she had previously led. She knew the decision would bring some retaliation and remembers it with both pride for her courage and regret because of the losses it brought.

Legal categories surgically separate human rights or IHL violations from the everyday life in which they are embedded, both before and after the events. A focus on these violations entails the assumption that civilians are always innocent victims, erasing civilian participation in the war. Civilian collaboration is a fact of civil war and is generally both morally complicated and absent from legal representation of violations of the laws of war. In women's stories of displacement, collaboration is not presented as such but rather as fraught stories of limited choices and revealing silences. A vigorous literature on civil war around the world has shown that civil war murders rely heavily on information provided by civilians, frequently malicious information provided by neighbors and family members using armies to settle local feuds or access the wealth of others.[8] Collaboration can also come from a deeply felt conviction that an insurgency will right historic wrongs, from a desire for the order promised by government troops, or from revenge for the violence of an enemy army.[9] Collaboration is always suspect, and even remaining silent and compliant to the demands of passing soldiers can create the illusion of collaboration, with all its social consequences.

These everyday decisions, to collaborate or to resist, to leave or to stay, and the ideas about one's self that emerge from them, are the complicated moral entanglement of everyday life in civil war. The loss of amor propio that comes from the inability to act in a way one finds recognizable, the failure to protect one's children from soldiers, the bargains that are experienced as freely undertaken but whose toll gangrenes family life; this is the density of everyday life that is extirpated by laws when they speak of war. Which is why the humanitarian regime that responds to displacement fails to see the strength that displacement entails, the agency of those who decide to flee, and the centrality of the virtue they appreciate the most: strength, strength to survive and reconstruct their lives after fleeing the war.

Displacement as an Identity and as an Experience

When people flee war, they acquire a legal identity: they became IDP after Law 397. Forced internal displacement is both a war crime, defined as such in our criminal code, and the origin of a legal identity that grants special rights. Internally displaced people are "special subjects of constitutional protection," and the Constitutional Court has enumerated the long list of state duties toward them. Most of these rights center around immediate relief and poverty alleviation and follow the humanitarian logic of compassion, idealization of the victim, and denial of their agency, critiqued by Didier Fassin (2012). Complicity with the war is never a legal issue, although it remains fodder for rumor and speculation, especially among the street-level bureaucrats who distribute resources to displaced people and frequently mistrust them for misdemeanors such as lying on their forms or taking more aid than they are meant to. Victims of forced displacement, as they are called since the 2011 Victims' Law, are expected to be virtuous, in the sense that they do not lie to the government, do not take more than their share, and generally behave like the poor who are deserving of relief. Compassion flows then toward people traveling what one commentator described as the road with no return to poverty (Ibáñez 2008), a compassion that grounds the special rights the law grants displaced people.

Displacement, however, has a different dimension in women's narratives of life after the war. It clearly offers the possibility of making life anew in the slums of a city or a large town, away from the armies. The initial years present the most difficult challenge: the absence of food and the need for cash in order to eat is a new and terrifying experience for displaced peasants, sometimes more traumatic than war. There is no right to food per se, and hunger is a constant and feared companion, especially hunger in small children, and the task of rebuilding life begins with finding food at any price. But finding food can also be the recovery of a moral agency that is degraded by the limited choices of war. One woman described finding food for her children as her duty, but also the process that reveals she is strong, and in this respect superior to men in a deeply patriarchal society:

> We carry the heaviest burden when we arrive, because men despair, and they leave, or go and find work, but we, women, we have to stay. We fight, we wash, we iron, we stomp the earth, we do what we have to do. Because [*pause*] even if we have to live off trash, we are here [*emphasis*], and we do everything we can because we have children who say everyday Mami, we are hungry. We are strong because our children say we are hungry. And we find food, we find *panela*, we find bread. But men they say I have no food for you. But with patience we don't eat no, we say just one bite and that's all, I am taking this home because my daughter, my son is there and I am taking this home even if my stomach is empty.

Her story, told emphatically and with some pride, illustrates the centrality of the recovery of a moral sense of who one is after the war, and the location of this recovery in the small acts such as feeding children who are hungry. It is similar to what Veena Das (2007) describes as the descent to the ordinary. The location of this descent to the ordinary begins with flight and is located in the context of decades of massive rural immigration to the cities. It involves undertaking a series of activities that remain in the margins of legality, described as informal rather than illegal: selling food and wares in the street without a permit, squatting on plots of land not meant for urbanization, building houses there initially out of wood planks, cardboard, and plastic sheets. These activities can in the end provide for a satisfactory result: three-story houses made of brick and mortar with indoor plumbing and electricity and rooms to let, children in school, families with subsidized health insurance, legalized neighborhoods with public services, and enough cash for food for all, a process that, with little help from the state, is an effective reconstruction from below.

Displaced people do not reconstruct from scratch. They build on dense family and neighborhood networks that allow them to make a living in the streets and slowly improve their slum houses with little police interference in either activity. After the mass migrations of La Violencia, the poor, especially in the Andean region of Colombia most affected by that civil war, developed a rich cultural tradition for rebuilding life after displacement with very little help from governments or charity. This tradition includes knowledge and vocabularies for informal street selling and other forms of informal labor (known as *rebusque*, loosely translated as "earnestly looking for something") protected by street networks. Likewise, there is a tradition of squatting that includes land invasions and building shelters and informal provisions of public services and the recourse to various forms of community organizing and solidarity in emergencies and eventual interpellation of the state for aid and subsidies.

In this cultural world of the rural poor fleeing the war strength is the most valued virtue, strength to take care of oneself and others, expressed as the capacity to rebuild life and provide it stewardship. "In the country I was useful for all manner of things," one woman said, expressing the growth of her self-understanding as strong, "and now I am in the city, where there are so many needs." She went on to describe how she had created a successful pillow-making business in the slums, and also described herself as "una mujer de superación," a woman who can overcome, oriented toward the future rather than the past. Her situation was far from ideal, as her description also included lapses into despair and failure as part of the life of a woman such as herself, but the thread that held the story together was her capacity to overcome. Self-description as strong enough to move on is frequent among displaced women, as is that of being *del campo*, from the countryside. But stories of their lives hardly ever include the term *forcibly displaced*, although the category was frequently used in relationships with donors and the government.

Strength is expressed as community leadership, as it extends in concentric circles: strong women take care of themselves, their immediate family, their extended family, their neighbors, their barrio. Helping others is not only an expression of strength; it also brings the relief of not being always faced with one's own pain and loss, but focusing if only for a few hours on others. Generosity has of course intrinsic value, frequently religious, but part of the satisfaction lies in recovering a sense of being a person that has the capacity to help, and in that sense, the capacity to live life in terms one finds morally acceptable. Generosity is a moral exchange that affirms the value both of the person who gives and the person who receives. Overcoming, rebuilding amor propio, reconstructing life after the war is also expressed in care of others. Taking care of others is an expression of identity and a source of both agency and pleasure, valued experiences lost in war. This is not to say that reconstruction after forced displacement is marked solely by the recovery of moral agency and the pleasures of virtue. Instead a close look at the margins of cities built by hand by people fleeing the war reveals a sobering fact: war is people, and it goes where they go.

War Is People, and It Goes Where They Go

Patterns of migration frequently mean people from the same war-torn regions meet again in the places where they find refuge. They know who collaborated with each armed actor, a private knowledge they do not share with NGO or government officials but that does shape their lives after the war and fuels hatred and mistrust within community organizations. Rather than the subtle exclusions described in Kimberly Theidon's (2012) *Intimate Enemies*, however, what I saw was a lot of fear: women who feared their former neighbors and who described being afraid to leave the house. They especially feared their neighbors' children who had joined various armies and returned to their families, former soldiers whose own rebusque frequently entailed the use of weapons.

These young men, ubiquitous in my fieldwork, civilians looking like soldiers dressed as civilians, are frequently loosely referred to as *los mismos* (the same men). They do look like the same men who terrorized displaced peasants, and frequently look and act like paramilitary armies. When they are known los mismos, children of the women in the neighborhood, they are called gangs; when they come from other cities, other neighborhoods, they are called the old derisive name for paramilitary soldiers, *paracos*, also a word in Spanish for a wasp's nest. The frequent violent deaths of these young men are widely accepted as just deserts, negligible deaths because they occur *entre ellos mismos* (between each other). These are the deaths that come hand in hand with the emergent war against organized crime, whose everyday life, symbols, and soldiers build on the very recent past in ways we still don't fully recognize yet.

I first met los mismos when doing research on a notable group of displaced women, the Liga de Mujeres Desplazadas, who, among other achievements, had built their own neighborhood in the outskirts of Turbaco, a town in northern Colombia. When I first met the women, they were worried because there was a motorcycle-taxi station at the entrance of their neighborhood making them feel unsafe. They identified the drivers as *paracos* and as *los de la moto*, since their usual mode of transportation was motorcycles. The fear was so great that if they ran into a *paraco* driving his motorcycle in the countryside they would immediately hide in the bush or in the fields, fearing death.

Paramilitary armies demobilized between 2005 and 2006, under the transitional justice regime set up by the Justice and Peace Law, but in many parts of the country demobilization came after the paramilitary alliance of soldiers, drug traffickers, landowners, transnational companies, and wealthier townspeople had won the war. They had enshrined authoritarian social orders, melding anticommunism with traditional gender and racial orders, and even after the war with the paramilitary was formally over and the death toll had decreased dramatically, former soldiers and young men emulating them still maintained the order the paramilitary fought so hard to enshrine.

The persistence of the paramilitary, however, is not limited to the reproduction of the social order they established. It is also deeply linked to a form of government that is known as a mafia and certainly not limited to Italy. Mafia scholars point to the vital role mafias play in economic markets as they regulate economic transactions and protect the mafia's clients from their enemies (Gambetta 1993). Mafia-like services are desperately needed where there is no other regulator of economic transactions and no other protector of wealth; they are needed in the wide swaths of the country dedicated to cocaine trafficking, as well as in the informal economy of the street rebusque and the building of illegal slums. Too frequently los mismos regulate everyday life in a complicated persistence of the civil war in towns and subnational capitals, as well as in the informal barrios of the capital, the new home of displaced people suspected by the locals of being guerrilla sympathizers.

The impact of the mafias and their relationship to former paramilitaries remains practically invisible for postconflict laws and institutions. For years the government refused to acknowledge the persistence of former paramilitary groups and changed their name; first the police called them criminal bands (*bacrim* for short), then illegal armed groups (GAI, in Spanish), and more recently post-demobilization groups. The 2016 peace agreement ordered the creation of a special prosecutors' unit focused on dismantling "post-demobilization paramilitary groups" but it has yet to understand these groups' relation to the mafias that control local governments. Instead both los mismos and emerging groups of former guerrilla soldiers are depicted as engaged only in illegal enterprises, especially cocaine and mining, and separate from legal economies and democratic government.

This limitation of the phenomenon to cocaine and illegal mining makes such groups' involvement in local governments invisible in a way displaced women then find difficult to name. One woman, explaining why demanding health care from the local health care provider was impossible, told a long story of using every legal way of asking for services, only to find herself under threat from the men on the motorcycles. The threats implied that criminal organizations with ties to both former paramilitary structures and the local government controlled the health care provider, and any investigation into this matter or further demands for services would be dangerous. "This is the life of victims," she then told me, explaining that she had "already fled violence" and was too terrified to insist on her rights. Her story illustrates how the generous legal frame of the Victims' Law, which gives her special rights to access health care and other services, can be useless when faced with local power balances. Current laws that respond to organized crime or corruption are not equipped to understand this as "the life of victims": to understand the economic and political links between former paramilitary armies and mafias that control local governments, as well as the particular vulnerability of displaced people faced with these criminal organizations.

As displaced people fled to towns and cities where the state was present and the war was left behind, they ran into the turf of mafias of different sizes; demobilized paramilitary soldiers, and increasingly demobilized guerrillas, followed the same path. The state was present in these places, but mafias do not rule in the state's absence; they rule in intimacy with public officials, bribing the police and other law enforcement as well as syphoning public rents for their private enjoyment. The expansion of state presence and the end of insurgencies does not solve the problem of mafias that only become stronger as the state expands, feeding both from illegal markets and from the state trough. Young men who know how to use guns find employment at their service and, if their training was in the war, can easily reproduce the reasons that justified violence against civilians in the war, a suspect political identity. Community organizing, journalism, and other civic engagements still set the ground for accusations of being "too political" and thus open to the stigma that heralds violent death. Townspeople rarely rebel; the stigma naturalizes murder, accepted as a small price to pay for an order that is also known as peace or postconflict.

Mafias and young men with guns have a complicated relationship to the democratic politics that is imagined as the end of violence. Subnational politicians cement their power on clienteles of poor people and middle-class public employees who access subsidies and jobs through the protection of the politician's network. Insertion into clientelist networks is one more form of rebusque, and the experience is not much different from insertion in networks that support selling food and contraband goods in the street or building informal housing from scraps. Some politicians have alliances with the mafias, and the nature of these alliances, and their proclivity to violence and to reproduction of the authoritarian social orders defended by the paramilitary, depend on complex local histories displaced peoples must learn to navigate with no help from the law, which simply says the war is over and the new problem is crime.

Conclusion

The vocabulary and the narrative that human rights and humanitarian law provide for war is rooted in the rejection of war and unchecked violence. It expresses the normality of a state that follows in the wake of war, setting up a dominion made legitimate by the bare limits laws set to violence. The expansion of human rights and humanitarian legal regimes is embedded in the expansion of state presence and action, made legitimate by law. Hence the rule of law remains the aspiration of postconflict laws and institutions, both in Colombia and globally, as if war were merely lawlessness, and laws the definitive remedy.

It is a well-known fact that the rule of law, insofar as it mostly limits both state power (human rights law) and what armies can do legally (humanitarian law), sets the stage for the violence that can be exercised within the law. Criminal law remains the clearest example of the complicity between the rule of law and the brutality of state power. On the other hand, in the wake of war the rule of law appears, as E. P. Thompson famously said, and remains an unqualified human good, providing some protection against violence. Postconflict laws in Colombia have been prolific in affirming the need for a rule of law that sets some limits on violence; beyond those limits, laws have also promoted social programs for reconstruction.

The imprint of these laws, and the faith that they will cement peace, extends well beyond state capacity for implementation. In the aftermath of civil war, legal regimes also provide a narrative about war, as well as a language of reconstruction. For the past twenty years this narrative has described the harms of civilian suffering during war, equating their status as civilians with innocence, ignoring the active role civilians play in war and the fluid boundaries between wartime violence and the violence that so often erodes peace in the years, sometimes decades following a civil war. Laws providing reconstruction measures have also ignored civilian agency by focusing on humanitarian relief and poverty alleviation through institutions that ignore civilian reconstruction after the war.

The institutions that today materialize the aspirations of postconflict laws are shaped by this underlying vision of war. The current program, rooted in the mid-1990s' response to massive internal displacement, finds its full expression in the complex system of agencies that emerged from displaced people's special rights to humanitarian aid, poverty-alleviation programs and social services, and subsidies for survivors of the war, as well as from the complex apparatus of transitional justice emerging from the Justice and Peace Law, the Victims' Law, and the final peace agreement. Twenty years of laws and institutions layered over each other are premised on the sharp distinction between victims and victimizers, a distinction that resonates with international human rights and humanitarian laws and with the global push for the rights of victims.

The current program has had little interest in or understanding of the experience of civil war beyond the scripted declarations by victims confirming the need for compassion and aid. It has no interest in everyday life and little understanding of the stigma and shame that come from the loss of moral agency in war and its aftermath, the centrality of networks of affect and loyalty that build informal cities and informal markets, and no appreciation for the strength and generosity that help life thrive outside state purview. These laws, to be sure, provide a complex vocabulary and a narrative for the aftermath of war, but tell a single story: the expansion and imposition of state rule, the rule of law as the only alternative to horror, the equation between suffering in war and absolute innocence. What ordinary people know of war, and their evaluation of the importance of the things that happened in everyday life, seems, as the war wanes, destined for the dustbin of history.

The continuities and discontinuities of war do reveal an alternative, or the need for an alternative. The seeds of violence are sown in everyday life, expressed in ordinary language that can capture the porous nature of civil war and peace, the waxing and waning of the greed and the grudges and the hatreds that lead to violence, the possibility of reconstruction. Postconflict laws and institutions might be more effective in laying the groundwork for peace if they addressed the loss of moral agency in war, if they allowed civilians to work through the shame and the stigma of collaboration, if they built on the strength of leaders with amor propio, recognized the power of rebusque, and tended to the networks of care and collaboration as the ground for a legitimate state. For example, this is what one of the more successful institutions of the power-sharing deal of 1959, the Frente Nacional, did, by creating bipartisan community action boards known as Juntas de Acción Comunal to coordinate local action on schools, roads, and social services. The institution was so successful that today one out of every five Colombians is still affiliated with a junta, and sadly, its leaders are regularly targeted for threats and murders by los mismos attempting to establish territorial control.

The current challenge to peace is the fragility of state territorial control when faced with mafias financed, at least in part, by the booming cocaine trade and mafias that freely use the armed power and experience of former soldiers. This challenge is shared by other countries that must face globally the impossibility of consolidating a state in a context of prohibition. As to mafias and the persistence of los mismos, former paramilitary and now guerrilla soldiers, postconflict laws might do a better job ensuring peace if they unearthed the political and economic links between armies and civilians who found a way to profit from war and who use former soldiers as weapons. Persistent violence linked to the cocaine trade is at the heart of the impossibility of peace, especially if peace is defined as the rule of law promised by a state that cannot deliver in those areas of the country where territorial control is already exercised and lavishly financed by avid cocaine markets. In these places only community leaders, many of them from the surviving Juntas de Acción Comunal, defend the rule of law and its promise of peace.

Paradoxically, depicting armies and soldiers as the only victimizers, civilians as victims, and grounding humanitarian relief and poverty alleviation on compassion closes the way to postconflict laws and institutions that might bring the end of war. This narrative, sponsored by international human rights and humanitarian legal regimes, fails to address the seeds of war that lie in everyday life, that is, in the life lived by civilians, in the experience of collaboration and the promise held by reconstruction. The current legal regime, mirroring international law, does not address the persistence of old hatreds and greed for others' land and pretends the rule of law has no rivals once the soldiers are gone. More dangerously, it depletes the virtuous strength of those who can and do take care of the weaker members of their communities, undermining their legitimacy as leaders by suspecting foul play, setting the stage for their demise to be replaced by state agencies doling out subsidies and aid. Facing the role civilians play in war, and its persistence, might be the only way to cement peace at last; it would require speaking publicly, through law, about the subtleties of civil war, about the difficult choices, about the money and the greed, the hatred that persists from generation to generation, the innocence that was lost, and, most important, the amor propio and the possibility of collaboration that can be regained.

Notes

1. In the 1990s I was engaged in legal reform, especially for women's rights in the wake of Colombia's progressive 1991 constitution. After getting my doctoral degree in the United States (Harvard 2007), I taught for a decade at the Universidad de los Andes Law School in Bogotá, while writing about social movement faith in the constitution and about "bottom-up" uses of and faith in law reform from a sociolegal perspective. Caught up in this faith, I am now a judge in the Justice Chambers of the Special Peace Jurisdiction created by the 2016 Peace Agreement with the former FARC guerrillas, hoping legal regimes can, and will, provide a powerful narrative for a successful postconflict transition.

2. Given the secret nature of US support for counterinsurgency operations in Latin America, and its persistence under the mantle of the war on drugs, there is a certain difficulty in tracing its history. We do know that in 1959 the United States sent a Special Survey Team with experience in the Philippines, Vietnam, and Korea to train Colombian forces (Rempe 1995). These tactics were surmised in the adage of winning "hearts and minds," requiring the combination of development assistance designed to address grievances and, covertly, a focus on the identification and elimination of civilians that might be either guerrillas passing as civilians or civilians advancing communist ends by seeding discontent through so-called subversive activities. This approach, together with a labeling of grids of areas of combat and others of pacification tested and developed by the French in Algeria, remains at the core of generally failed counterinsurgency operations around the world.

3. Notably, *tutela*, a demand for a writ of protection which has both generous standing rules and gives judges extraordinary powers to right human rights wrongs. To date Colombians have used it over eight million times since 1991 (in a country of approximately fifty million people).

4. The Victims' Unit reports 7,371,504 victims of forced displacement. See statistics at Red Nacional de Información, Reporte General, January 1, 2020, https://cifras.unidadvictimas.gov.co/Home/General.

5. The regime mirrored Francis Deng's Guiding Principles on Internal Displacement adopted by the United Nations that same year, granting IDP a full guarantee of human rights and making the state the guarantor of these rights. See United Nations High Commissioner for Refugees 2004.

6. Over thirty thousand people, soldiers and civilian supporters, signed up for the benefits of the law, including sentences no longer than eight years for the most heinous crimes. Victims flocked to the hearings and gave their testimonies in a national campaign that even announced on television which commander was coming up for trial. Judicial decisions took almost ten years, hearings extended over days and weeks, and most final decisions are over a thousand pages long.

7. Full disclosure: this is the transitional justice system where I am currently a judge, after thirteen years of being a professor at the Law School at Universidad de los Andes in Bogotá.

8. Stathis Kalyvas (2006) inaugurates the field, populated by many of his students.

9. Elizabeth Wood (2003), for example, has a detailed description of this type of support in El Salvador.

REVOLUTION 8

BEHROOZ GHAMARI-TABRIZI

In the summer of 1978, a nationwide revolt was gathering steam toward a full-scale revolution in Iran. The crowds of youth, elderly, men, women, the able and disabled—an entire nation marched in the streets, raising their clenched fists, shouting, "The shah must go!" The island of stability in the region, that which President Jimmy Carter had saluted a few months earlier at a royal court reception in Tehran, was witnessing the largest revolutionary gatherings in world history. More than 10 percent of the entire population actively participated in the Revolution, five times more than that of the French and ten times more than that of the Russian revolutions, and shouted in curious unison, "Neither Western, nor Eastern, Islamic Republic!" Not only in its popularity but also, and more important, in its objectives the Revolution in Iran was unprecedented. It called for the establishment of an Islamic government—a demand that even its main advocates articulated in ambiguous terms. The revolution unfolded, in a Benjaminian sense, as a leap into the open sky of historical possibilities.

On the neighboring continent, a fierce debate, kindled by François Furet's (1981) *Penser la Révolution Française*, dominated the intellectual circles in Paris. Furet introduced a general skepticism about the significance and wisdom of revolutions in world history, consigning the French experience from a constitutive event of modern European history to an anomaly with everlasting tension between 1789 and 1793, between the French Revolution and the ensuing Reign of Terror. In post-1968 Europe, reading the revolution in the shadow of the gulag struck a chord with those who saw totalitarianism as an inherent feature of revolutionary impulse. Furet effectively cast doubt on what he called the Marxist "revolutionary catechism": an orthodoxy that situated the French Revolution as the harbinger of the looming bourgeois revolutions and the ensuing class conflicts that would inevitably lead to the establishment of socialism. Furet argued that thinking about revolution as a mythology of "new beginnings" carried out by "a nation in the vanguard of history" made it possible to "salvage the preeminent value of revolution as an idea." But that very idea, he wrote for a receptive intellectual community, lost its credibility after Solzhenitsyn's indictment of Soviet totalitarianism by "locating the Gulag at the very core of the revolutionary endeavor." Revolutionary atrocities, Furet insisted, could no longer be systematically absolved by references to "circumstances" and "external phenomena" (1981: 11, 12).

At the time when revolution, the event, was unfolding in Iran, revolution, the concept, was losing its explanatory significance in world history and its political appeal. Liberals understood revolutions as a tragic perversion of luminaries' attempt to reconstitute state institutions with reference to the principles of legitimacy and accountability. Recovering from the failed experiences of China and the Soviet Union, the retreating Left found it increasingly unthinkable to decouple revolution from its totalitarian corollaries. From its onset, the Iranian Revolution, particularly with its religious mode of expression, appeared to be consistent with the new skepticism about the emancipatory potential of revolutionary transformations. Leading social theorists regarded the Iranian Revolution and the way it politicized religion as "anti-movements" as a "counterrevolution," "regressive utopia," "a mythical quest for the Lost Paradise," and "the return of the repressed."[1]

The events of 1789, or more precisely 1793, turned the commonplace understanding of revolution against its original meaning of a natural "circular motion" into a progressive march toward the future. Revolution became a temporal abbreviation, a radical disruption in cyclical order of political formations, a rupture or alteration in the course of time.[2] By the beginning of the nineteenth century, revolution had already turned into a historical event with its own independent authority in shaping and giving legitimacy to political violence. For the first time, as Hannah Arendt (1990: 41) observes, "1789 generated a historical precedence for the transformation of revolution from a collective event for the restoration of an old order into its very opposite, a change so radical that [it] turned subjects into rulers." It spread its shadow over future revolutions and turned them into scripted social and political affairs with fixed causes and known outcomes that were steeped in the universal principles of eighteenth-century bourgeois Enlightenment thought.

What was lost in this transformation of the concept of revolution was the singularity and ambiguity with which this temporal rupture was associated. Not only was the French Revolution singular, but it also operated with a great degree of ambiguity, to the extent that Diderot famously pondered, "What will succeed this revolution? Nobody knows" (cited in Koselleck 2004: 24). Marx was perhaps most significantly responsible for turning that ambiguity into the revolutionary certainty of bourgeois universalism that he transformed into a historical prelude to the looming proletariat revolution. By the early twentieth century, the specter that haunted Europe had turned into a discursive assertion that only showed to the rest of the world the predestined unfolding of their histories. "Intrinsically," Marx (1978: 296) wrote in 1867 in the preface to the first German edition of *Capital*, "it is not a question of the higher or lower degree of development of the social antagonisms that result from the natural laws of capitalist production. It is a question of these laws themselves, of these tendencies working with iron necessity towards inevitable results. The country that is more developed industrially only shows, to the less developed, the image of its own future."

Revolutionary moments, *like a thunderbolt from the blue*, tear open the world of possibilities—possibilities that are articulated, albeit in ambiguous terms, in public imaginations of the good life. Revolutionary moments, from the time of the French Revolution to the recent Arab uprisings, have also been stifled by institutional restrictions, discursive confinements, and the demands of postrevolutionary realpolitik. Such demands often compel revolutionary subjects to abandon their essential desire for *possible* realities and instead become content, as Robert Musil ponders in *The Man without Qualities* (1943), with a pragmatic sense of *real* possibilities.

Where do we stand today in relation to what political theorists began to explore in the 1970s about the end of revolutions? Are all the revolutions after 1789 staged to repeat the same drama, borrow lines and symbols from the same cast and production? Are we losing the ability to imagine that *another world is possible* with expressions and desires that do not map onto a temporal geography invented during the age of revolutions? Seventeen eighty-nine became the ground zero of history, an absolute beginning with universal claims on culture and morality—the way Voltaire envisioned: *one geometry, one morality*. A revolution, that in reality was both singular and ambiguous, gained historical certainty and universal transformative authority from Paris to Peking, from Moscow to Mogadishu. Increasingly revolution turned into a discourse that no longer reflected its formative impulse to alter the temporal map of history. The discursive containment of revolution has led to the realization of what Rousseau feared in the mid-eighteenth century about the emergence of a particular form of authority that penetrates mankind's innermost thoughts and desires.

Much has been written about the paradoxical core of the Enlightenment: its substantive emancipatory outlook and its instrumental oppressive practice. Enlightenment thought advocated a secular eschatology that promoted the pursuit of worldly happiness against the Christian submission to divine providence. It fostered the desire for earthly gratification against the hope for heavenly salvation. Yet revolutions around the globe, most significantly the Haitian Revolution that inaugurated the nineteenth century, most profoundly expressed a public imagination that rested upon a commitment to the world of possibilities with competing visions of good society. By the mid-twentieth century those utopian visions that primarily emerged through the spirit, or what Derrida called the "metaphysics," of the project of Enlightenment gradually became associated with totalitarianism. The inescapable association between utopia and terror, between the imagined good society and totalitarianism, formed the foundational block of all that was revolutionary.

Imagining the good society, one can argue, is the essence of distinctly *political* thought. Karl Mannheim once predicted that the fading of the desire to reconstitute the *totality* of the existing order and the abandonment of the idea of the good society would lead to the disappearance of revolution and utopian thinking, a practice that he considered to be the very foundation of politics. In his vision, however, the good society is conceivable only with reference to a history that leads to an ultimate end. Without that end, Mannheim (1985: 253) warned, "The frame of reference according to which we evaluate facts vanishes and we are left with a series of events all equal as far as their inner significance is concerned."

Revolutionaries often justified the atrocities committed in the name of revolution by references to that "ultimate end"—those who stood in its way acted against the demands of progress and historical inevitabilities. Revolutionary anticipation, and the uncertainty that defines it, yielded to a predestined goal the terms of which were set from a universal position of exteriority with ambivalence toward the contingencies that inform the particularities of any historical moment. Such a disconnect inhibited societies from recognizing their own narrative abilities in envisioning and articulating alternative political, economic, and cultural relations outside universal claims that have conditioned the existing orders. Ernst Bloch went even further to suggest that a society dispossessed of the narrative skill to envision alternative political, economic, and cultural relations is dead.

However, Bloch's vision of utopia and the revolutionary act that leads to its realization was distinct from Mannheim's, in that he linked the conception of utopia to the principle of hope. In order to delink revolution from terror, Bloch (1986) located the revolutionary core of utopian thinking in the "Not-Yet-Become" of folklore, in the popular desire to hope and strive for a better life expressed in myth, fairy tales, and daydreams.

In its earlier conceptions, revolution was not yet ossified in the realization of a new historical epoch the blueprint of which was already drawn. More care and credibility were given to a more playful and imaginative understanding of history that connected the experiences of life in the past to the possibilities of the yet-to-be-realized future, the creativity through the exercise of which revolutions unfold in a perpetual tension with a temporality that restrains any deviation from the imposed logic of historical necessities. Revolutions do not occur as a fulfillment of progressive inevitabilities. As Walter Benjamin (2006: 402) notes: "Marx said that revolutions are the locomotive of world history. But perhaps things are very different. It may be that revolutions are the act by which the human race travelling in the train applies the emergency brake." That image suggests that if humanity allows the train of history to follow its course, already laid down by the steel structure of the tracks, "we shall [be] hurled into catastrophe, the crash or the abyss" (Löwy 2013: 186).

Benjamin saw revolution as a moment of pause in, rather than acceleration of, historical time, a moment of reflection on the progressive temporalities that operate as second nature in modern times. In *On the Concept of History*, he advances a theory of class struggle against the reductionism that defined revolutionary politics in reference to mere "rough and material things." Courage, creativity, confidence, humor—fine and spiritual characteristics of struggle assert themselves in irreducible ways, in ways that reach far back into the mists of time: "Just as flowers turn their heads towards the sun, so too does that which has been turned, by virtue of a secret kind of heliotropism, *towards* the sun which is dawning in the sky of history. To this most inconspicuous of all transformations the historical materialist must pay heed" (Benjamin 1968: 255). Here Benjamin sees revolution as a moment of escape from linear progressive history, a moment of resurrection of historical possibilities that inform our action in different historical trajectories.

Revolutions have always spread at the threshold of a novelty with an inherent contradiction between the realization and the rejection of possibilities; between a pause and acceleration in historical temporality; between exits from and inclusion in history; and between the *particular* transformative experiences of life and the discursive demands of universal history. In the second half of the twentieth century, revolution increasingly became associated with terror and totalitarianism rather than with hope and emancipation. From a highbrow philosophical assertion, the end of history turned into an everyday reality that colonized the very essence of imagination and revolutionary thinking and acting. The ability to transcend the present and to think of the world anew appeared to be a story the end of which we already knew, so we told ourselves as the first act was unfolding. Despite restoring faith in the possibility of change, the transformative power of revolutionary imaginations and desires materialized through the imposition of existing possibilities.

Revolutions express a public desire to *make* history rather than reproducing it along the same prescribed futures. Revolutions open moments of possibilities to enact historical transformations without predetermined goals. But since the dawn of the age of revolutions, they have also been understood as "that transitory phase" that bridges one stage of history to another. Even Marx, *the* theorist of revolution, and his successors believed that revolution was a moment of transition, thus limiting the significance of politics to the *realization* of a predestined future. The evolutionary core of this radical ideology rendered public imagination as mere utopianism, thus confining politics in the prison house of a historical telos in which the present was comprehensible only as the future's past.

With Marx, revolution acquired a different meaning and its main historical significance shifted from a preoccupation with the exercise of freedom to the satisfaction of material needs. Marx transposed his youthful revolutionary élan to his later scientific economic theory and advanced a new ethos in which he understood revolution as the embodiment of historical necessity. Liberation, in the way Arendt distinguishes it from freedom, no longer appeared to be an act in contradistinction with tyranny.[3] When Robespierre spoke of the "despotism of liberty," he had no fear of being accused of speaking in paradoxes. "Condorcet summed up what everybody knew: The word *revolutionary* can be applied only to revolutions whose aim is freedom" (Arendt 1990: 24). With Marx, and later in practice with Lenin, revolution took one more step farther from the moment of generating conditions of possibility. Its role became to realize historical necessities and to liberate "the life process of society from the fetters of scarcity so that it could swell into a stream of abundance. Not freedom but abundance became now the aim of revolution" (64).

I began with the Islamic Revolution in Iran in 1979 and how it puzzled Western pundits and intellectuals who understood revolutionary movements only with reference to European experiences. They were confounded by the religious character of a historical movement that was hitherto understood as the most secular expression of social change. "Indeed," Arendt (1990: 63) insists, "it may ultimately turn out that what we call revolution is precisely that transitory phase which brings about the birth of a new, secular realm. But if this is true, then it is secularization itself, and not the contents of Christian teachings, which constitutes the origin of revolution."

European political philosophers who understood revolutions to be the ultimate manifestation of the incessant expansion of the secular realm saw in Iran only a counterrevolution, a momentary pause in the otherwise progressive march of history. From its earliest inception in 1977 a small but militant faction within the clergy, those who followed Ayatollah Khomeini, led the revolutionary movement that culminated in the Islamic Revolution of 1979 and the establishment of the Islamic Republic. Certainly many people of diverse walks of life and a variety of political parties participated in massive rallies and protests. But it was a religious disposition and the leadership of Ayatollah Khomeini that lent this movement an uncompromising revolutionary character. Unlike a commonplace conception of revolution as the expansion of secular space, it was Shi'ism that offered a cultural context and a shared language that defined, advanced, and sustained the revolution and the way people experienced it.

Shi'ism, and its emancipatory rearticulation by leaders such as Ayatollah Khomeini and Ali Shari'ati, afforded a political milieu to spread and perpetuate a movement with which massive numbers of people could identify in historically complex, politically ambiguous, and, to a large extent, inexplicable ways. Shi'ism gained constitutive significance in the revolution both as a feature of the popular culture and as a liberation theology. It gave substantive meaning to the desire for dignity and *fulfilling experience*,[4] something that had roots in the past and heralded a new dawn in the sky of history. Rather than a series of formal, theological, and legal principles, Shi'ism in the revolutionary context gave political expression to basic principles of a form of justice that corresponded to what Hegel termed *Sittlichkeit*—that is, the customs, norms, and expectations inherent in the conception of the good life.

No one is more responsible than Ali Shari'ati in advancing that particular political expression of Shi'ism. Shari'ati located his political agenda between two major trends in Iranian politics. He believed that while the institution of the clergy had degraded Islam into a culture of stagnation, the Iranian Marxist-Leninists had failed to appreciate indigenous cultural resources in the formation of a counterhegemonic ideology of emancipation. He inverted the Marxian conception of ideology as a system of illusory ideas in conflict with reality into a revolutionary *assertion* for the creation of new realities. These realities, he contended, will emerge only when a transformation of a revolutionary self debilitates the cultural and political foundations of inner justifications of oppression and mass consent.[5]

It was this preoccupation with legitimacy and mass consent that led Shari'ati to formulate his theory of *Islam as ideology*. He maintained that structures of domination were based upon the triangle of economic power, physical coercion, and inner ideological/cultural justification. He expressed the three elements of a "triangle of oppression" in Iran in different rhyming verses, *zar-zur-tazvir* (jewel-coercion-deception), *mālek-malek-mullah* (landed gentry–ruler–clergy), or *tigh-talā-tasbih* (sword–gold–the mullah's rosary), in each of which the clergy represented the institutional force behind the ideological (inner) justification of political and economic oppression.[6]

Shari'ati divided Shi'ism into two distinct forms of practice, one at the service of the successive royal courts and disengaged from transformative social concerns, and the other a reflection of the revolutionary core of the Islam of the disinherited. He called the former the Safavid Shi'ism and the latter the Alavid Shi'ism. In order to expose the repressive ideology of Safavid Shi'ism, Shari'ati took upon himself the task of rewriting the entire history of Shi'ism, to reclaim its original revolutionary core and to restore Alavid Shi'ism—the Shi'ism of Imam Ali, the Islam of the wretched of the earth.[7] He defined Alavid Shi'ism as an ideology of consciousness of the present time, a worldview through which Muslims claim a social location, class position, national condition, historical and civilizational direction. "Ideology," he remarked, "gives meaning to humankind's historical experience in the context of which one's ideals and values are constructed" (Shari'ati 1981: 28–29).

The anticolonial and liberation movements of the 1960s, especially that of Algeria and its effect on French progressive intellectuals with whom he strongly identified, profoundly informed Shari'ati's articulation of Alavid Shi'ism. But his contribution lies neither in his sophisticated knowledge of Western social thought nor in his thorough reexamination of Islamic theology. Rather, he was able to reimagine the concept of revolution and its universal historical claims in relation to specifically Shi'i references to the notions of justice and emancipation.

Shari'ati's intervention generated a weighty rift within Shi'i political thought. The most influential clerical guardians of the major seminaries mobilized to discredit his idiosyncratic discourse on revolutionary Islam as an attempt to undermine the age-old influence of the clergy. They chastised him for misusing the hadith (the Prophet's life narratives), for misappropriating the Qur'anic verses, and, most important, for his ambivalence toward Sunni-Shi'i differences. Ayatollah Naser Makarem-Shirazi (1972), one of Qom Seminary's emerging authorities in the early 1970s, argued that Shari'ati's views on the democratic nature of Islam were based on an unreliable hadith and on a misunderstanding of the notion of *ijmā'* (consultation). Furthermore, he called Shari'ati's praise of the Sunni Saladin, the Muslim warrior who defeated the Crusaders and retook Jerusalem in 1187, distasteful and damaging to the souls of his young followers. Makarem's critique represented a typical failure of the ulama to grasp Shari'ati's conception of Islam as a revolutionary ideology.[8]

Another important clerical figure and a trustee of Ayatollah Khomeini, Morteza Motahhari, also rebuked Shari'ati for politicizing Islam.[9] Although he shared the same pulpit with Shari'ati at Hosseiniyyeh-ye Ershād, he remained conspicuously apprehensive about Shari'ati's denunciation of the clergy. Motahhari asked his mentor in exile, Ayatollah Khomeini, to condemn Shari'ati's systematic critique of the clergy. Khomeini refused and transformed Shari'ati's incendiary intervention into his own revolutionary discourse on Islam and governance. But soon thereafter a number of grand ayatollahs launched a concerted defamation campaign against Shari'ati. They asked the shah and his secret police to stop what they called the spread of Shari'ati's poisonous words and deceptive books. At the same time, they also accused him of being a SAVAK collaborator whose mission was to destroy Islam from within. A long list of ayatollahs lent their support to a petition to prohibit their followers from attending his lectures and issued fatwas condemning his heresy (see Rahnema 1998: 272–75).

While Shari'ati tried to appease them, he was incensed by the ayatollahs' complacency in matters of injustice and tyranny. In a letter to Ayatollah Milani, who had earlier forbidden his followers from reading Shari'ati's books or attending his lectures, he lamented, "He still respects [the ayatollah]" and reminded him that his "presence offered hope and support to all the youth who desired a safe haven in these bewildering times." To have a better appreciation of Shari'ati's (1996) piercing language and affecting style, here is a long passage from his letter:

> Everybody is asking this question (and because of my gratitude towards you I have tried in vain to offer . . . a persuasive answer to them): Why is it that pious people such as yourself, who sit on the cathedra of the deputy of the Shi'i messiah (*imam-e zamān*) as a source of emulation, have not uttered a word about tyranny in this world? For eight years, the French army bloodied and massacred the Muslims of Algeria, wrecked their towns, tortured their rebels, but the Algerians carried on their fight heroically. Even the enlightened Christian priests in France sympathized with the Algerians. The existentialist Sartre and the anti-religion Ms. Simone de Beauvoir defended them and endangered their own livelihood for the sake of the Algerians' cause. Even the French communist Henri Alleg joined the Algerian resistance and made the atrocities of the French, their torture of the Algerian *mujahidin*, known to the world. You, one of the leaders of the Shi'i world[,] did not even issue a meaningless statement of sympathy with them. . . . For more than twenty years now the Muslims [*sic*] of Palestine have suffered at the hand of the Israelis. Their atrocities are so horrific that they compelled a young Japanese man to sacrifice his life bravely in defense of the Palestinians. But our clerical leaders do not show one-thousandth of the sensitivity they display in my condemnation in denouncing the brutalities of the Israelis. . . . It perturbs me deeply to witness that a great source of emulation writes on the pages of his book that "the Prophet has advised *those who eat melon would go to the heaven!*" And then you have the audacity to call me an "unfit element." (101–2)

Neither the Iranian Marxist-Leninist Left nor the clerical establishment understood Shari'ati's intention to transform Islam into a revolutionary *counterhegemonic* ideology. Whereas his religious lexicon troubled Marxist-Leninists, his idiosyncratic language, in borrowing freely from Rousseau, Marx, Imam Ali, and Abu Dharr, scandalized his clerical detractors. Shari'ati consciously developed his historiography (his *Islamology*), his conception of Safavid Shi'ism, and his emphasis on the cultural-ideological basis of domination in terms of the Gramscian *war of position*.

Like Gramsci before him, Shari'ati never abandoned the notion of revolution and remained committed to a *war of maneuver*. But he viewed a *war of position* as a strategy to restrain postrevolutionary violence. Independently from Gramsci, in his analysis of state power Shari'ati shifted the question of oppression under the shah from domination, as coercion, to leading, as coercion bolstered by consent. The state expands its authority, he maintained, not only through political violence but more importantly through the exercises of ideological domination in civil society, through the trinity of *este'mār*, *estesmār*, and *estehmār*, that is, colonialism, exploitation, and deception. He echoed the Gramscian idea that the state is not exclusively a gendarme–night watchman organization. Rather, its dominance is maintained by means of the institutions and relations of civil society— schooling, family, mosques and religious life, gender and ethnic identities, and so on, "in the web of existing social institutions, such as state; family; language; banks and insurance; retirement plans; saving accounts; and even lottery tickets" (Shari'ati 1971: 39). He understood that the response to the inevitability of postrevolutionary violence was to exercise "leadership before winning governmental power" (Gramsci 1975: 207).

Inspired by Marx's eleventh thesis on Feuerbach, Shari'ati described the philosopher and the *'ālem* as "observers of this world." In contrast, he believed, the responsibility of the "ideologue" is "to demand the good and to destroy evil, to criticize and to correct, to define the ideals for whose realization the masses should be organized." The Truth, he insisted, will emerge from neither scholastic debates nor scientific inquiry; "truth manifests itself only in action" (Shari'ati 1978: 14–19). Accordingly, the Islamic ideal was a society based on the worldview of *towhid* (the oneness of God). However, instead of a mere demarcation of Islam as a monotheistic religion, he regarded towhid as a weltanschauung that reflects a utopian egalitarian social relation based on the unity of Man, Nature, and God (Shari'ati 1981). He wrote:

> Social *towhid* negates the legitimacy of earthly gods and their authority in endorsing social orders that embody differences in class and other aspects of human life. In a word, a *towhidi* society negates human *shirk*.
>
> . . . *Shirk* is a world-view that justifies [social inequality] and attributes class-ridden social orders to the divine will. In this way, not only does it justify such an order, but also it worships it and calls it "natural" and "eternal." . . . The advocates of *shirk* "naturalize" social inequalities and create another god who forbids rebellion, and sanctifies the existing social orders. (Shari'ati 1981: 1:131–32)[10]

By politicizing towhid, Shari'ati called into question the authority of *ruhāniyat* as official exegetes of the Islamic canon. He understood that a legitimate imam is one who represents Islam in relation to contemporary contingencies.[11] But the kind of legitimate imam he had in mind was an intellectual who rejected the Iranian practice of either imitating the West or uncritically continuing old religious traditions. "Intellectuals are those who think in new ways," he wrote. "It does not matter if they are illiterate; or not knowledgeable in philosophy; or are not a *faqih*, a physicist, a chemist; or a literary connoisseur, or an historian. Intellectuals need to be conscious of their time, of their people, they need to know how to think and how to appreciate the responsibilities that critical thinking bestows on their shoulders, and be ready to accept the sacrifices the realization of those responsibilities demand[s] of them" (Shari'ati 1979a: 85).

To Shari'ati, intellectuals become organic not because they emerge from the classes they represent but because they accept the responsibilities that their position as public intellectuals demands. Therefore, he strove to create a new Muslim leadership of young revolutionaries who cast aside habitual blind emulation. His project was immensely successful. He never established a political party, but he considered his widely popular lectures to be the work of intellectual mobilization.

During his lecture series from 1967 to 1972, Hosseiniyyeh Ershād became the meeting place of a generation of young, otherwise Marxist, Muslim intellectuals who transformed the common understanding of Islam as the wisdom of ages into a dynamic (*puyā*) ideology of social change. In contrast to his detractors, he saw no contradiction in understanding Shi'ism as a revolutionary ideology that was rooted in the past but still could herald a just future. He grasped the Qur'an as a Divine but historical text, revealed in allegorical verses and relevant to generations in all ages.[12]

The religious character of the revolution in Iran revived an old notion of revolution as a phenomenon that weds the *longue durée* of people's historical consciousness of their own imagined selves with possible realities they desire. In this case, as Michel Foucault observed in Iran, Shi'ism was circularly transformed in a continuous theater from a self-regulating technique into a language of collective will. Iranians were dreaming, Foucault wrote in an essay during his visit to Iran in 1978. It was true, he observed, that there were economic difficulties, political repression, and corrupt administrations. It was also true that they knew they needed to change the whole country, its economic order, and political system. But, above all, they told themselves *we have to change ourselves*. "Our way of being, our relationship with others, with things, with eternity, with God, etc., must be changed, and there will only be a true revolution if this radical change in our experience takes place" (Foucault [1978] 2005: 256). Foucault called that radical change a *political spirituality*, a transformative experience that in practice gave rise to an unanticipated mode of being.

Foucault's enthusiasm for the revolution in its religious expression and his conception of political spirituality deeply puzzled the Parisian intellectual community. His friend Claude Mauriac recalls a conversation with Foucault about his support of a *political spirituality*:

MAURIAC: I read your paper in *Nouvel Observateur*, but not without surprise, I must say.

FOUCAULT: And you laughed? You are among those that I could already hear laughing.

MAURIAC: No . . . I only said to myself that as to spirituality and politics, we have seen what that gave us.

FOUCAULT: And politics *without* spirituality, my dear Claude? (Foucault [1978] 2005: 91)

In Iran, the revolution spread as a phenomenon of history and, at the same time, as a phenomenon that defied it. With all the ambiguities associated with their political discourse and religious expressions, Iranians intended to think of their future anew and refused to turn themselves into subjects of the discursive authority of a world that is perpetuated in tired conceptions of "history." The Iranian revolution unfolded without closing the window of possibilities, without subjecting the revolutionary movement to the logic of historical inevitabilities.

But the clerical leadership of the revolution as well as those who fought them afterward to undermine their political authority proved that Lenin, Mao, Stalin, and Castro were not the only ones who took a page from Robespierre's revolutionary handbook. The struggle to give voice to the revolutionary demands without ambiguity steadily eroded the condition of possibilities and brought the revolution from the threshold of a novelty back to the center of the realpolitik of postrevolutionary logic. The revolutionary Left saw the fleeting image of Kerensky on the face of Mehdi Bazargan, the provisional prime minister, and believed that they needed to radicalize the Iranian Revolution toward its own October. The Islamic regime advanced its own "despotic liberation," liberation from all they deemed un-Islamic. They followed the same nationalization and centralization scheme that other national liberation revolutions enacted. Gone was the *eros of creativity* that gave rise to the revolutionary impulse and the rhythm with which it unfolded. The final resolution to the ambiguity of the revolutionary dreams and the necessities of the project of state building was soon hammered out at the gallows.

More recently, the Arab uprisings that began in Tunisia in 2010 and spread throughout North Africa and the Middle East reminded us of the perils of the failure to recognize the significance of revolution as a moment of creativity rather than the realization of a historical necessity. Is it possible for a people to envision and desire futures uncharted by already existing schemata of historical progress and patterns of social change? Is it possible to think of dignity, equality, equity, justice, and liberty outside Enlightenment cognitive maps and principles? Is it possible to think of revolution not as a bridge but as an opening, a locomotive that lays down its own track?

The same kind of inexplicability of "the man in revolt" that puzzled Foucault thirty years earlier in Tehran, the same kind of transformative exuberance that he called *political spirituality*, and the same kind of ambiguity about the future direction of these uprisings that fascinated him during the Iranian Revolution seemed to define those moments. There was another important similarity in what was happening in 2010–11 with the Iranian Revolution of 1978–79. Pundits and scholars tried to make sense of this sudden upsurge of protest, analyze its causes, and attribute meaning to the demands of the insurgent masses in order to make these historical events *legible* to a global audience.

Unlike the Iranian Revolution thirty years earlier, the Arab uprisings not only overtook the streets of major cities and squares but also dominated the global mediascape that operated paradoxically both as an instrument of the effective dissemination of its existence and, at the same time, as a means of its discursive reticence. Although by and large the masses on the streets identified their movement as a call for human dignity (*kerāma*) and an end to social injustice and corruption (*kefāya*), only a few weeks after their emergence the news reports and scholarly analyses identified the moment as the "Arab Spring." In order to make a phenomenon legible, one has to operate within a recognizable assembly of points of reference. By naming it the Arab Spring, the uprisings entered a conceptual and discursive universe with a written past and a known future direction.

The Arab Spring was a discourse, in the making for five years, constructed to do exactly the opposite: close the window of possibilities and subject the uprisings to historical inevitabilities. After the massive rallies to condemn the assassination of the former Lebanese prime minister Rafik Hariri in February 2005, conservative as well as a number of liberal and Left columnists began to ponder the wisdom of George W. Bush's Middle East project. They considered the mass protests against the Syrian influence in Lebanon, the Cedar Revolution, an Arab Spring that heralded the fruition of the Bush policy of exporting democracy to the land of the unfriendly tyrants. In a self-congratulatory op-ed, the staunch conservative columnist Charles Krauthammer (2005) compared the Beirut protests to the 1848 revolutions that "did presage the coming of the liberal idea throughout Europe." "The Arab Spring of 2005," he proclaimed, "will be noted as a similar turning point for the Arab world."

The Arab Spring of 2005 did not materialize the way the pundits predicted. But the uprisings of 2010–11 turned into a full-bloom "spring," albeit a short-lived one. The dominant explanations of the uprisings interpreted this spring, whether it was a reference to Prague of 1968 or Europe of 1848, as a triumph of liberalism and the discovery of Enlightenment in the Arab world. In Alain Badiou's (2012: 48) words, "Our rulers and our dominant media have suggested a simple interpretation of the riots in the Arab world: what is expressed in them is what might be called a *desire for the West*." Not only did this view conflate competing interests of the uprising in a single reductionist desire for the West, but, more significantly, it subjected those who rose up to *make* history to the unfolding of its inherent logic.

The revolution in Iran spread as the struggle of a nation asserting itself for both an *inclusion* (in making history) and an *exit* (from terminal history). The indeterminacy of the revolutionary movement in Iran presented itself as a possible source of creativity and inspiration rather than an expression of backwardness finally unleashed against "progress." The narrative of Arab Spring denied the 2010–11 uprisings the *singularity* with which they could be comprehended and advanced outside the recognized patterns of revolutionary transformation. The discourse of Arab Spring devoured the Egyptian liberals and revolutionaries and denied them the impetus to articulate the significance of their uprising notwithstanding the burdens of a universal history. They considered any deviation from the conventional narratives of revolution to be a failure and inauthentic to their movement. The election of Mohamed Morsi of the Muslim Brotherhood invariably and quickly became the case in point. Even before the Morsi administration showed its incompetence and autocratic tendencies, liberals and many actors on the left regarded a Muslim Brother president as the epitome of *one step forward, two steps back*; thus their Orwellian jubilation over the July 2013 military coup to save democracy.

Liberal and Left parties hastily celebrated the Arab Spring as the end of the ideological significance of political Islam. They believed that these revolutions would restore the authority of secular politics that had been obscured by the Iranian Revolution since 1979. The secularists of the Left and the Right vowed that they would not allow Egypt to become a second Iran. Not thinking through the *singularity* of the Egyptian moment, they deemed irrelevant the conspicuous facts that the incompetent Morsi lacked anything in common with the charismatic Khomeini, that the Brotherhood institutionally lacked the same effective Shi'i clerical network, and that the Brotherhood's political philosophy shared no affinity with the Shi'i liberation theology.

I do not wish to suggest an intellectual commitment to a linear progressive conception of History was the reason a military coup in Egypt halted the Arab uprisings of 2010–11. But the desire to turn Arabs into legible subjects of the march of history rather than making history the subject of their uprising made the self-proclaimed secular actors ambivalent about, if not unashamedly promoting, a military intervention to save the nation from the "unyielding Islamist reactionaries."

On August 14, 2013, military forces massacred 1,250 brotherhood supporters in two protest camps in Cairo. After the massacre, the only audible voice was the sigh of relief of the former revolutionaries who thought that they had brought the nation from the brink of an electoral catastrophe back to the mainstream of history. *You can take the country back from a military junta, but you can't redeem the nation from the yoke of the Messengers of God.* While violence in the name of Allah appeared to be utterly unjustifiable, violence in the name of the "people" only contributed to historical progress. Egyptian radical secularists regarded any form of public religion to be offensive to their political, social, and aesthetic sensibilities. Talal Asad depicts this secular modernist attitude so aptly in Hilmi Namnam's (a well-known Egyptian journalist) praise of violence against Morsi supporters after the coup d'état:

> "No democracy or society," Namnam insists, "has ever advanced without shedding of blood." Namnam's concern is not simply to assert that the necessary price of progress is the physical elimination of its enemies but also suggest that progress is not a matter of completing a particular project but of an indefinite advance subject to transcendent principles and it is *this* that constitutes secularity, the real nature of society. . . . The deliberate violence of the progressive Egyptian movement is secular because it wants to make an increasingly better future in *this* world; the coercive activity of Islamists, by contrast, seeks conformity with a divine plan. It is motive not effect that distinguishes the two kinds of violence. (Asad 2015: 187)

Although the aspirations of the 2011 uprising were expressed neither in Islamic nor in secular terms, the election of Morsi to the presidency generated a bifurcated political stage. The binary generated alliances on the ground that otherwise one would deem implausible. As we know by now, the fragility of a secular coalition between the military and the Egyptian Left and liberals became evident soon after the coup. But the basic premise on which that coalition was justified remains in place on the ground and in intellectual circles. The binary conception of secular versus religious politics assumes actual uniformities on both sides of the dichotomy that correspond neither to a coherent conceptual project nor to the shared experience of a *particular* politics.

I shall conclude with a passage from Foucault's last essay on the Iranian Revolution, called "Is It Useless to Revolt?" Foucault (2001: 450) ends this passage with a rather biting question posed by Horkheimer:

> Then came the age of "revolution." For two hundred years this idea overshadowed history, organized our perception of time, and polarized people's hopes. It constituted a gigantic effort to domesticate revolts within a rational and controllable history: it gave them a legitimacy, separated their good forms from their bad, and defined the laws of their unfolding; it set their prior conditions, objectives, and ways of being carried to completion. Even a status of the professional revolutionary was defined: By thus repatriating revolt, people have aspired to make its truth manifest and to bring it to its real end. A marvelous and formidable promise. Some will say that the revolt was colonized in Realpolitik. Others that the dimension of a rational history has been opened to it. I prefer the naive and rather feverish question that Max Horkheimer once posed: "But is this revolution really such a desirable thing?" (Foucault 2001: 450)

Instances abound when historians, political actors, intellectuals, and all those who give voice to revolutionary desires render them as demands that are legible only with reference to the inherent logic of linear historical progress. Revolution is the space of engagement with politics in its imaginative and uncertain terms, a space that allows thinking about possible realities without the inhibiting constraints of real possibilities. Rather than a temporal abbreviation and a violent realization of a predetermined future, in this chapter I argued that revolution ought to be understood as a moment of creative pause and a transformative politics the outcome of which needs to be negotiated in practice. The Iranian Revolution as well as the Arab uprisings of 2010–11 generated in fleeting moments the possibility of a different kind of revolutionary politics that did not simply reflect the unfolding of a universal temporality. Revolutions might fail, but the experience of *becoming* in a revolutionary moment gives rise to a transformed subject whose relation with history will permanently change.

Notes

1. For a review of these claims, see Ghamari-Tabrizi 2004.

2. For a genealogy of the term and its historical appropriation, see Koselleck 2004: 43–57.

3. Arendt (1990: 29) argues, "It may be a truism to say that liberation and freedom are not the same; that liberation may be the condition of freedom but by no means leads automatically to it; that the notion of liberty implied in liberation can only be negative, and hence, that even the intention of liberating is not identical with the desire for freedom."

4. I am using "fulfilling experience" here in reference to Benjamin's (2004: 43) conception of revolution, as an act of self-presence without reservation for the realization of a wish.

5. Shari'ati had a Weberian understanding of the relations of domination. Although he seldom makes references to his sociology, he uses Weberian method throughout his treatises and lectures. In relation to the idea of mass consent and how state power is perpetuated, Weber (1958: 78) argues, "If the state is to exist, the dominated must obey the authority claimed by the powers that be. When and why do men obey? Upon what inner justifications and upon what external means does this domination rest?"

6. Although occasionally Shari'ati compromised the content of his discourse for its poetic form, he believed that his rhyming allegories greatly deepened their rhetorical power.

7. The result of this endeavor was a three-volume book, *Islam-shenāsi* (*Islamology*), which was originally delivered in a series of lectures at Hosseiniyyeh Ershād in Tehran from February to November 1972 (Shari'ati 1981).

8. For a summary of early clerical reactions to the rise of Shari'ati's influence, also see Rahnema 1998: 206–9, 266–76.

9. In an interview Motahhari confided in Shahrough Akhavi (1980: 144) that "Dr. Shari'ati brought pressure to bear on the political aspect [of the Hosseiniyyeh's activities]." Hamid Algar (1980: 47) also narrates an encounter with Motahhari in which he remarked, "Dr. Shari'ati was an instrumentalist in the sense that he used religion as an instrument for his political and social objectives."

10. *Shirk* is the idea of polytheism. Shari'ati uses the term here to refer to societies that are stratified by class and race.

11. For his innovative use of the notion of *imamat*, see Alijany 2006. Here we also see the similarity between Khomeini's late fatwas on the qualities of the *vali-ye faqih* and Shari'ati's conception of imam.

12. Shari'ati (1979b: 71) remarked, "The language of religion, and particularly the language of Semitic religions, in whose prophets we believe, is a symbolic language that expresses meaning through images and symbols—the finest and most exalted of all the languages that humankind has ever invented."

CORRUPTION 9

CAROLINE HUMPHREY

In the contemporary world, we see corruption on multiple scales. On the one hand, it is held to be a single phenomenon that is a global problem: it is calculated to be on the rise in this country or that, or is uncovered in vast shady deals that link offshore havens with internationally linked companies. On the other hand, corruption is a relation between individuals in their particular circumstances and can consist of something as tiny as the meaningful wink of an eye. This essay draws attention to the fact that different modes of reckoning are involved at the various scales and that they can be radically incongruent with one another. Of course, it is true that in some cases corruption manipulates huge sums of money, vast resources, or great political power, and in others small bribes or local threats, but the size of the loot is not the point made here. It is rather the scale of the social relations envisioned. On different scales the techniques of understanding, assessing, practicing, and experiencing corruption are dissimilar, and I argue that the means used on one scale, say, statistical measures, tend to obscure the character of another, which might be primarily political in character. I shall take the case of Russia and look at corruption, that is, any activities that might be known by this term, throughout society, discussing them at three scales: the global, the national, and the intimate. In such a large and complex political formation there certainly must be other scales or frameworks that make sense of corruption in their own ways, particularly those of religious communities with distinctive definitions of *corrupt*, but for the sake of simplicity I will discuss only the three mentioned. I will suggest that the means of knowledge production used in global assessments of corruption have only limited purchase in Russia, but that, paradoxically perhaps, the intimate scale is not only found in humble localities but is also a vibrant and powerful technique in the metropolis, at the very heart of government.

Corruption, though, is always a morally loaded word, and this fact presents us with another dimension to be considered. It is one of those words commonly used by individuals and institutions with agendas and aimed at persuasion. An "ideological word," as Epstein (1995: 105) puts it, does not simply describe an action that people take, such as "to walk," nor at the other end of the spectrum is it just a value judgment like "beautiful" or "harmful." This class of words indicates at the same time an action and a value judgment on that action. This is why such words are so prevalent in the language of governments that are placing emphasis not on the exchange of information but on controlling and steering the thinking of their listeners. An anthropological study of activities called corruption should, however, investigate the gap between an act and the judgment of that act that this word conflates. The point has been made many times that the very same activities that some people, almost always outside observers, label "corruption" may be described by the actors themselves in quite other, nonjudgmental or differently weighted ways (Parry 2000; Das 2015b; Mathur 2017; Smart 2018). This is why, when I write about corruption in the rest of this essay, I will mean "the phenomena called corruption in global media," leaving open both the vocabulary and the ethical judgments of actors. It is not just that the people involved may reject the idea of corruption as applying to their own practices, but that, even when some arrangement is called corrupt, the "badness" that is intrinsic to the term can refer to different moral principles. In other words, when the people in a given situation agree that some activity is morally offensive, their reason for feeling that way may differ greatly from the idea of wrongness applied by another group of people. After all, ethical values may pertain to moral absolutes (Lambek 2008)—but there are more than one of them. In fact, as the Russian material shows, the public probity discourse, in which certain activities are solemnly designated corrupt, is often relegated by actors as a mere shadow, while for them other, more pressing and vibrant but equally moral values prevail. Thus not just scale but also *perspective* must be central to our consideration of corruption, that is, perspective in a complex sense, indicating not only a distinction between first-person speaking for oneself and third-person speaking about others but referring also to the varying moral orientations of speech in a turbulent, postsocialist world of changed routines and conflicting values.

In contemporary Russia corruption is omnipresent, always as a murky and controversial imbroglio, an inextricable mixture of propositional facts, value judgments, and practices, all of which can be queried, subverted, laughed at, or cursed. In an attempt to gain some analytical purchase on this, I first outline three scalar modes that I hope will help make some sense of it and then address various perspectival views by which Russian observers and actors experience and react to it.

Three Scalar Modes of Conceiving Corruption

The simple question "What is corruption?" evokes answers that provide much insight into the issue of scale. On a global scale, the definition given by Transparency International is most widely accepted: "Corruption is the abuse of entrusted power for private gain." Two ideological words, *corruption* and *abuse*, point to (unspecified) moral condemnation. Following this general definition, Transparency International provides a knowledge structure starting with an array of sixty boxes that define different types of corruption (bribery, profit shifting, collusion, etc.). These definitions are then used to work out indicators, which enable calculation of the incidence of the various kinds of corruption in any country over a given period of time. The resulting scores are ranked, correlated with statistics from the World Bank, World Economic Forum, World Justice Project, and others, and changed year by year as each country is reckoned to become more, or less, corrupt. Let us call this conception Corruption 1. Russia does badly in these rankings: 135th out of 180 in the world in 2017, and well below the average for Eastern Europe and Central Asia.

Indicators are increasingly prevalent as a technique for assessing and promoting social justice policies around the world: there are indicators of rule of law, violence against women, economic development, and so forth. The idea is to provide quantifiable evidence that can make visible forms of violation and inequality that are otherwise obscured and thus to supply measurable data that can be used in global and national governance. Yet critics point out that the reliance on numerical representations of complex phenomena in effect sidelines political debate and replaces it with the technical expertise needed to devise and operate the indicators. Furthermore, in the effort to facilitate global comparisons, the indicators typically obscure their Western political-moral origins and rely on sources of information and practices of measurement that are themselves opaque (Merry 2011: S84). Corruption 1 thinking reaches Russia through a dedicated NGO and an academic Laboratory for Anti-Corruption Policy. But their impact is small. President Vladimir Putin recently acknowledged that "rapid success in fighting corruption in Russia should not be expected," though he thought it was worth trying (*Rossiyskaya Gazeta* 2016). Meanwhile the seeming precision that emerges from measurement appears as an enigmatic dance of statistics that impact international reputation but are not anchored in any understandable way to the corrupt activities in actors' own spheres.

However, if one searches online or in print media for "What is corruption?" using languages other than English or in relation to some particular region of the world, it becomes apparent that different countries tend to pick out divergent profiles of what constitutes such abuse. Let us call these answers Corruption 2. These are the versions of corruption that are publicly recognized in any given country, most written about in national media, subject to anticorruption campaigns, prosecuted in law, and analyzed in academic publications. I guess that if anyone were to put all these Corruption 2s together they would form a broad cluster, but they would do so in a way that is like Wittgenstein's "family resemblances," that is, as a series of overlapping similarities rather than having a single common core. Some cases taken from easily available dictionary or Wikipedia entries illustrate how national versions of Corruption 2 may diverge.

Corruption 2 in Russia emphasizes abuse of power by persons in authority. For example, "Corruption is a term that usually refers to the use by officials of their commanding power and assigned rights, as well as the authority and possibilities given by their official status, for the goal of personal advantage, contrary to law and moral principles. The corresponding term in European languages usually has a wider meaning derived from the original sense of the Latin word."[1]

Corruption 2 in India emphasizes illicit appropriation of central state funds by functionaries at lower levels and in various regions, preventing the resources from reaching the intended beneficiaries. For example, "The largest contributors to corruption are entitlement programs and social spending schemes enacted by the Indian government."[2] This is colloquially known as "eating money." As Prime Minister Narendra Modi kept repeating in his 2014 election campaign, "Neither will I eat, nor will I let others eat."[3]

Corruption 2 in the United Kingdom emphasizes cheating and subterfuge, and complicity in global flows of illicit capital, so as to undermine the "level playing field" of normal competitive capitalism. For example,

"Although the UK performs well on most standard corruption measures, there is a lingering feeling that beneath the surface there is an underlying corruption of cronyism and impunity that somehow feels uniquely British. Invisible, deniable, insidious, difficult to legislate against, sometimes appearing to do little harm except inexorably tilting the system in favour of its beneficiaries, sometimes doing great harm" (Barrington 2015).

Indicators do not figure widely in national discussions of Corruption 2, let alone the sixty Transparency International definitions. The configuration of governmental-public concern in each country is such that some types of corruption barely see the light of day while others loom as crises and important threats to society. The debate here is indeed primarily political, dealing with further ideological categories, such as probity, unfair advantage, or inequality, that are not self-evident, with the result that any attempt to translate them into numbers leads only to further controversy and accusations of bad faith.

Finally, there is what I call Corruption 3, the misdeeds that people in any given situation really mind, that they judge to be morally wrong, and that make them feel offended or ashamed or angry. In terms of perspective, this is unlike Corruption 2 because it is not a social diagnosis but a view taken from "inside" a group. In relation to scale, it does not take the form of a panoramic survey but comprises only what the person speaking can know about and pay attention to in the world outside. Unlike the broad judgments and characterizations of Corruption 2, this is a mode that is intrinsically diverse, minute, and self-referential. Nurit Bird-David (2018) has critiqued the "scale-blind" practice by certain anthropologists who somehow make comparable the imaginative world and lifeways of a tiny group—let's say a hamlet of twelve households of hunter-gatherers in India—and some large modern society, or even "the West." She argues that large-scale thinking is a different mode, involving classified, serialized, and standardized entities, whereas the small scale deals in the here-and-now singularity of people, a matrix of close kin, and the presence of a nonhomogeneous diversity of living beings in the vicinity. Taking my cue from this, I suggest that there are "inside" views of corruption, where ethical judgments and emotions arise from particular small-scale possibilities of knowability. Here we find distinctive, intimate modes of practice that are nonregularized and may be transgressive in relation to the practices of Corruption 1 and 2. However, this emphatically does not mean that great actors, such as the president of Russia, cannot adopt a small-scale mode, as will be shown later. So I should clarify, because this differs from Bird-David's discussion of a tiny south Indian forager community, that I am not suggesting that the three scalar modes correspond to different cultures, economies, or types of social existence. In a country like Russia, which has universal education and is saturated with media, very few people, if any, are so cut off as to be entirely *limited* to Corruption 3 thinking. Instead people could in principle adopt the kind of thinking of any of the three modes according to the circumstances and their interlocutors.

People use the everyday vernacular when railing about crooked actions, and so it is relevant that *korruptsiya* is not a native Russian word and has a heavy foreign-sounding feel to it. Avoiding its implicitly authoritarian tone, there is a whole other vocabulary that people use far more readily. The moral values Russians refer to come in a language specific to Russia, with meanings derived from the historical buildup that native words have. A historical aftereffect of the fact that contemporary Russia is a postsocialist country is that for many ordinary people one primary ethical value is *spravedlivost'* (fairness or justice), which is exactly what they lament was lost with the collapse of the socialist institutions that offered, or now seem to have offered, ways of getting redress for wrongs. Fairness is of course not the only ethical principle people may refer to. Shortly I will therefore attempt to provide evidence for the slightly complex point that one key phrase by which people express real anger at activities that in English might be called *corruption* is interpreted in different ways, according to which moral idea is given priority. This phrase is in Russian "brat' ne po chinu" (to take not according to [your] rank). "Taking" (*brat'*) and "thief" (*vor*) are the everyday idioms most commonly used for corruption, which is why they have been taken up and deployed by the opposition leader Alexei Navalny in his slogan-denunciation of Putin's government ("swindlers and thieves"). *Chin*, another ancient word, means "rank," and a *chinnovnik* is a government official. If we return to the Russian official version of Corruption 2, according to which a person with government office should not "take" for personal advantage at all, the Corruption 3 offense of "taking not according to rank" suggests a strange contrary idea, particularly if fairness is what the speaker has in mind. Could it be that in intimate-scale thinking there is nothing so problematic—and even something somehow fair—about "taking *according to* rank"?

Small-scale delineations of corruption are part of, and inseparable from, the existing weave of close social relations and cultural practices of the actors, and so it is unsurprising that they are extremely heterogeneous. The reasons people give for why they find some action to be truly abhorrent ("corrupt") differ in various social circles inside Russia, as I will show. And if we make a comparison between countries, the same point applies even more strongly. This essay is not intended as a global survey, but to illuminate the Russian material by means of contrast let me briefly mention the case of China. Ethnographic studies indicate that, even though China also has an unequal and rank-conscious society, the cardinal small-scale moral fault post-Mao is a different one from Russia's. It is to default on your network of personal mutual help (*guanxi*) and the associated cultivation of human sentiments (*renqing*) (Yan 2014). Now many outside observers, and some Chinese sociologists, have taken these very *guanxi* networks, because they are informal and nontransparent, to constitute corruption in themselves (see discussion in Osburg 2013 and Smart 2018). But that is to adopt Corruption 1 thinking. Intimate-scale corruption in contemporary China is something else: it is the unforgivable twisting of *guanxi* in such a way as to emerge triumphant, to disable your erstwhile friends and cause them to lose power, prestige, and face (*mianzi*). In Russia, taking advantage of a friend's trust is also despicable, but the whole ambiance, vocabulary, and moral import of such an act is different, since it would be viewed as a private betrayal with far fewer social implications of loss of prestige and face.

The Sociopolitical Environment of Corruption in Russia

In order to appreciate why "taking not according to your rank" has become so offensive in Russia—and by this I mean really abhorrent, so much so that people have been killed for this reason—we need to understand certain key political-economic changes that have taken place in the past fifteen years or so. This will give a background explanation of why it is that, amid the clashing waves of Corruption 2, notably the fluctuation of various governmental anticorruption campaigns versus Navalny's movement to unmask and attack that same government for its outrageous venality, what most deeply concerns both Russian rulers and other social groups is none of these campaigns. Instead the evolving sociopolitical environment supplies rationales for intimate versions of Corruption 3 that increasingly diverge in perspective according to the power status of the speaker. Two important recent processes provide my grounds for making these rather cryptic statements. The first of these is the legal reform of administrative ranks under Putin and Medvedev in 2003–4, and the second is the monetization of government that increased markedly from Putin's second presidential term (2004–8).

The reform of bureaucratic ranks sounds arcane—but it was not an empty exercise (*Rossiyskaya Gazeta* 2004). Russian observers (Kordonskii 2008, 2012; Zygar' 2017) argue that the Putin-Medvedev administration, facing the chaotic loss of state sovereignty of the Gorbachev and Yeltsin eras, tried consciously to re-create Russian greatness on the model of the tsarist empire, which was structured by a system of social estates. Until 1917 Russian society was divided hierarchically into nine estates (*sosloviya*, pl. *soslovie*), each of which was subdivided into further ranked subgroups. This was an imperial vision, a legal structure that almost entirely set aside ethnicities, provinces, and religions and instead categorized subjects by birth according to the service of their group to the sovereign, the tsar, and the state. The hierarchy was given by the value accorded by the sovereign to each service (military, religious, agricultural, mercantile, etc.), and the estates were allocated responsibilities, rights, privileges, and exemptions correspondingly. The estates were not equal before the law, nor were their equivalents in Soviet times, and nor are they today. It is true that in the 2003–4 reform the terms "service" (*sluzhba*) and "office" (*dolzhnost'*) were used rather than "estate," but the underlying rationale was the same as earlier: to create a legalized, hierarchical order with rules regulating recruitment to, promotion in, and exit from each status. Two things about these reforms are relevant to the question of corruption. First, the social reality of "estates" as a *system* of collective and internally ranked bodies that are not equal before the law spread, according to the sociologist Simon Kordonskii, far beyond the core services of the bureaucracy, the army, the police, and so forth, extending to all state employees, from forestry inspectors to teachers and doctors, all state dependents, such as pensioners, invalids, and prisoners, and the businesses that are state-owned or reliant on state contracts. This is the large majority of the population. Second, the reform was not just to systematize the ranks across the various professions but also to set out, in a further series of laws, the extraordinarily elaborate signs of differentiated status and esteem, such as titles, dress uniforms, or medals, on the one hand, and the real benefits, like special accommodation, cars and drivers, immunity from prosecution, or free medical treatment, on the other.

Many of the social collectivities that Kordonskii calls "estates" are direct descendants of their Soviet equivalents, and they are celebrated in the same ways. One of these is the annual festive "day of the firefighter," "day of the customs official," and so forth, when the members hold parties and receive congratulatory cards. Today there seem to be far more of these celebratory days than in Soviet times. No service should be forgotten, so virtually every date in the year is dedicated to one (or more) of them. In such ways each profession is told, or tells itself, about its specific value to Russia and the worthiness of the members providing the services.

How does this relate to corruption? An estate's interest lies in obtaining the best possible share of Russia's resources in return for their services. Initially this comes from the state in the form of salaries, allocated housing, and other benefits. But invariably this is seen as insufficient, less than our services are worth. Kordonskiĭ (2008) argues, on the basis of years of detailed fieldwork all over Russia, that an immeasurably larger income is taken by each estate as "rent"—resources acquired from other, less powerful estates for services rendered, an income that is seen as "our due." Some of this is legal; a fascinating appendix to his book details the federal laws entitling members of the FSB (the security service) to commandeer land, goods, buildings, transport, tax benefits, and so forth from any state or nonstate institution. But estates also obtain resources by means that are illegal, such as bribes and kickbacks. From a global perspective, these methods are called "corruption." But from an internal perspective they are the activity of acquiring what the members see as their "fair" (*spravedlivoe*) share of the limited total amount of resources, an income that should be distributed within the estate according to its interior ranks. So what I am suggesting is that a sense of entitlement, collectively cultivated, provides a rationale whereby people can easily assume that "fair" is more than they receive in meager wages. At the same time, it is "unfair" if some other group seems to have more resources or income than is appropriate for their status, and therefore it is legitimate to "take" anything they possess above that level.[4] Many people feel that this situation is unfortunate in a general way. But perhaps it is because the underlying idea of rank is that it reflects *worth* (that is, worth to Russia, to us, and therefore moral and emotional as much as functional), that it only arouses outrage when an individual or a group violates the norms and extorts *far more* than the standing of that profession warrants.

From the government perspective, the illicit externalities of the estate system have been tacitly almost normalized. The rulers of post-Soviet Russia, including Yeltsin and Putin, have not seriously attempted to change the state of affairs. Yeltsin wrote in his memoirs:

How can you force a bureaucrat not to take bribes to feed his family when he earns only 5,000–6,000 rubles per month but is involved in monitoring multi-million ruble transactions? Naturally, the only way is to raise his salary . . . but the State Duma, other politicians and the general public were always sharply opposed. And how could you raise the salaries of the bureaucrats when other state employees, like teachers and doctors, were paid so little? . . . It's probably not just a question of laws. Our mentality itself forces ordinary businesspeople and government clerks to give and take bribes; ever since the Soviet era we've been taught to get around bans and regulations by paying under the table. (Yeltsin 2000: 234–35)

Subsequently Putin is said to have openly supported the proposal around 2011 of the then mayor of Moscow, Gavriil Popov, that bureaucrats should have the right to take "commission" on contracts they approve (Pavlovsky 2014: 55; see also *Argumenty i Fakty* 2010).

The consequence, since the system of "taking according to rank" has been left in place, is that in each town and city there are going rates for bribes, kickbacks, "purchase" of posts, undercover fees for entrance to prestigious colleges, and so forth. There are many firms and institutions that resist and employ transparent contracts and recruitment, but to remain altogether free of the system is almost impossible. The rates go up and down, depending on the state of the local economy. The tariffs are much higher in Moscow than anywhere else, and this is related to the second important development in recent years: the *monetization of government*. In the early 2000s senior functionaries, according to the political journalist Mikhail Zygar' (2017), were not too cunning. The bribes they took from companies were still things like glamorous foreign holidays with their families. That cost the firm a maximum of several thousand dollars, when the contract received in return was worth millions (94). But the next ten years were golden ones for the Moscow power-bureaucracy: their numbers grew three and a half times, and soon many officials understood what their power to say yes or no was really worth. What was the point of taking little offerings in kind (*podachki*) from multimillionaires when they could become one themselves (95)?

Now all this time Russian governments have been promoting anticorruption campaigns. These campaigns are publicized in would-be Transparency International terms, that is, Corruption 1, but they actually operate as Corruption 2 events, in accordance with the accepted rules of the game in Moscow (Ledeneva 2006). In September 2016 Dmitry Zakharchenko, acting head of the Interior Ministry's Main Directorate for Economic Security and Countering Corruption, was arrested on charges of bribery and abuse of power. Officially earning less than US$52,000 a year, Zakharchenko was found to be keeping over US$122 million in rubles and other currencies in one of his many apartments, while his father, mother, four ex-wives, and one daughter had millions in foreign bank accounts. Being actually in charge of Countering Corruption must have been only too tempting, since he only had to warn, for example, a bank that its license was going to be revoked to be able to extract large sums from the frightened bankers, while they hastened to steal billions of rubles from the bank's accounts (RT 2017). It fits with Corruption 2–scale estate thinking that the huge sums found in Zakharchenko's keeping were widely suspected not to be his alone but to be the *obshchak* (common kitty) of his confreres and, as Navalny commented, must have been subject to "work ethics," that is, kept within normative boundaries, since they were well below the vaster sums that could be amassed by someone in the most elevated service, the FSB.[5] Evidently Zakharchenko was just one of many officials doing this kind of thing. Only some are picked off and prosecuted, and obviously not always by the Countering Corruption Directorate! We have to assume that arrests are made essentially for reasons other than the economic crime itself.

This is where we begin to see that the expression "taking not according to rank" can be interpreted in different ways. The supreme moral principle at work in ruling circles, especially in the past few years, is not fairness— anything but—but *vernost'* or *loyal'nost'* (loyalty to a leader or patron). The vital vector here is power rather than money as such, and "rank" implies appropriate subordination. Thus the accusations of corruption that are encoded in the expression "taking not according to rank" can take two divergent, almost opposed perspectival forms. One view, prevalent among the political elite, pastes the corruption label on venality that *defies* loyal adherence to rank; the other, found among everyone else, becomes enraged at the excessive overuse of rank to others' detriment.

Corruption Up Close: In the Center and in the Periphery

In the small circles of top politicians, businessmen, and officials, who regularly alternate places, who know one another intimately, and who dine together in the latest fashionable restaurants, the vectors of power contrive to punish anyone who steps out of line, gets too pushy, starts babbling about democracy, or gives evidence of the slightest disloyalty to the patron at the top. This is also a matter of scale: the vocabulary is an indicator of the tiny number of people envisaged. The group surrounding a paramount boss is called *komanda* (crew, team) or *dvor* (court or household), and within it incidents are resolved according to the logic of closeness to the leader. Membership of such a household is often assimilated with governmental posts, and the state corporations whose resources are then available for raiding are known as *koshel'ki* (little purses) (Gaaze 2016). Bureaucratic protocol is bypassed, or literally overwritten, by the personal and informal, such as encrypted messages or the unsigned, undated, handwritten note, passed also by hand. This last practice, ubiquitous in the top echelons, sharply distinguishes the small scale from any public operation on Corruption 2 scale, for only intimates can recognize the handwriting, decipher the scrawl, and understand the urgency. In one example of such a note the president scribbled over a formal printed letter to two close subordinates (Gaaze 2016: 116). The recipients must have understood that Putin was annoyed: "How can we go on working like this?" he scribbles. He adds a heavy-handed date, doubly underlined, by when his order must be fulfilled, and he adds a peremptory PS: "Look into [what's going on] between Rosneft and Gazprom." In this "household," as Konstantin Gaaze describes it, there are many faults among the courtiers that could end up with an indictment for corruption: too many personal resources, inability to adapt to the leader's swerves in policy, overplaying "closeness" in a way that becomes uncomfortable, or the brazen immodesty of maintaining one's own separate court. But there is an underlying moral idea here: loyalty—despite temptations—to the leader.

I move now to provincial Russia, where ethnographic materials enable me to distinguish the perspectives of the agents of corruption from those who are its victims.[6] In the provinces, regional bosses follow Putin's leadership style as best they can, but the data available to me come from low in the hierarchy, where officials interact directly with ordinary citizens. The voices of these agents give evidence of the estate rationale described earlier, but they also suggest new insights about how it may combine with parochial versions of power—loyalty scenarios. My first case shows how that combination in effect relegates indicators of probity, that is, administrative and legal requirements that may have derived distantly from the precepts of Transparency International, to an irritating and irrelevant hindrance.

In the Siberian town of Ulan-Ude and, in fact, throughout Russia, the tax inspectorate is a prime example of an estate-type body. The payment required to get a job there is so large that a substantial loan must be taken out, which is paid up the chain to the directors, and everyone realizes that the loan can be paid back only by the illicit income of the junior as soon as he has a post. Here is the voice of a tax inspector:

> The fact is that the tax inspectorate is an elite organization, and I am proud to work there. It's not just in our case that they put in their own people—all organizations do that. Because people try to work in an atmosphere of security and calm, and that can only be obtained if the staff are, well, close relatives, whom you can rely on. If I were the boss, I would also insert only my own team [komanda], because only they can be trusted to support me against enemies and accusations. This is what allows us to survive in difficult times at our deserved level [na dostoinom urovne].

He then explained how people who do not play the game, awkward people, the crazies who insist on honesty, are demoted into secretarial roles, where it is not possible to extract money. Or they are jettisoned without remorse, since that frees up another post from which all seniors stand to benefit.

Another tax inspector described his attitude to the law:

> Yes, the tax inspectorate is prestigious, but our salaries are insufficient, and naturally everyone has a passion to raise his takings. You know, there are many ways to enrich yourself. Without stepping on "that" [eto, "the law"], or even if you do step on it, well our criminal code is "square" as they say, and therefore . . . nothing has . . . tfu . . . tfu . . . [spits for luck] . . . consequences . . . [laughs]. If you take me, for example, I am one of the inspectors for private enterprise. I have a private practice, basically, consisting of all the small farmers who trade on the town's central market. Of course, I have to show the results demanded of me by my bosses. And the trader naturally does not want to have to pay all his income in taxes. So I lower his income for him on paper. The taxable sum will appear much less. And naturally, he will be very grateful to me. . . . So it's "I for you and you for me." You understand of course. If it's not money he gives me, it's goods.

Anton Oleinik (2011: 102–9) argues that the enjoyment of sheer power *for its own sake* is a primary value in contemporary Russia, more even than economic gain. Much ethnographic evidence supports this idea, which, if true, of course makes nonsense of the prevailing version of Corruption 2, namely, the view that the abuse of power is universally morally abhorrent. What, in fact, if some people actually take pleasure in the abuse of power? If this enjoyment is pervasive in certain organizations and drives the systems whereby they reproduce themselves, surely this indicates the presence of structural violence. The power vectors of the aptly named "forces" (*sily*), such as the FSB, army, and police, run outward and downward from a central concentration to the tiniest locales. This is why it is important to understand the motivations revealed by the speech of perpetrators and not only those of the victims and outsiders—on all scales. My interviewees indicate that no relation is too petty to give rise to the satisfying feeling of domination, as a conversation with another of the Ulan-Ude tax inspectors shows:

INSPECTOR: If I'm letting someone know he has to pay, well, how can I put it [*laughs*]? They bring it to me themselves. You don't have to say a word. It's in their consciousness. . . . They are ready to do anything to keep in good relations with the powers [*s vlastami*]. This applies to everyone, beginning with the grannies who sell seeds in the market and ending with the big Chinese traders.

RESPONDENT: The grannies? What can they pay?

INSPECTOR: Oh, the grannies are not so innocent. They also sell sourdough, they know what to cut it with, false substances . . . so you can get them for that. Oh yes, they give the dosh [cash] to us; they just wrap it up with the seeds so it all looks very innocent and couldn't be recognized as a bribe. You can do even better getting things out of them with their old Soviet mentality; they were brought up to strive to the utmost and they're scared [*laughs*]. But we have so many sources. The Japanese car method is very serious here, the peak of prestige you could say. Every man's dream is to have a good car. You can buy a car from those guys for a fifth of the market price—that will give the milk cow freedom to trade for six months. Or you can get it for free for a certain period. The time depends on your service position, and the differentiation of ranks is very marked. As a first-rank inspector, I can get a certain car for six months, but a third-rank officer, he can only get that car for a month and a half, or if he's careful for two months. You won't go to him [the "cow"] again for a certain period. But you have him in dependency. Of course, for this you have to know him, what he is capable of, and he has to know you. It's a matter of psychology, you have to know who is breathing what. Taking money without knowing what the person expects is very dangerous. You should take only from people who are dependent on you.

And the higher bosses also want to eat—not just bread and butter but also blood. A chief won't go himself. He's careful to send a deputy. But that will be a close trusted inspector in person, not his deputy or a still lower man because he [the chief] does not want too many people to know about it. He needs to keep the chain short in order to set up a reliable feeding trough [*kormushka*]. He's ready to do anything to keep it operating and to fend off the other "forces" from feeding there too. As for the traders, either they pay up or they cease trading. It's as simple as that.

The citizens of Ulan-Ude accepted as a sad fact of life that they had to pay up to the officials and inspectors. If asked by someone from outside, they would dutifully recognize this as *korruptsiya* in the sense of Corruption 2, but inside they rarely talked that way, since after all most of them were givers and takers of bribes themselves. Some even laughed and said it's not a problem; it's the best way to get things done. It's just a problem for the poor people, the ones who can't afford to pay up. This kind of response suggests that the word *korruptsiya* comes without attachment to any moral moorings. Instead, I suggest, another vocabulary brings into view a different, "realistic," as people say, moral horizon.

A word that springs readily to older people's lips when lamenting the present by comparison with the relatively strict Soviet era, with its laughably small bribes, is "ugliness" (*bezobrazie*, literally "without form"), which also connotes "mess," "outrage," or "disgrace." Meanwhile *beschinstvo* (literally "[acting] without [observation of] rank"), which used to mean improper behavior infringing accepted norms of rank (*chin*), has come to connote wild acts without regard to any rules at all. The people responsible are *nakhal*—presumptuous, brash, brazen, demanders of too much. But *nakhal* is not altogether negative. "Oh, you *nakhal!*" a father might exclaim almost admiringly to his bold-as-brass son. One of the examples of present-day *bezobrazie* that people "take realistically" is the intense pressure on the newcomers in hierarchies such as the customs service or the border guards, forcing them to compete with one another, to conjure up fake diplomas to get a promotion, and to join hostile groups, each struggling to get access to "the most delicious slices of the pie," that is, payments from big businessmen.

In Zabaikal'sk, an impoverished border town near Ulan-Ude, the customs service, according to local accounts, has split into three "clans," the most senior one appointed from and attached to Moscow, a second similarly linked to the regional center, Chita, and a third made up of local Buryats, who are kept in the lower ranks because of ethnic discrimination. The senior officers can become very wealthy in local terms, and young boys dream of getting a place in the service, but still the buccaneering times of the early 2000s, when the tax inspectors blithely expressed their thoughts, have ended. Fifteen years later the local economy is more depressed. The atmosphere is tenser, the divisions have congealed, the illegalities are better hidden, and the potential crackdowns seem more threatening. In Zabaikal'sk around 2016, all of the customs officers, even the Russians, consulted local Buryat shamans. Why? To get protection from the black magic and curses that the "clans" of officers cast on one another. A particularly bitter misfortune, seen by the victim as caused by deliberate magic rather than bad luck or his or her own carelessness, is when an indictment for corruption falls on one's head. Some local people deplore such "ugly" relations, which are rife with mutual suspicion, avarice, and servility, but even so, most simply accept this as the situation within which they have to make a hard living—and they can laugh at its absurdities. For example, the customs officials take money from traders for lowering the tariffs due at the border, but they pay the shaman only with the goods they manage to confiscate. It was once a matter of much amusement when a shaman's fee was a mass consignment of *dutiki* (brightly colored padded nylon winter boots) in many sizes; the shaman gave them out to the people of his village, with the result that everyone from that village appeared for months wearing exactly the same boots.

What is the quality of such laughter? It seems to me like amusement at the irony of the entire situation, in which lofty statist morality coexists as a shell within which other ethical concerns perforce prevail. Bayar, for example, was a Buryat customs officer with a prosperous lifestyle based almost entirely on taking bribes at the border, but he was aware that his ethnicity would prevent him from rising high in the service. He had hung on the wall of his flat a large poster in Russian of the "Moral Code of the Customs Officer." This is typical Corruption 2 material, instructing officers to observe professional standards of propriety, display "collectivism" toward colleagues, be patriotic, follow the law, and respect the attributes of statehood and the traditions and symbolism of the customs service. Bayar said he should know the Code by heart because he had to recite it to a qualifying commission. "Do you really know it by heart?" my amazed friend asked. "Yes," Bayar replied, "I must." But he disobeyed it every day. What concerned him was not that contradiction but that the Buryats in the service had to work harder and more carefully, to be wary of dummies and traps set for them by their enemy-colleagues. Therefore he was determined to focus his efforts only on watertight, trustworthy, high-yielding deals. There was a morality here: it was honesty, friendship, and mutual reinforcement within his own small "clan" and the select traders they had cultivated. This was compatible with Bayar's acceptance of his group's lowly status in the customs service and his knowledge that stepping out of line, "taking not according to rank," would be punished—whether by magic or other means.

Some Concluding Observations

In taking Russia as our example, we are looking at a polity where the leadership, far from determinedly attacking corruption, as in Singapore, Georgia, or Rwanda, instead, while routinely condemning it, in fact richly taps into it in the service of other pressing careerist and geopolitical goals. Most of the population has been convinced by Moscow's chosen political priorities, and therefore, drives to destabilize the government by invoking public anger at sleaze have not yet succeeded. I have attempted to analyze the ambivalence of this situation by suggesting the existence of three different modes by which corruption can be conceptualized and practiced in the same society. We could say that the oppositionist Navalny has attempted to use the quotidian language of Corruption 3 ("swindlers and thieves") in order to attack governmental Corruption 2. But the problem for him is that the two modes operate on different planes, with dissimilar moralities. This can be seen in the contradictory reactions (platitudinous moralizing, amazed laughter, disgust, fear) to what are, in a way, multiscalar events of an ersatz kind: the televised arrests of high politicians, when close-ups of the banknotes hidden in shoe boxes are beamed into each home. Corruption 2 maxims are assumed to be hypocritical and are easily overlaid by the viewer's thought: after all, looking around the world, why shouldn't our leaders be rich? This situation may change in the future, but meanwhile there is one question that requires some kind of answer: What is it that energizes the systemic presence of corruption throughout so many sectors of society? My answer has two aspects. The first concerns the way in which "corrupt" activities are not separated by actors from the struggle for life itself, and the second relates to the framework within which that struggle is currently conceived.

Maybe there is a connection between the half-admiration for the impenitent *nakhal* and the physicality of the images whereby illicit activities are imagined. This goes back to the notion of administrative "organs," which—in fact since Gogol's time—have been described as "feeding" at their troughs (*kormushki*), and continues with the bread, butter, and blood mentioned by respondents as their food, the tax inspector's milk cows, and the *navar* (greasy surface of soup) with which these cows are said to "fatten" and "warm" the organs. Such quasi-biological imagery was omnipresent in the early 2000s, when several respondents insisted that bribery is "natural." One woman, a low-paid hired worker in Ulan-Ude, said, "You know, it's in our mentality, it's in the ancestry, in the blood, and in nature [*v rode, v krove, i v prirode*] from ancient times. So how can I know whether it's a way of life that ought to be like that? True I was educated in Soviet times, so I know bribery is not right—but life makes me do it. Anyway, when you give from your soul . . . that's not a bribe. And if it's a question of life and death, I'd give to anyone!"

Here we can begin to perceive a reversal of conventional (in the West) vectors of virtue. It is as though these people are saying, *From our very lives we are giving the means of life.* A comment made to me recently, for example, was that it was positively virtuous, an act of charity, to bribe a badly paid nurse who was caring for your health. And all this "giving" and "taking" vitalizes that disgraceful, formless world of ours where the *nakhal* are reaching out to grab what they can. One banker laughed, "It's a crime *not to take*! I regard all that [he was referring to kickbacks for providing a loan] as an award [*nagrazhdenie*]." Of course, what is seen as an "award" to the recipient can be regarded as an "offering from below" (*podnoshenie*) by the givers. But both views are consistent with the quasi-biological imagery of a world of ebullient, pulsating action that is nevertheless hypersensitive to status, a world in which the simple transaction between equals that is, at least hypothetically, the basis of capitalism does not exist.

These respondents are again the best guide to the sociopolitical framework in which corruption in their view has to happen. They accepted that almost all resources belong to or are controlled by the state. Because these resources were doled out by state bodies, it was assumed they were finite and scarce. And because access was limited, actors took it for granted that gatekeeping officials would be powerful. What differentiates today from Soviet times is that instead of allocation being regulated by an austere and distant plan, it is now an intense struggle—in which we ourselves rush to take part. As one manager of an office equipment company said:

An official who sits in a chair, however honest he is, sooner or later he will be in a position where he has to make a decision. If the decision depends personally on him, that is where bribery will come in. It's elementary, like the rules of the road. If there is a plain no-entry sign, then no one can drive there. But in Russia we put an old boy to stand by the sign with a stick and we have to ask him whether we can enter or not. Sooner or later, honest, honest, honest as he may be, he'll act on the basis of friendship. And we ourselves will start to make offers to him, because we want to go down the road. It's the same everywhere in the economy. As soon as you get a list of exceptions or privileges, Afghan veterans let's say, or Russian Orthodox clergy, then it turns out they can go down the road, but I can't. . . . Why should I have to pay when they don't?

It was not the fact that there are high and low, rich and poor in Russia that angered this man, nor even corruption as such, which he regarded as inevitable or "immortal," as he put it. It was that the life struggle had been set up to be unequal, the rules were not the same for everyone. In ordinary people's accounts, Russian citizens share with the low-income Indian citizens described by Veena Das (2015b: 333) the thought that corruption is not an attribute of persons but an attribute of the tangle of relations in a particular environment. Yet it seems that the aspiration in Russia is subtly different from that described by Das for India: it is not for a "purified polity" (322) but for a just and fair one. *Corruption* as a term in the lexicon for our world needs to be understood critically, in such a way that can take account of such differences.

Notes

1. Wikipedia, "Коррупция," accessed May 2018, https://ru.wikipedia.org/wiki/коррупция. My translation.

2. Wikipedia, "Corruption in India," accessed September 24, 2020, https://en.wikipedia.org/wiki/Corruption_in_India.

3. "Na khaunga, na khaane doonga," quoted in Mathur 2017: 1796.

4. In the case of businesses and self-employed people working outside the estate system, that is, those working in the part of the market that is most independent of the state, their entire enterprise is fair game (Oleinik 2011).

5. See photographs at Naval'nyi 2016.

6. Ethnographic quotations derive from a research project on bribery conducted in the Buryat Republic (Russia) and in Mongolia in 2002–3. Interviews were recorded by colleagues from the locale, some of whom were close to and trusted by the interviewees. The respondents were from all the local ethnicities, were both rural and urban, aged from young children to pensioners, and covered a wide range of occupations, from bankers to manual workers. The interviews are of their time; see the text concerning ways in which the situation changed by 2017 and 2018.

OPENNESS 10

TODD SANDERS AND ELIZABETH F. SANDERS

In March 2017, for the first time in its 140-year history, the *Washington Post* added an official slogan to its familiar masthead: "Democracy Dies in Darkness." Social media came alive. Though many saw the addition as an indirect—and fitting—reply to President Donald Trump for his frequent attacks on the *Post* and other "fake news media," the newspaper said otherwise: it had borrowed the slogan and had chosen it long before the election. Jeff Bezos, the paper's owner, had in fact used the phrase in an interview the previous May. "I think a lot of us believe this," he said then, "that democracy dies in darkness, that certain institutions have a very important role in making sure that there is light" (Farhi 2017). Bezos reportedly heard it from Bob Woodward, the legendary investigative reporter and *Post* associate editor, who used the phrase in a 2015 talk on his latest book about Watergate. Woodward, for his part, claims he read it years earlier in a judicial opinion in a First Amendment case. "It goes way back," Woodward said. "It's definitely not directed at Trump. It's about the dangers of secrecy in government, which is what I worry about most. The judge who said it got it right."[1] Thus if the *Post*'s first-ever slogan captures the zeitgeist for many, it is also as old as its message is clear: darkness and secrecy threaten democracy, while light and openness make it stronger.

Yet this urge to open, so vital these days to many, points to a tension at the core of liberal democracy: if openness is the goal, how are we to manage necessary closures? Not everything, after all, can or should be opened up. Openness's others—concealment, opacity, ambiguity, and secrecy—are essential to the realization of public goods such as privacy and intellectual property rights, commercial value, safety, and security. Openness must be both championed and contested. But as controversies attending

Wikileaks and whistleblowers, NSA spying and Facebook data-harvesting attest, there are no simple formulas by which to achieve apposite openness, and no enduring solutions. What works at one time and place seems suspect at another. Changing public expectations around democratic participation, technological innovations, and the waxing and waning of trust in our public and private institutions ensure that openness continues to be actively pursued, while also being difficult to define and achieve. One casualty of this complexity is any easy equation relating democracy, openness, and light.

In what follows we explore some of the complexities, complications, and contradictions that pursuing openness entails today. We do so by attending closely to particular Euro-American institutions concerned with science for governance. These institutions are engaging with a new push for openness, avidly debating the changing knowledge and governing practices that it entails. For some, this push is about embracing the possibilities that inhere in our rapidly advancing information technologies: more democratic politics and more innovative sciences. For others, it is the necessary antidote to an erosion of trust in our public institutions—science and government among them. Yet whatever the motivations, the means by which openness is being realized are remarkably similar. We might also say they have a distinctly twenty-first-century texture.

For the institutions we examine, opening is today about anatomizing—exposing, detailing, and documenting—the processes by which knowledge and decisions are made. It demands probing, ever deeper, into those processes, laying bare the routines, procedures, and practices that in times past were inaccessible to many. But more than this, opening means extending an invitation to participate in, and not merely spectate, these newly visible processes. "Open data," which many governments and sciences are increasingly pursuing, encapsulates what is on offer.[2] It promises to harness the power of information infrastructures so that anyone—scientists, policymakers, journalists, ordinary citizens—can access raw data, reproduce analyses, double-check conclusions, and thus trust scientific findings and government decisions. By opening up processes, democracy and science will thrive. That, at least, is the plan.

But institutionalizing new practices of openness is rarely simple. That tension, that question of how to manage necessary closures, turns out to be devilishly complex in practice. As we shall see, "opening up" is reworking many things: the roles that citizens, experts, and their knowledges play in decision making; what science is, who is allowed in, and who gets to say; and the basis on which the public trusts science and accords it a privileged role in democratic governance. Adding to the complexity is the moral matrix with which we began: for democracy to thrive, we must throw open the doors and let in light. Yet as opening shifts the balance, sometimes subtly, between what can legitimately be open and closed, and what openness and its others might mean, some are caught unprepared. Formerly tenable positions suddenly seem morally dubious and generate suspicion. Defending these positions becomes a morally complicated enterprise.

To explore these issues, we consider two controversies. The first is Climategate, that infamous scandal that followed the unauthorized release of thousands of private emails and documents from the Climatic Research Unit at the University of East Anglia in England. Climategate did many things. Chief among them was to capture and crystallize—if momentarily—a shift in public thinking around openness, scientific practices, and democratic governance. Our second example is the US Honest and Open New EPA Science Treatment (HONEST) Act of 2017, a bill introduced to the US Congress to ensure that the Environmental Protection Agency base future regulations on open science. Since its introduction in 2014 as the Secret Science Reform Act, the HONEST Act has proven to be a lightning rod for debates over what science is, its role in governance, and who gets to say. Together these examples provide insights into the curious alliances, novel tensions, and surprising paradoxes that contemporary practices of openness sometimes entail. They show, too, how much the grounds on which science for governance works are shifting and how hard it can be to defend long-standing scientific practices, which are increasingly cast as secretive, suspect, and morally untenable.

One story commonly told about these controversies is familiar: science is under siege. For liberal pundits, this has much to do with the resurgence of right-wing populism in North America and Europe and the antiestablishment, antielite, and antiscience agendas that come with it. Our intervention complicates such explanations. As we shall see, an "openness" lens casts these controversies in a particular hue, and partisan explanations in a peculiar light. We will argue that although many of our institutions, including science for governance, are being seriously challenged at the moment, the recent push for openness is itself contributing substantially to those challenges. But first, a few words about openness in government and science today.

Practicing Openness in Government and Science

Western liberal democracies have long been bound up with ideas of openness. Yet these days we find very particular expressions of "open government," ones that emerge from older precepts and practices but also differ markedly from them. Consider President Obama's 2009 Memorandum on Transparency and Open Government, which provides one familiar expression of open government today: transparency, participation, collaboration. *Transparency* promotes accountability by ensuring that government agencies rapidly disclose information and data to the public; *participation* invites citizens in to contribute ideas and expertise to executive departments and agencies so government can make better policy; *collaboration* ensures that executive departments and agencies cooperate among themselves and with nonprofit organizations, businesses, and the private sector. Obama's memorandum was given bite by the US Office of Management and Budget's Open Government Directive, which instructed executive departments and agencies "to take immediate, specific steps to open their doors and data to the American people" (US Department of State n.d.).[3]

The British government is making similar moves, committed as it is "to being the most transparent government in history" (UK Cabinet Office 2016). At the time of writing, Britain, a cofounder of the Open Government Partnership, is in the midst of its third Open Government National Action Plan.[4] Central to the plan is the idea that "governments and institutions work better for citizens when they are transparent, engaging and accountable" (UK Cabinet Office 2016). This is why the British government has made over twenty-seven thousand data sets—and more—available online; strengthened its Freedom of Information Act's code of practice and other rules and laws that enable citizens to hold public authorities to account; and has done so, through the UK Open Government Network, in collaboration with ordinary citizens. As the minister for the cabinet office and paymaster general put it, "Open government means accepting that we don't have all the answers, and putting data and power in the hands of people who might. . . . [T]his is about continuing to change the way we govern. We want to build a Britain where the citizen is editor as well as a reader, where we use data to make decisions, and where a free society, free markets and the free flow of information all combine to drive our success in the 21st century" (UK Cabinet Office 2016).[5]

Here as elsewhere good governance means open governance. And in this context, openness means letting people in: to inspect, use, and challenge government information, tools, and data; and to witness, at close range, the wheels of government as they turn. Openness is an invitation to participate in, and thus trust, the democratic process.

For scientists, openness is at once an epistemic and a political virtue. The British Royal Society's centuries-old motto, *Nullius in verba*—Take nobody's word for it—implies that good science is open science, that to be trusted, science must be open to critical scrutiny. In a recent report, the society reaffirmed the place of open inquiry at the heart of the scientific enterprise. Yet times are changing, they observed, and what scientific openness means in practice is changing with them. Today openness means attending closely to scientific processes. This era requires "a more intelligent openness: data must be accessible and readily located; they must be intelligible to those who wish to scrutinise them; data must be assessable so that judgements can be made about their reliability and the competence of those who created them; and they must be usable by others" (Boulton et al. 2012: 7).

The Royal Society is not alone. Openness is currently a matter of concern for many in the scientific research ecology: scientists, research funders, journal editors, and research users variously situated in universities, government, nonprofit organizations, professional associations, and industry. Some speak of an open science movement. Others practice Open Science. Many simply reassert the importance of openness, while reworking what it means in practice. They are variously committed to open-source software and/or open data, and for varied reasons.[6]

For some, open science is the answer to the "reproducibility crisis": a loss of confidence among some biomedical and behavioral scientists in the reliability of published research findings in their fields. This crisis has occasioned media attention, parliamentary inquiries, multi-stakeholder meetings, and new research programs that examine the conduct of diverse sciences and scientists. One outcome is that five thousand scientific journals and organizations have signed up to and are variously implementing the 2015 Transparency and Openness Promotion guidelines. These guidelines encourage a greater anatomization of the research process in published reports and the provision of research data and codes in accessible, reusable formats on publication. For many journals—including flagship journals such as *Nature* and *Science*—such openness is becoming the default requirement.

Open science, say some, will also accelerate the pace of scientific discovery and innovation. Consider the Center for Open Science (n.d.), a nonprofit organization established in 2013. "Wouldn't it be great if solutions for our most pressing challenges could be found faster and cheaper? They can. OPEN SCIENCE." The center spearheaded the development of the Transparency and Openness Promotion guidelines and also supports the Open Science Framework, a free open-source software platform for managing scientific workflow. It is developing electronic platforms to facilitate and accelerate interdisciplinary communication and a hub where researchers can store and share files, protocols, and data. The head of the Chan Zuckerberg Initiative agrees. They "want all of biomedical science to be faster, more robust, shareable and scalable" and aim to "be a leader in bringing biology towards the level of sharing that's expected in the physical and computer sciences" (Bargmann 2018: 21). To this end, the initiative is funding both scientific infrastructure projects and software engineers and computational biologists who are working on new data platforms and tools for biomedical science.

For still others, open science stands to strengthen civil society, or even to remake it independent of corporate and state power (see Kelty 2008). Open source, for example, invites tech-savvy publics to inspect, copy, use, modify, and share software's source code—to be, that is, editors, creators, and collaborators, not just readers, in the public sphere. And open source and open data are mandated more and more by national funding bodies, since these practices "reduce barriers to communication, foster S[cience] & E[ngineering] research, and provide a platform for innovation that will contribute to the economic prosperity and well-being of American citizens" (National Science Foundation 2015: 2).

In short, our institutions of science and government are engaged in similar projects of opening—employing similar means, sometimes to similar ends, even while their ends and contexts may also differ. Yet open science and open government also explicitly encounter each other whenever and wherever evidence-based policymaking—another emblem of this era of openness—is being negotiated. The resulting interferences can amplify contestations and highlight the stakes in further opening and democratizing our institutions. Adding to the mix is the fact that science in this context is underdetermining, often uncertain, and most know this. This makes controversies surrounding science for governance particularly instructive.

Climategate

When the UK Freedom of Information Act (FOIA) and the Environmental Information Regulations (EIR) came into effect in January 2005, climate change skeptics in Britain and elsewhere were ready. Some had been requesting for years—to little avail—that scientists at the Climatic Research Unit (CRU), University of East Anglia, release their raw data and data sets, as well as their email correspondence related to the Fourth Assessment Report from the Intergovernmental Panel on Climate Change (IPCC). The new legislation, which had jurisdiction over British public authorities—including universities—promised to facilitate their efforts. Yet initially at least, it did not. As FOIA and EIR requests multiplied—for data, weather station identifiers, emails, methodologies, and computer code—CRU scientists, supported by their university, regularly found reasons to deny the requests: confidentiality agreements existed between CRU and different national meteorological organizations that supplied the data; it would adversely affect intellectual property rights or international relations; the data and code were already publicly available elsewhere; IPCC work was exempt from any particular nation's freedom of information requests. Off the record, but not for long, CRU's scientists were anxious and frustrated that they were faced with enabling the very people who they believed sought to undermine their work.

Then came the hack, or the leak, or the unauthorized disclosure, as some less presumptively called it. It happened in late November 2009, when thousands of private emails, text files, PDFs, Word documents, spreadsheets, and source code were taken from a CRU backup server and made public on the internet. "We feel that climate science is, in the current situation, too important to be kept under wraps," said an anonymous post on a climate-skeptic blog, along with a link to the data. "We hereby release a random selection of correspondence, code, and documents. Hopefully it will give some insight into the science and the people behind it."[7]

Almost immediately climate skeptics' worst suspicions were confirmed. The emails, said skeptics in the blogosphere, revealed much about climate science, none of it noble: leading climate scientists had deliberately and systematically manipulated climate data, arbitrarily adjusted them, cherry-picked them, misrepresented them, hidden them, lost them, and, when necessary, deleted them to support their predetermined conclusions about global warming. Some email snippets went viral ("Mike's *Nature* trick" to "hide the decline" in proxy temperatures derived from tree ring analysis). What's more, skeptics charged, the emails showed that climate scientists had schemed to keep contrary views out of peer-reviewed publications and the IPCC's Fourth Assessment Report.

If the conspiracy seemed large, which to many it did, the implications were larger still. This is because the CRU was no bit player in climate change science but a vital node in the network. It had pioneered work in two areas: using tree ring data to estimate the earth's temperature over the last millennium and instrumental temperature measurements to calculate how much the average temperature of the earth's land mass was changing. Relatedly, through years of labor, it had compiled the world's first and most comprehensive gridded data set of surface temperatures. CRU's work was significant and cited prominently in IPCC assessments. To lose trust in CRU was to lose trust in climate science, the IPCC's conclusions, and any future climate policies.

Eight separate official inquiries investigated the allegations raised by Climategate. In Britain, two were commissioned by the University of East Anglia (Muir Russell et al. 2010; Oxburgh et al. 2010), while the House of Commons Science and Technology Select Committee conducted its own.[8] Inquiries operated independently, and their remits complemented rather than replicated one another. The Independent Climate Change E-mails Review, for instance, led by Sir Muir Russell, considered the scientists' behavior—their honesty, rigor, and openness—by scrutinizing CRU's processes, procedures, and data-handling practices, whereas the Scientific Assessment Panel, chaired by Lord Oxburgh, examined the integrity of their publications, asking whether scientists had dishonestly selected, manipulated, or presented climate data to support predetermined conclusions. These inquiries were composed of eminent scientists, senior civil servants, and seasoned administrators. The parliamentary inquiry, for its part, dwelt on the accuracy and availability of data, data sets, and computer code, asking how accessible CRU's data and methodologies actually were.

In the end, all official inquiries into Climategate exonerated CRU scientists of any deliberate scientific malpractice. The emails, they agreed, made sense in context; they were evidence not of conspiracies and scientific misconduct but of science in action. The honesty, rigor, and integrity of the scientists were not in doubt. Nor was their science. Consequently the IPCC's conclusions on global warming remained robust. On these fronts, the inquiries concluded, skeptics were simply wrong.

Curiously enough, though, climate skeptics were on other fronts—punning aside—all too right. For they had long insisted, in word and in deed, that climate science should be open to scrutiny. Others agreed, including the scientists, policymakers, members of Parliament, civil servants, and others involved in official inquiries into Climategate. The Independent Climate Change E-mails Review roundly criticized the "ethos of minimal compliance (and at times non-compliance) by the CRU with both the letter and spirit of the FOIA and EIR" (Muir Russell et al. 2010: 93). The House of Commons inquiry panned the CRU and University of East Anglia for their "culture of non-disclosure." A major finding of both inquiries was that CRU and the University of East Anglia had to open up.

Yet not any old openness would do. Rather, the inquiries proffered their vision of openness and clear recommendations on how to achieve it: CRU scientists must make all their data public—including raw data—as well as the methods by which they reached their conclusions. They should have done so long ago. This was not about making scientific findings available but laying bare, in a timely manner, the processes of their production. This is precisely the sort of openness that climate skeptics and others had been after all along.

For the Oxburgh Panel, this meant archiving data and algorithms and documenting expert judgments made during data handling and analysis. The Independent Climate Change E-mails Review, for its part, pointed to NASA's Goddard Institute for Space Studies as one promising model: they had made the source code for their own gridded data set publicly available. The review also singled out a recent US National Academy of Sciences report and urged CRU scientists to heed its advice: "The default assumption should be that research data, methods (including the techniques, procedures and tools that have been used to collect, generate or analyze data, such as models, computer code and input data) and other information integral to a publically reported result will be publically accessible when results are reported" (Muir Russell et al. 2010: 104).

One reason to open up climate science in this way was to strengthen it. Making data and methods readily available was necessary, the inquiries maintained, so that others—whoever, wherever, and whenever they were—could in principle replicate and validate CRU's findings (see, e.g., Muir Russell et al. 2010: 36, 49; Oxburgh et al. 2010: 3).[9] Inquiries were subtle on the question of replication. In its own trial analysis of CRU's Land Temperature Record (CRUTEM), for instance, the Independent Climate Change E-mails Review found that because 90 percent of the raw primary instrumental temperature data were publicly available, and the required computer code was straightforward and easy to write, any independent researcher could, as they had done, test CRUTEM analysis "quite precisely" and obtain "very similar" results. This was one form of replication. In this context, however, the review stressed the need for higher standards of disclosure to enable more precise replication: CRU's climatologists should have made available an unambiguous list of *all* the stations used in each version of CRUTEM so that anyone could in principle trace their exact steps from start to finish. This could only strengthen the science.

But there was another reason the inquiries insisted that CRU open up like this: because the world was changing, even if many climatologists hadn't noticed. If ever there were times when scientists and bureaucrats worked behind closed doors in the public interest, when experts said and people did, when the public trusted experts to work that way, disinterestedly and for the greater good, those times were gone. Garnering trust these days—particularly trust in science for governance—required more work. It meant not waiting for Freedom of Information requests to act, but proactively opening up; it meant making all methods and data widely usable and publicly available in good time so that others could interrogate them; it meant being open, in short, precisely as the inquiries had prescribed. Unduly withholding information, or hiding behind confidentiality agreements, expertise, or the IPCC, was indefensible. The fact that "it is not standard practice in climate science to publish the raw data and the computer code in academic papers" was no defense either.[10] It had *to become* standard practice. Given their work's public, political, and policy import, CRU scientists would have to learn to live life in a fishbowl.

Their failure to do so, the inquiries noted, had had dire consequences. It had fueled suspicions and accusations that climatologists were up to no good, that they were doing secret science because they had something to hide, namely, the fact that their science was unsound, biased, ideological, and interested. Though these suspicions and accusations proved baseless, the conditions that enabled them stood to dent public trust in climate science and thus its usefulness for policy. Openness would not guarantee trust, but not being open enough was bound to generate distrust. CRU scientists, said the inquiries, were the architects of their own problems.

The Liberal Democrat MP and chair of the House of Commons Science and Technology Committee from 1997 to 2010, Phil Willis, captured the tenor in his summary of the House of Commons inquiry: "Climate science is a matter of global importance. On the basis of the science, governments across the world will be spending trillions of pounds on climate change mitigation. The quality of the science therefore has to be irreproachable. What this inquiry revealed was that climate scientists need to take steps to make available all the data that support their work and full methodological workings, including their computer codes. Had both been available, many of the problems at CRU could have been avoided" (UK Parliament 2010).

CRU climatologists and University of East Anglia administrators accepted the inquiries' mixed findings with grace. CRU's director, Phil Jones—"We have maintained all along that our science is honest and sound"—felt vindicated. The university's vice-chancellor responded to the main criticism of the Independent Climate Change E-mails Review: "We accept the report's conclusion that we could and should have been more proactively open, not least because—as this exhaustive report makes abundantly clear—we have nothing to hide. The need to develop a culture of greater openness and transparency in CRU is something that we faced up to internally some months ago and we are already working to put right" (University of East Anglia 2010).

And they did put things right when, a year later, the UK information commissioner compelled them under threat of law to release their comprehensive gridded data set of surface temperatures. The commissioner's ruling did not come from nowhere; it was the outcome of an appeal against an earlier freedom of information request that the university had denied. It had cited specific regulations to justify that denial: the information was already publicly available and easily accessible; there would be adverse effects on international relations, on the interests of the information provider, and on intellectual property rights. The commissioner, however, was not satisfied with the university's reasoning around those regulations, wherein "the threshold to justify non-disclosure is a high one." He ruled that even if most of the data were publicly available elsewhere, CRU had a duty to make *all* the data available; that CRU had not shown that releasing their data would adversely affect international relations or data providers; and that "their" data were not theirs but were the property of the public authority that employed them. The commissioner gave the university thirty-five days to release their massive, gridded data set, which they did—thirty-four days later.

If this was our new world of openness, then previous settlements over the relations among science, policy, politics, and varied publics were clearly under revision, or gone. Conventional scientific practices were under serious strain as many more publics were welcomed in. Yet one might wonder how the climatologists could have missed this world in the first place, and the diverse constituencies busily making it. One answer is that climate science had since the 1980s moved from being a relatively unglamorous, secluded science to one of immense public interest, and the climatologists suddenly found themselves in the limelight and unprepared. They knew their science. But they were now in a domain of science for governance, where public accountability worked differently. Here, in their newly found workplace, people wanted in, and were morally and legally entitled to be in: to see and scrutinize the science that stood to shape their lives. Conventional scientific modes of accountability and work practices were misaligned with the prevailing "openness" requirements and all too easily signaled "secrecy," "hiddenness," "bias," "interests," "ideology," even "conspiracy." Doubling down on science-as-usual made matters worse.

Truth be told, though, CRU scientists' task was never simple, not least because they were moving into a realm that was itself in motion. Expectations and practices of openness in science for governance were under revision. New legislation had come into effect; demands for evidence-based policy were growing; the blogosphere was spawning new forms of sociality and skepticism; professional scientific societies were doing the same; and much besides. For these scientists, it was the perfect storm, but a fast-changing one too. Under such conditions it would not have been obvious what, if any, settlement over openness might eventually transpire, or how exactly one should navigate in the interim.

Though the inquiries brought the Climategate affair to a close, the settlement in question is still under negotiation and revision—including in places where science for governance has been the main preoccupation all along. On this score, the HONEST Act proves instructive.

The HONEST Act

For the past few years, American lawmakers have been working hard to legislate open science for open government. In March 2017 the HONEST Act (H.R. 1430) passed in the US House of Representatives. Its aim was clear: to require that the Environmental Protection Agency (EPA) make regulations based on "the best available science" and that the underlying scientific and technical information be specifically identified and "publicly available online in a manner that is sufficient for independent analysis and substantial reproduction of research results." The act further specified what "scientific and technical information" includes: materials, data, and associated protocols to understand, assess, and extend conclusions; computer code and models involved in the creation and analysis of such information; recorded factual materials; and detailed descriptions of how to access and use such information.

The chairman of the House Committee on Science, Space, and Technology, Congressman Lamar Smith, explained the rationale:

> The American people foot the bill for the EPA's billion dollar regulations and they have the right to see the underlying data. If the EPA has nothing to hide, and if their data really justifies their regulations, why not make the information public? Data sharing is becoming increasingly common across scientific disciplines. The legislation requires that EPA science be available for validation and replication. Americans impacted by EPA regulations have a right to see the data and determine for themselves if the agency's actions are based on sound science or a partisan agenda. The bill ensures transparency and accountability. The American people deserve the facts. And so does good policy. (Committee on Science, Space, and Technology 2014)

This probably sounds familiar. The act is in tune with the times and could easily have come from British Parliament or the US National Academy of Sciences. But it didn't. It came from Lamar Smith, a Republican representative from Texas. It was cosponsored by twenty-eight fellow Republicans in the House and widely endorsed by conservatives and industry. When it passed in the House, it did so along largely party lines. The HONEST Act has a history too. It began life as the Secret Science Reform Act of 2014, a bill that twice passed in the House but died in the Senate. That act also garnered support from conservative forces: industry groups ranging from the US Chamber of Commerce to the American Chemistry Council; select Ivy League professors, scientists, and physicians; and former EPA officials. In its travels, the act has changed. Its latest iteration is less sweeping and includes some outs: "any personally identifiable information, trade secrets, or commercial or financial information obtained from a person and privileged or confidential, shall be redacted prior to public availability."

Supporters of both bills worried, and still do, about technocracy and the creeping administrative state. Mindful of the gray zones between rule-making and lawmaking, many see the EPA as pushing a liberal agenda and using environmental and health sciences that cannot be adequately scrutinized to do so. The HONEST Act, they insist, would ensure that the EPA is more accountable to the publics it serves, that their regulations are made above board, based not on special interests or politicized science but on the best available science. It would do so by laying bare the EPA's regulatory process—including the processes of production of the science that underpins regulations—for anyone to see and contest. Open science for open governance. Or as Congressman Smith put it, "The days of 'trust me' science are over" (Committee on Science, Space, and Technology 2017).

But not everyone agrees. Given its origins and history, the HONEST Act is for many a dishonest act, another unwelcome offensive in the "Republican war on science" (Mooney 2005). Democrats, journalists, scholars, scientists, and environmentalists routinely condemn the bill, arguing that its supporters misunderstand science and are pushing a "nakedly antiscience agenda" (*Scientific American* 2017: 10) to further right-wing politics. If the bill were to become law, critics charge, it would ensure that EPA regulations are based on less science, not more, worse science, not better, and severely curtail the EPA's ability to fulfill its statutory duties.

Criticisms of the HONEST Act vary. Most, however, paint it in one of three ways, and sometimes all three at once: as unworkable, undesirable, unnecessary. On the unworkability front, opening data creates problems. How might one protect the privacy of individuals who participate in the large-scale epidemiological, medical, and public health studies that the EPA relies on to make regulations? How to protect trade secrets? Commercial and financial information? Clearly not all data can be opened up. But where are the limits? Who would have access to which data? And crucially, who decides? If studies whose data were not fully available were disallowed, the EPA's ability to use "the best available science" to make rules would be compromised. Then there are the costs: implementing the act would be expensive, and the bill makes inadequate budgetary provisions. The act's language, many agree, is also unworkable, since it lacks precision on key scientific concepts such as reproducibility, independent analysis, materials, and data. For scientists, these concepts are complex and invite many questions. What do *reproducibility* or *independent analysis* mean in practice? What about science that cannot be strictly replicated—the science, say, surrounding the Deepwater Horizon Gulf oil spill? Would that too be disallowed in EPA rulemaking? And what of those sciences for whom reproducibility is not common practice, or even an aspiration? These vital questions, critics argue, cannot be left to legislators to answer.

Even if the HONEST Act were workable, for many it remains undesirable. This is because, critics claim, it politicizes science. Science works best—and best serves government—when politics are kept at bay. "I've always had a hard time understanding why members of Congress like to tell scientists how to conduct their research," said Democratic Congressman Bill Foster, who is also a physicist. "Scientists should set the standards for research.

Not politicians" (Atkin 2017). On this score, the American Association for the Advancement of Science's objection to the HONEST Act speaks for many: "We urge caution in setting laws that submerge science beneath politics."[11]

Finally, many suggest that the HONEST Act is unnecessary because our existing scientific institutions, procedures, and control mechanisms work fine. The Environmental Data and Governance Initiative (EDGI), an organization set up by academics and nonprofit employees to promote open and accessible government data and evidence-based policymaking, explains its opposition to the HONEST Act this way: "While EDGI supports improvements to transparency in the EPA's scientific decision-making processes and recognizes the importance of public data accessibility, it also recognizes that the EPA already has processes in place to ensure the quality and relevance of data used in decision-making, including internal and external peer review and review by scientific advisory boards" (Underhill et al. 2017: 7). Science advocacy groups express similar views, as did the director of the Center for Science and Democracy at the Union of Concerned Scientists in regard to the Secret Science Reform Act: "Most often, it is not the raw data and materials the public and decision makers need access to, but the studies that have gone through the scientific process, with peer review and its checks and balances. To ensure science-based decision making, the relevant science must be reviewed by experts in the field. This is the important watchdog role that ensures it is the best available science, not the examination of raw data by politicians. Access to this synthesis of scientific information is what should be of public concern" (Rosenberg 2014).

The cumulative effect of such criticisms is to suggest that it is scientists who should manage the scientific process, while only the outcome should concern everybody else. The suggestion is that scientists are best positioned to understand the intricacies of, and to adjudicate over, complex questions surrounding their work practices; that science and scientists must remain autonomous and untainted by politics to do so; and that scientists, through peer review and scientific advisory boards, should evaluate and warrant scientific knowledge. Many criticisms of the HONEST Act thus converge around a familiar position: "Trust Science."

But it is this position, and the particular institutional arrangements it defends, that the current push for openness challenges. It isn't simply a matter of science under siege by ideologically inspired antiscience forces. As we noted at the outset, many institutions, governments, scientists, and others these days are rather certain that science and its inner workings can be, should be, and must be further opened to scrutiny and wider participation, and for myriad reasons. What's more, institutional practices are changing accordingly, if sometimes subtly, cautiously, and not without resistance (see, e.g., Pels et al. 2018; International Consortium 2016). The US National Science Foundation and National Institutes of Health have made open access, data preservation, and data sharing central pillars of their funding practices. The US-based Bill and Melinda Gates Foundation and UK-based Wellcome Trust have done the same. The European Commission also recently moved to make open data the default for its Horizon 2020 program, one of the biggest research funding programs in the world. Researchers may legitimately demur, but open data is now the default in such settings. Closures must be defended.

So too for our institutions of government, which share so many of their knowledge practices with scientific institutions (and, of course, that are often one and the same). This includes the EPA, which, in its own inquiry into Climategate, endorsed the Independent Climate Change E-mails Review's recommendations for "greater transparency in the future in this area of climate research" (US Environmental Protection Agency 2010: 49582). It, too, is institutionalizing forms of openness that inch ever closer to those envisioned by the HONEST Act. On her appointment as EPA administrator in 2009, Lisa Jackson (2009) reaffirmed the agency's long-standing commitment to openness: "I have the utmost confidence in the ability of the EPA's workforce to promote full public involvement and openness in all EPA affairs. I believe this will enhance the credibility of the Agency, boost public trust in our actions and improve the quality of our decisions. In short, we will let more sunlight into our Agency."

According to the "U.S. Environmental Protection Agency Open Government Plan 4.0" (2016b), thousands of EPA data sets were publicly available online; the agency had "made a major step towards systematizing Open Data as a key tenet of the Agency's operating principles"; and the public was being invited to participate in EPA rulemaking processes through www.regulations.gov. (The site solicits public input but does not identify or make publicly available the scientific data underpinning proposed rules.) In line with other research-funding agencies and current legislation, the agency was also taking steps to increase public access to EPA-funded science, including to peer-reviewed publications *and* digital research data (US Environmental Protection Agency 2016a).

Yet there are no inevitabilities. With the election of Donald J. Trump as president and the appointment of a new EPA administrator, academics, hackers, coders, archivists, and librarians—including many opponents of the HONEST Act—rushed to rescue government scientific data from EPA servers, worried it would soon be secreted away.[12] As one librarian and co-founder of Data Refuge told the *New York Times*, "No one would advocate for a system where the government stores all scientific data and we just trust them to give it to us" (Harmon 2017).

As of now, the HONEST Act's future is unclear as the bill sits idle, awaiting its moment in the Senate. Yet the wider conversation over openness, trust, science, and governance carries on. One only need mention the OPEN Government Data Act, part of the Evidence-Based Policymaking Act, which garnered broad bipartisan support in Congress and was signed into law by President Trump in January 2019. Building on President Obama's Open Data Policy (Obama White House 2013), the law requires federal agencies to publish much of their data proactively online in open, machine-readable, nonproprietary formats. In this conversation participants, willing and un-willing alike, are engaging on shifting and at times uncomfortable ground. Previous arrangements of what is legitimately open and closed, what these terms might mean, what science is, and its role in governance are being questioned, rearticulated, and remade. Under such conditions it can be difficult to argue persuasively for trust in long-standing scientific knowl-edge practices—peer review and other forms of expert assessment—which from certain angles increasingly appear retrograde, atavistic, elitist, even antidemocratic. In today's world such arguments also all too readily trans-mogrify into defenses of secrecy, hiddenness, treachery, interests, and conspiracy and rapidly power down. Just ask CRU climatologists. Gaining one's footing on such shifting terrain and mustering compelling argu-ments for what have become "closures" is no mean feat. Paradoxically, for those working to reassert the value of scientific expertise, expert judgment, and conventional scientific knowledge practices in policy settings, open-ness is creating dark times indeed.

Conclusion

Openness is today a word on many lips: those of journalists, politicians, policymakers, philanthropists, skeptics, scientists, IT experts, scholars, bureaucrats, reactionaries, reformers, revolutionaries, and the rest. It in-dexes a value that many are mulling over, talking about, and working in varied ways to achieve. Moreover, as we have seen, myriad projects of open-ing are reshaping our world. In the case of science for governance, existing institutional arrangements are unraveling; new standards of practice are being implemented; weighty, protracted negotiations are underway over what science is, who will trust it, and under what conditions, and where science stops and policy, politics, and varied publics begin—all arguments over how, precisely, power will be exercised in today's world. There is much of import to consider right there.

Yet these issues resonate widely. Rapidly changing communication and information technologies, for instance, and the new ways of connecting, sharing, and participating they enable, are essential ingredients in our examples. The practices that are redefining openness in science and government would be impossible without them. But while these technologies promise much, they also bring new perils. In today's digitally mediated world, our actions and interactions generate digital traces that themselves become valuable data—raising anew urgent questions about surveillance, access, ownership, protecting citizens' privacy, and the health of democracy. Small wonder, then, that shortly after the European Union announced that open research data were the default of their Horizon 2020 program, their General Data Protection Regulation—which reasserts individual rights to privacy—came into effect; or that Facebook's CEO, Mark Zuckerberg, was in 2018 called before Congress to explain how data were harvested from millions of Facebook users, an act that may have affected the outcome of a US presidential election. Controversies over openness and its others take many forms, unfold in many settings, and are unlikely to vanish anytime soon.

Attending to novel practices of openness and its others also invites us to see so much more than "climate denial" or "partisan politics" at work in the Climategate controversy or the much-contested HONEST Act. It allows us to follow important currents rippling through our institutions, to notice institutional entanglements, rather than beginning with institutional specificities and separations. We can move from British parliamentary inquiries to US congressional legislation, from "science" to "governance" and back again. We can see multiple similar yet never quite the same projects of opening unfold and fuel each other. In so doing we can observe, unfazed, that the *Washington Post* and Congressman Lamar Smith, climate skeptics and data-rescue activists, are drawing from the same script: all worry deeply about the dangers of secrecy in government; all toil untiringly, in the name of democracy, to ensure there is light. Suddenly, popular stories about a post-truth, antiscience Right that operates in the shadows, and a truthful, pro-science Left that does not, seem a lot more complicated.

Notes

We are grateful to participants in the IAS's Words and Worlds workshop and particularly to Didier Fassin, Veena Das, and Jonathan Pugh for their close readings of this chapter. The chapter draws on research supported by the Social Sciences and Humanities Research Council of Canada.

1. According to the *Post*'s media reporter, Paul Farhi (2017), Woodward appears to be referring to Judge Damon J. Keith of the US Court of Appeals for the 6th Circuit, who ruled in a pre-Watergate-era case that government could not wiretap individuals without a warrant. Judge Keith's wording in the ruling was "Democracy dies in the dark."

2. The primary concern in this chapter is with planned, overt data collection for science and governance, not with the covert collection of citizens' digital traces that become (meta)data.

3. For the original directive, see Obama White House 2009. Throughout his tenure, President Obama was strongly committed to open government. He issued several such memoranda, including on the Freedom of Information Act, which he said must be administered "with a clear presumption: In the face of doubt, openness prevails." Presidential Documents, Memorandum of January 21, 2009, 74 *Federal Register* 4681, January 26, 2009.

4. The Open Government Partnership is a multilateral initiative cofounded in 2011 by Brazil, Indonesia, Mexico, Norway, the Philippines, South Africa, the United Kingdom, and the United States. To date, over seventy countries have endorsed the Partnership's Open Government Declaration and announced their country-specific action plans. See their website, https://www.opengovpartnership.org.

5. For open data and information portals, see https://data.gov.uk and https://www.gov.uk. On the UK Open Government Network, see https://www.opengovernment.org.uk.

6. While open access forms part of this suite of concerns, our interest in this chapter is the recent preoccupation with process and, with that, open-source software and open data.

7. FOIA (comment 10), response to "Open Letter on Climate Legislation," *Air Vent: Because the World Needs Another Opinion* (blog), November 17, 2009, https://noconsensus.wordpress.com/2009/11/13/open-letter/#comments.

8. House of Commons Science and Technology Committee 2010.

9. Also see House of Commons Science and Technology Committee 2010: 10–11.

10. House of Commons Science and Technology Committee 2010: 18–19.

11. American Association for the Advancement of Science, letter, March 28, 2017, https://www.aaas.org/sites/default/files/s3fs-public/HR%25201430%2520HONEST%2520Act%2520Multisociety%2520Letter%2520of%2520Concern.pdf.

12. One year on, one organization involved in data rescue found that no climate data sets had so far been removed or deleted from federal websites under the Trump administration (Rinberg et al. 2018: 8).

RESILIENCE

11

JONATHAN PUGH

Stop calling me resilient. Because every time you say, "Oh, they're resilient," that means you can do something else to me.

FROM A POSTER QUOTING TRACIE WASHINGTON OF
THE LOUISIANA JUSTICE INSTITUTE, AFTER HURRICANE
KATRINA HIT NEW ORLEANS IN 2005

Over the past twenty years there has been a "spectacular rise" in the use of the term *resilience* across the natural and social sciences, media, and international policy debates (Brown 2014: 1). Today, whether one reads about cultivating resilience in victims of environmental disasters, schoolchildren, small islands, Indigenous communities, or national economies, the call from many policymakers, academics, and international interventions is for us all to become more resilient to the increasing social and environmental precarity that is said to define the contemporary era. The word *resilience* comes from the Latin word *resilire*. Back in the seventeenth century, *resilire* meant the ability of physical materials to rebound and recoil into their original shape after becoming deformed (Reid 2017). But in contemporary times, the idea that individuals and communities should learn to become resilient has gained growing importance. There has been a massive shift in focus and tone of engagement across a broad spectrum of political positions toward cultivating individual, social, and environmental resilience. In some cases, the shift toward resilience has been more at the individual level and focused on the psychologization and individualization of social issues concerning vulnerability and trauma (Fassin and Rechtman 2009). In others, the concern of this chapter, the emphasis is more on community resilience, as when the leading resilience scholar, Neil Adger (2000: 347), defines *resilience* as "the ability of groups or communities to cope with external stresses and disturbances as a result of social, political and environmental change."

The specific focus of this chapter is community resilience to environmental precarity. Particular attention will be paid to the shifting nature of resilience and environmental precarity debates in Western international intervention and academic literature. The main critique of resilience in what follows is that resilience tends to shift the focus of attention away from the perpetrators to the victims of environmental precarity. Resilience frameworks often narrowly focus on developing the resilient capabilities of the victims of environmental precarity themselves rather than engaging in the more politically charged stakes, and deeper structural conditions, which brought about environmental precarity in the first place. In tracking the longer history and evolution of resilience paradigms over time, the chapter brings such concerns right up to the present by discussing how this situation is potentially being made worse by recent debates in Western academia and international policy. While often well-meaning, these debates now increasingly celebrate the resilient capacities of nonmodern and Indigenous peoples. Not only does this run the risk of repeating history by once again reductively romanticizing the Indigenous subject; it can also become a way of obfuscating the West's responsibility for global environmental change, as well as downplaying the importance of alternative political imaginaries from around the world that do not wish to reduce human lives to merely being resilient. The final parts of the chapter ground such concerns through the prism of the small island, arguably the emblematic figure of resilience debates today.

The Rise of Resilience

When thinking through the rise and proliferation of resilience in environmental debates and Western international intervention, it is useful to stand back and spend some time unpacking the historically changing conditions on the international stage, which made the rise of resilience possible in the first place. Back in the 1980s the situation was rather different from the resilience programs of today, which, as noted, focus on cultivating the resilient capabilities and capacities of victims of environmental precarity. Back then, Western international development programs had a more inverted approach and tended to hold that problems in the functioning of government in the Global South lay in blockages created by national elites rather than the resilience of local communities themselves. Between the 1980s and early 2000s, the West's approach to intervention in the Global South was one of liberal interventionism—from structural adjustment programs in Latin America and the Caribbean to the invasion of Iraq and Afghanistan—which sought to export and install liberal institutions around the world. Formal institutional frameworks were seen as determining the outcomes of social interaction. Governments that were part of systems of colonialism, hierarchy, domination, and exploitation became the focus of functional organization and strategic allocation (Chandler 2016).

But since the 1990s this approach, which focused on formal institutional frameworks as determining outcomes of social interaction, has been widely seen as failing, as illustrated in the debacles of Bosnia, Kosovo, Iraq, and Afghanistan and in liberal internationalist state building more generally. In such cases there has been a deepening malaise not only from outside the liberal tradition but from within the liberal project itself. Here both liberals and their critics have recentered on the value of working with civil society instead. In his book *At War's End*, Roland Paris (2004) argues that liberal internationalists underestimated the blockages coming from local agency and society at large, which prevented the operation of liberal institutional frameworks (Pugh 2014). This reversal of approaches focused on how people in the Global South were instead embedded in complex social and cultural practices (later to be expanded to the complexity of human-environment relations, discussed later) and that these first needed to be understood in detail before liberal state building could take place. For liberal internationalists there had been too much democracy promotion in societies that were problematic, aliberal, or dysfunctional. What was first needed, therefore, was for these societies to build their effective capacities for action at the level of community and civil society (Chandler 2016).

When now turning to understand how changing debates about the environment fed into this evolving situation, and what was eventually to become the rise of resilience paradigms, it is useful to be reminded of Michel Foucault's (2008: 16) statement, "Nature is something that runs under, through and in the exercise of governmentality." What Foucault means by this deceptively straightforward statement is that economic actions work through the sense that they appeal to an underlying "natural law" (as one example, Foucault cites populations moving to locations where they receive increased wages), and people and governmentalities are seen to "succeed" or "fail" according to these "natural" laws. As explained, as the 1990s progressed the idea that local communities are best placed to develop their own capacity building became increasingly *naturalized* in this way from a broad range of political perspectives. This was given further and particular impetus as changing debates about the environment in the 1990s also increasingly understood human-nature entanglements as complex and nonlinear too. These similarly questioned the frameworks of reasoning of Western modernity, linear pathways of control, and, in particular, from the perspective of these environmental debates, the coherence of a human/nature divide that had hitherto been central to the notion of "Western, rational, man." Through the pioneering work of such writers as Ilya Prigogine and Isabelle Stengers (1984), exemplified in chaos and complexity theory, the predictive outcomes of modern and rationalist models in both nature and society began to be seriously questioned. For Prigogine and Stengers, complexity means that the inputs into a system will not necessarily produce proportionate outcomes, and we cannot know these outcomes in advance because systems are nonlinear. As the 1990s progressed, environmental debates drew upon such developments and foregrounded how life was increasingly held to be complex, not closed off but open-ended, full of unpredictable and immanent possibilities. Through these debates in both the social and environmental sciences during this time, socio-ecological systems were thus increasingly held to act as complex and evolving integrated systems that could not be understood or controlled in the same way as older Western modern frameworks of reasoning. As these concerns for complexity invaded contemporary life, becoming dominant at the level of ontology across a wide range of academic disciplines, policymaking debates, and practices, they influenced the nature of political economy and the rising prominence of the resilience paradigm.

Back in the 1990s, an emphasis on community resilience, often defined as the capacity to buffer change and precarity, emerged from these debates as an *active response* to the waning confidence in top-down intervention and frameworks of modernity in the Global South. Debate often reflected the approaches of prominent scholars such as Ulrich Beck (1992), and the United Nations (2004: chap. 1, §1, 17) defined resilience as "the capacity of a system, community or society to resist or change in order that it may obtain an acceptable level of functioning and structure." During these earlier phases of the rise of the resilience paradigm, debate sought to highlight the role of community-environment relations in order to develop better, more efficient, and reflexive ways that challenged the linear, top-down, and reductionist approaches of modernity. For these earlier approaches to resilience, the task was to *actively* build community capacity as a means to manage the unfolding of environmental precarity and change. At this time, concerns such as global warming were still being framed in terms of how resilience had the possibility of managing or holding them back. The question was often less one of believing in or denying global warming, as most of these debates had already accepted that global warming was happening. What was now at stake was nothing less than a reconfiguration of human-nature relations themselves through a growing awareness of and attention to the complexity of human-nature entanglements and how resilience could be cultivated within them (Pugh 2014). These earlier resilience approaches therefore did just enough to problematize modernist understandings of the human/nature divide, while retaining the human subject (often still carrying some of the legacies of "Western, rational man") as being able to understand human-environment processes (Chandler 2016). The goal was to learn how to become more resilient in order to reach some sort of "happy ending" given the growing and worrying evidence of global environmental change and precarity around the world. With some helpful stewardship (usually in the form of non-Indigenous intervention from development agencies), people from around the world would learn to adapt and adjust to the changing global environment through the resilient governance of feedback loops in the awareness that the interconnections between human actions and global effects can be seen, understood, and acted on (Chandler 2018). The concern was how to learn to become resilient through a growing awareness of the empirical entanglements between humans and nature associated with such growing concerns as global warming, rising sea level, hurricanes, increased levels of risk, and environmental degradation more generally.

Here resilience found strong purchase because it thereby played into the waning faith in Western modernity, while notionally foregrounding the need for local communities (often seen as being oppressed by modernity and colonialism) to now draw on their own resources to adapt, adjust, and bounce back from environmental precarity. In making this switch to facilitated resilience, the focus of international intervention increasingly became about how local communities can be helped to become resilient themselves. New resilience programs and governmental rationalities were rolled out and naturalized on a massive scale in the 1990s and seen to succeed or fail accordingly. By the new millennium, resilience was rapidly becoming a prominent governmentality across a wide range of academic disciplines, media, and international policy debates, as new "natural laws" were seen to have taken hold to mediate relations at the socio-ecological level.

In order to support the proliferation of the resilience paradigm, exemplars of resilience were needed and, indeed, rolled out on a massive scale on the international stage. As I examine in more detail later, it is in particular due to their vulnerabilities, including isolation, limited resources, sea-level rising, and global warming, that the acronym SIDS (Small Island Developing States) was appropriated by many advocates of resilience as emblematic of the new resilience paradigm. Only a year after *Time* magazine heralded *resilience* as the buzzword for our time, the United Nations designated 2014 the International Year of the SIDS. In March 2015 Cyclone Pam devastated Vanuatu and impacted the neighboring island states Tuvalu and the Solomon Islands—it was the second most intensive storm ever measured in the Southern Pacific. More recent years have seen the relationship between resilience and islands gathering apace. Today the presidency of international climate change meetings, such as the United Nations Climate Change Conference in 2017, is not held by the United States, the United Kingdom, or Germany but by small islands like Fiji. In the same year, hurricane after hurricane battered the small islands of the Caribbean—Anguilla, Barbuda, Dominica, Puerto Rico, Saint Kitts and Nevis, Saint Martin, Turks and Caicos, and the British Virgin Islands, among many other smaller islands. The devastation was brutal, challenging crucial island electricity and water supplies as hurricanes relentlessly pounded the region. Ten hurricanes hit the Atlantic in ten weeks, breaking a 124-year-old record. For the first time two category 5 hurricanes, the most severe, hit the Caribbean one after the other. The images that flashed across media, social network feeds, and in international policy and academic debates alike were described by many academics and policymakers as illustrative of how the small island has become symbolic of the need for resilience.

The New Stakes of Resilience in the Anthropocene

Environmental debate today is particularly fast-moving, and the contemporary stakes and frameworks of resilience are changing as a result. It is important to pick up and engage these changes in some depth if we are to develop a more complete and comprehensive picture of resilience, in particular its potentially negative consequences, in contemporary times.

The Anthropocene—a concept coined by Eugene Stoermer in the 1980s and popularized by Paul Crutzen (2002) in the 2000s—is a disputed term that refers to a new geological epoch in which human activity is seen to have profound and irreparable effects on the environment. Distinguished from the Holocene, the term *Anthropocene* comes from the ancient Greek word for "human," *anthropos*, and as the website Welcome to the Anthropocene (n.d.) says, there is now "overwhelming global evidence that atmospheric, geologic, hydrologic, biospheric and other earth system processes" have been transformed by human actions since at least the Industrial Revolution. This attention to a new epoch in which humanity's impact on the earth means that natural processes can no longer be separated from historical, social, economic, and political effects has further, and even more powerfully challenged the older Western modernist understanding of the nature/culture divide. As Dipesh Chakrabarty (2009) pointed out in his seminal essay on the Anthropocene, nature can no longer be understood as operating on fixed or natural laws, while politics and culture can no longer be understood as operating in a separate sphere of autonomy and freedom.

Contributing to these shifting stakes, many of the leading contemporary environmental philosophers of the Anthropocene today, like Timothy Morton (2013: 15), now interestingly characterize the Anthropocene as a new "Age of Asymmetry." This is because although the human species may have played a large part in unleashing the Anthropocene's forces of global warming, rising sea levels, and hurricanes, it seems increasingly apparent that we have little power to control these changes. Compared to these newer ways of approaching environmental debate in the work of such influential and prolific authors as Morton, even the relatively recent models of resilience discussed earlier, and developed only a few years ago, are now increasingly seen as out of touch with the tide of environmental change. They are being troubled and questioned as a result. There is a growing concern in both environmental philosophy and, importantly, in international policy (see later discussion) that these older ways of thinking about resilience now imply too much of a "happy ending." Saliently, the argument is increasingly being made that older approaches to resilience still carry too much of the tone of a Cartesian rational man able to develop effective stewardship over the environment (Chandler 2018: 4).

Perhaps one of the most famous illustrations of this in recent contemporary environmental philosophy is Isabelle Stengers's (2015) reinvoking of the name "Gaia" as an operation, event, and eruption against humanity's impact on a planetary scale. For Stengers, the power unleashed by the

Anthropocene has become too rich and too intense for feedback loops of resilience, and her influential work demonstrates the increasing need for alternative ways of attuning to these forces. Indeed, for many similarly attuned authors today, even the term *Anthropocene* has become rather awkward because even as "we" (read: modern, Western man) claim the power of the human over nature, the agency of Gaia is increasingly being revealed in the form of global warming, hurricanes, rising sea level, and other uncontrollable forces. These recent interjections thus importantly switch the register of attention and tone of debate much more obviously toward the intensification and unpredictability of forces in the Anthropocene, and their influence is increasingly widespread.

The influential philosopher and anthropologist Bruno Latour (2017), for example, took Stengers's work on Gaia as the central theme for his 2013 Gifford Lectures. Among other developments, this has now permitted Latour to move on somewhat from his older actor-network theory framings of human-nature entanglements, so that today it is the intense ungraspable forces of Gaia that make the "reenchantment" of the world and our adaptation to it so difficult in the manner of older ways of framing the human-nature relations and resilience. On the one hand, all life today already exists *within* global warming, so that global warming has burned right through old frameworks of geography and modernity that separated out nature as something that existed "over there." But on the other hand, global warming also demonstrates the intensification and richness of forces beyond human control in the Anthropocene, which means that, while profoundly real, global warming is never present to us or for us and is fixed in some way (Morton 2013). For these and other influential environmental philosophers of the Anthropocene, like Anna Tsing (2015), debate has therefore now very much shifted to how "we" (Western moderns) are *already* living "life in the ruins"—the argument being that the exuberant confidence of Western modernity in a human/nature divide and the associated powers of control can now be consigned to history. Here the Anthropocene is heuristically invoked to finally reveal the human/nature divide to be what it always was: a fiction. As a result, much contemporary literature, from a broader range of academic and policy backgrounds, is now caught up in the search for alternative ontologies, ethics, and politics.

Here, as I said, it is really important to note that such debates are not confined to the sometimes abstract and dense writing styles of critical Western environmental philosophers. Indeed they now very much play out in concrete and salient ways through the shifting stakes of recent international policy debates. One reflection of the limits of the late modernist perspective of relational harmony that characterizes these influential debates is the increasing shift toward the importance of Indigenous knowledge, and here the figures of the island and island community are being invoked once again. But this time the stakes are being reframed in terms of offering alternatives to modernity and in terms of island Indigenous communities, and islanders themselves as being better attuned to the conditions of the Anthropocene (Chandler and Pugh 2018). As a joint UNESCO and UN report states, "Indigenous societies have elaborated coping strategies to deal with unstable environments, and in some cases, are already actively adapting to early climate change impacts. While the transformations due to climate change are expected to be unprecedented, Indigenous knowledge and coping strategies provide a crucial foundation for community-based adaptation measures" (Nakashima et al. 2012: 6).

A celebration of indigeneity is today widely reflected in international policy, for example, in the work of the Intergovernmental Panel on Climate Change (IPCC), where islands figure particularly prominently. Indigenous knowledge was acknowledged in the IPCC's Fourth Assessment Report as "an invaluable basis for developing adaptation and natural resource management strategies in response to environmental and other forms of change" (Parry et al. 2007: 15.6.1). Recognition was reaffirmed at IPCC's Thirty-Second Session (Nakashima et al. 2012), and consideration of traditional and Indigenous knowledge was included as a guiding principle for the Cancun Adaptation Framework adopted at the 2010 United Nations Framework Convention on Climate Change Conference. The IPCC's Working Group II contribution to the Fifth Assessment Report also includes local and traditional knowledge as distinct topics in chapter 12 on human security (Nakashima et al. 2012).

As Elizabeth Hall and Todd Sanders (2015) saliently remark, today much international environmental policy literature on climate change frames Indigenous peoples as different from the modern, and in particular because Indigenous peoples are said to build up knowledge of their environment through generations. Indigenous communities are said to be less likely to see the world in terms of Western modernity's more linear causes and effects, numerical precision and control, and the modern binary of human/nature. As Julian Reid (2017) also says, both academic and policy debate follow now-familiar lines here, with the Douglas Nakashima et al. (2012: 8) report *Weathering Uncertainty* saying that "despite their high exposure-sensitivity, indigenous peoples and local communities are actively responding to changing climatic conditions and have demonstrated resourcefulness and resilience." The Indigenous subject has become a high-value figure to international policymakers because Indigenous peoples are perceived to be resourceful in the face of the environmental uncertainties of global warming.

Anthropologists have played a particularly important role in the advancing of such Indigenous alter-politics. Indeed many of the arguments against the human/nature divide were already being developed by anthropologists like Eduardo Viveiros de Castro (1998) and Tim Ingold (2002) at the same time as debates about global warming and the Anthropocene were growing apace. Here the (re)discovery of the Indigenous subject by Western anthropology has increasingly emerged as a "solution" to the crisis of faith in Western modernity. For Ingold, it is the Indigenous subject's "ontology of dwelling" that is today more accurate than Western ontology and its mistaken founding postulate of a mind detached from the world. Similarly for Déborah Danowski and Viveiros de Castro (2016), the Indigenous subject has never been modern and, therefore, has never had a human/nature divide to lose (unlike those who still problematically hold on to Western modernity in the Anthropocene).

The inversion is then being made, increasingly it seems, that if Western modernity and the associated modern frameworks of reasoning led to the Anthropocene, then "we" (Western moderns) should turn to the figure of the Indigenous subject for inspiration. Chandler and Reid well summarize these shifting stakes:

> The reason why indigenous ways of being are feted is for the specific attributes of coping with natural or environmental problems, which are seen to evade the grasp of modern science and technology. When nature was seen as a passive object open to modernist understanding and appropriation, indigenous ways of being were seen to lack history and agency. Today, the tables are turned. . . . The collapse of the nature/culture divide and the focus on the previously ignored liveliness, power and agency of natural forces, previously thought to be passive, innate and lacking in agency, has transformed the understanding of indigeneity. The indigenous are the anthropocenealogists of non-modern ontology; they can teach the moderns how to see the non-human differently. (Chandler and Reid 2018: 9–10)

Again, it is the small island in particular that recurrently features in international policy debates, as "the idea of isolation, relative or absolute, sits well with the idea that indigenous knowledge and practices move intact between generations" (Hall and Sanders 2015: 442). While island cultures living in close relation to nature are argued to be most at threat from the forces of the Anthropocene, at the same time, because they are said to have become adaptive over generations, islanders are also argued to be particularly resilient. Thus, whereas in previous phases of resilience the focus on small islands adapting to disasters, environmental precarity, and becoming resilient tended to be framed in terms of the application of non-Indigenous forms of reason, today the recognition that we are all *already* in the Anthropocene is now leading to a different set of assumptions and practices, reconfigured in terms of greater awareness of islanders' resilience themselves.

Critically Disrupting the Figure of the Island

Given these shifting debates that increasingly solidify the role of the island as an exemplar of the Anthropocene, it is useful to be reminded that the figure of the island has often been something of a placeholder for Western culture's anxieties, projections, and concerns more generally over history. In 1516 the political theorist Thomas More employed the island as a backdrop and bounded place to explore his ideals of utopia. The island of Shakespeare's *Tempest* was a stage set for questions of political theory, rule, and authority to play out. In Daniel Defoe's *Robinson Crusoe*, the island was a place to explore questions of boundedness, escape, and control over others. In writing from Homer to Gilles Deleuze, the island has loomed large in Western discourse and literature. As John Gillis (2004: 1) accurately observes, Western culture not only thinks about islands; it "thinks *with* them." Our times of global environmental insecurity and change are no different. Today the problems faced by those living on small islands are not framed in terms of their problems alone but rolled out on the international stage as reflective of the wider need for new approaches to human-environment relations, Indigenous reasoning, and resilience paradigms more generally. This "island effect"—the capacity of islands to be exemplars of global environmental change—has meant that people in many other parts of the world similarly threatened are seen to be highly likely to derive important insights from island experiences (even as small islands present diverse sets of social, cultural, and political economic circumstances; Baldacchino and Royle 2010; Grydehøj 2017).

But as the following brief anecdote from my own research shows, we are not only critically at risk of being faced with the deadpan expression of the islander who has just recently been told, "Over to you to attune to global warming, then." We are also going to have to engage this deadpan expression itself with a serious sense of moral and ethical responsibility (Pugh 2017).

It is 8:30 a.m. one morning in April 2014. I am sitting waiting in the reception room of the town planning office of Saint Lucia, which is located on the waterfront of the capital of this Caribbean island, Castries. Having lived on the island for a number of years and studied it for nearly twenty, I've interviewed dozens of town planners on the changing character of Caribbean island planning. At this moment I am watching Mr. Bean on the overhead TV with the new receptionist at the desk, who does not know me, while trying my best to explain to both the receptionist and a member of the general public who is also waiting to see a town planner that I am not a hotel developer but interested in doing academic research. I am not sure whether they believe me, or perhaps they think it is perfectly possible to be both. But as my ability to shape their understanding of who I am and take hold of the situation starts to unravel, a town planner walks from another room and over to greet me with a deadpan expression. As Kathleen Stewart (2011: 452) usefully reminds us, an "atmosphere is not an inert context but a force field in which people find themselves. It is not an effect of other forces but a lived affect—a capacity to affect and to be affected that pushes the present into a composition, an expressivity, the sense of potentiality and event." This planner knows that I am here to update my ongoing research on the changing nature of town planning and environmental management in Saint Lucia. When we sit down in the planning office and after a few brief pleasantries about how planning systems are changing in the present era, the planner lowers his voice and, again with a deadpan expression, slowly says, "There is resilience, and then there is *resilience* . . ."

Explaining the difference, the planner talked about how he had higher hopes for postcolonial independence than being "merely resilient" (in the contemporary sense of resilience governmentality), saying, "Our independence was supposed to break with history. Resilience does not do that." The resilient subject "merely rides the waves of catastrophe and change," while the subject of postcolonial independence "sought to seize history, and transform it." Indeed the people of the Caribbean have quite obviously already lived their lives in the ruins of modernity and colonialism and through a postapocalyptic experience; from Frantz Fanon to Marcus

Garvey and Bob Marley, they have sought to develop more affirmative alternative political imaginaries from these experiences. My ethnographic encounter thus demonstrates how contemporary resilience as a "naturalized" form of governmentality plays out between a grasping hand that today reductively romanticizes the islander as being resilient in the Anthropocene and its unraveling in everyday life as islanders seek out higher and more politically transformative horizons themselves. The deadpan expression of the planner becomes an impasse and injunction for the island to not be straightforwardly appropriated, read, and naturalized, as the figure of the island so often has been throughout colonial history.

Such concerns raised suggest the need to reflect more deeply on how resilience paradigms operate as contemporary forms of violence. On the one hand, there is rightly deep concern for how the Anthropocene was significantly brought about by Western modernity, and in particular through Western modernity's elevation of a human/nature divide where man was posited as being able to control nature. It is also right that much Western critical theory and international policy is responding to this and now searching for alternative frameworks of reasoning and ontology to engage. But on the other hand, as I said earlier, the figure of the island, and indeed the Indigenous subject, has often been reduced to a scene where Western anxieties are projected and played out, and today such legacies continue to be at work—this time through the reductive romanticizing of island and Indigenous communities as better attuned to the unpredictable forces of the Anthropocene. As my Saint Lucian interviewee interjects into such debates with his uncomfortable bodily expressions and words, history is once again repeating itself as the features of the islander and Indigenous subject are reductively grasped and categorized in new ways.

Such critical perspectives require a renewed concern for disciplines like anthropology and ethnography, which have (no doubt well-meaningly) contributed to this negative situation. It becomes necessary to explore, in more nuanced and effective ways, how the dominant Western framings of resilience and indigeneity unravel and unfold in the everyday, how they are shot through with impasses and deadpan expressions such as the one I described, even as they seek to naturalize the figure of the island and the Indigenous subject in new ways.

Here, as the anthropologist Veena Das (2007) has demonstrated many times, the relations we encounter during ethnographic and anthropological research in the field are lived out through such awkward atmospheres as the one between the Saint Lucian planner and myself that do not always congeal into something coherent like a political act of resistance or uprising. But they nevertheless illustrate the ongoing struggle over what Stanley Cavell (1996), in a related but different way from Foucault (2008), calls an appeal to "natural" laws. I tend to think of my encounter with the Saint Lucian civil servant around contemporary resilience paradigms in terms of what Cavell (1996: 330) calls, after Ludwig Wittgenstein, a tension that pervades agreements in "forms of life"—between a "conventionalised, or contractual, sense of agreement" and a "biological or vertical sense of form of life" which contests "its sense of political or social conservatism." What is at stake in the Saint Lucian planner's interjection is, on the one hand, the contestation of a conservative contract that has emerged recently around resilience and indigeneity in Western discourse and, on the other hand, a more spiritual, vertical struggle against this naturalization. Here the planner's interjection—"There is resilience, and then there is *resilience . . .*"— also brings to mind a much longer Caribbean history, where the majority of people who have lived in Saint Lucia (slaves) have struggled through colonialism and modernity against particularly oppressive "naturalizations" of their human life, being reduced to "savage" subjects, endowed with less capacity for rational thought than moderns. But the planner's interjection further suggests that today, in the Anthropocene, new forms of naturalization are at work and playing through contemporary resilience and related debates, this time romanticizing and imbuing islanders and Indigenous subjects with special qualities, more attuned and resilient to the Anthropocene, which the Western subject is by contrast seen as lacking.

Giving the growing prominence of these contemporary frameworks there is a real risk of not actually engaging the diverse historical and geographical contexts of different islands around the world and their wide range of political and social struggles. Perhaps worse still, imbuing islanders and Indigenous subjects with resilient powers can facilitate the regressive withdrawal of the West from what are, of course, the deeply connective and connecting structural problems of the Anthropocene. As the quote with which I opened this chapter exemplifies, resilience often works to shift the focus of attention from the perpetrators to the victims in this way, downplaying wider structural oppressions, legacies, and colonial relations.

The foregrounding of these struggles as everyday practices could not be more important when we return to the hurricane-ravaged Caribbean of 2017. After Hurricane Irma struck the region in that year, 95 percent of the Caribbean island of Barbuda's buildings were damaged, 60 percent of the island's population became homeless, and a two-year-old child was tragically killed.

While 1,800 people were transported to nearby Antigua, and offers of help came in from around the world, on September 11 the prime minister announced "access restrictions on islanders wanting to return to Barbuda" (George 2017). On September 12 a local newspaper ran a short article reporting that the government was seeking to make "changes to a historical law governing land distribution on Barbuda." This was a "closed-doors decision" which sought to "alter the 2007 Barbuda Land Act and end communal ownership of land," thereby opening "the door for private and foreign land ownership" (George 2017).

In many Caribbean islands land laws have often been hard won by populations emerging through emancipation from slavery. The struggle against colonialism meant the struggle for land and landownership. In Barbuda, like many other Caribbean islands, the tradition of common land is thus "deeply engrained" (George 2017). Yet, as Naomi Klein (2007) demonstrates well in *The Shock Doctrine*, too often today crises like hurricanes and environmental disasters more generally work to the benefit of powerful international agents that brush aside such long-held struggles against colonialism for the sake of acting "urgently." In the Caribbean, islanders can be displaced and cherished land laws won through emancipation and independence overturned for the sake of inviting quick foreign investment after disaster strikes. Powerful hotel chains, offshore banks, and other international agents seize this opportunity to dismiss land laws and legacies of postcolonial struggle because of the apparent need to act now. Saliently here for the critical argument I am making, the dominant narrative of island resilience that circulated after the hurricanes hit the Caribbean in 2017 offers little as a counter-response. Being encouraged to be more adaptive and attuned to the environment rather than developing politically counterhegemonic movements is a much more impoverished form of politics, even a form of violence against islanders themselves when we consider the longer struggles of colonialism. The circumstances of Barbuda are clearly far more politically charged and about postcolonial struggles than islanders merely learning to become resilient to environmental catastrophe, adapting and bouncing back. The political stakes are much higher and more firmly those of a continued struggle for postcolonial self-determination. As in the case of one of Barbuda's neighbors, Saint Lucia, islanders need far more progressive and politically transformative ideals than mere resilience.

As a final illustration of this, the legacies of island colonialism have been made particularly apparent in the case of Puerto Rico, one of the many other islands devastated by the hurricanes of 2017. Puerto Rico has been subjected to a long history of US imperialism and colonialism, since at least the Spanish-American War, when the island was caught up in struggles over Cuba. The island was also famously treated as a US military training ground for many years in the twentieth century. But what is positive about the case of Puerto Rico after the hurricane crisis, when compared to the lesser-known situation of Barbuda, is that colonial and imperialist legacies have been picked up by US media coverage on CNN, PBS, and other outlets. In particular, a strong media narrative has foregrounded how the Trump administration's poor response to the crisis still today makes Puerto Rico feel like a second-class US territory. Media commentary has regularly drawn our attention to how "the island's status as a United States territory—and by extension, its peculiar and colonial relationship with the United States—has been exposed to the rest of the world like the roots of the trees left bare from the force of [Hurricane] Maria's winds and rain" (Vega 2017).

Puerto Rico is not a fully incorporated territory of the United States but is rather what is called a free associated state. This means that by law Puerto Ricans are US citizens, but they are not represented in Congress, do not vote for the president, are disenfranchised at a national level, and remain massively in debt, to the tune of billions upon billions of dollars, to the United States. Because Puerto Rico is not fully incorporated into the United States, it cannot declare bankruptcy in the same way as, say, a US city, and the island's debt burden therefore remains. But compared to other Caribbean islands hit by hurricanes that year, mainstream media narratives have been less inclined to focus on the need for Puerto Ricans to become more resilient and adaptive to this environmental catastrophe. Rather, they have more positively foregrounded these strong colonial legacies and power structures that today keep Puerto Ricans down, suggesting how the crisis could "signal a new political awakening among Puerto Ricans eager to examine the colonial status of the island and prevent further economic and cultural erosion" (Vega 2017). Shortly after the hurricane hit the island, the media did much to foreground Puerto Rican activists' concerns that "the world has found out in the past few days what our history has always stubbornly made visible to us" (Vega 2017).

While change is frustratingly slow for Puerto Ricans themselves, more generally speaking, we can therefore see that such debates hold out the *possibility* of going beyond the reductive narrative of islanders merely being resilient, adapting and bouncing back to some sort of status quo. Indeed although Barbuda has received less coverage, the *New York Times* has recently foregrounded the complexities of island resilience there too (Collier, DeKornfield, and Laffin 2017). Explaining how prominent figures such as Robert De Niro might be seeking to acquire land in Barbuda for hotel development, deeper questions of who owns land have been opened up for wider debate and linked to colonial legacies and contemporary power structures. Such coverage, which opens up the complexities of island life beyond the many contemporary stereotypes and caricatures of islanders' resilience, increases the possibilities for potentially more politically progressive horizons and higher aspirations for island futures.

Conclusion

The rapidly changing environment of the planet and the term *Anthropocene* rightly suggest that a critique of Western modernity is now badly needed. But the increasingly prevalent and inverted switch to romanticize the Indigenous subject and the small island as taking on the burden of becoming resilient themselves, in both critical literature and international policy, offers a worryingly impoverished counternarrative. This inversion, as I have explained, is more of a reflection of how the term *Anthropocene* is increasingly being appropriated and put to use within Western discourse. It is reflective of an appropriate critical anxiety about how Western modernity is in ruins but also of an associated move to elevate the role of the "nonmodern" and "Indigenous" as "alternative solutions," thereby shifting focus largely from the perpetrators to the victims. This chapter has in response invoked examples of small islands that return us to these contemporary debates with a certain deadpan expression, suggesting that resilience and associated debates often offer little transformative weight and power when it comes to the massive political might of the industrially polluting nations of the world and the continued, powerful colonial legacies that have given rise to the Anthropocene. Many islanders are of course extremely resilient and continue to be so in the face of seemingly unsurmountable forces. As an op-ed in the *New York Times* asserts, "In Puerto Rico, we invented resilience" (Giusti-Cordero 2017). But my growing sense is that many islanders around the world are becoming wary of this reductive trope that is being projected onto them, and there is a need to treat their deadpan expressions with the serious moral respect they deserve. Islanders' political and social struggles, like those of all of us, are complex and multifaceted. It is these contingencies that need to be explored rather than reductively romanticizing islanders and Indigenous subjects, as has so often happened in history, or imbuing them with special powers that Westerners do not believe they possess. The salient question now, as for so many others writing in this collection, is once again how we take contemporary crisis as an opportunity to develop some new and different political horizons.

Note

I would like to acknowledge Todd Sanders, Veena Das, Didier Fassin, and Munirah Bishop for their careful reading, useful insights, and comments on earlier drafts of this chapter.

INEQUALITY

RAVI KANBUR

12

Any discussion of inequality must begin by asking *inequality of what?* and *inequality between whom?*. On the *what*, my focus will be on economic inequality, specifically inequality of income. On the *between whom*, I will consider inequality within nations and inequality between nations. So I will be viewing economic inequality primarily through the lens of the world as a whole and the nation-states that compose it. And I will be interested in the implications for inequality of different degrees of openness of borders between nation-states. The openness of borders can refer to goods or to people. I will restrict my attention to movements of people and, furthermore, to movement based on economic incentives. Thus I will focus on economic migration and not on refugees fleeing war and persecution.

To set up the issues I want to discuss, I start very simply with income inequality. I leave to one side the many criticisms of a sole focus on an economic measure. I have myself been such a critic. But I cannot help noticing that many such critics are quite willing to use headline economic numbers, like the share of income going to the top 1 percent, without withering criticism when it fits their narrative. Anyway, I leave also to one side many technical issues on how this data is generated and the measures formulated.[1] For now, suppose that every individual in the world can be given a number, their "income," that measures in some fashion their economic well-being. Line up all individuals in the world from lowest to highest income. The spread of this distribution of income, and there are many statistical measures of this spread, is the degree of income inequality in the world as a whole.

Now divide the world up into nation-states, which is where the constituent parts of the global data come from. Each nation-state will have its average income (its income per capita) and its own spread around its own average, which is the inequality within that nation-state. It should be intuitive that inequality across individuals in the world as a whole is attributable to two elements. First is the fact that there is a spread in average incomes across nation-states: some countries are richer than others, and there would be inequality in the world as a whole even if there was no inequality within each nation-state. But, second, there is indeed inequality within each nation-state, and each of these within-nation inequalities contributes to world inequality. Leaving aside various technical details, then, inequality across all individuals in the world as a whole can be "decomposed" into (1) inequality within nation-states and (2) inequality between nation-states.

What are the basic facts on levels and trends in these two constituent components and in global inequality overall? Average national incomes have evened out in the past quarter century. China, India, Vietnam, and others have had spectacular growth rates in comparison with the rich countries. Even Africa, with its failing states, took advantage of the commodity boom and, until recently, was growing at a fast clip on average. Thus inequality between nations declined. The pattern within nations is nuanced but is dominated by rising inequality in the United States and in other large economies, such as China and India, so that the component of world inequality within nations has risen.

Thus the two components of global inequality have moved in opposite directions in the past quarter century. The net effect is an empirical matter. As a matter of fact, world inequality overall has decreased. Put another way, reducing inequality between China and the United States more than compensated for increasing inequality within China and the United States. However, despite having declined, inequality between nation-states continues to be by far the larger of the two components of global inequality. Differences across countries in their per capita national incomes account for close to three-quarters of the inequality across all individuals in the world, down from over four-fifths a quarter of a century ago (see Lakner and Milanovic 2016).

These stylized facts of world income distribution and its evolution raise many questions: What explains the large gaps between rich and poor countries? Why, after four decades of decline after World War II, has inequality within rich countries increased in the past three decades? Why has inequality increased in some developing countries, such as China and India, but actually declined in others, such as Brazil? Each of these questions is worthy of a separate extended investigation, but my entry point of within-nations and between-nations inequality explores the intersection between inequality and another increasingly vexed issue of our time: migration across borders.

This intersection is driven by concerns of both within-nation and between-nation inequality. It is argued that rising inequality in rich countries such as the United States is at least partially the result of heavy immigration of unskilled labor, bringing downward pressure on local wages and thus upward pressure on inequality within the receiving country. However, such migration relieves labor market surplus in developing countries and is argued to be good for their development, and the global reallocation of labor from low-productivity to high-productivity locations to be good for the world economy as a whole. But at the same time the outmigration of skilled labor such as doctors and nurses from poor countries is held to be detrimental to the development of these countries and thus mitigates narrowing between-nation inequality. These conflicting forces need to be examined conceptually and empirically to explore the linkages between cross-border migration and inequality.

The large difference in average income enjoyed by someone born in a rich country compared to a poor one, which is the largest component of global inequality, also raises the question of the legitimacy of these income differences. Some refer to the gap as a "citizenship rent," highlighting that the individual in question did not do anything to earn it but merely had the good fortune to be born into it.[2] One way to address this misfortune of birth for those in poor countries could be to allow free migration across borders, which could be argued to neutralize the luck of the draw at birth. Should, then, national borders be much more open to migration? Underpinning these questions is the fundamental issue of the moral salience of the nation-state. Its instrumental salience may be weakened by globalization in the flow of capital and technology, but its moral salience is at the heart of the discourse on inequality in a global perspective, either explicitly or, often, implicitly. Indeed it is the weakening of instrumental saliency that is raising anew the matter of moral saliency.

What would be the answer to the question of open borders from the perspective of inequality—inequality between nations and inequality within nations? I begin the discussion with the impact of open borders on inequality between nations, then take up an issue of great import in the current political climate: the impact of open borders and immigration on inequality in receiving countries. I then consider the issue of outmigration and its impact on sending countries.

Open Borders and Inequality between Nations

A standard characterization of economists is that they have too much respect for the operation of markets and for the incentives that markets create for the efficient allocation of economic resources. This "invisible hand" mentality is criticized by other social scientists and by many economists themselves. They argue that not only does a sole focus on economic efficiency neglect the distribution of the gains from efficiency but that the free operation of markets does not guarantee economic efficiency. Efficiency through the operation of markets is guaranteed only when a range of conditions is met, including that there should not be impediments to the free operation of markets, preventing goods from moving to where they would be most desired and factors of production such as labor moving to where they would be most productively deployed. But these conditions are not met in practice. Competition is not free but is riddled with market power, and the movement of goods and people is not free. Such sentiments questioning the efficient operation of markets are themselves present in Adam Smith, and such analysis has won many Nobel prizes in economics. However, the basic instinct of economists to consider negatively impediments to movement of goods and people across markets perseveres, often bringing them into conflict with those who support regulation of markets within national borders, often with equity goals in mind.

But national borders are also impediments to the free movement of goods, services, and factors of production across markets. Taking the world economy as a whole, the "invisible hand" perspective would balk at any restriction on free global movement. There is a long history of promoting free trade in goods across national borders as a means to global economic efficiency and protectionism as a means of supporting domestic production and industry. Great political battles have been fought over free trade. The *Economist* magazine was founded in 1843 to argue for the repeal of the protectionist Corn Laws in Britain. Its original name, the *Economist: A Political, Commercial, Agricultural and Free-Trade Journal*, lays out its perspective very clearly. The issue of free trade led to a great political split in Britain in the early 1900s over "imperial preference." The young John Maynard Keynes, then a student at Cambridge, was on the side of free trade, equating it with free thought; in 1903 he wrote to a friend, "Sir, I hate all priests and pro-tectionists. . . . Down with pontiffs and tariffs" (quoted in Skidelsky 1983: 227). But then in 1944, at the Bretton Woods Conference that shaped the postwar order, Keynes battled for imperial preference to protect British markets from the onslaught of the emerging world economic power, the United States.

Coming to the twenty-first century, there is now little doubt on the role that trade in goods, especially access to markets of rich countries, has played in the spectacular economic growth of poor countries in Asia and elsewhere, growth that has narrowed economic inequality between them and the rich countries of the world. For example, over the four de-cades since the start of economic opening-up in 1978, China's growth of per capita income has approached an average of 10 percent per year, which means that it is now more than fifty times its value at the start of this pro-cess. The growth in trade volume has been even more spectacular, doubling every four years, and China is now the largest exporter in the world.[3] How-ever, while trade flows have been rightly lauded as the basis of narrowing inequality between nations, capital flows, especially flows of "hot money," have been blamed for global instability. They led to the Asian financial crash of 1997. Global financial interlinkages in the early 2000s meant that the collapse of the US subprime mortgage market in 2008 fed through to the world at a rapid pace and led to the global recession of 2008–9, from which the world is only just now beginning to recover. And many of the poorest economies of the world were hardest hit by the global recession.

Thus removing impediments to the free movement of goods has had a positive impact on the world economy as a whole and on inequality be-tween nations in our era of globalization, while deregulating the move-ment of capital has led to instability in the global economy with negative impacts on the poorest economies. The freer movement of goods and capital has also tied the hands of governments to introduce redistributive taxation—witness the race to the bottom in corporate tax rates—thereby furthering rising inequality. But this still leaves open the crucial question of the openness of the world economy to movements of labor between na-tions and what impact this is having and could have on global economic efficiency and equity.

The global economic efficiency answer to the question of open bor-ders for movement of people is straightforward. In the economic analy-sis frame, borders are a market distortion. They stand in the way of free movement of a factor of production. They put costs in the way of a "willing buyer–willing seller" transaction. They impede movement of labor from a low-productivity to a high-productivity location. Indeed the issue is often put in terms of incomplete globalization. Trade openness has globalized the markets for goods, and financial flows are globalized as well; what remains to be globalized is the labor market.

These and many other such characterizations capture the essence of many quantitative calculations on the global economic benefits from the opening of borders to the movement of labor. The actual numbers of cross-border migrants is in fact quite low, although it has been increasing:

> The current global estimate is that there were around 244 million international migrants in the world in 2015, which equates to 3.3 per cent of the global population. A first important point to note is that this is a very small minority of the global population, meaning that remaining within one's country of birth overwhelmingly remains the norm. The great majority of people in the world do not migrate across borders; much larger numbers migrate within countries (an estimated 740 million internal migrants in 2009). That said, the increase in international migrants has been evident over time—both numerically and proportionally—and at a greater rate than had been anticipated by some. For example, a 2003 projection was that by 2050 international migrants would account for 2.6 per cent of the global population or 230 million (a figure that has already been surpassed). In contrast, in 2010, a revised projection for 2050 was 405 million international migrants globally. (International Organization for Migration 2017: 2)

The low number of international migrants elicits different responses, ranging from *If it is so low, then why is there so much concern about it?* to highlighting that the very smallness of the amount of cross-border flows is an indication of impediments to the efficient allocation of global labor. The huge benefits at the individual level from migration are also highlighted in quantitative analyses of wage differentials across countries, correcting for differences in education and training. Lant Pritchett's work (2010) is representative of this type of analysis. Here are his estimates of wage differentials in terms of purchasing power parity (PPP) dollars:

> The data allowed us to estimate the wage ratios of observably equivalent workers in the United States and 42 developing countries. . . . The apparently same worker from these countries makes *five times* as much in the United States as in his home country—that is, on average an annual wage income that is $15,000 (PPP) higher. Even if the estimates of wage

differences of observably equivalent workers are discounted by a factor of 1.5 to adjust for selection and the costs of moving, the gains in wages to a low-skill worker are $10,000 (PPP). Not only is the world not flat, it is not a curb nor a barrier. Rather, the world has a massive cliff at the U.S. border (and, one suspects, most other rich industrial countries have similarly sized cliffs). (271–74)

If the huge wage differentials are an indication of productivity differentials, then the numbers given by Pritchett and elsewhere hold out the potential for efficient reallocation of the global workforce across countries. And indeed a stream of global economic models does just this, albeit taking on complexities in a much more elaborate manner. Open borders are a boon for global growth and productivity. Frédéric Docquier, Joël Machado, and Khalid Sekkat (2015: 303) are fairly typical in terms of their methods but also in terms of their conclusions: "In our benchmark framework, liberalizing migration increases the world GDP by 11.5–12.5 percent in the medium term."

But what should also be intuitively clear is that permitting open borders, as in this exercise, will also tend to lower the between-nations component of inequality, other things being held constant. Labor markets will tend to tighten in the sending poor countries, and additional labor will tend to hold down wages in the richer receiving countries. The consequences of the latter for within-country inequality in the rich country will be taken up presently, but the effect on inequality between countries is the component of global inequality that has indeed decreased in the past quarter century of globalization of good markets, and these calculations show that inequality would decline further if borders were opened up to free movement of people.

Despite the narrowing of between-country inequality over the past quarter century, the gaps remain large, as shown in Pritchett's (2010) wage data and in Christoph Lakner and Branko Milanovic's (2016) calculation that close to three-quarters of inequality among all individuals in the world is accounted for by differences in the average incomes of the countries in which they live. Full opening up of all borders to all movement would, according to economic calculations, improve global efficiency *and* reduce between-country economic inequality as commonly measured. There is one further line of argument for open borders, and it flows from a philosophical tradition that holds that it is not equality of outcome that matters but equality of opportunity. The modern literature on this owes much to the foundational papers by Ronald Dworkin in the 1980s (reprinted in Dworkin 2000), and the economics literature owes much to the development and formulation by John Roemer (1998). The essential distinction is that between two types of determinants of variations in outcome across individuals, labeled "circumstance" and "effort." Circumstance is that which is beyond the control of the individual; effort is that which is not. Thus the amount of variation in outcome that can be attributed to circumstance is, in this argument, "inequality of opportunity."

Recall that three-quarters of the inequality in income across individuals is accounted for by the countries where they live. There will be some adjustment for the fact that some individuals do not live where they were born, but we know that these constitute only 3.3 percent of all individuals in the world. This is what leads Milanovic to argue as follows:

> When income differences among countries are large, then a person's income depends significantly on where they live, or indeed where they are born, since 97 percent of the world's population live in the countries where they were born. The citizenship premium that one gets from being born in a richer country is in essence a rent, or if we use the terminology introduced by John Roemer in his *Equality of Opportunity*, it is an "exogenous circumstance" (as is the citizenship penalty) that is independent of a person's individual effort and their episodic (that is, not birth related) luck. (2016: 132)

Faced with these strong philosophical and normative arguments, Milanovic considers three options along a spectrum: "unrestricted movement of labor," "limited but higher level of migration than what currently exists," and "keep[ing] the flow of migrants at the current level or an even lower level" (154). He goes for the middle option: "The first option seems to me to be unattainable, and the third . . . inferior in terms of efficiency . . . and equity" (154).

However, while the case for open borders appears to be strong in terms of its contribution to reducing global inequality and the advancement of a particular conception of equality of opportunity, is the opposition to it in receiving countries merely xenophobia? And is the case for greatly increased outmigration also self-evidently dominant? The next two sections take up these questions in turn.

Immigration and Inequality

If immigration is so small (around 3 percent of the world's population has migrated across borders) and if it is such a good thing (raising world GDP and reducing global inequality, if quantitative economic models are to be believed), then why does it cause such angst in the world, and why is it resisted so strongly in receiving countries? There are many possible reasons for in-migration to have become such an explosive issue in the rich receiving countries of Europe and in the United States: identity anxiety, racism, populism, and more. But the possible wage effect on natives and the greater demands on public services could be economic channels that link to the rise of inequality within rich nations. The rise of within-nation inequality cannot be ignored politically, nor perhaps even ethically, even though it is dominated by declining between-nations inequality and an overall decline in global inequality.

The same economic models that show the benefits of international migration to world GDP and world inequality also, by the very same logic, highlight issues of rising inequality in migrant-receiving countries. Marco Delogu, Frédéric Docquier, and Joël Machado (2013: 32) build an elaborate model of international and intergenerational migration and its consequences and simulate the effects of liberalized migration policies: "In sum, we demonstrate that the long-run gain from liberalizing cross-border migration exceeds by far the short-run effect, and its magnitude is in line with what was found in previous studies. However the mechanism and the distribution of the gains are different. . . . The main winners are future generations of people originating from poor countries. This makes it difficult to find redistributive policies to compensate the losers, i.e., the current generations of low-skilled nationals residing in high-income countries."

But how can it be that a movement of less than 3 percent of the world's population can have a significant impact? The answer is that these moves are not spread evenly across the world but are concentrated in certain recipient countries: "The United States of America has been the main country of destination for international migrants since 1970. Since then, the number of foreign-born people residing in the country has almost quadrupled—from less than 12 million in 1970, to 46.6 million in 2015. Germany has been the second top country of destination since as early as 2005, with over 12 million international migrants residing in the country in 2015" (International Organization for Migration 2017: 18). Indeed close to 15 percent of the population of the United States and Germany is now foreign born. The basic economics of labor markets suggests that an increase in the supply of labor to such an extent in a national labor market will have a depressing effect on wages, all else being held constant. George Borjas's (2003: 1370) famous study ignited debate among economists in the United States: "Between 1980 and 2000, immigration increased the labor supply of working men by 11.0 percent. . . . My analysis implies that this immigrant influx reduced the wage of the average native worker by 3.2 percent. The wage impact differed dramatically across education groups, with the wage falling by 8.9 percent for high school dropouts, 4.9 percent for college graduates, 2.6 percent for high school graduates, and barely changing for workers with some college."

As might be expected, such studies can be and have been challenged (with response in return) on methodological grounds. Thus David Card (2009: 19) is representative of a school of analysis that does not find much impact of immigration on US inequality: "These comparisons suggest that the presence of immigration can account for a relatively small share (4–6 percent) of the rise in overall wage inequality over the past 25 years."

Notice that both Borjas (2003) and Card (2009) find an effect of immigration in receiving-country inequality, in this case the United States. Card argues that the effect is relatively small compared to other factors. Here the debate flows into a wider discussion on the central role of technological change in explaining rising inequality in the United States and other countries. The question had been *Trade or technology?* as the major cause behind the stagnation of wages in the US economy. David Autor (2014: 843) quotes a range of studies suggesting that in the United States "about two-thirds of the overall rise of earnings dispersion between 1980 and 2005 is proximately accounted for by the increased premium associated with schooling in general and postsecondary education in particular." This rise in the skill premium is attributed to rising demand for more educated labor in an era of technical change that is displacing basic labor.

However, even if immigration is quantitatively the smaller causal factor in explaining rising inequality in the narrow economic sense, it clearly has an outsized role in political discourse. Why? One reason could be that the real concern is about rising inequality, but the causality is misperceived as being predominantly through immigration rather than technological change or employer power. If this is the case, then perhaps merely providing information, for example publicizing the sorts of studies just discussed, might correct the misperception. But one fears that there is something deeper and more disturbing at the root of the misperception, which is a nativist concern about the increasing heterogeneity and diversity of the population.

There are many ways to discuss or characterize this phenomenon and its manifestations. Consider the following example. Let there be one thousand people in the population of working age, but only nine hundred jobs to go around. Let the population be completely homogeneous. Then a random allocation of jobs to people has an argument to be a fair distribution of jobs across people. No matter what happens, one hundred people will be without a job, but the chance of unemployment is one in ten, the same for everybody. Now suppose that people are tagged by their group type, A and B. Let the allocation still be random, but now the chances are that at least one B will have a job when an A does not. It is easy to see then how a political entrepreneur could try to sell the narrative that the reason A does not have a job is because B has one. In the ex-post sense this is true because there are fewer jobs than people, even though in the ex-ante sense the allocation was a fair random allocation of jobs across all people. It should also be clear that if the A-B distinction has sociopolitical salience, then, almost by definition, the argument that the ex-ante allocation was fair would not sway a member of either group who did not have a job, comparing himself or herself with a member of the other group who has a job. The jobs case is relevant but not unique. One thousand households to be allocated nine hundred public housing units, as is the case in many European countries, would have the same effect, as would overcrowded public schools or public health facilities.

What is the answer to these social tensions? In the examples given, the tensions would not arise if there was not a resource constraint—if there were enough jobs, houses, schools, and hospitals for everybody. And this is indeed an important lesson: the unemployment rate is not just an indicator of the waste of economic potential; it is also a harbinger of social tension. But the groupings have to be socioculturally salient to give the inequality of unemployment traction in creating this type of tension. Reduction of the salience of different types of cleavages would also reduce the collateral effect of economic inequality. But many if not most of these cleavages, like race in the United States, are long-lived and historical and move in geological time relative to the fast pace of economic change. For this reason, addressing those cleavages is also a long, slow process.

And therein lies the rub. It can be argued, indeed it has been argued, that high and fast rates of immigration introduce new social and cultural cleavages at a pace quicker than can be absorbed and can overwhelm previous mechanisms of reducing historical divisions, which of necessity have an effect over the long term. The net result is rising tension and a fraying of the redistributive social compact, designed for a more homogeneous society.

There is some evidence for these sorts of mechanisms in operation during periods of rapid immigration. Marco Tabellini (2018) looks at the period of mass migration in the United States in the late nineteenth and early twentieth centuries, which changed the composition of the US population dramatically: "In 1870, almost 90% of the foreign born came from Northern and Western Europe, whereas less than 5% of immigrants had arrived from Southern and Eastern Europe. . . . By 1920, however, the situation had changed dramatically, with the share of migrant stock from new source countries being as high as 40%. Europeans from new regions were culturally farther from natives and significantly less skilled than those from old sending regions" (6). This inflow had positive consequences for the economy. But Tabellini also documents the backlash that culminated in the US Immigration Acts of 1921 and 1924: "I show that immigration had a positive and significant effect on natives' employment and occupational standing, as well as on economic activity. However, despite these economic benefits, the inflow of immigrants also generated hostile political reactions, inducing cities to cut tax rates and limit redistribution, reducing the vote share of the pro-immigration party, and increasing support for the introduction of immigration restrictions" (38–39).

From our perspective the key finding is on the limiting of redistribution as diversity grew. Thus the causal chain is now not just from immigration to falling wages to rising inequality, but also from immigration to rising diversity to falling redistribution to rising inequality. There is some evidence for the negative impact of heterogeneity on solidarity in general, going back at least to the work of Robert Putnam (1995). But the more recent wave of immigration to Europe has led to similar arguments being made, for example by Paul Collier (2013), who also relies on evidence from Africa that, all else equal, ethnic heterogeneity has a negative impact on economic growth. Alberto Alesina, Johann Harnoss, and Hillel Rapoport (2018: 4) use attitudinal surveys in Europe to quantify the effect of immigration on attitudes toward redistribution: "We find robust evidence consistent with group loyalty and labor market effects of immigration. Native citizens' demand for income redistribution decreases . . . when the share of foreigners increases. . . . Tellingly, group loyalty effects are stronger for natives who think that immigrants negatively affect the quality of life in natives' home countries."

Faced with rapid immigration and growing sociocultural heterogeneity in the United States and Europe, many political philosophers have gone back to the basic arguments for and against restricting immigration into a nation-state. Among the best known of the recent contributions is that of David Miller (2016), which sets itself against a stream of thinking, such as that of Joseph Carens (1987), that argues strongly for open borders. As characterized by Eszter Kollar (2017: 726), "The underlying motivation of David Miller's inquiry into the political philosophy of immigration in his *Strangers in Our Midst* is to shift the burden of proof from advocates of closed borders to those of open borders. He argues that the democratic political community has the right to control its border to determine who to let in and on what grounds, as long as good reasons are given to the migrants at their doorstep. Consequently, the burden of proof is on theorists of free movement to show that limiting this collective right is justified."

Miller's thesis has led to an intensive debate and critique by theorists of democracy, including that by Kollar (2017).[4] But it clearly echoes, in the groves of academe, sentiments found on the streets of Trump-voting America and Brexit-voting Britain. On his conception, a democratic polity has the right to exclude immigrants for reasons of public policy, except perhaps for humanitarian reasons. And if that public policy reason is the mitigation of inequality, then inequality and open borders intersect once again, and none too comfortably for a cosmopolitan liberal perspective.

Outmigration and Inequality

So much for the consequences of migration for receiving countries. What about the sending countries? Surely there must be benefits all around in the poor countries that export their labor to rich countries? The migrants themselves clearly benefit, taking advantage of the huge wage differentials discussed earlier, which are the very cause of economic migration in the first place. And perhaps those who do not migrate benefit as well, partly as labor supply pressure is relieved in the sending country's labor market, and partly because of remittances from the migrants, which benefit the family and the community left behind. On average, therefore, the sending country would tend to benefit from outmigration. At least, that is the core argument for open borders as seen from the sending country's perspective, and even from the perspective of inequality between nations. But what about inequality within the sending country?

The counters to the simple argument that outmigration benefits the sending country begin with the notion of *selectivity* in migration. Migrants are not simply a representative draw from the sending countries' populations. While in absolute numbers unskilled and low-education workers dominate the pool because their base numbers are so large, often it is the skilled and educated who migrate disproportionately. And even if migration was representative of the sending country's population, the economic implications of an outmigration of skilled labor, a "brain drain," could be significant. Gillian Brock and Michael Blake put it in stark terms:

> Japan has around twenty-one physicians per ten thousand people, while Malawi has only one physician for every *fifty thousand* people. . . . These facts are troubling in themselves. They become even more troubling when we start asking *why* nations like Malawi have so few physicians. The answer, it seems, is not that citizens of developing countries have no interest in becoming physicians or a lack of opportunity for medical training. In fact, many developing societies spend a great deal of money training new physicians, and spots in medical schools are avidly sought in these countries. The reason for the low numbers of physicians has much to do with what medical training provides: namely, the opportunity to *leave* the developing society and enter into a more developed one. . . . No matter how much a developing country invests in medical education, it is unlikely to obtain an adequate stock of medical personnel. (2015: 1–2)

As Brock and Blake emphasize, this selectivity in migration ends up contributing to health inequality across rich and poor countries. And it can also be argued that it contributes to health inequality in the sending country, since the few medical personnel who remain are very likely to end up catering to the needs of the wealthy in their country.

The brain drain concern on the sending country's side is only sharpened in the current conjuncture, where rich receiving countries either already operate "points-based" immigration systems, which select in favor of skilled labor, or are moving in that direction. This tendency of rich countries to "cream off" the talent that poor countries spend huge resources training has been a concern of economists for a long time. As far back as the 1970s, Jagdish Bhagwati put forward a proposal for what became known as the "Bhagwati tax," which would impose a tax on countries receiving skilled labor to be remitted back to sending countries (see Bhagwati and Partington 1976) in compensation for the costs of training and the loss of services of those skilled workers.

More recently, however, some economists have emphasized an intriguing "brain gain" counterargument, which goes as follows. Consider the situation in which the stock of medical doctors or nurses, say, is determined not just by government expenditure but by individual decisions on whether to take up the training, with its personal cost of time and money. The cost-benefit of this choice is determined in part by the probability that after training the individual can "escape" to the higher paying markets of a rich country. But this probability depends on the restrictiveness of the quota system in place for immigration to these countries. As this quota system is relaxed, a higher number of individuals will want to train for the higher skill level. Although a higher proportion of this larger number will leave, this could still result in more doctors and nurses in the country of origin. As might be imagined, there is some controversy over empirical testing of the brain-gain hypothesis. A review by Docquier and Rapoport (2012: 681) concludes, "The recent empirical literature shows that high-skill emigration need not deplete a country's human capital stock and can generate positive network externalities."

But there are counterarguments, as indicated by Brock in her contribution to Brock and Blake (2015: 260–61): "However, the brain gain is not always beneficial to source countries, as enhanced training can be skewed towards usefulness in the targeted destination countries. . . . Even when there is a notable brain gain, there is considerable variation in whether it is significant [enough] to outweigh other factors."

Added to Brock's arguments is the weight of further inequality considerations. The acquisition of skills is generally biased toward those who can afford the short-term costs. Thus it will be typically the already wealthy who will acquire the skills demanded. Those who successfully migrate will send remittances back to their already wealthy families, and so on. While the relationship between remittances and inequality in sending countries is complex, there are certainly situations in which outmigration can increase and has increased source-country inequality (Docquier, Rapoport, and Shen 2010).

All of this is typically set in the framework of asking the question whether the rich countries should restrict immigration. Collier (2013), for example, argues that restrictive immigration policies will benefit receiving rich countries, but they could also benefit sending poor countries. But the question could equally well be posed as whether poor countries should restrict emigration. Here the arguments for freedom of movement clash against the arguments for the social benefits of such restriction to sending countries. As Blake puts it in his debate with Brock (Brock and Blake 2015: 286–87): "Whatever can be done to keep the 'best' of a given population in its home jurisdiction must be compatible with the rights of people to seek their own happiness, to form new relationships, and to decide for themselves where they will do both. If people are not happy with the society where they are, they have the right to leave." Thus even if the brain drain, as its name suggests, makes the sending country worse off on average and increases inequality in that country, Blake would argue against restrictive emigration. Indeed it seems as though whether outmigration reduces or increases source-country inequality, reduces or increases receiving-country inequality, reduces or increases inequality between nations, on this view restricting outmigration is on a different moral plane. Its impact on inequality is at best secondary and complementary to the central argument based on the rights of people. There does indeed seem to be more to the world than the narrow economic conceptions of inequality within and between nations, and the sum of those two as global inequality.

Conclusion

Starting with inequality, I have attempted to explore the intersection between two discourses that have become prominent in analysis and policy. First is the evolution of global inequality. Inequality has been taken to mean a narrow economic conception of inequality of income. This allows us to focus on global inequality as composed of inequality between nations and inequality within nations, and to consider the evolution of each component in recent decades. Second is the troubled and explosive issue of cross-border migration. In light of recent backlashes against in-migration to rich countries, the question arises as to whether borders should be significantly more or less open to economic migration than they are.[5] While response and resistance to migration can be discussed from many perspectives, I have focused on the implications of open borders for economic inequality in its within-nation and between-nations dimensions.

By and large, economic models predict a decline in global income inequality as borders become more open to the movement of people. This is mainly because such opening narrows income gaps between nations, which is by far the largest component of global inequality. But opening borders can have significant distributional consequences within receiving countries and within sending countries. Clearly the migrants themselves benefit as they move to higher incomes. But their presence could lower incomes for some in receiving countries, and their absence could negatively affect those left behind in sending countries. It is these within-nation inequality consequences that drive the politics of the open-borders question and that are also at the heart of the philosophical and ethical discourse on open borders.

Beyond the narrow economic analysis of open borders and inequality are deeper questions of the rights of individuals to move to destinations of their choice and the rights of nation-states to restrict the right to enter or to leave. Against a thoroughgoing cosmopolitanism and global equality of opportunity view, which would make place of birth irrelevant to prospects faced by individuals, are arguments that a democratic polity has the right to restrict entry and that this is indeed the essence of democracy, or that a state has the right to restrict exit if that exit will have negative consequences for those left behind. However, despite its narrowness and, ultimately, incompleteness in addressing the question of open borders, I hope this paper has shown how an economic inequality perspective can help to structure arguments in favor of and against openness, at the very least as an entry point into a broader discourse.

Notes

1. The data sources are typically national household surveys that collect information on household income and expenditure. In fact, for most countries information on "income" inequality is actually inequality in monetary expenditure across households. Total monetary household expenditure is corrected for price variations across space and time in order to arrive at "real" consumption. Rural-urban and regional price indices are used to make these corrections, raising technical issues of their own. The severity of the problem is magnified when comparing across countries. The use of official exchange rates to convert rupees and cedis into a common unit of account, usually dollars, is problematic because of the vagaries of exchange rate determination. So a direct method is used with data from the International Comparisons Project, which collects price information around the world and generates conversion factors known as "purchasing power parity" (PPP). These PPP conversion factors are meant to convert one rupee into an equivalent purchasing power compared to one cedi, but technical issues abound in developing these factors. There are many other substantive and technical issues in household surveys, such as undersampling of the very rich. Nevertheless, if we wish to discuss economic inequality at the global level, these are the issues we have to confront. For a good discussion of these, see Atkinson 2017.

2. The phrase is used by Milanovic 2016.

3. The Chinese growth experience is reviewed in Fan et al. 2014.

4. In particular one might argue that we cannot simply cordon off the nation-state as the boundaries of democratic practice when completely undemocratic

means were employed to subvert the development of free markets or democracies in other places, giving advantages to the countries that are presently rich as a result.

5. I emphasize again that issues of refugee migration are not addressed in this chapter.

CRISIS 13

DIDIER FASSIN

One day in August 2017, as I was beginning to reflect on the pervasiveness of the language of crises, I conducted an online search in the *New York Times* archive, which I limited to articles published in the newspaper during the previous twenty-four hours. It provided thirty-six occurrences of the word *crisis* either in the title or in the description. They included a "diplomatic crisis" ongoing with North Korea about nuclear weapons, a "political crisis" in Venezuela following the election of a Constituent Assembly, a "cash crisis" in Yemen on the side of the Saudi-supported government, a "refugee crisis" in India as a result of the massive displacement of Rohingyas, a "citizenship crisis" in Australia after the discovery of several lawmakers' binationality, a "currency crisis" in Nigeria associated with an economic recession, an "opioid crisis" declared a national emergency in the United States, a "domestic crisis" caused by the US president's complacency toward alt-right violence in Virginia, a "subway crisis" as a result of the aging and congestion of the transportation system in New York City, a global "doping crisis" in track and field sports exacerbated by the Russian case, and of course various mentions of the 2008 "financial crisis," the Greek "debt crisis," the Syrian "humanitarian crisis," and even a reference to the "identity crisis" experienced by a character on the television series *Game of Thrones*. This list, which is more evocative of Jorge Luis Borges's fictitious Chinese encyclopedia, with its hilarious classification of animals, than of material for a potential research program, should, however, not be taken lightly. The word *crisis* is part of the common vocabulary and shared imaginary of contemporary societies. One can regard it as a sign of the times, this expression being understood in its literal sense: it signals something about the present. We thus live in a world *of* crises. But does this mean that we also inhabit a world *in* crisis? We should certainly be prudent in establishing an equivalence between the two.

Does the ubiquity of the notion of crisis, its self-evidence, its rhetorical effectivity, and its social success signify a new "age of anxiety," as in W. H. Auden's ([1947] 2011) eponymous eclogue—anxiety about the world and us, which remains to be specified? I will address this question from three successive perspectives. I will first conduct a philological exploration of the development and intersection of the two notions, showing the relevance of such exercise to unpack the historical link between crisis and critique. I will then turn to a sociological inquiry and address critically the question of a world of crises, asking more precisely how crises come into being. I will finally propose an anthropological inquiry and suggest ways to ponder the possible meanings of a world in crisis from a critical perspective.

Crisis and Critique

The word *crisis* has its origins in the Indo-European root *krei*. In particular, in ancient Greek, the verb κρίνω (*krinō*) means "to separate," "to distinguish," "to choose," as well as "to judge," "to decide," "to resolve," "to interpret" (Bailly 1935: 1137). It thus implies a dual aspect of discrimination among ideas, things, and people, and of determination in front of a situation, a conflict, a crime. It has an analytic dimension (to separate) and a normative one (to judge). Derived from it, the noun κρίσις (*krisis*) means the act of distinguishing and of deciding as well as the crucial phase of a war or of a disease, the two meanings being closely connected: it is at this dramatic juncture that the right judgment and relevant action prove determining. Two elements are therefore linked and frequently confused: the existence of a pivotal moment in the evolution of an event (we would describe it today as *critical*, in the sense of "qualifying as a crisis") and the evaluation of this event in order to adjudicate (we would also define it as *critical*, but this time in the sense of "developing a critique"). Most important, *crisis* and *critique* are etymologically linked: the critical event calls for a critical interpretation, which eventually leads to a response.

According to Reinhart Koselleck's ([1982] 2006) classic essay in conceptual history, there were three contexts in which the verb κρίνω (krinō) or the noun κρίσις (krisis) were generally used: legal, religious, and medical. In the legal realm, they meant balancing the pros and cons, differentiating between good and bad, and settling the case, which could concern an offense, an election, a battle; they carried a positive value associated with justice. In the religious field, they generally referred to the Last Judgment of the Christian doctrine, with the idea that the ultimate determination between salvation and damnation could be anticipated by one's conduct during one's life; they consequently involved both individual conscience and collective destiny. In the medical domain, as represented by the *Corpus Hippocraticum*, they indicated simultaneously the juncture in the development of an illness that could result in life or death for the patient and the decision made by the physician that could influence this outcome. Both could be recurrent as the disease developed, and Galen later extended the notion to chronic conditions.

From ancient Greek, the word *crisis* was eventually adopted in the various European languages, but it is only from the seventeenth century on that its meaning was progressively extended beyond the religious and medical realms. The introduction of the term to describe political events in the eighteenth century is remarkable as it signals the emergence of a philosophy of history, which offers numerous variations. It points to the acknowledgment of moments of transition when the breakdown of the present marks a rupture with the past and announces changes for the future, with possible teleological implications. In 1762 Jean-Jacques Rousseau (1979: 158) wrote in a premonitory way, "We are approaching a state of crisis and the age of revolutions." Seventeen years later the French Revolution started. This event became the paradigmatic case of a crisis leading to a drastic transformation of the state of the world, in which Thomas Paine, whose journal was titled the *Crisis*, optimistically saw the promise of the end of tyranny and oppression, while Edmund Burke mournfully deplored the destruction of the traditional social order and legitimate political institutions. Interestingly, the use of the word to designate economic events, which has become so widespread today that it sometimes does not even need to be specified by an adjective, occurred relatively late, in the nineteenth century, with the parallel rise of capitalism and political economy, the former being accompanied by recurrent crashes, the latter being used to explain them. Whereas the new idea of the cyclical character of economic crises became commonplace among theorists, their reading of them differed radically. For liberals, such as Julius Wolf, they were necessary events with positive effects as they corrected the deficiencies of the system. For Marx and Engels, on the contrary, they signified the demise of capitalism and rendered the coming of revolutions inexorable. Finally, in the twentieth century, the word *crisis* pursued its generalization, with a dissemination in the moral and intellectual worlds, especially during the interwar period, when, most notably, Paul Valéry's ([1919] 1977) *Crisis of the Mind* and Edmund Husserl's ([1936] 1970) *The Crisis of the European Sciences and Transcendental Phenomenology* offered tragic perspectives on the values and knowledge of their time, respectively. But, as mentioned earlier, almost any human activity or social fact can today potentially be described as being in crisis.

As Friedrich Nietzsche showed, philology has much to teach us about our present, and notably about the buried meanings of the words we use and of the imaginaries we share. With respect to crisis, what can we therefore learn from this outline of the etymology of the term and the development of the idea? At least three things.

First, the original meaning of the word indissociably links a critical moment and the critical assessment of it, or said otherwise, crisis and critique. Contemporary crises inextricably associate the two dimensions: there is an actual situation, which is considered to be problematic, and there is the account of it, which makes it exist through various forms of argumentation and representation. Both these processes are crucial: the evidence of the crisis has to be established, but the crisis has to be exposed to become imaginable. The ecological crisis is thus made possible by the conjunction of the emission of greenhouse gases causing global warming and inadequate policies aggravating it, on the one hand, and of the measurement and interpretation of the phenomenon by scientists, the production of a language, of tables and graphs, of images and narratives, on the other hand. Think of Naomi Oreskes and Erik Conway's (2014) *The Collapse of Western Civilization*, which proposes a dark view of our world from our future in a science fiction essay, or of Dale Jamieson and Bonnie Nadzam's (2015) *Love in the Anthropocene*, whose short stories less tragically imagine life in societies where nature has been entirely dominated.

Second, a tension that traverses the religious and medical uses of the word develops into the modern age between two philosophies of history, with two contrasted representations of crisis as a unique decisive moment or as multiple and possibly recurrent events. The first version, teleological, in its secularized variations regarding the economic realm offers opposite views on the fate of capitalism: the millenarian *Grand soir* and the Second International's *Lutte finale* promise its irremediable collapse, whereas the assertive "end of history" announces its ultimate victory. But it has more mundane expressions through the definitive diagnoses formulated by so-called declinists, for whom crises signal the inevitable termination of an era when things were better. The second version, pragmatic, is typically illustrated by the notion of cyclical economic crises that are supposed to regulate the flaws of capitalism and ultimately improve its efficacy and profitability. It operates as a normalization of the repeated phenomena of crash or recession, thus avoiding major changes in the system responsible for them and trivializing their human consequences. As shown by Adam Tooze (2018), the shock of the 2008 financial crisis has been profitable in the long run to banks, companies, and shareholders, while its effects in terms of eviction, pauperization, and marginalization of vulnerable populations remain largely unaccounted for. Today not only does the periodic foretelling of a new coming crisis not generate political responses to prevent it, but continuing deregulatory policies even tend to precipitate it. This tension between teleological and pragmatic versions can be illustrated by the irreconcilable analyses of Wolfgang Streeck's (2016) *How Will Capitalism End?*, which argues that the crisis of the system is critically beyond remedy, and Luc Boltanski and Eve Chiapello's ([1999] 2006) *The New Spirit of Capitalism*, which suggests that the system always overcomes its crises by integrating the critiques formulated against it.

Third, the contemporary understanding of the word and the idea of crisis is the result of relatively recent developments. In this sense, viewing the state of the world in terms of crisis, that is, of dramatic ruptures into the normal course of things that will bring about serious disorder and call for urgent solution, would be a signature of Western modernity. However, the lack of a term does not necessarily indicate the absence of the notion that it names. We have too little knowledge of the way dramatic moments such as the 1348 Great Plague in Europe, which killed dozens of millions of people and provoked major demographic, social, economic, political, and cultural disruptions, or the 1521 fall of the Aztec Empire, which led to the destruction of one of the richest pre-Columbian civilizations as well as the exploitation and evangelization of the native population, were experienced and represented to be certain that a sense of crisis was absent. But in fact, what authorizes scholars to affirm that crisis is a modern concept is that they indissociably connect it with critique. And they do so in two ways. In Koselleck's ([1959] 1988) *Critique and Crisis*, the development of critical thinking is the far-reaching consequence of the ascent of absolutism to put an end to the wars of religion, as was already argued by Hobbes, since a separation was then established between individual conscience and sovereign power. But instead of remaining in the private domain it had been assigned, critique progressively expanded into the public sphere, thus shifting from moral judgment to political contestation, eventually provoking a crisis, which is epitomized in France by the 1789 Revolution and the decapitation of the monarch. In Michel Foucault's (1997) "What Is Critique?," conversely, it is the crisis caused by the excesses of the practices of governing by the king as well as by the church and the discontent they generated that is at the source of critique as the art of not being governed in this way. This approach is explicitly inscribed in the lineage of Kant's "What Is Enlightenment?," which is a protest against the restrictions on freedom of his time and a call for the emancipation of human beings from their state of minority. In other words, we could say that, for Koselleck, critique preceded crisis and was destructive, while for Foucault, crisis called for critique and was productive. The opposition between the two is in part methodological, as the Begriffsgeschichte of the former is quite distinct from the genealogical approach of the latter, and in part ideological, as one denounces the Enlightenment while the other praises it. One could, however, wonder with Talal Asad (2013) whether making critique a signature of Western modernity is not ignoring older traditions, from Diogenes the Cynic to Étienne de la Boétie, as well as traditions elsewhere, for instance in the rich heritage of Arab and Farsi thinking or Muslim and Jewish theology.

Thus far the etymological and genealogical approach has mostly allowed me to explore the complex relations between crisis and critique, their concomitant emergence, the lasting traces of their original meanings, and their problematic interaction in modern times. But I have yet to show how critique can help us apprehend better what we call crises. A sociological and anthropological approach will contribute to this endeavor. Indeed we can assume that sociology will contribute to our comprehension of the world *of* crises (plural), that is, the existence of crises in the world, whereas anthropology will advance our understanding of the world *in* crisis (singular), that is, the centrality of the language of crisis in the world.

A World of Crises

So, a world of crises. According to our philological inquiry, in order to exist, a crisis must logically combine two elements: the presence of a situation that disrupts the supposedly normal order of things and its recognition as such. Let us call the former an objective fact and the latter a subjective one.

In a study I conducted a few years ago on child lead poisoning, I showed how a long-ignored problem could suddenly become a public health crisis

(Fassin and Naudé 2004). In most countries, the contamination of children by lead particles is mainly due to old paints that were widely used in housing during the twentieth century. Although their toxicity has been known since the 1890s, aggressive advertising campaigns conducted by the lead industry, which covered up the dangers of the metal, considerably delayed the official banning of these paints, which took place in 1949 in France and 1978 in the United States. In poor neighborhoods, however, children who lived after these dates in dilapidated homes with old deteriorated paints continued to be exposed to the risk through the ingestion of flakes and the inhalation of dust. Consequences could be lethal in the most serious cases, but for the majority of affected children they consisted in neurological damage leading to cognitive disability, behavioral disorder, and educational underachievement. When a case was diagnosed in Lyon in 1981, a clinical review in the French medical literature found only ten cases in the previous twenty-five years, leading the authors to conclude that lead poisoning was extremely rare among children. Less than two decades later, in 1999, a report written by experts from the French National Institute for Health estimated that eighty-five thousand children between one and six years old, representing 2 percent of their age group, suffered from lead poisoning, these children belonging almost exclusively to disadvantaged migrant families.

From then on the exceptional disease was turned into a silent—or even silenced—epidemic. It became a public health national priority. The discrepancy between the two figures—ten in twenty-five years becoming eighty-five thousand—was obviously due not to a sudden increase in the number of children poisoned by lead but to the identification of the issue by the medical community via population screenings. In other words, the problem had been there, but it had not been problematized, to use Foucault's vocabulary. There are several reasons for this negligence, the most significant ones being the social and spatial marginalization of the affected groups, mainly Africans living in rundown apartments and decaying squats, and the lack of interest of public authorities for their material and sanitary conditions. Symmetrically, there are also reasons it suddenly came to be apprehended, the most important of them being the mobilization of physicians, social workers, and, above all, members of humanitarian and human rights organizations who carried out epidemiological surveys, visited foreign programs, and pressured an initially reluctant French government. The public health crisis thus resulted from the conjunction of two facts: the existence of bodies poisoned by a toxic metal and the recognition of the reality of this poisoning. The first one can be analyzed in terms of social production: What produced lead poisoning, and why were poor migrant children especially affected? The answer to these questions involves the sociohistorical study of public housing and immigration policies of the past half-century. The second one can be grasped in terms of social construction: How was the epidemic discovered and interpreted, and by whom? The answers to these questions imply an investigation into the encounter between public health techniques and public health activists.

As a general statement, we can say that any crisis can be analyzed from the dual perspective of its social production (What caused the problem?) and its social construction (How did it come to be problematized?). In many cases, the two anticipated elements—the problem and its problematization, to use Foucault's wording—are thus combined to engender the crisis. But what happens when this is not the case? What happens when the problem is not problematized, or when the problematization does not correspond to an actual problem? In the first configuration, that of an alarming situation that does not get recognition, can we still speak of a crisis? That is, can a crisis be considered to exist without being named or perceived? In the second configuration, that of an alarming imaginary that does not rely on a matter of fact, what does such disconnection tell us about this crisis? That is, how to interpret a crisis with no evident ground? To answer these two series of questions, we have to take seriously the making of crises. Through which processes, involving which politics of truth, do crises come, or not, into being?

The relevant concept here is that of authorship. In his *Dictionary of Indo-European Concepts and Society*, Émile Benveniste ([1969] 2016: 429–30) traces the Latin meaning of the word *auctor*, the one "who founds, who guarantees, and finally who is the author," with the primary sense of "cause to appear," and he adds that "this is how the abstract *auctoritas* acquired its full force" as "a gift which is reserved to a handful of men who can literally 'bring to existence.'" Indeed "every word pronounced with *authority* determines a change in the world." But according to Alain Rey ([1992] 2006: 2:265), *auctor* also gave *auctorare*, "to guarantee" on the basis of this authority and, from there, "to allow," "to legitimize," "to authorize." In the case of crises, to interpret the first configuration, that of crises made invisible (drowned migrants in large numbers, for instance), one has to ask who has the authority to declare the existence of a crisis, and who does not, whereas to analyze the second configuration, that of crises grossly fabricated (exaggeration of the reality of immigration, for example), one has to ask what the affirmation of the existence of a crisis authorizes and, conversely, what it censures.

Consider the problem of police violence as an illustration of a crisis made invisible. When I conducted an ethnography of law enforcement, and more specifically of anticrime units in the banlieues of Paris (Fassin [2011] 2013), I could hardly ignore it, not only for its empirical presence during my fieldwork but also because I started my research a few months before the 2005 riots erupted throughout the country in reaction to the death of two adolescents chased by police officers and ended it a few weeks before the 2007 more local but more fierce riot started subsequent to the death of two youths run down by a police car in what looked like a deliberate act. In fact, since the 1980s, nearly each time someone was killed as a result of an inter-action with law enforcement agents—this someone being almost always a young man of African origin—urban disorders occurred. By contrast, in the United States, where multiple serious episodes of civil unrest had taken place in the 1960s in Watts, Detroit, Baltimore, and Newark, the situation had apparently been pacified in disadvantaged neighborhoods during the past half-century, with the notable exception of the 1992 Los Angeles riots after the acquittal of the officers who had assaulted Rodney King. The re-markable dissimilarity between the two countries led several scholars to develop various hypotheses to account for it, notably the better represen-tation of racial minorities in local politics, their increased access to courts of law, their progressive integration into police departments, their involve-ment in nonviolent organizations, and, more critically, the consequence of mass incarceration, which had removed the most vehement individu-als from the public spaces. Then, in August 2014, Michael Brown was shot dead by a police officer. The Ferguson riots started, the Black Lives Matter movement developed, and as the killing of mostly young African Ameri-can men by law enforcement agents made the news on a quasi-daily basis, protests and sometimes riots multiplied across the country. The crisis in policing became a major issue, leading to public debates, federal investi-gations, reform proposals, and defiant reactions from police departments and unions. Studies revealed that on average more than three people were killed by law enforcement agents every day in the United States. But beyond these tragic events, the experience of a majority of black people, especially men, with the police was one of ordinary physical, verbal, and moral abuse, with harassment via stop and frisk, humiliation by demeaning comments and racist slurs, recurrent citations and summons for low-level offenses generating fines, fees, and sometimes jail for nonpayment. Prima facie, we could think that the police crisis in the United States typically combines the two elements previously evoked, objective and subjective: a situation of multifaceted violence and its identification by the society at large. And we could argue that there was no such crisis before Ferguson because there was no problematization of the problem or, to put it straightforwardly, no perception of the issue. But this reasoning would ignore the fact that, as multiple testimonies reveal, this awareness did exist among black communities long before it became mainstream knowledge. It existed through literature, organizations, intellectuals, and multiple other channels—but was simply ignored by the majority. African Americans often expressed their surprise that people would suddenly discover what they had always known by experience: the banality of police abuses against them. This dissociation leads to the important conclusion that the problematization of the issue had been socially and racially segmented.

The question therefore becomes: Who has the authority to name a crisis? Obviously not everyone does. Indeed the recognition of a situation as crisis can be disregarded on the grounds that it comes from a minority who has little access to the public sphere. But evidence of this disparity in authorship over the word *crisis*, that is, in the ability to bring a crisis into existence, is not limited to inequalities within countries; it is also true for inequalities between countries. In 2015, at the height of the so-called migrant crisis in Europe, at a time when images of long lines of migrants walking along the roads and of people pressed against barbed wires, falsified statistics and dramatic graphs, distressing discourses and shocking phrases made the headlines of newspapers across the planet, one country had more asylum seekers than the whole European continent. It was South Africa, where the number of persons applying for refugee status exceeded one million, the largest proportion being from Zimbabwe. Relative to its population, this was ten times more than Europe and twenty times more than France. But who ever heard about a migrant crisis in South Africa? Yet in the research I carried out there during that period (Fassin, Wilhelm-Solomon, and Segatti 2017), I realized how critical the situation was for the authorities of the country, torn between respect for international law and flare-ups of xenophobic violence, and above all for the migrants, who illegally occupied abandoned buildings, survived with the meager sums obtained from begging, and constantly feared police raids in their squats and harassment in the street. But neither the South African government nor the Zimbabwean asylum seekers could make their crisis come into being in the global public sphere. They did not have the authority to do so. A critique of crises should therefore question not only the conditions of possibility of crises but also their conditions of impossibility. What are the unsettling or harrowing situations that never come into being for lack of an authorized agency? The "repression of voice," which Veena Das (2007: 6) worries about as she accounts for the wounds and losses of Indian women, should be a concern for what regards not only individuals but also communities. One task of the critic is to give voice to those who do not have authority to have their crisis acknowledged and to thus contribute to bringing to existence untold crises: the crises of the dominated.

But symmetrically, there are crises that are fabricated by the dominant, in the sense that they do not rely on the facts that are allegedly at stake, either because they merely do not exist or, more often, because they are distorted. On July 14, 2001, French president Jacques Chirac began the ritual televised interview for the celebration of Bastille Day with a long evocation of what he described as a major rise in crime and violence, declaring that it had reached an unbearable level as people in cities and even the countryside lived in "fear," a word that he uttered seven times. Speaking of "people being assaulted and young women being raped," he interpreted this situation as a consequence of the "lacking authority of the state" and called for a "zero tolerance" policy. This interview is believed to have launched and definitely oriented the presidential campaign, which for the first time under the Fifth Republic was focused on "insecurity." Yet, remarkably, there did not exist any statistical evidence of an increase in crime, for which several indicators even showed a decline over the years. Only anecdotal facts abundantly covered by the media and commented on by right-wing politicians could explain the sudden progression of the so-called sentiment of insecurity among people who, most of them, had never been personally exposed to any such violence. Rather than the famous Tocqueville paradox, according to which the more an unpleasant phenomenon declines, the less it is accepted, as many commentators suggested, it was more trivially a matter of mere manipulation of the opinion for political purposes. And the promotion of fear that had been initiated had the expected effect: the president was reelected. Significantly, his first campaign, five years earlier, had been on what he had designated as the "social fracture" between the poor and the wealthy. The shift from inequality to insecurity marked a crucial transformation in the public sphere. As economic disparities, which had been deepening since the 1980s, were not addressed by the government, the latter turned to the war on crime. Law and order substituted for social justice. During the following decade of right-wing government, the prison population increased by 52 percent, leading to an extreme overcrowding the appalling consequences of which I have analyzed in my ethnography of a correctional facility (Fassin [2015] 2016). This dramatic evolution in incarceration rates is not, however, equitably distributed across the social spectrum. There is an increase in convictions for minor offenses such as marijuana possession, driving with a suspended license, and misdemeanors, while convictions for economic and financial crime decline. Thus the social categories affected by the growing economic disparities are the same that are specifically targeted by the new policies. The declared security crisis consequently had for effect the invisibilization of inequalities, the criminalization of the disadvantaged, and ultimately the substitution of the growing penal state for the waning welfare state.

The general question that can be drawn from this case is therefore: What does the naming of a crisis authorize, and what does it censure? The fact of not only labeling it but also interpreting it gives the power to transform the representation of the world and act in consequence according to one's interests or to the interests of the group with whom one is allied. Those who are granted such authority define the problems, decide the stakes, and determine the solutions. By doing so, they discard alternative ways of construing, explaining, and responding to the situations faced. An interesting case is that of humanitarianism, whose language has imposed itself in recent years as an effective way of characterizing crises. Describing a situation as a humanitarian crisis can justify a military intervention, as was the case in Libya in 2011, when the newly voted United Nations doctrine called "responsibility to protect" was invoked for the first time as Benghazi was allegedly the theater of a forthcoming massacre—a threat later known to have been forged. Conversely, it can avoid taking sides in a conflict, as is the case today in Yemen, where the depiction of the civil war as a humanitarian crisis, which it is undeniably, allows Western states to affirm their neutrality while eluding their own responsibility in the massacre of populations—since they actively support the coalition's deadly operations. The affirmation of a humanitarian crisis calls for immediate responses and gives a moral tonality to the politics deployed. By calling the tragic landslide that caused the death of tens of thousands of people in Venezuela on December 15, 1999, a humanitarian crisis, the government, led by the recently elected Hugo Chávez, obtained a large popular consensus as he declared a state of emergency and mobilized the army in the rescue operation, a gesture that would have been much more difficult to legitimize in another context. As I found in the research I conducted in the aftermath (Fassin and Vasquez 2005), the sense of urgency and the appeal to emotions, which this language induced, was crucial in the compassionate militarization of the response to the disaster. More generally, referring to a situation as a crisis always brings into play both a temporality, that of urgency, and an affectivity, which can take a wide range, from empathy to fear. Both this temporality and this affectivity generally serve interests and strengthen powers. As Joseph Masco (2017: S75) wrote about the way "the nuclear danger and the climate danger" are addressed in the United States, "crisis talk seeks to stabilize an institution, practice, or reality rather than interrogate the historical condition of possibility of endangerment to occur." It is therefore another task of the critic of crisis to ask which agents benefit from it and what are their hidden agendas.

A World in Crisis

So much for the world *of* crises. What about the world *in* crisis? It would seem strangely contrarian to deny that there is today a general sense that the present moment offers certain particular traits in terms of the quality, intensity, and spread of its crises, whether one considers the late recognition of the human imprint on the planet's sustainability; the amplification of forced migrations caused by conflicts, persecution, or poverty; the multiplication of radical religious, ethnic, or nationalist movements; the deepening of inequality within and across societies; the questioning of knowledge, truth, and simply facts associated with the dissemination of conspiracy theories; the rise of xenophobic populism and its electoral successes. But should we assume that all these crises have a common denominator, let alone a common determinant? Can their multiplication be reduced to a sort of metacrisis that would encompass the variety of specific crises discussed until now?

There is a double paradox here: one semantic, the other epistemological. First, while crises have been construed on the background of and in contrast with normalcy (a crisis is a rupture in the normal order of things), a world in crisis would imply the normalization of crisis (there would be no outside of crisis; it would become the new normal). Second, whereas I have argued that crises were the result of a social construction (critique should therefore uncover what is at stake in the process, in particular in terms of power relations and hidden agendas), the idea of permanent crisis would tend to essentialize it (as an immanent production of contemporary societies). The critical theory of the Frankfurt School has attempted to surmount these paradoxes by thinking in terms of "social pathologies" rather than "crisis" and by giving those what Axel Honneth (2009: 21) calls "an explosive charge" derived from their "socially effective rationality" and therefore potential for change. If we were to adopt this perspective, the omnipresence of a representation of a world in crisis could reflect two possible realities, which are distinct but partially linked. The first one, objective, would reveal the crisis of capitalism or, more generally, of the rational foundations of contemporary societies. The second one, subjective, could indicate the awareness of this crisis by both those who benefit from the system and those who suffer from it. While I am not convinced by the former, which has been announced too many times to be entirely credible, I have provided some empirical evidence of the latter, against the too easily invoked idea of false consciousness. But it is a different path that I will follow: critical social science rather than critical theory.

The ubiquity of the representation of the world in terms of crisis can be seen as a form of life in the sense that Wittgenstein gave to this phrase, that is, an agreement in the ordinary language that allows human beings to share common understandings in most of the situations they encounter. When we speak of crisis, we think that we comprehend something of the world and that this comprehension is shared. When we hear journalists, politicians, social scientists, or lay people describing a given situation as a crisis, we apprehend more or less what they are talking about. From the perspective I propose, the question, then, is less to wonder whether what they say about a specific crisis or a possible general crisis is true, or not, than to examine the sort of truths that are delivered through their enunciation. As Janet Roitman (2014: 94) writes in her *Anti-Crisis*, in which she discusses at length and in depth the 2008 financial and economic crisis, "The point is to observe crisis as a blind spot, and hence to apprehend the ways in which it regulates narrative constructions, the ways in which it allows certain questions to be asked while others are foreclosed." Critique resides indeed in the deconstruction of crisis as a given. It goes further than what Jacques Derrida (2002: 71) writes in the context of the economic recession of the early 1980s: "The representation of crisis and the rhetoric it organizes always have at least this purpose: to determine, in order to limit it, a more serious and more formless threat, one which is in fact faceless and normless. By determining it as crisis, one tames it, domesticates it, neutralizes it—in short, one economizes it." While the naming of a situation as crisis can have this reassuring function of cognitive appropriation of uncertainty, I showed earlier that it also has other social and political functions. Understanding who has the authority to articulate the existence of a crisis, and who does not, and what this diagnosis authorizes, and with which purposes, allows us to recognize that some of the most serious issues of our time are not phrased in terms of crisis, on one side, and that the making of crises obeys logics having little to do with the problems at stake, on the other. Such critique is potentially productive. As Rodrigo Cordero (2017: 33) writes, "crisis is a moment that triggers socially reflexive processes of social criticism" that in the end can "create spaces for political innovation." For this critical process to be effective in the approach to the contemporary crisis, I suggest three methodological precautions.

First, we should avoid the singularization of crisis, which comes down to subsuming all crises under one single phenomenon. It seems more heuristic to specify distinct crises and analyze how they relate to each other. If the United States is considered to be confronted with a major crisis of its governance and even identity under the present administration, we have to go beyond this immediate apprehension and connect the democratic issue, which is characterized by the disenfranchisement of six million citizens, the abstention of half of the constituency, the financialization of election campaigns, the representatives' dependency on lobbies, and the politicization of the judicial institution; the social question, which is expressed through the deepening of inequalities in all aspects of life, the marginalization of minorities, and the stigmatization of immigrants; and the flourishing of the economic and financial system, which mostly benefits a powerful minority. The crisis is neither general nor universal, and the election of the current president did not create, as is often said, but instead revealed the democratic issue and social question by turning them into a crisis.

Second, we should caution against presentist tendencies, manifest in the implicit idea that we live in a unique moment when our societies are facing one ultimate crisis. There is a long history of such moments, and the twentieth century, with two world wars, several genocides, a brutal decolonization, a major financial crash, has had its share of them. Definitive diagnoses and gloomy predictions abound in the writings of intellectuals repetitively depicting a tragic present and announcing a crepuscular future. Suffice it to read past works and newspapers in difficult times to see the recurrence of the theme from the aftermath of World War I with its so-called lost generation to 9/11 attacks purportedly signaling a clash of civilizations. There are specificities in the present moment to which we must be attentive, with the consequences of climate change for the most vulnerable populations, the inextinguishable greed of capitalism, and the progress of threatening ideologies, but they do not call for a teleological reading.

Third, we should beware of an ethnocentric perspective, which has been all too common in the conversation on crisis in the Western world. Most interpretations of the perils of the present moment came after two unexpected events, the vote for Brexit in the United Kingdom and the election of Donald Trump in the United States, concomitant with the rise of authoritarian regimes in Europe, while the so-called migrant crisis was exclusively seen from a Western perspective as if the Global South was on the verge of invading the Global North. But what do we know about the crisis lived in African countries, such as the Democratic Republic of the Congo or the Central African Republic, where civil wars have caused millions of victims? How can we think of crisis in places where people say that they have not experienced anything else for decades, such as Argentina, which has recurrently been confronted with economic instability for most of the past eighty years, or Palestine, whose inhabitants have been under Israeli occupation and oppression for seventy years? And how should we reflect on contexts in which the discourse on crisis is censured, as is the case in China? We therefore need to provincialize the Western crisis and, for instance, remember that 9/11, before being a tragic attack in the United States in 2001, had been in 1973 a military coup that terminated democracy in Chile and had received the support of the government of the United States. One crisis can sometimes conceal another.

With these three caveats in mind, we can understand how difficult it is to answer in a nondisappointing way the question of whether we are entering one of these delicate moments in history when "the old is dying and the new cannot be born," in Gramsci's words. Social scientists are neither oracles nor prophets. They can only scrupulously examine the world as it is, faithfully account for what people have to say about it, mindfully formulate what they have understood of it, and ultimately open their analysis to public discussion.

Note

The research in this essay forms part of a program funded by the Distinguished Scholar Award that I received from the Nomis Foundation. I am grateful to my coeditor, Veena Das, for her insightful comments on an earlier version of this text and to my colleagues in the School of Social Science at the Institute for Advanced Study for our enriching discussions as part of the program on Crisis and Critique that I have run in collaboration with Axel Honneth during the year 2018–19.

REFERENCES

Abu-Lughod, Lila. 1990. "The Romance of Resistance: Tracing Transformations of Power through Bedouin Women." *American Ethnologist* 17, no. 1: 41–55.

Acemoglu, Daron, and James A. Robinson. 2012. *Why Nations Fail: The Origins of Power, Prosperity, and Poverty.* New York: Crown Business.

Adger, W. Neil. 2000. "Social and Ecological Resilience: Are They Related?" *Progress in Human Geography* 24, no. 3: 347–64.

Agamben, Giorgio. 2003. *State of Exception.* Translated by Kevin Attell. Chicago: University of Chicago Press.

Akhavi, Shahrough. 1980. *Religion and Politics in Contemporary Iran.* Albany, NY: SUNY Press.

Alesina, Alberto, Johann Harnoss, and Hillel Rapoport. 2018. "Immigration and the Future of the Welfare State in Europe." Paris School of Economics, Working Paper no. 2018–04. https://ideas.repec.org/p/hal/psewpa/halshs -01707760.html.

Algar, Hamid. 1980. *The Islamic Revolution in Iran.* London: Open Press.

Alijany, Reza. 2006. *Bad-Fahmi-ye yek towjih-he nā movaffaq* [The misinterpretation of an unsuccessful justification]. Tehran: Kavir.

Alpes, Maybritt J. 2017. *Brokering High-Risk Migration and Illegality in West Africa: Abroad at Any Cost.* Abingdon, UK: Routledge.

Anderson, Perry. 2000. "Renewals." *New Left Review* 1: 1–20.

Appiah, Kwame Anthony. 2005. *The Ethics of Identity.* Princeton, NJ: Princeton University Press.

Appiah, Kwame Anthony. 2006. *Cosmopolitanism: Ethics in a World of Strangers.* New York: Norton.

Arato, Andrew. 2017. *The Adventures of the Constituent Power: Beyond Revolutions? Comparative Constitutional Law and Policy.* Cambridge: Cambridge University Press.

Arendt, Hannah. 1961. "What Is Authority?" In *Between Past and Future: Six Exercises in Political Thought*, 91–141. Cleveland, OH: Meridian.

Arendt, Hannah. 1990. *On Revolution.* New York: Penguin.

Argumenty i Fakty. 2010. "Gavriil Popov: Korruptsiyu v rossiiskoi stolitse mozhno pobedit'." October 6. http://www.aif.ru/gazeta/number/376.

Asad, Talal. 2003. *Formations of the Secular: Christianity, Islam, Modernity*. Stanford, CA: Stanford University Press.

Asad, Talal. 2013. "Free Speech, Blasphemy, and Secular Criticism." In *Is Critique Secular?: Blasphemy, Injury and Free Speech*, edited by Talal Asad, Wendy Brown, Judith Butler, and Saba Mahmood, 14–37. New York: Fordham University Press.

Asad, Talal. 2015. "Thinking about Tradition, Religion, and Politics in Egypt Today." *Critical Inquiry* 42, no. 1: 166–214.

Atkin, Emily. 2017. "'Republicans' War on Science Just Got Frighteningly Real." *New Republic*, March 9.

Atkinson, A. B. 2017. *Monitoring Global Poverty: Report of the Commission on Global Poverty*. Washington, DC: World Bank.

Auden, W. H. (1947) 2011. *The Age of Anxiety: A Baroque Eclogue*. Princeton, NJ: Princeton University Press.

Austin, J. L. (1962) 1975. *How to Do Things with Words*. Oxford: Oxford University Press.

Autor, David H. 2014. "Skills, Education, and the Rise of Earnings Inequality among the 'Other 99 Percent.'" *Science* 344, no. 6186: 843–51.

Badiou, Alain. 2012. *The Rebirth of History: Times of Riots and Uprisings*. New York: Verso.

Bailly, Anatole. 1935. *Dictionnaire grec-français*. Paris: Hachette.

Baldacchino, Godfrey, and Stephen A. Royle. 2010. "Postcolonialism and Islands: Introduction." *Space and Culture* 13, no. 2: 140–43.

Bargmann, Cori. 2018. "Three Ways to Accelerate Science." *Nature* 553, no. 7686: 19–21.

Barrington, Robert. 2015. "How Corrupt Is Britain?" *HuffPost Blog*, May 22. https://www.huffingtonpost.co.uk/robert-barrington/corruption-britain_b_6911052.html.

Batalvi, Shiv Kumar. 2009. *Birha Tu Sultan*. Amritsar, India: Lok Prakashan.

BBC News. 2017. "Poland MPs Back Controversial Judiciary Bill." July 15. https://www.bbc.com/news/world-europe-40617406.

Beck, Ulrich. 1992. *Risk Society: Towards a New Modernity*. London: Sage.

Beck, Ulrich. 2016. *The Metamorphosis of the World: How Climate Change Is Transforming Our Concept of the World*. Cambridge: Polity.

Bell, Christine, and Jan Pospisil. 2017. "Navigating Inclusion in Transitions from Conflict: The Formalised Political Unsettlement." *Journal of International Development* 29, no. 5: 576–93.

Benjamin, Walter. 1968. "Theses on the Philosophy of History." In *Illuminations: Essays and Reflections*, translated by Harry Zohn, 253–64. New York: Schocken.

Benjamin, Walter. 2004. *Selected Writings*. Vol. 1, *1913–26*, edited by Marcus Bullock and Michael W. Jennings. Cambridge, MA: Belknap Press of Harvard University Press.

Benjamin, Walter. 2006. *Selected Writings*. Vol. 4, *1938–40*, edited by Howard Eiland and Michael W. Jennings. Cambridge, MA: Belknap Press of Harvard University Press.

Benoist, Jocelyn. 2010. *Concepts: Introduction à l'analyse*. Paris: CERF.

Benveniste, Émile. (1969) 2016. *Dictionary of Indo-European Concepts and Society.* Translated by Elizabeth Palmer. Chicago: Hau Books.

Bhagwati, Jagdish, and Michael Partington, eds. 1976. *Taxing the Brain Drain.* Vol. 1, *A Proposal.* Amsterdam: North Holland.

Bhargava, Rajeev, ed. 1998. *Secularism and Its Critics.* New Delhi: Oxford University Press.

Bilgrami, Akeel. 2011. "Gandhi's Religion and Its Relation to His Politics." In *The Cambridge Companion to Gandhi,* edited by Judith M. Brown and Anthony Parel, 96–116. Cambridge: Cambridge University Press.

Bilgrami, Akeel. 2014. *Secularism, Identity, and Enchantment.* Cambridge, MA: Harvard University Press.

Bilgrami, Akeel, ed. 2016. *Beyond the Secular West.* New York: Columbia University Press.

Bird-David, Nurit. 2018. "Size Matters! The Scalability of Modern Hunter-Gatherer Animism." *Quaternary International* 464: 305–14.

Bloch, Ernst. 1986. *The Principle of Hope.* Vol. 1, translated by Neville Plaice, Stephen Plaice, and Paul Knight. Cambridge, MA: MIT Press.

Boltanski, Luc, and Eve Chiapello. (1999) 2006. *The New Spirit of Capitalism.* Translated by Gregory Elliott. London: Verso.

Bondi, Marina, and Mike Scott, eds. 2010. *Keyness in Texts.* Amsterdam: John Benjamins.

Borjas, George. 2003. "The Labor Demand Curve *Is* Downward Sloping: Reexamining the Impact of Immigration on the Labor Market." *Quarterly Journal of Economics* 118, no. 4: 1335–74.

Boulton, Geoffrey, Philip Campbell, Brian Collins, Peter Elias, Wendy Hall, Graeme Laurie, Onora O'Neill, Michael Rawlins, Janet Thornton, Patrick Vallance, and Mark Walport. 2012. *Science as an Open Enterprise.* Report 02/12. London: Royal Society Science Policy Centre.

Bourdieu, Pierre. 1994. "Rethinking the State: Genesis and Structure of the Bureaucratic Field." Translated by Loïc J. D. Wacquant and Samar Farage. *Sociological Theory* 12, no. 1: 1–18.

Brock, Gillian, and Michael Blake. 2015. *Debating Brain Drain: May Governments Restrict Emigration?* Oxford: Oxford University Press.

Brown, Katrina. 2014. "Global Environmental Change I: A Social Turn for Resilience?" *Progress in Human Geography* 38, no. 1: 107–17.

Brown, Wendy. 2018. "Neoliberalism's Frankenstein: Authoritarian Freedom in Twenty-First Century 'Democracies.'" In *Authoritarianism: Three Inquiries in Critical Theory,* edited by Wendy Brown, Peter E. Gordon, and Max Pensky, 7–43. Chicago: University of Chicago Press.

Bruhn, Kathleen. 2012. "'To Hell with Your Corrupt Institutions!': AMLO and Populism in Mexico." In Mudde and Kaltwasser 2012: 88–112.

Brunner, Otto. 1992. *Land and Lordship: Structures of Governance in Medieval Austria.* Translated by Howard Kaminsky and James Van Horn Melton. Philadelphia: University of Pennsylvania Press.

Butler, Judith. 2008. "Sexual Politics, Torture and Secular Time." *British Journal of Sociology* 59, no. 1: 1–23.

Card, David. 2009. "Immigration and Inequality." *American Economic Review* 99, no. 2: 1–21.

Carens, Joseph. 1987. "Aliens and Citizens: The Case for Open Borders." *Review of Politics* 49, no. 2: 251–73.

Cassin, Barbara, Emily Apter, Jacques Lezra, and Michael Wood, eds. 2014. *Dictionary of Untranslatables: A Philosophical Lexicon.* Princeton, NJ: Princeton University Press.

Cavell, Stanley. 1996. "Declining Decline." In *The Cavell Reader,* edited by Stephen Mulhall, 321–53. Oxford: Blackwell.

Cavell, Stanley. 2010. "The Touch of Words." In *Seeing Wittgenstein Anew,* edited by William Day and Victor J. Krebs, 81–100. Cambridge: Cambridge University Press.

Center for Open Science. n.d. "Mission." Accessed August 27, 2019. https://www .cos.io/about/mission.

Çetin, Fethiye. 2012. *My Grandmother: An Armenian-Turkish Memoir.* Translated by Maureen Freely. London: Penguin.

Chabal, Patrick, and Jean-Pascal Daloz. 1999. *Africa Works: Disorder as Political Instrument.* London: James Currey.

Chakrabarty, Dipesh. 2009. "The Climate of History: Four Theses." *Critical Inquiry* 35, no. 2: 197–222.

Chandler, David. 2016. "How the World Learned to Stop Worrying and Love Failure: Big Data, Resilience and Emergent Causality." *Millennium: Journal of International Studies* 44, no. 3: 391–410.

Chandler, David. 2018. *Ontopolitics in the Anthropocene: An Introduction to Mapping, Sensing and Hacking.* Abingdon, UK: Routledge.

Chandler, David, and Jonathan Pugh. 2018. "Islands of Relationality and Resilience: The Shifting Stakes of the Anthropocene." *Area* 52, no. 1: 65–72. https:// doi.org/10.1111/area.12459.

Chandler, David, and Julian Reid. 2018. "'Being in Being': Contesting the Ontopolitics of Indigeneity Today." *European Legacy* 23, no. 1: 1–18.

Chauveau, Jean-Pierre. 2018. "Autochtonie nomade et État frontière—Conflit et post conflit en Côte d'Ivoire au prisme de la question agraire." https://doi. org/10.13140/RG.2.2.28573.20964.

Chauveau, Jean-Pierre, and Koffi Samuel Bobo. 2003. "La situation de guerre dans l'arène villageoise: Un exemple dans le Centre-Ouest ivoirien." *Politique Africaine,* no. 89: 34–48.

CNN. 2016. "Nigel Farage: This Will Be a Victory for Real People." June 23. https:// www.youtube.com/watch?v=k-KolaQhNSQ.

Cohen, David W., and E. S. Atieno Odhiambo. 1992. *Burying SM: The Politics of Knowledge and the Sociology of Power in Africa.* London: Currey / Heinemann.

Collier, Neil, Ora DeKornfield, and Ben Laffin. 2017. *No Man's Land: Barbuda after Irma. New York Times* Documentaries, November 26. Available at https://desdemonadespair.net/2017/11/video-no-mans-land-barbuda-after.html.

Collier, Paul. 2013. *Exodus: How Migration Is Changing Our World.* Oxford: Oxford University Press.

Committee on Science, Space, and Technology. 2014. "Committee Approves Bill to Prohibit EPA from Using Secret Science." June 24. https://republicans-science .house.gov/news/press-releases/committee-approves-bill-prohibit-epa -using-secret-science.

Committee on Science, Space, and Technology. 2017. "House Approves HONEST Act." March 29. https://republicans-science.house.gov/news/press-releases /house-approves-honest-act.

Cordero, Rodrigo. 2017. *Crisis and Critique: On the Fragile Foundations of Social Life.* New York: Routledge.

Crutzen, Paul J. 2002. "Geology of Mankind." *Nature* 415, no. 23. https://doi.org/10 .1038/415023a.

Cumings, Bruce. 2016. "American Responsibility and the Massacres in Cheju." *World Environment and Island Studies* 6, no. 4: 203–9.

d'Allonnes, Myriam Revault. 2006. *Le pouvoir des commencements: Essai sur l'autorité.* Paris: Éditions du Seuil.

Danowski, Déborah, and Eduardo Viveiros de Castro. 2016. *The Ends of the World.* Cambridge: Polity.

Das, Veena. 1976. "Masks and Faces: An Essay on Punjabi Kinship." *Contributions to Indian Sociology* 10, no. 1: 1–30.

Das, Veena. 2007. *Life and Words: Violence and the Descent into the Ordinary.* Berkeley: University of California Press.

Das, Veena. 2012. "Ordinary Ethics." In *A Companion to Moral Anthropology,* edited by Didier Fassin, 133–49. London: Wiley Blackwell.

Das, Veena. 2014. "Action, Expression, and Everyday Life: Recounting House-hold Events." In *The Ground Between: Anthropologists Engage Philosophy,* edited by Veena Das, Michael Jackson, Arthur Kleinman, and Bhrigupati Singh, 270–306. Durham, NC: Duke University Press.

Das, Veena. 2015a. *Affliction: Health, Disease, Poverty.* New York: Fordham University Press.

Das, Veena. 2015b. "Corruption and the Possibility of Life." *Contributions to Indian Sociology* 49, no. 3: 322–43.

Das, Veena. 2017. "Techniques of Power and the Rise of the Grotesque." Theorizing (Dis)Order: Governing in an Uncertain World (seminar), World Peace Foundation, Tufts University, Medford, MA, March 15. https://sites.tufts .edu/reinventingpeace/2017/03/15/techniques-of-power-and-the-rise-of-the -grotesque/.

Das, Veena. 2020a. "Corona Policy Must Factor in Scientific Uncertainty." *Deccan Chronicle,* May 24.

Das, Veena. 2020b. *Textures of the Ordinary: Doing Anthropology after Wittgenstein.* New York: Fordham University Press.

Das, Veena, and Ashis Nandy. 1985. "Violence, Victimhood, and the Language of Silence." *Contributions to Indian Sociology* 19, no. 1: 177–95.

Debos, Marielle. 2016. *Living by the Gun in Chad: Combatants, Impunity and State Formation.* London: Zed.

Delafosse, Maurice. (1912) 1972. *Haut-Sénégal-Niger.* Paris: Maisonneuve.

de Lagasnerie, Geoffroy. 2015. *L'Art de la révolte: Snowden, Assange, Manning.* Paris: Fayard.

de la Torre, Carlos, ed. 2014. *The Promise and Perils of Populism: Global Perspectives.* Lexington: University Press of Kentucky.

Delogu, Marco, Frédéric Docquier, and Joël Machado. 2013. "The Dynamic Implications of Liberalizing Global Migration." IRES Discussion Paper no. 2013-29, Université Catholique de Louvain.

Derrida, Jacques. 2002. *Negotiations: Interventions and Interviews, 1971–2001.* Edited and translated by Elizabeth Rottenberg. Stanford, CA: Stanford University Press.

Detienne, Marcel. 2003. *Comment être autochtone: Du pur Athénien au Français raciné.* Paris: Seuil.

Devji, Faisal. 2012. "Leaving India to Anarchy." In *The Impossible Indian: Gandhi and the Temptation of Violence,* 151–84. London: Hurst.

de Waal, Alex. 2015. *The Real Politics of the Horn of Africa: Money, War and the Business of Power.* Cambridge: Polity.

de Waal, Alex. 2019. *Sudan: A Political Marketplace Framework Analysis.* World Peace Foundation Occasional Paper no. 19. Somerville, MA: World Peace Foundation.

Diamond, Larry. 2015. "Facing Up to the Democratic Recession." *Journal of Democracy* 26, no. 1: 141–55.

Die Presse. 2016. "Staatsanwaltschaft ermittelt gegen Mitglieder von 20 Wahlbehörden." August 10. https://www.diepresse.com/5066434/staatsanwaltschaft-ermittelt-gegen-mitglieder-von-20-wahlbehorden.

Docquier, Frédéric, Joël Machado, and Khalid Sekkat. 2015. "Efficiency Gains from Liberalizing Labor Mobility." *Scandinavian Journal of Economics* 117, no. 2: 303–46.

Docquier, Frédéric, and Hillel Rapoport. 2012. "Globalization, Brain Drain and Development." *Journal of Economic Literature* 50, no. 3: 681–730.

Docquier, Frédéric, Hillel Rapoport, and I-Ling Shen. 2010. "Remittances and Inequality: A Dynamic Migration Model." *Journal of Economic Inequality* 8, no. 2: 197–220.

Donatelli, Piergiorgio. 2015. "Perfectionist Returns to the Ordinary." *MLN* 130, no. 5: 1023–39.

Dorn, Aaron van, Rebecca Cooney, and Miriam Sabin. 2020. "COVID-19 Exacerbating Inequalities in the US." *Lancet* 395, no. 10232: 1243–44.

Du Bois, W. E. B. 1903. *The Souls of Black Folk.* Chicago: A. C. McClurg.

Dunbar-Ortiz, Roxanne. 2018. *Loaded: A Disarming History of the Second Amendment.* San Francisco: City Lights.

Duyvendak, Jan Willem, Peter Geschiere, and Evelien Tonkens, eds. 2017. *The Culturalization of Citizenship: Belonging and Polarization in a Globalizing World*. London: Palgrave.

DW.com. 2018. "Viktor Orban: Era of 'Liberal Democracy' Is Over." May 10. https://www.dw.com/en/viktor-orban-era-of-liberal-democracy-is-over/a -43732540.

Dworkin, Ronald. 2000. *Sovereign Virtue: The Theory and Practice of Equality*. Cambridge, MA: Harvard University Press.

Epstein, Mikhail. 1995. "Relativist Patterns in Totalitarian Thinking: The Linguistic Games of Soviet Ideology." In *After the Future: The Paradoxes of Postmodernism and Contemporary Russian Culture*, translated by Anesa Miller-Pogacar, 101–63. Amherst: University of Massachusetts Press.

Euripides. 1995. *Selected Fragmentary Plays*. Vol. 1, translated and edited by C. Collard, M. J. Cropp, and K. H. Lee. Warminster, UK: Aris and Phillips.

Ewald, Paul. 2011. "Evolution of Virulence, Environmental Change, and the Threat Posed by Emerging and Chronic Diseases." *Ecological Research* 26, no. 6: 1017–26.

Fan, Shenggen, Ravi Kanbur, Shang-Jin Wei, and Xiaobo Zhang, eds. 2014. *The Oxford Companion to the Economics of China*. Oxford: Oxford University Press.

Farhi, Paul. 2017. "The *Washington Post*'s New Slogan Turns Out to Be an Old Saying." *Washington Post*, February 24.

Faris, Rob, Hal Roberts, Bruce Etling, Nikki Bourassa, Ethan Zuckerman, and Yochai Benkler. 2017. "Partisanship, Propaganda, and Disinformation: Online Media and the 2016 U.S. Presidential Election." Berkman Klein Center, August 16. https://cyber.harvard.edu/publications/2017/08/mediacloud.

Fassin, Didier. (2011) 2013. *Enforcing Order: An Ethnography of Urban Policing*. Cambridge: Polity.

Fassin, Didier. 2012. *Humanitarian Reason: A Moral History of the Present*. Translated by Rachel Gomme. Berkeley: University of California Press.

Fassin, Didier. 2015. "Can States Be Moral?" In *At the Heart of the State: The Moral World of Institutions*, edited by Didier Fassin, ix–xii. London: Pluto.

Fassin, Didier. (2015) 2016. *Prison Worlds: An Ethnography of the Carceral Condition*. Translated by Rachel Gomme. Cambridge: Polity.

Fassin, Didier. 2017. "Donald Trump à la Maison Blanche: Ubu Président." *Libération*, January 19. https://www.liberation.fr/debats/2017/01/19/donald-trump-a -la-maison-blanche-ubu-president_1542677.

Fassin, Didier. 2020. "L'illusion dangereuse de l'égalité devant l'épidémie." Lecture, Collège de France, April 16. https://www.college-de-france.fr/site/didier -fassin/L-illusion-dangereuse-de-legalite-devant-lepidemie.htm.

Fassin, Didier, and Anne-Jeanne Naudé. 2004. "Plumbism Reinvented: Childhood Lead Poisoning in France, 1985–1990." *American Journal of Public Health* 94, no. 11: 1854–62.

Fassin, Didier, and Richard Rechtman. 2009. *The Empire of Trauma: An Inquiry into the Condition of Victimhood.* Translated by Rachel Gomme. Princeton, NJ: Princeton University Press.

Fassin, Didier, and Paula Vasquez. 2005. "Humanitarian Exception as the Rule: The Political Theology of the 1999 'Tragedia' in Venezuela." *American Ethnologist* 32, no. 3: 389–405.

Fassin, Didier, Matthew Wilhelm-Solomon, and Aurelia Segatti. 2017. "Asylum as a Form of Life: The Politics and Experience of Indeterminacy in South Africa." *Current Anthropology* 58, no. 2: 160–87.

Fisher, Mark. 2009. *Capitalist Realism: Is There No Alternative?* Winchester, UK: Zero Books.

Flint, Julie, and Alex de Waal. 2008. *Darfur: A New History of a Long War.* London: Zed.

Flores, Reena. 2016. "Donald Trump Attacks Republicans, Democrats Alike." *CBS Weekend News*, May 7.

Foa, Roberto Stefan, and Yascha Mounk. 2016. "The Danger of Deconsolidation: The Democratic Disconnect." *Journal of Democracy* 27, no. 3: 5–17.

Foucault, Michel. 1978. *The History of Sexuality.* Vol. 1, *An Introduction*, translated by Robert Hurley. New York: Pantheon.

Foucault, Michel. (1978) 2005. "Iran: The Spirit of a World without Spirit." In *Foucault and the Iranian Revolution: Gender and the Seductions of Islamism*, edited by Janet Afary and Kevin Anderson, 250–60. Chicago: University of Chicago Press.

Foucault, Michel. 1997. "What Is Critique?" In *The Politics of Truth*, edited by Sylvère Lotringer, 41–81. Los Angeles: Semiotext(e).

Foucault, Michel. (1999) 2003. *Abnormal: Lectures at the Collège de France, 1974–1975.* Translated by Graham Burchell. London: Verso.

Foucault, Michel. 2001. "Is It Useless to Revolt?" In *Power: The Essential Works of Foucault, 1954–1984*, edited by James Faubion, 449–53. New York: New Press.

Foucault, Michel. (2003) 2006. *Psychiatric Power: Lectures at the Collège de France, 1973–1974.* Translated by Graham Burchell. New York: Picador.

Foucault, Michel. 2008. *The Birth of Biopolitics: Lectures at the Collège de France, 1978–1979.* Translated by Graham Burchell. Basingstoke, UK: Palgrave Macmillan.

Fraenkel, Ernst. 2017. *The Dual State: A Contribution to the Theory of Dictatorship.* New York: Oxford University Press.

Frum, David. 2018. *Trumpocracy: The Corruption of the American Republic.* New York: Harper Collins.

Fueyo, Jesús. 1968. "Die Idee des 'Auctoritas': Genesis und Entwicklung." In *Epirrhosis: Festgabe für Carl Schmitt*, edited by Hans Barion, Ernst-Wolfgang Böckenförde, Ernst Forsthoff, and Werner Weber, 213–36. Berlin: Duncker and Humblot.

Furedi, Frank. 2018. *Populism and the European Culture Wars: The Conflict of Values between Hungary and the EU.* New York: Routledge.

Furet, François. 1981. *Interpreting the French Revolution*. Translated by Elborg Forster. Cambridge: Cambridge University Press.

Gaaze, Konstantin. 2016. "Rukopisnoe pis'mo kak praktika rossiiskoi pravitel'nost." *Sotsiologiya Vlasti* 28, no. 4: 104–31.

Gambetta, Diego. 1993. *The Sicilian Mafia: The Business of Private Protection*. Cambridge, MA: Harvard University Press.

Gandhi, Mohandas Karamchand. 1909. *Hind Swaraj*. Cambridge: Cambridge University Press.

Gellner, Ernest. 2006. *Nations and Nationalism*. 2nd ed. Ithaca, NY: Cornell University Press.

George, Tim. 2017. "Barbudan Land Ownership: A 200-Year-Old Freedom Put at Risk Following Hurricane Irma." *Open Democracy*, September 22. https://www .opendemocracy.net/beyondslavery/tim-george/barbudan-land-ownership -200-year-old-freedom-won-by-emancipated-slaves-and-.

Geschiere, Peter. 2009. *The Perils of Belonging: Autochthony, Citizenship, and Exclusion in Africa and Europe*. Chicago: University of Chicago Press.

Geschiere, Peter, and J. Gugler, eds. 1998. "The Urban-Rural Connection: Changing Issues of Belonging and Identification." *Africa* 68, no. 3: 309–19.

Geuss, Raymond. 2008. *Philosophy and Real Politics*. Princeton, NJ: Princeton University Press.

Ghamari-Tabrizi, Behrooz. 2004. "Contentious Public Religion: Two Conceptions of Islam in Revolutionary Iran." *International Sociology* 19, no. 4: 504–23.

Giebler, Heiko, and Wolfgang Merkel. 2016. "Freedom and Equality in Democracies: Is There a Trade-off?" *International Political Science Review* 37: 594–605.

Gillis, John Randall. 2004. *Islands of the Mind: How the Human Imagination Created the Atlantic World*. New York: Palgrave Macmillan.

Ginsburg, Tom, and Alberto Simpser, eds. 2014. *Constitutions in Authoritarian Regimes*. Cambridge: Cambridge University Press.

Giusti-Cordero, Juan. 2017. "In Puerto Rico, We Invented Resilience." *New York Times*, October 24. https://www.nytimes.com/2017/10/24/opinion/puerto-rico-hurricane-resilience.html.

Grydehøj, Adam. 2017. "A Future of Island Studies." *Island Studies Journal* 12, no. 1: 3–16.

Guyer, Jane. 1993. "Wealth in People and Self-Realization in Equatorial Africa." *Man*, n.s. 28, no. 2: 243–65.

Guyer, Jane. 2004. *Marginal Gains: Monetary Transactions in Atlantic Africa*. Chicago: University of Chicago Press.

Habermas, Jürgen. 1975. *Legitimation Crisis*. Boston: Beacon.

Habermas, Jürgen. 1985. "Civil Disobedience: Litmus Test for the Democratic Constitutional State." *Berkeley Journal of Sociology* 30: 95–116.

Hall, Elizabeth F., and Todd Sanders. 2015. "Accountability and the Academy: Producing Knowledge about the Human Dimensions of Climate Change." *Journal of the Royal Anthropological Institute* 21, no. 2: 438–61.

Hall, Stuart. 1988. *The Hard Road to Renewal: Thatcherism and the Crisis of the Left.* London: Verso.

Harmon, Amy. 2017. "Activists Rush to Save Government Science Data—If They Can Find It." *New York Times*, March 6. https://www.nytimes.com/2017/03/06 /science/donald-trump-data-rescue-science.html.

Hilgers, Mathieu. 2011. "L'autochtonie en milieu urbain ouest-africain: Éléments pour une approche comparative." In *Une anthropologie entre pouvoirs et histoire— Conversations autour de l'œuvre de Jean-Pierre Chauveau*, edited by E. Jul-Larsen, P. J. Laurent, P. Y. Le Meur, and E. Léonard, 383–405. Paris: Karthala.

Hill, Ken, W. Selzer, J. Leaning, S. J. Malik, and S. S. Russell. 2008. "The Demographic Impact of Partition in the Punjab in 1947." *Population Studies* 62, no. 2: 155–70.

Hobbes, Thomas. 1996. *Leviathan.* Edited by J. C. A. Gaskin. Oxford: Oxford University Press.

Honneth, Axel. 2009. *Pathologies of Reason: On the Legacy of Critical Theory.* Translated by James Ingram. New York: Columbia University Press.

Horkheimer, Max. 1947. *Eclipse of Reason.* New York: Oxford University Press.

Horkheimer, Max. 1985. "Die Rackets und der Geist." In *Gesammelte Schriften*, vol. 12, *Nachgelassene Schriften 1931–1949*, ed. Gunzelin Schmid Noerr, 287–91. Frankfurt: Suhrkamp.

House of Commons Science and Technology Committee. 2010. *The Disclosure of Climate Data from the Climatic Research Unit at the University of East Anglia.* March 31. HC 387-1. London: Stationery Office Limited.

Huntington, Samuel P. 1996. "Democracy for the Long Haul." *Journal of Democracy* 7, no. 2: 3–14.

Huq, Aziz, and Tom Ginsburg. 2018. "How to Lose a Constitutional Democracy." *UCLA Law Review* 65. https://papers.ssrn.com/sol3/papers.cfm?abstract_id =2901776.

Husserl, Edmund. (1936) 1970. *The Crisis of European Sciences and Transcendental Phenomenology.* Translated by David Carr. Evanston, IL: Northwestern University Press.

Ibáñez, Ana María. 2008. *El desplazamiento forzado en Colombia: Un camino sin retorno a la pobreza.* Bogotá: Universidad de los Andes.

Ingold, Tim. 2002. *The Perception of the Environment: Essays on Livelihood, Dwelling and Skill.* London: Routledge.

International Consortium of Investigators for Fairness in Trial Data Sharing. 2016. "Toward Fairness in Data Sharing." *New England Journal of Medicine* 375, no. 5: 405–7.

International Organization for Migration. 2017. *World Migration Report 2018.* http:// publications.iom.int/system/files/pdf/wmr_2018_en.pdf.

Jackson, Lisa P. 2009. "Transparency in EPA's Operations." EPA.gov, April 23. https://19january2017snapshot.epa.gov/sites/production/files/2014-02 /documents/transparency_in_epas_operations.pdf.

Jackson, Stephen. 2006. "Sons of Which Soil? The Language and Politics of Autochthony in Eastern D. R. Congo." *African Studies Review* 49, no. 2: 95–122.

Jamieson, Dale, and Bonnie Nadzam. 2015. *Love in the Anthropocene.* New York: OR Books.

Jarry, Alfred. (1894) 2003. *Ubu Roi.* Translated by Beverly Keith and Gershon Legman. Mineola, NY: Dover.

Kalyvas, Stathis. 2006. *The Logic of Violence in Civil War.* Cambridge: Cambridge University Press.

Kang, Han. 2016. *Human Acts: A Novel.* Translated and introduced by Deborah Smith. New York: Hogarth.

Kelty, Christopher M. 2008. *Two Bits: The Cultural Significance of Free Software.* Durham, NC: Duke University Press.

Kessler, Glenn, Salvador Rizzo, and Meg Kelly. 2018. "President Trump Has Made 6,420 False or Misleading Claims over 649 Days." *Washington Post,* November 2.

Khan, Mushtaq. 2018. "Power, Pacts and Political Settlements: A Reply to Tim Kelsall." *African Affairs* 117, no. 469: 670–694.

Khosla, Gopal Das. 1989. *Stern Reckoning: A Survey of the Events Leading Up to and Following the Partition of India.* New York: Oxford University Press.

Kim, H. J. 2014. *The Massacres at Mt. Halla: Sixty Years of Truth Seeking in South Korea.* Ithaca, NY: Cornell University Press.

Kim, Nan. 2016. *Memory, Reconciliation, and Reunions in South Korea: Crossing the Divide.* Lanham, MD: Rowman and Littlefield.

Kim, Seong Nae. 2019. "Placing the Dead in the Postmemory of the Cheju Massacre in Korea." *Journal of Religion* 99, no. 1: 80–97.

Klein, Naomi. 2007. *The Shock Doctrine: The Rise of Disaster Capitalism.* New York: Metropolitan Books/Henry Holt.

Kleinman, Arthur, and Joan Kleinman. 1996. "The Appeal of Experience, the Dismay of Images: Cultural Appropriations of Suffering in Our Times." *Daedalus* 125, no. 1: 1–23.

Koh, Sungman. 2018. "Trans-Border Rituals for the Dead: Experiential Knowledge of Paternal Relatives after the Jeju 4.3 Incident." *Journal of Korean Religions* 9, no. 1: 71–103.

Kojève, Alexandre. 2014. *The Notion of Authority (A Brief Presentation).* Edited by François Terré. London: Verso.

Kollar, Eszter. 2017. "Global Equality of Opportunity and Self-Determination in the Context of Immigration." *Critical Review of International Social and Political Philosophy* 20, no. 6: 726–35.

Kordonskii, Simon. 2008. *Soslovnaya struktura postsovetskoi Rossii.* Moscow: Institut Fonda Obshchestvennoe Mnenie.

Kordonskii, Simon. 2016. *Socio-Economic Foundations of the Russian Post-Soviet Regime: The Resource-Based Economy and Estate-Based Social Structure of Contemporary Russia.* New York: Columbia University Press/Ibidem Press.

Koselleck, Reinhart. (1959) 1988. *Critique and Crisis: Enlightenment and the Pathogenesis of Modern Society*. Cambridge, MA: MIT Press.

Koselleck, Reinhart. 2004. *Futures Past: On the Semantics of Historical Time*. Translated by Keith Tribe. New York: Columbia University Press.

Koselleck, Reinhart. (1982) 2006. "Crisis." Translated by Michaela Richter. *Journal of the History of Ideas* 67, no. 2: 357–400.

Krauthammer, Charles. 2005. "The Arab Spring of 2005." *Seattle Times*, March 21.

Kwon, Heonik. 2006. *After the Massacre: Commemoration and Consolation in Ha My and My Lai*. Berkeley: University of California Press.

Kwon, Heonik. 2008. *Ghosts of War in Vietnam*. Cambridge: Cambridge University Press.

Kwon, Heonik, and Seong Nae Kim. 2018. "Guest Editors' Introduction." In "Religions in Cold War Korea and Peace Keeping" (special issue), *Journal of Korean Religions* 9, no. 1: 5–10.

Laclau, Ernesto. 1977. *Politics and Ideology in Marxist Theory: Capitalism—Fascism—Populism*. London: New Left Books.

Lakner, Christoph, and Branko Milanovic. 2016. "Global Income Distribution: From the Fall of the Berlin Wall to the Great Recession." *World Bank Economic Review* 30, no. 2: 203–32. https://doi.org/10.1093/wber/lhv039.

Lambek, Michael. 2008. "Value and Virtue." *Anthropological Theory* 8, no. 2: 133–57.

Lambek, Michael. 2010. "Toward an Ethics of the Act." In *Ordinary Ethics: Anthropology, Language, and Action*, edited by Michael Lambek, 39–63. New York: Fordham University Press.

Landau, David. 2012. "Abusive Constitutionalism." *UC Davis Law Review* 47, no. 1: 189–260.

Latour, Bruno. 2017. *Facing Gaia: Eight Lectures on the New Climatic Regime*. Cambridge: Polity.

Ledeneva, Alena. 2006. *How Russia Really Works: The Informal Practices That Shaped Post-Soviet Politics and Business*. Ithaca, NY: Cornell University Press.

Lefort, Claude. 1998. *Democracy and Political Theory*. Translated by David Macey. Cambridge: Polity.

Leftwich, Adrian, ed. 2015. *What Is Politics? The Activity and Its Study*. Cambridge: Polity.

Lemaitre, Julieta. 2009. *El Derecho como conjuro*. Bogotá: Siglo del Hombre.

Lemaitre, Julieta. 2019. *El Estado siempre llega tarde*. Buenos Aires: Siglo XXI and Editores Uniandes.

Lemons, Katherine. 2019. *Divorcing Traditions: Islamic Marriage Law and the Making of Indian Secularism*. Ithaca, NY: Cornell University Press.

Lentz, Carola. 2013. *Land, Mobility, and Belonging in West Africa*. Bloomington: Indiana University Press.

Levitsky, Steven, and Daniel Ziblatt. 2018. *How Democracies Die*. New York: Crown.

Locke, John. 1950. *A Letter on Toleration*. Indianapolis, IN: Bobbs-Merrill.

Locke, John. 1988. *Two Treatises of Government*. Edited by Peter Laslett. Cambridge: Cambridge University Press.

Loraux, Nicole. 1996. *Né de la terre: Mythe et politique à Athènes*. Paris: Seuil.

Loraux, Nicole. 2000. *Born of the Earth: Myth and Politics in Athens*. Ithaca, NY: Cornell University Press.

Löwy, Michael. 2013. *On Changing the World: Essays in Political Philosophy from Karl Marx to Walter Benjamin*. Chicago: Haymarket Books.

Lukes, Steven. 2005. *Power: A Radical View*. 2nd ed. London: Palgrave.

Lyman, Rick, and Joanna Berendt. 2015. "As Poland Lurches to Right, Many Look on in Europe with Alarm." *New York Times*, December 14. https://www.nytimes.com/2015/12/15/world/europe/poland-law-and-justice-party-jaroslaw-kaczynski.html.

Mac Ginty, Roger. 2012. "Against Stabilization." *Stability* 1, no. 1: 20–30.

Magyar, Bálint. 2016. *Post-Communist Mafia State: The Case of Hungary*. Budapest: CEU Press.

Mair, Peter. 2013. *Ruling the Void: The Hollowing-Out of Western Democracy*. London: Verso.

Makarem-Shirazi, Naser. 1972. "Āyā hokumat-e islami bar pāye-ye shurāst?" [Is Islamic state based on democratic councils?]. *Maktab-e Islam* 13, no. 1: 76–78.

Mannheim, Karl. 1985. *Ideology and Utopia: An Introduction to the Sociology of Knowledge*. New York: Harvest/HBJ Book.

Manski, Charles F. 2020. "COVID-19 Policy Must Take All Impacts into Account." *Scientific American*, March 28. https://blogs.scientificamerican.com/observations/covid-19-policy-must-take-all-impacts-into-account/.

Marcuse, Herbert. 1972. *A Study on Authority*. Translated by Joris De Bres. London: Verso.

Marshall-Fratani, Ruth. 2006. "The War of 'Who Is Who': Autochthony, Nationalism, and Citizenship in the Ivoirian Crisis." *African Studies Review* 49, no. 2: 9–43.

Marx, Karl, and Friedrich Engels. 1978. *The Marx-Engels Reader*. 2nd ed. Edited by Robert C. Tucker. New York: Norton.

Masco, Joseph. 2017. "The Crisis in Crisis." *Current Anthropology* 58, Suppl. 15: S65–S76.

Mathur, Nayanika. 2017. "Eating Money: Corruption and Its Categorical 'Other' in the Leaky Indian State." *Modern Asian Studies* 51, no. 6: 1796–817.

Mbembe, Achille. 2000. "A propos des écritures africaines de soi." *Politique Africaine* 77: 16–43.

Mbembe, Achille. 2017. *Critique of Black Reason*. Translated by Laurent Dubois. Durham, NC: Duke University Press.

McGovern, Mike. 2011. *Making War in Côte d'Ivoire*. Chicago: University of Chicago Press.

Meaney, Thomas. 2018. "The Dark European Stain: How the Far Right Rose Again." *New Statesman*, September 12.

Merrill, John. 1980. "The Cheju-do Rebellion." *Journal of Korean Studies* 2, no. 1: 139–97.

Merry, Sally Engle. 2011. "Measuring the World: Indicators, Human Rights, and Global Governance." *Current Anthropology* 52, Suppl. 3: S83–S95.

Milanovic, Branko. 2016. *Global Inequality: A New Approach for the Age of Globalization.* Cambridge, MA: Belknap Press of Harvard University Press.

Miller, David. 2016. *Strangers in Our Midst: The Political Philosophy of Immigration.* Oxford: Oxford University Press.

Minow, Martha. 1992. "Surviving Victim Talk." UCLA *Law Review* 40: 1411–41.

Minow, Martha. 1998. *Between Vengeance and Forgiveness: Facing History after Genocide and Mass Violence.* Boston: Beacon Press

Moffitt, Benjamin. 2016. *The Global Rise of Populism: Performance, Political Style, and Representation.* Stanford, CA: Stanford University Press.

Monga, Célestin. 1995. "Cercueils, orgies et sublimation: Le coût d'une mauvaise gestion de la mort." *Afrique 2000* 21: 163–72.

Mookherjee, Nayanika. 2015. *The Spectral Wound: Sexual Violence, Public Memories, and the Bangladesh War of 1971.* Durham, NC: Duke University Press.

Mooney, Chris. 2005. *The Republican War on Science.* New York: Basic Books.

Morton, Timothy. 2013. *Hyperobjects: Philosophy and Ecology after the End of the World.* Minneapolis: University of Minnesota Press.

Mouffe, Chantal. 2018. *For a Left Populism.* London: Verso.

Mudde, Cas, and Cristóbal Rovira Kaltwasser, eds. 2013. *Populism in Europe and the Americas: Threat or Corrective for Democracy?* Cambridge: Cambridge University Press.

Muir Russell, Alastair, Geoffrey Boulton, Peter Clarke, David Eyton, and James Norton. 2010. "The Independent Climate Change E-mails Review." July. http://www.cce-review.org/pdf/FINAL%20REPORT.pdf.

Müller, Jan-Werner. 2011. *Contesting Democracy: Political Ideas in Twentieth-Century Europe.* London: Yale University Press.

Müller, Jan-Werner. 2016. *What Is Populism?* Philadelphia: University of Pennsylvania Press.

Nakashima, Douglas, Kirsty Galloway McLean, Hans Thulstrup, Ameyali Ramos Castillo, and Jennifer Rubis. 2012. *Weathering Uncertainty: Traditional Knowledge for Climate Change Assessment and Adaptation.* Paris: UNESCO.

Narayanan, Vidya, Vlad Barash, John Kelly, Bence Kollanyi, Lisa-Maria Neudert, and Philip N. Howard. 2018. "Polarization, Partisanship and Junk News Consumption on Social Media during the 2018 US Midterm Elections." Data memo 2018.1. Oxford Computational Propaganda Project. February 6. http://comprop.oii.ox.ac.uk/research/polarization-partisanship-and-junk-news/.

National Science Foundation 2015. "Today's Data, Tomorrow's Discoveries: Increasing Access to the Results of Research Funded by the National Science Foundation." NSF 15–51. March 18. https://www.nsf.gov/pubs/2015/nsf15051/nsf15051.pdf.

Naval'nyi, Alexei. 2016. "Dvadtsat' polkovnikov Zakharenko—indesatsiya vsem pensioneram." September 10. https://navalny.com/p/5043/.

Nola Defender. 2015. "Don't Call Me Resilient." August 28. https://www.noladefender.com/2015/08/28/uncategorized/don-t-call-me-resilient/.

North, Douglass. 1991. "Institutions." *Journal of Economic Perspectives* 5, no. 1: 97–112.

Obama White House. 2009. "Transparency and Open Government." January 21. https://obamawhitehouse.archives.gov/the-press-office/transparency-and-open-government.

Obama White House. 2013. "Open Data Policy: Managing Information as an Asset." Memorandum M-13-13. May 9. https://obamawhitehouse.archives.gov/sites/default/files/omb/memoranda/2013/m-13-13.pdf.

Ober, Josiah. 2017. *Demopolis: Democracy before Liberalism in Theory and Practice.* Cambridge: Cambridge University Press.

Oleinik, Anton. 2011. *Market as a Weapon: The Socio-Economic Machinery of Dominance in Russia.* New Brunswick, NJ: Transaction.

Oreskes, Naomi, and Erik Conway. 2014. *The Collapse of Western Civilization: A View from the Future.* New York: Columbia University Press.

Orr, David W. 2016. *Dangerous Years: Climate Change, the Long Emergency, and the Way Forward.* New Haven, CT: Yale University Press.

Osburg, John. 2013. *Anxious Wealth: Money and Morality among China's New Rich.* Stanford, CA: Stanford University Press.

Oxburgh, Ron, Huw Davies, Kerry Emanuel, Lisa Graumlich, David Hand, Herbert Huppert, and Michael Kelly. 2010. "Report of the International Panel Set Up by the University of East Anglia to Examine the Research of the Climatic Research Unit." April 12. http://www.ossfoundation.us/projects/environment/global-warming/summary-docs/investigation-reports/SAP.pdf.

Panizza, Francisco, ed. 2005. *Populism and the Mirror of Democracy.* London: Verso.

Paris, Roland. 2004. *At War's End: Building Peace after Civil Conflict.* Cambridge: Cambridge University Press.

Park Ch'ansik. 2011. "4.3 saja e taehan kiŏk pangsik ŭi pyŏnhwa: Cheju chiyŏngmin ŭl chungsimŭro" [Changes in the way of remembering the dead of Jeju 4.3: With a focus on the Jeju people]. *Kwa yŏksa* 11: 89–103.

Park, Soul. 2010. "The Unnecessary Uprising: Jeju Island Rebellion and South Korean Counterinsurgency Experience, 1947–48." *Small Wars and Insurgencies* 21, no. 2: 359–81.

Parry, Jonathan. 2000. "The 'Crises of Corruption' and 'the Idea of India': A Worm's-Eye View." In *Morals of Legitimacy: Between Agency and System,* edited by I. Pardo, 27–55. New York: Berghahn.

Parry, Martin L., Osvaldo F. Canziani, Jean Palutikof, Paul J. van der Linden, and Clair E. Hanson, eds. 2007. *Contribution of Working Group II to the Fourth Assessment Report of the Intergovernmental Panel on Climate Change.* Cambridge: Cambridge University Press.

Patel, Kamla. 2006. *Torn from the Roots: A Partition Memoir*. Translated by Uma Randeria. Delhi: Women Unlimited.

Pavlovsky, Gleb. 2014. "Putin's World Outlook." *New Left Review* 88: 55–68.

Pels, Peter, Igor Boog, J. Henrike Florusbosch, Zane Kripe, et al. 2018. "Data Management in Anthropology: The Next Phase in Ethics Governance?" *Social Anthropology* 26, no. 3: 391–413.

Piot, Charles. 2010. *Nostalgia for the Future: West Africa after the Cold War*. Chicago: University of Chicago Press.

Pitkin, Hanna. 1964. "Hobbes's Concept of Representation, I." *American Political Science Review* 58, no. 2: 328–40.

Pospisil, Jan. 2019. *Peace in Political Unsettlement: Beyond Solving Conflict*. London, Palgrave Macmillan.

Prigogine, Ilya, and Isabelle Stengers. 1984. *Order out of Chaos*. Toronto: Bantam.

Pritchett, Lant. 2010. "The Cliff at the Border." In *Equity and Growth in a Globalizing World*, edited by Ravi Kanbur and A. Michael Spence. Washington, DC: World Bank Commission on Growth and Development. https://openknowledge .worldbank.org/bitstream/handle/10986/2458/548910PUB0EPI11C10Dislosed 061312010.pdf?sequence=1&isAllowed=y.

Pritchett, Lant, Kunal Sen, and Eric Werker. 2018. "Deals and Development: An Introduction to the Conceptual Framework." In *Deals and Development: The Political Dynamics of Growth Episodes*, edited by Lant Pritchett, Kunal Sen, and Eric Werker, 1–38. Oxford: Oxford University Press.

Przeworski, Adam. 1991. *Democracy and the Market: Political and Economic Reforms in Eastern Europe and Latin America*. New York: Cambridge University Press.

Przeworski, Adam. 2018. *Why Bother with Elections?* Cambridge: Polity.

Pugh, Jonathan. 2014. "Resilience, Complexity and Post-Liberalism." *Area* 46, no. 3: 313–19.

Pugh, Jonathan. 2017. "Postcolonial Development, (Non)Sovereignty and Affect: Living On in the Wake of Caribbean Political Independence." *Antipode* 49, no. 4: 867–82.

Putnam, Robert. 1995. "Bowling Alone: America's Declining Social Capital." *Journal of Democracy* 6, no. 1: 65–78.

Rahnema, Ali. 1998. *An Islamic Utopian: A Political Biography of Ali Shari'ati*. London: I. B. Tauris.

Rancière, Jacques. (2005) 2014. *Hatred of Democracy*. Translated by Steve Corcoran. London: Verso.

Rauch, Jonathan, and Benjamin Wittes. 2017. "More Professionalism, Less Populism: How Voting Makes Us Stupid, and What to Do about It." Center for Effective Public Management at Brookings, May. https://www.brookings.edu /wp-content/uploads/2017/05/more-professionalism-less-populism.pdf.

Rawls, John. 1973. *A Theory of Justice*. Oxford: Oxford University Press.

Reid, Julian. 2017. "'We the Resilient': Colonizing Indigeneity in the Era of Trump." Institute for Interdisciplinary Research into the Anthropocene, October 11.

https://iiraorg.com/2017/10/11/we-the-resilient-colonizing-indigeneity-in -the-era-of-trump/amp/.

Rempe, Dennis. 1995. "Guerrillas, Bandits, and Independent Republics: US Counter-Insurgency Efforts in Colombia 1959–1965." *Small Wars and Insurgencies* 6, no. 3: 304–27.

Revel, Jean-François. 1983. *Comment les démocraties finissent*. Paris: Grasset.

Rey, Alain, ed. (1992) 2006. *Dictionnaire historique de la langue française*. Paris: Le Robert.

Rinberg, Toly, Maya Anjur-Dietrich, Marcy Beck, et al. 2018. "Changing the Digital Climate: How Climate Change Web Content Is Being Censored under the Trump Administration." Environmental Data and Governance Initiative, January 10. https://envirodatagov.org/publication/changing-digital-climate/.

Roberts, Margaret. 2018. *Censored: Distraction and Diversion inside China's Great Firewall*. Princeton, NJ: Princeton University Press.

Rodgers, Daniel T. 1987. *Contested Truths: Keywords in American Politics since Independence*. Cambridge, MA: Harvard University Press.

Rodríguez-Garavito, César, and Diana Rodríguez-Franco. 2015. *Radical Deprivation on Trial: The Impact of Judicial Activism on Socioeconomic Rights in the Global South*. Cambridge: Cambridge University Press.

Roemer, John E. 1998. *Equality of Opportunity*. Cambridge: Cambridge University Press.

Roitman, Janet. 2014. *Anti-Crisis*. Durham, NC: Duke University Press.

Rosanvallon, Pierre. 2018. *Good Government: Democracy beyond Elections*. Translated by Malcolm DeBevoise. Cambridge, MA: Harvard University Press.

Rosenberg, Andrew. 2014. "The Secret Science Reform Act: Perhaps We Should Just Call It Catch-22," *Union of Concerned Scientists* (blog), February 18. https://blog .ucsusa.org/andrew-rosenberg/the-secret-science-reform-act-perhaps-we -should-just-call-it-catch-22-417.

Rossiyskaya Gazeta. 2004. "Federal'nyi zakon ot 27 iyulya 2004 g. N 79-F3 O gosu-darstvennoi grazhdanskoi sluzhbe Rossiiskoi Federatsii." July 31. https://rg.ru /2004/07/31/gossluzhba-dok.html.

Rossiyskaya Gazeta. 2016. "Putin Does Not Believe in a Swift Victory over Corruption." *Russia Beyond*, January 26. https://www.rbth.com//news/2016/01/26 /putin-does-not-believe-in-a-swift-victory-over-corruption_562523.

Rousseau, Jean-Jacques. (1762) 1979. *Émile, or On Education*. Translated by Allan Bloom. New York: Basic Books.

Rousseau, Jean-Jacques. 1993. *The Social Contract and Discourses*. Translated by G. D. H. Cole. London: J. M. Dent/Everyman.

RT. 2017. "Abuse of Office, Bribes, and Embezzlement: Top 5 Russian Corruption Scandals." December 18. https://www.rt.com/politics/413538-top-5-recent -russian-corruption/.

Runciman, David. 2015. "Rescuing Democracy in the Age of the Internet." *Ethics and International Affairs*, September. https://www.ethicsandinternationalaffairs .org/2015/rescuing-democracy-age-internet/.

Sadurski, Wojciech. 2018. "How Democracy Dies (in Poland): A Case Study of Anti-Constitutional Populist Backsliding." *Sydney Law School Research Paper* 18/01.

Sayeed, Mohammad. 2017. "Citizenship, Community, and Urban Spaces: A Case Study." PhD diss., University of Delhi.

Scheffer, Paul. 2000. "Het Multiculturele Drama." nrc/*Handelsblad*, January 29 and March 25. https://www.nrc.nl/nieuws/2000/01/29/het-multiculturele-drama -a3987586.

Scheppele, Kim Lane. 2013. "The Rule of Law and the Frankenstate: Why Governance Checklists Do Not Work." *Governance* 26, no. 4: 559–62.

Schmitt, Carl. (1922) 2005. *Political Theology: Four Chapters on the Concept of Sovereignty*. Translated by George Schwab. Chicago: University of Chicago Press.

Scientific American. 2017. "A Fix for the Antiscience Attitude in Congress: A Group of Objective Expert Advisers Should Counsel the Senate and House Science Committees." October 1. https://www.scientificamerican.com/article/a-fix -for-the-antiscience-attitude-in-congress/.

Scott, James C. 1998. *Seeing Like a State: How Certain Schemes to Improve the Human Condition Have Failed*. New Haven, CT: Yale University Press.

Scott, James C. 2009. *The Art of Not Being Governed: An Anarchist History of Upland Southeast Asia*. New Haven, CT: Yale University Press.

Scott, James C. 2017. *Against the Grain: A Deep History of the Earliest States*. New Haven, CT: Yale University Press.

Selby, Don. F. 2018. *Human Rights in Thailand*. Philadelphia: University of Pennsylvania Press.

Shari'ati, Ali. 1971. *Tashayyo'-e Alavi va Tashayyo'-e Safavi* (Alavid Shi'ism and Safavid Shi'ism). Tehran: Hosseiniyyeh Ershad.

Shari'ati, Ali. 1978. *Shi'eh* (Shi'ism). Vol. 7 of *Collected Works*. Tehran: Hosseiniyyeh Ershad.

Shari'ati, Ali. 1979a. "Intellectuals and Their Responsibilities in Society." In *Collected Works*, 20:18–110. Tehran: Hosseiniyyeh Ershad.

Shari'ati, Ali. 1979b. "Man and Islam." In *On the Sociology of Islam*, translated by Hamid Algar, 70–81. Berkeley, CA: Mizan Press.

Shari'ati, Ali. 1981. *Islam-shenāsi*. 3 vols. Tehran: Ershad.

Shari'ati, Ali. 1996. "Nāmeh beh Ayatollah al-Uzma Milani" (Letter to the Grand Ayatollah Milani). In *Collected Works*, 34:98–103. Tehran: Qalam.

Shear, Matthew. 2017. "How Far Will Sean Hannity Go?" *New York Times*, November 28. https://www.nytimes.com/2017/11/28/magazine/how-far-will-sean -hannity-go.html.

Sherman, Gabriel. 2017. "'I Have Power': Is Steve Bannon Running for President?" *Vanity Fair*, December 21. https://www.vanityfair.com/news/2017/12/bannon -for-president-trump-kushner-ivanka.

Shin, Gi-Wook, Soon-Won Park, and Daqing Yang, eds. 2007. *Rethinking Historical Injustice and Reconciliation in Northeast Asia: The Korean Experience*. London: Routledge.

Shin, Ki-young. 2006. "The Politics of the Family Law Reform Movement in Contemporary Korea: A Contentious Space for Gender and the Nation." *Journal of Korean Studies* 11, no. 1: 93–125.

Skidelsky, Robert. 1983. *John Maynard Keynes: Hopes Betrayed, 1883–1920*. London: Macmillan.

Smart, Alan. 2018. "The Unbearable Discretion of Street-Level Bureaucrats: Corruption and Collusion in Hong Kong." *Current Anthropology* 59, Suppl. 18: S37–S47.

Smith, William. 2011. "Civil Disobedience and the Public Sphere." *Journal of Political Philosophy* 19, no. 2: 145–66.

Snyder, Timothy. 2018. *The Road to Unfreedom: Russia, Europe, America*. New York: Tim Duggan Books.

Stengers, Isabelle. 2015. *In Catastrophic Times: Resisting the Coming Barbarism*. Translated by Andrew Goffey. London: Open Humanities Press. http://openhumanitiespress.org/books/download/Stengers_2015_In-Catastrophic-Times.pdf.

Stewart, Kathleen. 2011. "Atmospheric Attunements." *Environment and Planning D: Society and Space* 29, no. 3: 445–53.

Streeck, Wolfgang. 2014. *Buying Time: The Delayed Crisis of Democratic Capitalism*. London: Verso.

Streeck, Wolfgang. 2016. *How Will Capitalism End? Essays on a Failing System*. London: Verso.

Tabellini, Marco. 2018. "Gifts of the Immigrants, Woes of the Natives: Lessons from the Age of Mass Migration." MIT, May 19. http://economics.mit.edu/files/13646.

Taylor, Charles. 2007. *A Secular Age*. Cambridge, MA: Belknap Press of Harvard University Press.

Taylor, Charles. 2017. "Is Democracy Slipping Away?" Social Science Research Council, February 7. https://items.ssrc.org/is-democracy-slipping-away/.

Theidon, Kimberly. 2012. *Intimate Enemies: Violence and Reconciliation in Peru*. Philadelphia: University of Pennsylvania Press.

Tooze, Adam. 2018. *Crashed: How a Decade of Financial Crises Changed the World*. New York: Viking.

Tsing, Anna L. 2015. *The Mushroom at the End of the World: On the Possibility of Life in Capitalist Ruins*. Princeton, NJ: Princeton University Press.

Uitz, Renáta. 2015. "Can You Tell when an Illiberal Democracy Is in the Making? An Appeal to Comparative Constitutional Scholarship from Hungary." *International Journal of Constitutional Law* 13, no. 1: 279–300.

Uitz, Renáta. 2016. "National Constitutional Identity in the European Constitutional Project: A Recipe for Exposing Cover Ups and Masquerades." *Verfassungsblog*, November 11. https://verfassungsblog.de/national-constitutional

-identity-in-the-european-constitutional-project-a-recipe-for-exposing
-cover-ups-and-masquerades/.

UK Cabinet Office. 2016. "Policy Paper: UK Open Government National Action Plan
2016–18." May 12. https://www.gov.uk/government/publications/uk-open
-government-national-action-plan-2016-18/uk-open-government-national
-action-plan-2016-18.

UK Parliament. 2010. "Disclosure of Climate Data from Climatic Research Unit at
the University of East Anglia." March 31. https://old.parliament.uk/business
/committees/committees-a-z/commons-select/science-and-technology
-committee/inquiries/uea/.

Underhill, Vivian, Megan Martenyi, Sarah Lamdan, and Andrew Bergman. 2017.
"Public Protections under Threat at the EPA: Examining Safeguards and
Programs That Would Have Been Blocked by H.R. 1430." Environmental Data
and Governance Initiative. https://envirodatagov.org/publication/public
-protections-under-threat/.

United Nations. 2004. *Living with Risk: A Global Review of Disaster Reduction Initiatives*. New York: United Nations.

United Nations Framework Convention on Climate Change. 2010. "Report of the
Conference of the Parties on Its Sixteenth Session, Held in Cancun from
29 November to 10 December 2010: Part I: Proceedings." https://unfccc.int
/documents/6525.

United Nations High Commissioner for Refugees. 2004. "Guiding Principles on
Internal Displacement." September. http://www.unhcr.org/protection/idps
/43ce1cff2/guiding-principles-internal-displacement.html.

United Nations Office for Disaster Risk Reduction. n.d. "Making Cities Resilient:
2030 Is Here." Accessed December 28, 2017. https://www.unisdr.org/we
/campaign/cities.

University of East Anglia. 2010. "The UEA's Response." July 7. https://www.uea.ac
.uk/about/media-room/press-release-archive/statements/cru-statements
/muirrussellreport.

Uprimny, Rodrigo, and María Paula Saffon. 2006. "Justicia Transicional sin
Transición." In *¿Justicia transicional sin transición? Verdad, justicia y reparación
para Colombia*, edited by Catalina Botero, Esteban Restrepo, and Maria Paula
Saffon, 109–38. Bogotá: DeJuSticia.

Urbinati, Nadia. 2014. *Democracy Disfigured: Opinion, Truth, and the People*. Cambridge, MA: Harvard University Press.

Urbinati, Nadia. 2015. "A Revolt against Intermediary Bodies." *Constellations* 22:
477–86.

US Department of State. n.d. "Open Government Initiative." https://www.state
.gov/open-government-initiative/.

US Environmental Protection Agency. 2010. "Denial of the Petitions to Reconsider
the Endangerment and Cause or Contribute Findings for Greenhouse Gases

under Section 202(a) of the Clean Air Act." August. https://www.govinfo.gov/content/pkg/FR-2010-08-13/pdf/2010-19153.pdf.

US Environmental Protection Agency. 2016a. "Plan to Increase Access to Results of EPA-Funded Scientific Research." November. https://www.epa.gov/sites/production/files/2016-12/documents/epascientificresearchtransperancyplan.pdf.

US Environmental Protection Agency. 2016b. "U.S. Environmental Protection Agency Open Government Plan 4.0." September. https://19january2017snapshot.epa.gov/sites/production/files/2016-09/documents/2016epaopengovplan4_0draft091516update1.pdf.

Valéry, Paul. (1919) 1977. "Crisis of the Mind." In *Paul Valéry: An Anthology*, translated by Denise Folliot and Jackson Matthews, edited by James Lawler, 94–107. Princeton, NJ: Princeton University Press.

VanAntwerpen, Jonathan. 2007. "Introducing the Immanent Frame." *Immanent Frame* (blog), October 18. http://tif.ssrc.org/2007/10/18/25/.

Vega, Tanzina. 2017. "Puerto Rico Has a Long Way to Go before Being 'OK.'" CNN, October 8. http://edition.cnn.com/2017/10/08/opinions/puerto-rico-not-okay-vega-opinion/index.html.

Verfassungsblog. 2017. "Debate: Constitutional Courts and Populism." May 4. http://verfassungsblog.de/category/debates/constitutional-courts-and-populism-debates/.

Viveiros de Castro, Eduardo. 1998. "Cosmological Deixis and Amerindian Perspectivism." *Journal of the Royal Anthropological Institute* 4, no. 3: 469–88.

Walzer, Michael. 1997. *On Toleration*. New Haven, CT: Yale University Press.

Warner, Michael, Jonathan VanAntwerpen, and Craig Calhoun, eds. 2010. *Varieties of Secularism in a Secular Age*. Cambridge, MA: Harvard University Press.

Weber, Max. 1958. "Politics as a Vocation." In *From Max Weber: Essays in Sociology*, edited and translated by H. H. Gerth and C. Wright Mills, 77–128. New York: Oxford University Press.

Weber, Max. 1978. *Economy and Society: An Outline of Interpretive Sociology*. Edited by Guenther Roth and Claus Wittich. Berkeley: University of California Press.

Welcome to the Anthropocene. n.d. http://www.anthropocene.info/ (accessed October 29, 2020).

Williams, Raymond. (1976) 2014. *Keywords: A Vocabulary of Culture and Society*. Oxford: Oxford University Press.

Wittgenstein, Ludwig. (1953) 2009. *Philosophical Investigations*. Translated by G. E. M. Anscombe. Revised by P. M. S. Hacker and Joachim Schulte. Malden, MA: Wiley-Blackwell.

Wittgenstein, Ludwig. 1980. *Culture and Value*. Translated by Peter Winch. Chicago: University of Chicago Press.

Wood, Elisabeth Jean. 2003. *Insurgent Collective Action and Civil War in El Salvador*. Cambridge: Cambridge University Press.

Yan, Hao, Allen Lavoie, and Sanmay Das. 2017. "The Perils of Classifying Political Orientation from Text." *Linked Democracy: Artificial Intelligence for Democratic Innovation* 8, no. 858: 38–50.

Yan, Yunxiang. 2016. "Old and New Moralities in Changing China." Interview with Charles Stafford. *Anthropology of This Century*, no. 15. http://aotcpress.com/articles/moralities-changing-china/.

Yeltsin, Boris. 2000. *Midnight Diaries*. London: Weidenfeld and Nicholson.

Zygar', Mikhail. 2017. *Vsya kremlevskaya rat': Kratkaya istoriya sovremennoi rossii*. Moscow: Intellektual'naya literatura.

CONTRIBUTORS

BANU BARGU is an associate professor in the Department of History of Consciousness at the University of California, Santa Cruz. She is a political theorist with a focus on modern and contemporary political thought and critical theory. She is the author of *Starve and Immolate: The Politics of Human Weapons* (2014) and editor of *Turkey's Necropolitical Laboratory: Democracy, Violence, and Resistance* (2019).

VEENA DAS is Krieger-Eisenhower Professor of Anthropology at Johns Hopkins University. She is a Fellow of the American Academy of Arts and Sciences and a Corresponding Fellow of the British Academy. Her most recent books are *Affliction: Health, Disease, Poverty* (2015) and *Textures of the Ordinary: Doing Anthropology after Wittgenstein* (2020).

ALEX DE WAAL is the executive director of the World Peace Foundation, a research professor at the Fletcher School of Law and Diplomacy, Tufts University, and a Professorial Fellow at the London School of Economics. He has worked on the Horn of Africa and on humanitarian issues since the 1980s as a researcher and practitioner. His most recent books are *The Real Politics of the Horn of Africa: Money, War and the Business of Power* (2015) and *Mass Starvation: The History and Future of Famine* (2018).

DIDIER FASSIN is James D. Wolfensohn Professor at the Institute for Advanced Study, Professor to the Annual Chair in Public Health at the Collège de France, and a director of studies at the École des hautes études en sciences sociales. He works on political and moral issues, notably inequality, punishment, and immigration. He recently authored *Life: A Critical User's Manual* (2018) and *The Will to Punish* (2018).

PETER GESCHIERE is emeritus professor of the anthropology of Africa at the University of Amsterdam and Leiden University. He has undertaken historical-anthropological fieldwork in Cameroon and elsewhere in West and Central Africa. His publications include *The Perils of Belonging: Autochthony, Citizenship and Exclusion in Africa and Europe* (2009) and *Witchcraft, Intimacy, and Trust: Africa in Comparison* (2013).

BEHROOZ GHAMARI-TABRIZI is a professor of Near Eastern studies and the director of the Sharmin and Bijan Mossavar-Rahmani Center for Iran and Persian Gulf Studies at Princeton University. He works on topics related to social theory and Islamist political thought and is currently conducting a comparative study of philosophy of history and political theory of Walter Benjamin and Ali Shari'ati. He is the author of *Foucault in Iran: Islamic Revolution after the Enlightenment* (2016) and *Remembering Akbar: Inside the Iranian Revolution* (2016).

CAROLINE HUMPHREY is an anthropologist who has researched a wide range of topics, including Soviet and post-Soviet provincial economy and society; Buryat and Daur shamanism; Jain religion and ritual; trade and barter in Nepal; environment and the pastoral economy in Mongolia; and the history and contemporary situation of Buddhism, especially in Inner Mongolia. Currently she is completing a project on sociopolitical interactions on the Russia-Mongolia-China border. Her most recent books are *A Monastery in Time: The Making of Mongolian Buddhism* (2013) and *Trust and Mistrust in the Economies of the China-Russia Borderlands* (2018).

RAVI KANBUR is T. H. Lee Professor of World Affairs, International Professor of Applied Economics and Management, and a professor of economics at Cornell University. His research is focused on the theory, empirics, and policy dimensions of inequality and poverty. His most recent books are *The Quality of Growth in Africa*, coedited with Akbar Noman and Joseph E. Stiglitz (2019), and *Climate Justice: Integrating Economics and Philosophy*, coedited with Henry Shue (2019).

JULIETA LEMAITRE is a judge at the Justice Chambers of the Colombian Special Jurisdiction for Peace and a faculty member of the Law Department at Los Andes University in Colombia. Her academic work uses a sociological and historical approach to the study of law and violence. She is currently the investigating judge for the peace jurisdiction's first macro-case: charges against the policy and practice of kidnapping brought against former guerrilla leaders. She has recently authored *La Paz en Cuestión* (2011) and *El Estado Siempre Llega Tarde* (2019).

UDAY S. MEHTA is Distinguished Professor of Political Science at the Graduate Center, CUNY. In 2002 he was named a Carnegie Foundation scholar. He is currently completing a book on the moral and political thought of M. K. Gandhi. He has authored *The Anxiety of Freedom: Imagination and Individuality in Locke's Political Thought* (1992) and *Liberalism and Empire: A Study in Nineteenth-Century British Liberal Thought* (1999).

JAN-WERNER MÜLLER is Roger Williams Straus Professor of Social Sciences and a professor of politics at Princeton University. His books include *Contesting Democracy: Political Ideas in Twentieth-Century Europe* (2013) and *What Is Populism?* (2017).

JONATHAN PUGH is Reader in Island Studies, School of Geography, Politics and Sociology, Newcastle University. He has just finished the monograph *Anthropocene Islands: A Critical Agenda for Island Studies in the Anthropocene*, which will be published in 2021.

ELIZABETH F. SANDERS is an assistant professor at the Dalla Lana School of Public Health and the Department of Anthropology at the University of Toronto. She previously worked as a public health physician and epidemiologist. Her research interests include science, expertise, and public policy.

TODD SANDERS is an associate professor of anthropology at the University of Toronto. He has long-standing interests in African and Euro-American knowledge practices. His publications include *Anthropology in Theory: Issues in Epistemology* (with H. L. Moore, 2014) and *Beyond Bodies: Rainmaking and Sense Making in Tanzania* (2008).

INDEX

Chakrabarty, Dipesh, 231

Chan Zuckerberg Initiative, 210

chaos, 52, 136–37, 139–40, 228. *See also* complexity

charismatic authority, 80

Chauveau, Jean-Pierre, 101

Chávez, Hugo, 44, 47, 272

Chiapello, Eve, 265

children: and lead poisoning, 266–68; as victims, 22, 27–29, 35, 150–51; and war, 24, 153, 155, 158–59. *See also* motherhood

Chile, 276

China, 2, 39, 124, 167, 191, 244, 247, 259n3, 276

Chirac, Jacques, 271

Christianity, 11, 121n1, 169, 263

chronocentrism, 124

citizenship, 86, 92, 96–102, 106, 261

Citizenship Act (India), 2

Citizenship Amendment Act (India), 11

citizenship rent, 16, 245, 250

civil disobedience, 57, 60n24

civilians, 13, 143–45, 152, 155, 159, 161–64, 165n2, 165n6

civility, 51, 114

civil war: and civilian collaboration, 155; definition of, 144, 152; depictions of, 152, 272; effects of, 162–63; victims of, 149. *See also* war

class differences, 73, 77, 146, 170, 271

Class Struggles in France, 1848 to 1850, The (Marx), 77

climate change: as a crisis, 264; effects of, 225, 230, 238–39, 264, 273; framings of, 15, 229, 232–34; responsibility for, 226, 236; skeptics of, 211–13

Climategate, 15, 207, 211–16, 220

Climatic Research Unit (CRU), 207, 211–13

Clinton, Hillary, 43

cocaine trade, 147–50, 164

Cold War, 41, 84, 91–94, 146–47. *See also* Soviet Union (USSR)

Collapse of Western Civilization, The (Conway), 264

collective, 44, 62, 68–70, 74, 79, 81, 113. *See also* individuals; polity

Collier, Paul, 254, 257

Colombia: civil war of, 12, 143, 146–50; Constitutional Court, 148, 156; constitution of, 150, 164; final peace agreement and, 162; Justice and Peace Law of, 148, 159, 162; laws and, 148, 155–56, 397; Victims' Law, 149, 156, 160, 162; Victims' Unit, 151–52, 165n3

colonial, 9–10, 22–24, 30, 87–90, 92, 101, 126, 237, 241. *See also* colonialism; decolonization

colonialism: legacies of, 23, 103, 126, 239–40, 275; organization of, 10, 276; paradox of, 88–89; ruins of, 236, 238–39. *See also* colonial, decolonization

Comment les démocraties finissent (Revel), 58n1

commodification, 12, 131–33, 135, 141, 143. *See also* marketization

communism, 10, 13, 77–78, 146. *See also* capitalism; economics

community resilience, 225–26, 228

complexity, 118, 133, 137, 206–7, 227–29, 241, 249. *See also* chaos

Comprehensive Peace Agreement (CPA), 127–31

concepts, 2–6

conceptual history, 262–63

conflict: consequences of, 105; forms of, 59n13; moralization of, 43; as part of democracy, 55; and religion, 103, 109–10

Constituent Assembly of India, 22, 30

Constitution of India, 22

context: and authoritarianism, 62–64, 272; and belonging, 88–95; and democracy, 50–51, 80–85, 208–10; and imperialism, 116–17; and language, 262–63, 274, 276; and reality, 20–21; and religion, 105–12, 172–73; of victimhood, 27–29, 37n10, 238; and war, 149–50, 163. *See also* reality

Conway, Erik, 264

cooperation, 55, 130, 208

Corbyn, Jeremy, 54
Corbyn, John, 57
Cordero, Rodrigo, 275
coronavirus pandemic, 17–18
Corpus Hippocraticum, 263
corruption: accusations of, 57; attempts
   to fight, 179, 201; categories of, 186–87;
   194, 201; centering of, 139, 187; indicators of, 188–89; indictment for, 200; and
   morals, 185–86, 199; necessity of, 202;
   scale of, 185, 187–91, 195–201
cosmopolitanism, 83, 259. *See also*
   globalization
crisis: and critique, 262–66; dominance of,
   17, 262, 269, 273; etymology of, 262–64;
   invisibility of, 268–69, 276; naming of,
   54, 261, 263, 270, 274–75; repetition of,
   21, 265; rhetoric of, 40, 274
Crisis (Paine), 263
Crisis of the European Sciences, The (Husserl),
   264
Crisis of the Mind, The (Valéry), 264
critique, 4, 72–73, 76, 79, 124, 126–27, 135,
   141, 255, 262–66, 273–75
Critique and Crisis (Koselleck), 265
Crutzen, Paul, 231
Cuban Revolution, 146
culture: and citizenship, 96; definitions
   of, 97–99; hegemony of, 52. *See also*
   identity
Culture and Society (Williams), 3
culture wars, 48–50
Cyclone Pam, 230

Dagolo, Mohamed "Hemedti," 134
Danowski, Déborah, 234
Darfur, 12, 127–33
Darfur Peace Agreement, 132–33
Das, Veena, 157, 203, 237–38, 271
Data: collection of, 6, 141, 222, 223n2;
   openness of, 217, 220; ownership of, 215.
   See also big data
death: and civil war, 144–46; perception
   of, 37n7–37n8, 159, 161, 272; ritual

responses to, 25–26, 29–30, 154; terminology for, 24–25, 272. *See also* life
decentralization, 93–94
decolonization, 91–92, 275. *See also*
   colonialism
Defoe, Daniel, 235
deinstitutionalization, 140. *See also*
   institutions
Delafosse, Maurice, 88–89
Deleuze, Gilles, 235
Delogu, Marco, 251
democracy: and authoritarianism, 50, 64;
   claims of, 39, 58n1; disfiguration of, 62;
   forms of, 49, 51, 56, 140; future of, 53–57;
   legitimacy of, 72–74, 207; paradox of,
   70; participation in, 45, 76, 206, 208;
   perceptions of, 8, 39–40, 161; problems
   of, 40–41, 64, 275; theories of, 9, 74,
   139–40, 259n4; threats to, 43–50, 61–62,
   80, 142, 276. *See also* authoritarianism;
   illiberal democracy
Democratic Republic of Congo, 276
democratization of Africa, 89
Demosthenes, 85
Deng, Francis, 165n5
De Niro, Robert, 241
deregulation, 247
Derrida, Jacques, 169, 274
descent to the ordinary, 157
designed instability, 139
despotism, 75
development: and democracy, 53–56, 79;
   and disorder, 135–38; indicators of,
   187; language of, 49, 226–29; policies
   of, 15, 94–95, 130, 149, 165n2, 245; of
   society, 115
Dewey, John, 57
Dewinter, Filip, 96
Dharr, Abu, 175
dictatorship, 39, 139–40. *See also*
   authoritarianism
*Dictionary of Indo-European Concepts and
   Society* (Benveniste), 268
Dictionary of Untranslatables (Cassin et al.), 4

discourse: absences from, 31, 34, 37n8, 276; ambiguity of, 100–102; of human rights, 12, 30, 161–64; of official history, 8, 97–98, 145; and populism, 62–63, 80–81, 97; public forms of, 25, 54, 270; and religion, 118, 121; revolution as, 168–69. *See also* silence

Discourses on the Origin of Inequality (Rousseau), 73

disorder, 126, 135–40

displacement, 155–58. *See also* internally displaced people (IDP)

Docquier, Frédéric, 249, 251, 257

documents, 15, 24, 26–29, 90, 128–32, 207, 211

domination, 52, 65–67, 72, 125, 173, 175–76, 183n5, 198, 227

Donatelli, Piergorgio, 20–21

double consciousness, 126

doubt, 43, 67, 87, 97–98, 166, 223n3. *See also* suspicion

dual state, 52–53

Du Bois, W. E. B., 126

Dugin, Alexander, 42

Dworkin, Ronald, 249–50

Eboua, Samuel, 95

economics: crises of, 247, 265, 274; globalization of, 147; and inequality, 243; and morals, 14; systems of, 14, 160, 259n1; and war, 148. *See also* capitalism; communism; labor; protectionism

Economist, 246

egalitarianism, 63, 80–82, 176. *See also* equity

Egypt, 127

Eighteenth Brumaire of Louis Bonaparte, The (Marx), 77

Elias, Norbert, 114

El Salvador, 165n9

Engels, Friedrich, 263–64

English Civil War, 106–7, 111

Enlightenment, 167, 169, 180, 266

entitlement, 193

entropy, age of, 140

Environmental Data and Governance Initiative (EDGI), 219

environmental debates, 228

Environmental Information Regulations (EIR), 211

environmental philosophy, 231–32

environmental precarity, 226

Environmental Protection Agency (EPA), 207, 216–21

Epstein, Mikhail, 186

equality of opportunity, 250

equity, 63, 70, 130, 179, 246–47, 250. *See also* egalitarianism; inequality

Erdoğan, Recep Tayyip, 39, 41, 46–48, 80

Erechtheus (Euripides), 86–87

erotic imagery, 34

Ershād, Hosseiniyyeh, 177

ethics, 18, 26, 111, 136, 145, 186, 189–90, 200, 232, 236, 251, 258. *See also* morals

ethnicity, 8, 10, 44, 50, 88, 90, 100–103, 120, 146, 176, 192. *See also* identity; race

ethnic nationalism, 44, 50

ethnocentrism, 265–66

etymology, 10, 17, 58n5, 127–28, 188, 262–64, 266. *See also* language

Euripides, 85–87

European Commission, 51, 222

European New Right, 42

European Union, 47, 50–51, 94

everyday, the: and autochthony, 101; and the catastrophic, 20–23, 35; civil war as the, 152–55, 159–60, 163–64; descent to the ordinary and, 157; distortion of, 31, 33, 38n15, 93, 237–38; fragility of, 20–21; knowledge in the, 19–20, 35, 119; laws and the, 144, 151; as perilous, 18; vernacular of, 190. *See also* life

evidence: and belonging, 87–89, 99–102, 254; of climate change, 229, 264; of corruption, 187, 190, 196–98; and policymaking, 210, 216; of religious coexistence, 11; scarcity of, 31, 271; and victimhood, 28. See *also* data; facts

Indian Constitution, 103, 107
Indian-English relations, 116–18
Indian National Congress, 30
indigenous knowledge, 233–34
indigenous people, 15–16, 233–34, 237–38, 242
individuals, 11–14, 38n12, 43; inequality between, 248–50; and morals, 14; religious beliefs of, 106–8, 119, 177; rights of, 148, 218, 222, 223n1, 259; role of, 11, 43, 66, 112, 116, 185–86, 225–26, 271; and the state, 38n12, 74, 120. *See also* collective; populism; selfhood
Indonesia, 223n4
inequality: claims of, 63; of class, 73, 77; by design, 203; evidence of, 187; global scope of, 244–45, 258; and immigration, 251–55; of income, 243–44; and insecurity, 271; rises in, 16, 40. *See also* equity
Ingold, Tim, 234
innocent victims, 24–25
inordinate knowledge, 7, 19–20, 35, 36n3. *See also* knowledge
institutions: as constraints, 139; and democracy, 56, 139–40; emphasis on, 78, 137, 202, 206; exporting of, 227; stability of, 143, 273; trust in, 45, 62
intellectual property rights, 211. *See also* bureaucracy; deinstitutionalization; government, science
Intergovernmental Panel on Climate Change (IPCC), 211–12, 233
Interim National Constitution of Sudan, 129
internally displaced people (IDP), 148, 151, 155–58, 165n5. *See also* displacement
International Comparisons Project, 259n1
international intervention, 15, 124, 152, 164, 226–27, 229
international law, 143, 164, 231, 234
International Monetary Fund (IMF), 94
interregnum, 139–40
intimacy, 14, 22–23, 161, 185, 189–90, 195–96

Intimate Enemies (Theidon), 158
Iran, 13, 166–67, 172, 177–78, 180–83
Iranian Marxist-Leninists, 173, 175
Iraq, 139–40, 227
"Is It Useless to Revolt?" (Foucault), 182
Islam: ideals of, 173–74, 176; as ideology, 173, 175; politicization of, 174, 180; rituals of, 32; suspicion of, 10, 44, 98. *See also* Muslims
Islamic: republic, 166, 172; state, 127–128, theology, 173
Islamic Revolution, 17, 172
Islamology (Shari'ati), 183n7
island effect, 234–41
Israel, 276
Italy, 57
Ivory Coast, 83–84, 86–90, 92–94, 101

Jackson, Stephen, 100
Jamieson, Dale, 264
Jammu, 104
Japan, 23–24
Jbembe, Achille, 126
Jeju 4.3 incident, 7–8, 21–30, 33, 35–36, 37n9
Jones, Phil, 215
Judt, Tony, 41
Juntas de Acción Comunal, 163–64
justice: ideals of, 104, 110, 117, 172–74, 190, 262–63; transitional forms of, 37n9, 143, 149–51, 159–63; and victimhood, 25, 30
Justice and Equality Movement, 128–29

Kaczyński, Jarosław, 47
Kang, Han, 22
Kant, Immanuel, 266
Kanuda, Kenneth, 94
Kashmir, 104
Keith, Damon J., 223n1
Kenya, 95–96
Keynes, John Maynard, 130, 246–47
keywords approach, 2–4
Khalil Ibrahim, 129, 131
Khartoum Springs, 134

Khomeini, Ayatollah, 172, 174, 181

kin, 21, 25–26, 28, 31–32, 37n8, 189,

King, Rodney, 269

kinship, 29, 31, 33–34,

Klein, Naomi, 239

kleptocracy, 134, 139

knowledge: forms of, 20, 25–30, 34–35; modes of, 20; production of, 29, 35; reification of, 8; ritual forms of, 25–30. *See also* inordinate knowledge; reality; thought

Koh, Sungman, 24

Kojève, Alexandre, 67

Kollar, Eszter, 255

Kong, Han, 23

Kordonskiĭ, Simon, 192–93

Korean unification, 24. *See also* South Korea

Koselleck, Reinhart, 2–3, 262–63, 265–66

Kosovo, 227

Kwon, Heonik, 25–26, 32–33

labor: allocation of, 90, 248, 251–53; forms of, 157; markets of, 249

Laboratory for Anti-Corruption Policy, 188. *See also* economics; unemployment

Labour Party, 57

Laclau, Ernesto, 61

Lakner, Christoph, 249

land scarcity, 92–96

language, 4, 125, 127–31, 190. *See also* etymology; translation; words

Laplace, Pierre-Simon, 135

LA race riots, 269

Latin Christianity, 121n1

Latour, Bruno, 232

La Violencia, 147–49, 157

law: categories of, 155; faith in, 143, 150; language of, 150–51, 158; limits of, 151–52, 157; as a narrative, 144; priorities of, 151; and social hierarchy, 192–93; weaponization of, 51. *See also* legal; lawlessness

Law and Justice party (PiS), 47–48

lawlessness, 136–37

Lázár, János, 58n8

lead poisoning, 266–68

leaked information, 211–16

Lebanon, 179–80

Lega Norte, 97

legal, 12, 14, 18, 34–35, 50–53, 66, 73, 143, 146, 148, 150–152, 155–156, 160, 172, 192–193, 196, 262: apparatuses, 52; authority 52, 66–67, 72; category of victim, 21–22, 29–30, 160; normality, 52; order, 72–76, 82; reform, 148–149, 164, 191; regime, 143–45, 151–152, 161–162, 164. *See also* law; lawlessness

legitimacy, 66, 70–73, 79, 103–4, 164, 268

Legutko, Ryszard, 42

Lenin, Vladimir, 131, 171, 178

Le Pen, Jean-Marie, 85, 97

Le Pen, Marine, 61, 85–86

lexicon, concept of, 2–4

liberalism, 2, 40–42, 58n9. *See also* illiberal democracy

liberation theology, 172

Libya, 272

life: commoditization of, 135, 141–42; everyday aspects of, 17–21, 118–19, 159–60, 275; forms of, 2–5, 16–17, 106–9, 238; progress of, 170–71, 228, 232; repairing of, 33–35; stakes of, 83, 201–2, 263–64. *See also* death; everyday, the

Liga de Mujeres Desplazadas, 159

Lippman, Walter, 56

literature, 33, 41, 235, 264

Locke, John, 11, 71–72, 74, 104–5, 107, 122n3

longue durée, 6, 177. *See also* history

Loraux, Nicole, 86–87

los mismos, 159–60, 163

Louisiana Justice Institute, 225

Love in the Anthropocene (Nadzam), 264

loyalty, 47–48, 52, 55, 80, 195, 254

Machado, Joël, 249–51

Maduro regime, 150